W9-CCT-060

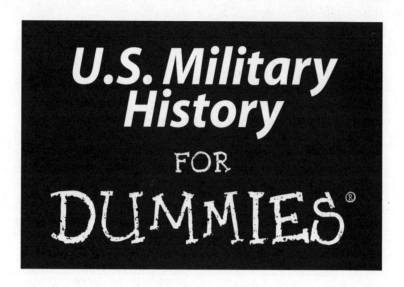

U.S. Military History

FOR

DUMMIES®

by John C. McManus, PhD

BICENTENNIAL
1807
WILEY
2007
BICENTENNIAL

Wiley Publishing, Inc.

U.S. Military History For Dummies®
Published by
Wiley Publishing, Inc.
111 River St.
Hoboken, NJ 07030-5774
www.wiley.com

WILEY

About the Author

John C. McManus, PhD, is an associate professor of U.S. m
at Missouri University of Science and Technology. He teach
Civil War, World War II, Vietnam, Americans in combat, and
of American military history. A prolific lecturer on military
received numerous awards for outstanding teaching.

He has written several books on the American military expe
The Deadly Brotherhood: The American Combat Soldier in Wo
Americans at D-Day; and, most recently, *Alamo in the Ardenn*
Story of the American Soldiers Who Made the Defense of Bast
is a member of the editorial advisory board at *World War II m*
served as an historical expert for numerous battlefield tours

He lives in St. Louis, Missouri, with his wife, Nancy.

Dedication

To the soldiers, sailors, Marines, Coast Guardsmen, and airmen who made this history.

To my students, whose insatiable curiosity about U.S. military history inspires me to keep learning more about it.

Author's Acknowledgments

My first word of thanks goes to Kurt Piehler, my colleague at the University of Tennessee, for laying the foundation for this project and making it possible. David Fugate and Ted Chichak, my literary agents, gave the project definition and purpose. I greatly appreciate their tireless work in making this book happen.

I am very grateful to editors Mike Baker and Stephen Clark, both of whom did an outstanding job. Their collective insight, wisdom, and passion for military history strengthened this book immeasurably. I appreciate the sharp eye of copy editor Vicki Adang, who improved my prose in myriad ways.

I would like to thank my colleagues in the Department of History and Political Science at Missouri University of Science and Technology, especially Larry Gragg and Russ Buhite, two of the finest historians in existence.

My final and most heartfelt word of thanks goes to my family for their love and support. My parents, Michael and Mary Jane; my brother, Mike; my sister, Nancy; my brother-in-law, John; my nieces, Erin and Kelly; and my nephew, Michael, are with me always. My wife, Nancy, love of my life, is the brightest light of them all. She has made all of my dreams come true. Thank you!

Publisher's Acknowledgments

We're proud of this book; please send us your comments through our Dummies online registration form located at www.dummies.com/register/.

Some of the people who helped bring this book to market include the following:

Acquisitions, Editorial, and Media Development

Project Editor: Stephen R. Clark

Acquisitions Editor: Mike Baker

Copy Editor: Victoria M. Adang

Editorial Program Coordinator: Erin Calligan Mooney

Technical Editor: Lee S. Harford, Jr., PhD, Army Reserve Historian

Editorial Manager: Christine Meloy Beck

Editorial Assistants: Joe Niesen, David Lutton, Leeann Harney

Cover Photos: © Gary Benson/Getty Images

Cartoons: Rich Tennant (www.the5thwave.com)

Composition Services

Project Coordinator: Lynsey Osborn

Layout and Graphics: Reuben Davis, Brooke Graczyk, Shane Johnson, Barbara Moore, Alissa Walker, Christine Williams

Anniversary Logo Design: Richard Pacifico

Proofreaders: John Greenough, Glenn McMullen

Indexer: Glassman Indexing Services

Publishing and Editorial for Consumer Dummies

Diane Graves Steele, Vice President and Publisher, Consumer Dummies

Joyce Pepple, Acquisitions Director, Consumer Dummies

Kristin A. Cocks, Product Development Director, Consumer Dummies

Michael Spring, Vice President and Publisher, Travel

Kelly Regan, Editorial Director, Travel

Publishing for Technology Dummies

Andy Cummings, Vice President and Publisher, Dummies Technology/General User

Composition Services

Gerry Fahey, Vice President of Production Services

Debbie Stailey, Director of Composition Services

Contents at a Glance

Table of Contents

Introduction

A merican military history is fascinating. Like any high drama, it has everything you can want in a story. It has tragedy. It has inspiring and not-so-inspiring leaders. It has heroes and villains. It has blood, sweat, and tears, but also humor, comradeship, and revelry. More than anything, American military history is about the ordinary American in extraordinary circumstances.

Perhaps that's why it's such a popular topic. Go to any average bookstore, and you'll see that books on military topics usually comprise anywhere from one-third to one-half of the history section. Go to the video store, and you can't help but notice the huge quantities of war movies and combat video games that clutter the shelves. Military stories sell, even if they're inaccurate or poorly told, as so many are.

Military history, though, is much more than just another entertaining diversion. It's the story of this country's past, present, and future. Anyone who wants to understand the first thing about American history, and even American society today, must know military history.

From the earliest days of the American colonies to our own time, warfare and the armed forces have had a major impact on everything that has happened. In colonial times, European settlers fought Native Americans for land. In later years, Americans did the same. Indians fought just as hard to hang on to their land, sometimes against whites, other times against other Native Americans. Americans earned their independence as a result of two wars with imperial Great Britain. Major disagreements about slavery, race, federal power, states' rights, and economics led to a ruinous war between northerners and southerners that marked the country forever. Generations later, America's participation in World War II transformed the country more than any other event, before or since. All these wars, like most, accelerated the pace of change.

Military history isn't just about wars, though. It's about average Americans and their lives. Who served in the armed forces and why? How closely do America's military forces reflect our society? Why do American soldiers risk their lives in combat? Do major American problems, such as drugs, racism, sexism, and corruption, carry over into military life?

Military historians debate these issues and so many others. They argue about everything from Robert E. Lee's decisions at the Battle of Gettysburg to the Army's treatment of female soldiers in the 1970s. They debate everything from the reasons for American victory in the Revolution to the reasons for American defeat in Vietnam.

In these troubled, warlike times, nearly everyone has an opinion about some aspect of American military history. If you're one of those people, then reading this book will let you know which of your opinions carry some weight and which may need some revising. The book also may provide you with some ammo to use in a debate over nearly any aspect of American military history.

About This Book

I teach U.S. military history at Missouri University of Science and Technology. Each year, when I get a new set of introductory students, their main complaint is that history is boring. To them, history is nothing more than a remote series of names, dates, and facts to be memorized for the test and then discarded. I actually don't blame them for feeling that way because that's how history is often taught and written. Well, the first thing I assure them — and you — is that history is not just names, dates, and facts. It is the story of people and the challenges of their times. History is about *why* and *how,* not *what* and *when.* The study of history is all about bringing people of the past to life. It's also about understanding what their experiences can teach us about ourselves and our own challenges. When I present history to my students that way, you'd be amazed at the transformation in their interest level. They actually start enjoying it.

History is for everybody, not just a few scholars in some little elitist club. This book is written from an inclusive perspective. Each chapter explains unfamiliar terms, breaks up complicated information into easily understandable groupings, and avoids arcane jargon. The other great thing about the book is that you don't have to read it chronologically, from the front cover to the back cover. You can start anywhere you want, skipping what doesn't interest you and concentrating on what does. Maybe you're only interested in the post–World War II period or the Civil War or the 18th century, or maybe you're into every aspect of American military history. No matter what your interests, you'll find something you like in this book. And I promise there won't be a test!

Conventions Used in This Book

I use the following conventions in this book to help you navigate your way:

> ✔ I *italicize* all new words and terms that are defined.
>
> ✔ I **boldface** keywords or the main parts of bulleted items.
>
> ✔ I use `monofont` for all Web addresses.
>
> ✔ Throughout the text, I sometimes refer to Native Americans as Indians.

What Not to Read

Although I cover the highlights of U.S. military history in this book, I just can't resist sharing some additional facts and anecdotes that enhance the story. I've put these interesting but nonessential tidbits in sidebars. You can skip the sidebars — shaded boxes that appear here and there — if you'd like.

Foolish Assumptions

The literature on American military history is enormous and growing each year. No one can possibly keep up with all of it. *U.S. Military History For Dummies* is designed for the reader who wants to be informed but without getting overwhelmed by the details. I don't claim to provide a description of every incident, battle, issue, or personality in American military history. The topic is way too large for that.

Because you picked up this book, I assume you're interested in a quick-hitting, lively, accurate overview of U.S. military history, and you probably fall into one of the following categories:

> ✔ You want a general overview of U.S. military history that answers the questions of who, what, where, why, when, and how.
>
> ✔ You want a compact reference guide to major subjects in American military history.
>
> ✔ You're interested in discovering how the military and warfare have shaped American life, society, politics, economics, and culture.
>
> ✔ You want to brush up on the topic without having to plow through scholarly minutiae, military-buff Web sites, or incomprehensible military terms.

How This Book Is Organized

I have organized this book into six major topical and chronological parts, each of which covers important aspects of American military history.

Part I: The Nitty-Gritty of U.S. Military History

This part gives you an overview of why military history is very important, why Americans fight wars, who we fight, and how all of this has affected the country's history. It introduces you to the key players in American military history, from politicians to generals to the warriors themselves. This part also explains the purpose, traditions, and unique missions of each of the armed services. Plus, it discusses what happens when those services actually get into combat as well as why American soldiers risk their lives in battle.

Part II: Born in War

Warfare created the United States. This part explains how a colonial war against the French and their Native American allies created the conditions that led to the American Revolution. It examines the important battles of the Revolution and how that defining event affected Americans, and explains why the American revolutionaries won. These chapters also discuss the many challenges the new nation faced, from dealing with Indians to Barbary pirates and another conflict with Great Britain.

Part III: Forged in War

With independence secured, the United States began to expand westward, all the way to the Pacific coast. This part examines a territorial war that the United States fought with Mexico and explains how this helped lead to the Civil War. It relates the main causes of the Civil War, chronicles the important battles, and shows how deeply the war affected nearly every American. The fighting and dying didn't end with the Civil War. After the war, the United States continued its relentless expansion west and, in so doing, battled with several proud Native American tribes. Finally, this part concludes with America's first real overseas war, a morally charged, brief tilt with Spain that led to the establishment of a small American empire in the Philippines.

Part IV: Going Global: The World Wars

This part examines the first half of the 20th century, when the United States became a leading world power. The Great War, or World War I, raged in Europe, and initially, the United States was inclined to stay out of it. But by 1917, the Americans willingly joined the war, and this part explains exactly how that happened, as well as what the war was like for Americans. The war's greatest tragedy is that it created the conditions for a much worse war, fought between 1939 and 1945, that we generally call World War II. One chapter examines the causes of that war and explains how the United States eventually got involved. Then, the next chapter describes the crucial battles of that colossal war, the horrible realities of combat, and the many ways that the war profoundly changed the United States forever.

Part V: Bearing Any Burden: The Cold War and the Unpaid Peace Dividend

This part covers the violent half century that followed World War II. The Cold War led the United States into two major wars on the Asian continent. In Korea, the United States joined with a coalition of other nations to keep Communist North Korea from conquering non-Communist South Korea. A decade later, the U.S. again sought to protect and secure a non-Communist ally, South Vietnam, against its Communist enemies in North Vietnam and an insurgency called the Viet Cong. This war was one of the longest, least popular, and least successful in which Americans fought. This part also covers the key Cold War events, from the American Marshall Plan for European recovery to the Cuban Missile Crisis, to the fall of the Berlin Wall. The final three chapters look at American involvement in the Middle East, from 1990 through the present, including protracted wars in Afghanistan and Iraq.

Part VI: The Part of Tens

This is often the most fascinating part of any *For Dummies* book. The Part of Tens gives me an opportunity to relate important information that doesn't quite fit into the flow of the book. The chapters contain top-ten lists on the best and worst generals in American military history and the best movies ever made on the topic. Each list is designed to provoke some thought, some debate, and perhaps inspire you to do more reading on the subject (maybe to create your own lists!).

Icons Used in This Book

Sometimes you may need some quick help in finding what's important. The icons designate passages about four subjects. These little pictures next to the text are easy to find and identify. Here's what each one represents:

This icon identifies military strategy used by U.S. commanders or their enemies to achieve their overall objectives. Often a commander's strategy is equivalent to his battle plan.

This icon gives you an interesting bit of historical information that adds to your knowledge and understanding of American military history.

This icon points out especially important information that you need to keep in mind as subsequent events unfold.

This icon gives you special details about the realities of the military experience. It provides a "you are there" sense of what battles were really like for the soldiers.

Where to Go from Here

This book is about war, politics, and combat throughout American history. It's designed for you to skip around, reading whatever interests you the most. If you're mainly interested in the early period of U.S. military history, then head over to Part II. If World War II is your thing, then you can jump ahead to those chapters. Perhaps you want to know more about the war on terror. If so, look at the later chapters of Part V. Or maybe you just want some quick information on how the military works and what combat is like. In that case, Part I is where you should start. If you just want intriguing and provocative tidbits on U.S. military history, the Part of Tens is the place to go. However, if you want to know it all, then start with the first chapter and read the book in order. Any way you choose to go, you can find plenty of information to fill in the gaps. Basically, it's your book, so read it — and enjoy it — however you want.

Part I
The Nitty-Gritty of U.S. Military History

"Join the war, man."

In this part . . .

*B*efore you can understand all the wars Americans have fought, you need to understand the military's background and the people who serve our country. In this part, you see why wars and the armed forces have been such an important part of the United States' history. You find out who has done the fighting and what it's really like. You even get a quick overview on what each of the services does and what makes each of them unique.

Chapter 1

Why This Stuff Is Important

In This Chapter

▶ Shaping the nation through war

▶ Seeing how wars of the past affect you today

▶ Meeting the storytellers of history

*T*he U.S. military doesn't exist, as some people argue, "to kill people and break things." Quite simply, it exists *to provide security for the American people.* Sometimes that does indeed mean killing people and breaking things. Other times, it means precisely the opposite. In World War II, the armed forces, in order to protect America, had to destroy the enemy's armed forces in conventional combat. However, during the Cold War, the military's primary focus was to prevent a catastrophic World War III by maintaining peace rather than making war.

Basically, U.S. military history is the story of how we've maintained our security and how we can continue to do so in the future. That means military history actually affects your life.

Security is *the* basic necessity of life. Without security, nothing works. Security is sort of like your health. If you don't have your health, you're in deep trouble. If you do, then it's easy to take it for granted. Imagine, for just a moment, if your life were devoid of security. For the purpose of self-defense, your home would be a bunker, with no creature comforts, not even electricity or indoor plumbing because those things are the product of stable communities and foresighted engineering. With no police, firefighters, or soldiers, your main focus would be to protect your family from predators. There would be no supermarkets, no Starbucks, no local mall, and (gasp!) no bookstores. Instead, your existence would be governed by the law of the jungle. Not a pretty picture, is it? Sadly, conditions similar to these exist in far too much of the world.

But Americans are fortunate. We enjoy relatively peaceful, stable lives that come from our collective security as a country. We live in safe homes, drive on regulated, fairly well-maintained roads, shop at secure businesses, and work in safe, peaceful jobs. In truth, none of these blessings can exist without — you guessed it — security. And, for America, that security comes from the armed forces, which are made up of individual Americans.

One of the most fascinating aspects of U.S. military history is that it's largely the story of ordinary Americans in extraordinary circumstances. Perhaps that's why most of us are so moved by it. Plus, if you know military history, you know American history, because they're closely intertwined. You also begin to understand where security — our most basic necessity — actually comes from.

The purpose of this chapter, then, is to explain what U.S. military history is, how profoundly it has affected our country's development, and why it's important to your life.

Shaping a Country through War

Americans like to think of themselves as peace-loving people. To some extent, the characterization fits. Most Americans tend to think of war as unusual and quite undesirable, something to be avoided if at all possible. To them, peace is the norm, war is the aberration. Security is a given. Violence and chaos are only frightful exceptions to an otherwise orderly existence. Throughout American history, only a minority of Americans have ever fought in combat. All of this is obviously a good thing.

However, there is no question that war is a central theme in American history. War created this country, shaped it, and propelled it into world-power status. It is literally impossible to study American history without studying war. By my count — and this is a conservative estimate — Americans have fought and died in well over 100 wars since colonial times. Those wars ranged in size from small skirmishes against Native American tribes to World War II, the largest conflict of all time. Like it or not, American history is really something of a Jekyll-and-Hyde duality between the peaceful and warlike sides of America. For this reason, military issues relate to almost every aspect of the American story. And this story that loops from the past into the present touches you in more ways than you may be aware.

Reaping the sociological and political rewards of war

Military conflict has decided a large number of major issues in U.S. history. That's the essential paradox of America. A country founded on notions of representative government, peaceful compromise, tolerance, and universal human rights nonetheless resolved many of its conflicts through violence. Here's a brief list that demonstrates the momentous effect of wars on the development of the United States as a nation:

- ✔ The **Revolutionary War** (see Chapters 6 and 7) created an independent American republic. The **War of 1812** (see Chapter 9) solidified that independence and gave Americans permanent control of the Mississippi River. This led to massive economic growth.

- ✔ **Wars against Native Americans** (see Chapters 8 and 12) led to the precipitous decline of Indian cultures in this country. Those wars also expanded the United States across the continent, creating a coast-to-coast nation built around the Constitution.

- ✔ A **war with Mexico** (see Chapter 10), fought in 1846 and 1847, won control of the entire Southwest for the United States.

- ✔ The **Civil War** (see Chapter 11) destroyed slavery, propelled race to the forefront as a thorny American issue, and guaranteed that the United States would develop as a free-market, capitalist, multiethnic republic.

- ✔ The **Spanish-American War** (see Chapter 13) led to colonial commitments for America overseas.

- ✔ **World War I** (see Chapter 14) created widespread disillusionment with the idea of war itself. It also furthered the idea that Americans should remain aloof from world affairs. This notion, known as *isolationism,* still exists in American political thought.

- ✔ **World War II** (see Chapter 16) turned the United States into a world-leading power of immense proportions. It also sparked major changes in race relations, gender roles, economic growth, political norms, and lifestyles.

- ✔ The **Vietnam War** (see Chapter 19) proved the limits of American power. It caused many Americans to question the country's basic morality. The war also spawned massive social protest movements, the ripples of which we still feel today.

Remember that those are just a few examples, among many. Nor do they even take into account the military's considerable peacetime impact on the American people throughout the span of U.S. history. The main point I'm conveying is that modern America is, to a great extent, the product of its martial past.

Reaping the innovations of war

Many things you encounter in your daily life eventually relate to military history or security. Indeed, I would venture to say that nearly every product you use is dependent, in some way, upon military security. Here are just a few examples:

- ✔ **Automobiles:** Every American automaker during World War II converted from the production of civilian cars to vehicles with a military purpose, such as tanks, trucks, planes, and jeeps. The Jeep and the Hummer originally were exclusively military vehicles. Also, civilian cars are, of course, dependent on oil-based petroleum for fuel. The United States has fought wars in the oil-rich Middle East and maintains a major military presence there to safeguard the world's oil supply.

- ✔ **Cotton:** This crop is, obviously, useful for making comfortable clothes. In the early 19th century, the South's economic system was heavily dependent upon slave-based cotton production for foreign markets. This led to the growth of a slavery-centered economy, political system, and culture in the South that ultimately clashed with the North's industrial, free-market economy, helping lead to the Civil War. The impact of the Civil War's outcome has continued into the present with civil rights being extended to all ethnic groups. And those cotton khakis you love originated from military uniforms.

- ✔ **Penicillin:** This was the wonder drug of the mid-20th century. Penicillin was so effective in fighting infections that it led to a dramatic rise in the production of antibiotics. What does penicillin have to do with U.S. military history, you may ask? The drug was developed during World War II for American military forces. The war also led to other major advances in medicine, including improved prosthetic limbs, reconstructive plastic surgery, better psychiatric care, and a slew of new surgical techniques that doctors still employ.

- ✔ **Detroit:** The city started as a French trading post. British soldiers and American militiamen captured it from the French during the French and Indian War. Later, the British and their Native American allies took the city from the Americans in the War of 1812. The Americans subsequently took it back. It's been part of the U.S. ever since and was a driving force (pun intended) in automobile manufacturing in the U.S. And without Detroit as part of the U.S., would we have ever had the Motown sound?

- ✔ **Insecticide:** During the Vietnam War and in the Pacific Theatre in World War II, American soldiers were issued bottles of insecticide to ward off mosquitoes, ants, leeches, and other tropical insects. Vietnam-era soldiers greatly prized their bottles of "bug juice" in the country's insect-ridden environment. Today, with the threat of bird flu and other mosquito-borne diseases, bug repellent is just as important. It's also nice to have along on picnics!

- ✔ **Kid Rock:** What, you may ask, can this pop icon anti-hero possibly have to do with the military? Kid Rock travels overseas to play free concerts for American troops, as do other entertainers such as Jay Leno, Gary Sinise, and Toby Keith. The greatest troop entertainer of all time was Bob Hope, who traveled tens of thousands of miles over the course of many decades to brighten the morale of Americans in uniform. Chances are, your favorite singer or actor may entertain the troops, at military bases here in the U.S. or overseas.

Seeing the Value of Understanding the Past

You may be tempted to say, "Well, that's interesting, but it's all in the past. Why is this stuff important to me now?" It's a good question, and it requires an equally good answer that I think can be summed up in a passage George Orwell wrote more than 50 years ago. "We sleep safe in our beds because rough men stand ready in the night to visit violence on those who would do us harm." This was true in Orwell's time, and it's certainly true now. Basically, it amounts to this: Without security, you have nothing; without an effective military, you have no security; without military history, you have no knowledge of what you must do to ensure your security.

History is not just about the past. It's about the present and the future, too. You've probably heard the old cliché that "those who don't learn from the past are doomed to repeat it." This statement is trite and even a little condescending, but sometimes it's actually true. Take, for example, the mistakes of American national security policymakers in the last half century. Since World War II, most American leaders have relied upon technology, air power, and sea power to fight America's wars, at the expense of ground power. Yet, most of our modern wars have actually been fought and won on the ground. As a result, Americans have usually been ill-prepared for the wars they fought, from World War II through now. The waste in American blood and treasure has been nearly incalculable. So, yes, it's a very good idea to learn from the past and apply it to the future.

We live in troubled, bloody times, and this is nothing new. The sad lesson of history is that human beings make war on one another. This has been true in most every culture, in every time period, and it's certainly true today. Closing your eyes and wishing away humanity's warlike tendencies won't make them extinct. The stark reality is that your security and mine are dependent upon those who serve in the United States armed forces. They are the "rough" men — and now women — standing ready to do violence against anyone meaning to harm us.

Make no mistake. The United States has plenty of enemies who readily kill Americans when given half a chance to do so (see Chapter 2). It doesn't matter whether you are a liberal Democrat, a conservative Republican, or anything in between. If you are an American, you are a target for a variety of enemies. Who keeps those enemies at bay so that we can enjoy secure, healthy lives? Those who serve in the U.S. military. They serve all over the world, on long deployments, in combat zones, far away from their families. They know the ache of loneliness and homesickness. They routinely risk their lives for us. In some cases, they lose their health or their lives in the line of duty. The least we can do is know what makes them tick. (Chapter 3 takes a look at who fights on our behalf, and Chapter 5 explains what they face in war zones.) If you know military history, you begin to comprehend those who ensure your security and how they accomplish that mission. What can be more important than that?

Listening to American Military Historians Tell the Story

History is the true story of real people told by other people *(historians)* who happened to come along later in time. All good historians are storytellers. Military historians tell stories about soldiers in uniform, the conflicts they fight, and the ways in which humanity is affected by military issues. American military historians have a lot to talk about, from the story of colonial militiamen to the 21st-century, all-volunteer armed forces and everything in between. The American military past is so enormous that an army of historians (pun intended) could study it for decades and not even come close to covering everything important. But we do our best!

Reporting tomorrow's history today

One good way to appreciate the vastness of American military history is to pick up a copy of today's paper, keeping in mind that today's news stories are tomorrow's history. Take note of every story that has some sort of military angle or topic, from the latest Army Corps of Engineers river project to reports of battles. Chances are you've located a fair number of military-oriented stories in your paper. For each one of those military stories, several others didn't get published. That's a lot of stories, right? Now multiply all of those stories by the full length of recorded American history, roughly 150,000 days. That gives you a sense of the enormity of U.S. military history and the challenge historians face in telling that aspect of the American story. So those historians tend to concentrate on what they feel is most important. They also focus on topics that are well recorded because they must have good sources to do their work.

Working the military history beat

American military historians work in a variety of places. Some, like me, are academics who teach at the higher-education level. Many work for the armed forces as official historians or as professors in service-run professional schools. Others work for the National Park Service as battlefield guides, rangers, and consultants. Quite a few work in the popular sector as analysts, authors, military magazine editors, historians for battlefield tour companies, memorabilia collectors, or as producers, writers, and hosts of movies and TV shows that cover military topics. Almost all American military historians *sub-specialize*. This means they develop expertise in one, or several, aspects of American military history. Here are just a few examples:

- ✔ Tom Fleming, although he has published books on nearly every time period in American military history, is best known for his excellent work on the American Revolution.
- ✔ Gary Gallagher and James McPherson are known as Civil War historians.
- ✔ Brian Linn is the foremost authority on the Philippine-American War.
- ✔ D'Ann Campbell is a leader in the field of American women and the military.
- ✔ Stephen Ambrose earned a reputation as the foremost chronicler of the American GI in World War II.
- ✔ Samuel Eliot Morison wrote the history of the United States Navy like no one else, before or since.
- ✔ Joseph Glatthaar is a pioneer in the study of African Americans in the military.
- ✔ Allan Millett is a leading authority on the history of the United States Marine Corps and also the Korean War.

So, as you can see, American military historians cover a wide variety of topics, practically everything from battles of the 19th century to the ways in which American education was affected by the growth of military bases.

HISTORIC TRIVIA

U.S. military historians may study all sorts of different subjects, but most fit into one of two categories.

- ✔ *Traditionalists* tend to focus on generals, senior leaders, and the narration of great battles. They describe strategy, tactics, and the influence of powerful individuals on the outcome of history. This is generally known as a "top-down" approach to history.
- ✔ The other category, more prevalent from the 1960s onward, is known as the "new" military history. This is a somewhat silly, vague term that refers to a "bottom-up" approach that is roughly akin to social history. In other words, these socio-military historians are primarily interested in the impact military history had on ordinary individuals, whether common soldiers or civilians. They approach military history by asking "What was it actually like?" Thus, for instance, some of these "new" military historians write battle histories from the perspective of those who did the actual fighting, often relating the horrible realities of combat.

You may be wondering which kind of historian I am. Definitely the latter. Generals are important, but in the end, U.S. military history is made by the average American in uniform and the everyday civilian on the home front.

Chapter 2

Why America Goes to War and Who We Fight

Since the 18th century, Americans have fought a variety of enemies. For the first 100 years of U.S. history, the country fought almost entirely against continental enemies, such as Native Americans, Mexicans, and colonial Europeans, normally for territory or national sovereignty. That changed at the turn of the 20th century, when the United States squared off in conflicts with overseas enemies such as Spain and Germany. By the middle of the 20th century and thereafter, Americans began to lock horns with ideological enemies such as Nazis, Communists, and Islamic radicals.

In this chapter, I examine the major reasons why the United States fights wars. I also give you a nice sense of the various enemies Americans have faced in combat. Overall, the chapter tells you everything you need to know about the why and the who in relation to American wars.

Why Do We Fight?

In the early 19th century, Karl von Clausewitz, a Prussian general and military strategist, summed up, in one sentence, the most famous explanation for war's existence. "It is clear that war is not a mere act of policy but a true political instrument, a continuation of political activity by other means." Is that really true? Actually, sometimes it is, and sometimes it isn't.

Throughout U.S. history, Americans have gone to war for a variety of reasons, ranging from political to economic to ideological, with a heavy emphasis on the latter. American wars have seldom been the result of dispassionate political calculation. This is because Americans tend to value individual human life because the country, after all, was founded on the idea of individual civil liberties. Obviously war destroys many of those individual lives. So, typically, Americans only support wars that appear to have some higher moral purpose than mere political maneuverings or economic gain. Of course, hard-core economic interests and power politics have sometimes been the real underlying reasons for our wars, leading to postwar disillusionment among many Americans, especially those who did the fighting.

The question of why we go to war provokes strenuous debate among American military historians. Some see our wars as the result of economic imperialism. They say that the United States always fights to expand its economic influence and enhance its own prosperity. Others argue that the United States has fought to spread its ideas and culture around the world. Other historians believe that self-defense and preoccupation with the security of the Western Hemisphere are the primary motivations for American wars. Thus, different historians often advance a variety of explanations for the same war.

The beauty of history is that there isn't always a 100 percent correct answer to every question. Sometimes, historical understanding comes from absorbing several possible explanations and deciding for yourself which makes the most sense. So, in this section, I relate several such explanations for American wars, with plenty of examples to explain what I mean.

When words fail: Politics

Our friend Clausewitz would, of course, champion a political explanation. He would say that Americans go to war when they find it necessary to advance their political agenda with violence, rather than peaceful persuasion. Sometimes this has been true. Political disagreements have indeed flared into outright warfare numerous times in American history:

- The American Revolution resulted from years of angry political debate between colonists and Great Britain. In fact, if you read the Declaration of Independence, you see that much of it is a listing of political grievances against King George III rather than a manifesto of great ideals. (Read about the United States' quest for independence in Chapter 7.)

- In the years leading up to the War of 1812, the United States attempted to resolve its differences with Great Britain by passing embargo laws to restrict American trade with Britain. When those laws failed to bring about the necessary political change in London that the Americans wanted, they declared war on Britain (Chapter 9 hits the highlights).

✔ A controversial election actually led to the Civil War. When Abraham Lincoln, an antislavery northerner, won the presidency in 1860, many southern slave states seceded from the Union rather than submit to his political authority. This secession, in turn, led to a terrible war that pitted the free-soil, free-labor, industrial, pro-Union political philosophy of the North against the proslavery, states' rights politics prevalent in the South (see Chapter 11 for more details).

✔ The United States entered World War I, in part, to support fellow democracies Britain and France. (Chapter 14 outlines the first World War.)

Economics: The root of all evil

Some historians argue that economics is the driving force behind all wars. They have a good point. From the ancient world until now, kingdoms, empires, nations, and interest groups have often fought for economic gain. In that sense, the United States is no different, even though American policymakers usually deny their economic motivations for war.

In reality, economics has been a major factor in nearly every American war, from the days when colonial Americans thirsted for control of French North American fur-trading routes to our own times when Americans demand open access to Middle Eastern oil. Time and time again in American history, U.S. soldiers have fought to protect the economic interests of their country:

✔ During the French and Indian War, many American militiamen fought in hopes of inheriting control of French fur-trading businesses (see Chapter 6).

✔ Some historians argue that the patriots of the American Revolution were primarily motivated by the economic advantages of separation from England (see Chapter 7).

✔ During the War of 1812, the main sticking point between the United States and Great Britain was the fact that the United States wanted to engage in free overseas trade without British harassment. When the Royal Navy continued to interfere with American trade in Europe, Americans opted for war (see Chapter 9).

✔ Economics was a major cause of the Civil War. The North's industrial, free-market, free-labor entrepreneurial economy clashed with the South's agricultural, plantation, slave-based economic system (see Chapter 11).

✔ From colonial times onward, economics was a major component of every American conflict with Indians because Americans often coveted resources they found on Indian land (see Chapters 8 and 12). For instance, the famous Battle of Little Bighorn in the summer of 1876 happened, in part, because American settlers discovered gold on Sioux Indian land.

✔ American desire to expand economically overseas and win access to foreign markets helped lead to the Spanish-American War (see Chapter 13).

✔ During World War I, American industrialists and bankers had an enormous stake in the Allied cause. Most historians believe this was a major reason why the U.S. entered the war on the Allied side. (Chapter 14 covers other reasons why the U.S. fought in World War I.)

✔ The U.S. fought in World War II, in part, to protect its overseas markets in Asia and Europe. (Chapter 15 explains the factors that led to World War II.)

✔ Economic historians argue that the Cold War resulted from America's desire to protect worldwide market capitalism against Communist encroachment (see Chapter 17). This led Americans into wars in such distant places as Korea and Vietnam (see Chapters 18 and 19).

✔ In 1990–1991, when Iraq took over Kuwait, the United States and a coalition of allies reacted with military force, not just to free Kuwait, but to protect the free flow of oil at market prices (see Chapter 20). Some commentators and historians claim that the United States invaded Iraq in 2003 to gain control of that country's oil resources (see Chapter 21).

Territory: Really major land grabs

Before the 20th century, the American desire to acquire territory caused several wars. From colonial times through the late 1890s, Americans were constantly on the move, expanding their influence, usually to the west. The American nation steadily grew from a seaboard collection of 13 original states to a bicoastal, continental colossus. To a great extent, this happened because of war.

Here's a good rule of thumb to keep in mind. From 1914 onward, Americans never fought a war to acquire territory. Before that time, they rarely fought a war in which they didn't win territory.

Here are several examples of wars Americans fought over territory:

✔ One of the main reasons for the French and Indian War in the 1750s was because Americans were moving west from the 13 seaboard British colonies, encroaching on French land (see Chapter 6).

✔ During the Revolutionary War, many patriots fought because they expected to gain land at the expense of Loyalists and pro-British Indian tribes (see Chapter 7).

✔ In 1803, the U.S. government bought substantial amounts of North American land from France in the Louisiana Purchase. Several years later, in the War of 1812, the U.S. fought to keep the British from encroaching on the Louisiana Purchase (see Chapter 9).

✔ Many times in the 19th century, Americans fought Indian tribes for their land (see Chapters 8 and 12).

✔ The best example of a territorial conflict is the Mexican-American War. This war originated from a disagreement between the two countries over a common border. The American president, James K. Polk, wanted to expand to the southwest, all the way to the Pacific Ocean. Much of that territory was under the loose control of Mexico, though. Polk attempted to purchase the land. When Mexico refused to sell, war soon followed. (Get more details in Chapter 10.)

✔ As a result of the Spanish-American War, the United States acquired Spain's former colonies in Puerto Rico, Guam, and the Philippines (see Chapter 13).

The Four Freedoms

In going to war, Americans usually rally around idealistic motivations rather than hard-core geopolitics. Knowing this, American leaders often articulate war objectives with high-minded rhetoric. For instance, during World War II, President Franklin D. Roosevelt often summed up American war aims in what he called the Four Freedoms. As Roosevelt outlined them, the Four Freedoms were

✔ Freedom of speech

✔ Freedom of worship

✔ Freedom from want

✔ Freedom from fear

The president declared that every human being had a right to these freedoms. His fondest hope was that the war would make this happen.

Norman Rockwell, in his own unique way, immortalized the Four Freedoms in a series of wartime paintings. You can see the paintings on the National Archives Web site at www.archives.gov/exhibits/powers_of_persuasion/four_freedoms/four_freedoms.html. You can also hear an excerpt of President Roosevelt's Four Freedoms speech on the site.

The thinking person's reason: Ideology

The United States is a constitutional republic founded on high-minded notions of inalienable human rights. In the broad sweep of human history, that's a rare thing. So it's only natural that Americans would fight and die for big ideas. Thomas Jefferson saw America as an "empire for liberty." Abraham Lincoln often referred to American representative government as a noble experiment that was the "last, best hope for the Earth." Cold War–era presidents such as Harry Truman, John Kennedy, and Ronald Reagan often contrasted American liberty with Communist tyranny. During the Global War on Terror, President George W. Bush described terrorist-sponsoring nations as an "axis of evil."

When Americans have felt that their ideals of liberty and justice were in danger, they have chosen to fight. Ideas, then, have been a powerful motivator for American wars. Fiery, patriotic rhetoric from politicians has often rallied Americans for war. Although sometimes the reasons for war went deeper than mere patriotic ideals, there is no doubt that idealism has been a major cause for most every war the United States has ever fought:

✔ Many patriots of the American Revolution were inspired by the ideals espoused in the Declaration of Independence, namely that all men were created equal and everyone was endowed with the right to life, liberty, and the pursuit of happiness. They believed that the British king and Parliament threatened those God-given liberties (see Chapter 7). Nearly every signer of the Declaration was a wealthy man with much property and treasure to lose by going to war. Many suffered terribly for joining the patriot cause. To them, the ideals of the Revolution were more important than mere dollars and cents.

✔ During the War of 1812, quite a few Americans fought to protect their national sovereignty. They felt that Britain had no respect for America's status as an independent nation. They decided that only war would force the British and other European powers to respect American sovereignty (see Chapter 9).

✔ A notion called *Manifest Destiny* was a strong motivator for American westward expansion and the ensuing conflicts with Indian tribes (see Chapter 12). Proponents of Manifest Destiny argued that the United States was a special country founded on liberty, and thus was destined by God to spread across the continent. Americans had a duty to "settle" the continent and disseminate their ideals far and wide, even if it meant killing Indians and pushing them off their land.

✔ During the Civil War, northerners and southerners believed they were fighting for freedom. Southerners equated states' rights with their individual liberties. In separating from the North, they believed they were carrying on in the tradition of Revolutionary War patriots who had chosen separation from England. Plus, most of the war was fought in the South, so rebels were often defending their very homes. Northerners equated the Union with the Constitution and thus their own liberty. They thought that if the South prevailed, the Constitution would forever be threatened. Later in the war, northerners also fought for the abolition of slavery — literally to free other human beings. (Chapter 11 covers all these points in greater detail.)

✔ A major cause of the Spanish-American War was American anger with Spain over its poor treatment of Cuban rebels who were fighting for independence from Spain. Americans thus fought Spain to free Cuba (see Chapter 13).

✔ In the wake of that war, President William McKinley decided to occupy the Philippines as an American colony to spread the "benefit of American culture, institutions, and ideas" to the Filipinos. The trouble was that many Filipinos wanted independence more than these "benefits." They chose to fight the Americans in what became known as the Philippine-American war (see Chapter 13).

✔ In World War I, a major American war aim was to "make the world safe for democracy" by ending German militarism. Many Americans viewed this conflict as the war to end all wars, a struggle that would secure worldwide democracy once and for all (see Chapter 14).

✔ World War II was among the most idealistic of all American wars. Nearly every American loathed Nazism and Japanese Fascism and believed the war must be fought to expunge this kind of tyranny from the earth (see Chapter 15). President Roosevelt articulated these notions in his Four Freedoms.

✔ During the Cold War, Americans saw Communism as a mortal threat to human liberty. This belief led to major American wars in Korea and Vietnam, along with small conflicts in a litany of other places (see Chapters 18 and 19).

✔ A major reason for the Persian Gulf War was the American desire to free Kuwait after the Iraqis gobbled that little country up in an unprovoked invasion (Chapter 20 has the details).

✔ Ideology was a major motivation for the Global War on Terror. In the wake of terrorist attacks on the United States in 2001, Americans saw Islamic radicals as a serious threat to American freedom. The desire to roll back such radicalism and spread American-style liberty was a powerful motivator for U.S. invasions of Afghanistan in 2001 and Iraq in 2003 (Chapter 21 covers both conflicts).

Which explanation for American wars do I prefer? I would have to say ideology. The United States grew out of the *Enlightenment,* an era of European history in which notions about inalienable human rights, representative government, and personal liberty were powerful agents for change. In fact, I would argue that, in all modern history since then, ideas, whether good or bad, are what really drive events. Think, for example, of the effect that Marxist ideas about inequality and ending human poverty, economic exploitation, and private property have had on modern history. American ideas of market capitalism and individual liberties have had a similarly massive influence on humanity. Americans are traditionally an idealistic lot. Not surprisingly, American leaders are the product of this idealism, as are their decisions for war.

Who Do We Fight?

Over the course of U.S. history, Americans have fought a variety of enemies. At times, bitter enemies — such as Britain, Germany, Italy, and Japan — have later turned into friends. The opposite has also been true. China went from a good friend in the early 20th century to an implacable foe after World War II. During World War II, the Soviet Union was an ally. But, after the war, the Soviets became public-enemy number one.

The United States has never had any continuous, traditional enemy. Over time, our enemies have fit into one of three categories: continental, overseas, and ideological. Enemies in the early days of American history were continental. As of the late 19th and early 20th centuries, we began to fight overseas enemies. In more modern times, America's enemies have all been ideological.

Continental enemies: Battling on our turf

From 1776 to about 1890, Americans were primarily fixated with expanding across the American continent. In fact, during that time, nearly every American war was fought here in North America, against enemies who were either threatening American sovereignty or competing for influence on this continent. These enemies fit into three subcategories:

Colonial European powers

Until the early 19th century, Britain, France, and Spain collectively controlled most of North and South America. Throughout the colonial period, Americans fought against the French, most notably from 1754 to 1763, in what became known as the French and Indian War. In the late 18th and early 19th centuries,

Americans at times engaged in small skirmishes with the Spanish in such places as Florida, Alabama, and Louisiana. The biggest tilts were, of course, against the British. Americans launched a revolution to be free from Britain. Later, from 1812 through 1815, they fought another war with the old mother country. (The chapters in Part II cover these wars.)

Native Americans

Native American tribes were the most powerful and feared continental enemies of the United States. Before 1890, as the U.S. relentlessly expanded westward, Americans fought a dizzying series of wars against various tribes. The deadliest, and most important, of these struggles were

- The Seminole Wars, 1817–1818, 1835–1842
- The Black Hawk War, 1832
- The Creek Uprising, 1835–1837
- The Dakota War, 1862
- The Black Hills War, 1876–1877
- The Nez Perce War, 1877
- The Apache Wars, 1864–1886

Eventually, through sheer determination, economic power, and ruthlessness, the United States overwhelmed all these tribes.

Continental competitors

In 1821, Mexico won its independence from Spain. The Mexicans believed they had inherited significant portions of the Spanish empire — roughly today's southwestern part of the U.S. — that lay right in the path of American westward expansion. This disagreement between Mexicans and Americans over who should control the Southwest led to a war between the two countries that the United States won decisively. (Chapter 10 addresses this war with our neighbor to the south.)

There's another wrinkle to this subcategory. From 1861 to 1865, during the Civil War, Americans were actually continental competitors with other Americans. Over the course of those four bloody years, northerners and southerners fought to determine whose vision would prevail for America. Southerners wanted their own independent nation based on an agricultural system of slave labor. Northerners wanted one indivisible nation based on free-labor capitalism and industrialization. The North's vision prevailed. (Chapter 11 has the ugly details.)

Overseas enemies: Fighting on foreign soil

After 1890, the United States fought all of its wars overseas. With the continent fully under control, Americans now became interested in overseas markets for their products and world-power status for their nation. Indeed, the goal of American policymakers was to fight their enemies not here on U.S. soil, but far from American shores.

The U.S. has battled with the vast majority of its overseas enemies because of ideological differences. However, from 1898 through 1918, the U.S. fought three overseas wars in which ideology was not the major point of contention:

- The Spanish-American War (1898) was an imperial contest between a declining Spanish empire and a rising American economic superpower (see Chapter 13).
- The Philippine-American War (1899–1913) was the only time the United States ever fought to establish a colony overseas. The war led to 50 years of American colonial occupation in the Philippines (see Chapter 13).
- Although the United States hoped to spread democracy by entering World War I, Americans fought in that war mainly to prevent imperial Germany from dominating Europe (see Chapter 14).

Ideological enemies: Standing up for what we believe

From World War II through the present, Americans have fought against enemies whose ideologies differ dramatically from the American philosophy of free trade, individual liberties, and constitutional government. The U.S. has fought bitter, costly wars against Fascists, Communists, and radical Islamic fundamentalists (whom Americans generically call "terrorists").

Fascists

In World War II, the enemies of the United States were all Fascists. *Fascism* was an ideology that espoused racial supremacy, total government control at the expense of civil liberties, wars of conquest, and genocide against certain "inferior" ethnic groups, most notably Jews. Italy, Japan, and Germany were all controlled by such aggressive, conquest-minded Fascist governments, the most notorious of which was the Nazis in Germany. The Nazis plunged Europe into war, and the Japanese did the same in the Pacific. The United States participated in an Allied coalition that fought a successful two-front war to destroy Fascism once and for all. (Chapters 15 and 16 cover World War II.)

Communists

From 1945 through 1991, the United States was almost totally preoccupied with stopping the spread of Communism, yet another ideology that was opposed to American values.

Communism was based on the prolific writings of Karl Marx, a 19th-century social critic and philosopher. Communists believed that, in the emerging industrial world, capitalism and private property were inherently exploitive of the average person. Communists wanted to eliminate private property in favor of collective ownership through the government. They also derided religion as an "opiate of the masses." In other words, they believed that, throughout history, the elite simply used religion to exploit the poor and the weak.

Communists espoused something called the *dialectic* that basically meant that the triumph of world Communism was inevitable. Although Communists supported racial and gender equality, they viewed individual liberties as unimportant. Only the collective truly mattered. Communist parties in Russia, China, Korea, Vietnam, Cambodia, and Cuba all tried to create societal equality by force. As a result, millions perished.

The ideological differences between the capitalist United States and the Communist Soviet Union were a major cause of the long struggle known as the Cold War (see Chapter 17). The triumph of Communism in China ended the friendship between that country and the U.S. During the Cold War, Americans fought in such faraway places as Korea and Vietnam to prevent the spread of Communism (see Chapters 18 and 19). Americans also fought Communists in small proxy wars in such places as Laos, Afghanistan, El Salvador, Nicaragua, and Grenada. In the end, most Communist regimes collapsed under the weight of their own tyranny and economic failures. This included the Soviet Union in 1991.

Radical Islamic fundamentalists

With about one billion believers, Islam is one of the world's major religions. Islam is prevalent in the Arab Middle East, along with large portions of Africa and Asia. Members of this *monotheistic faith* (the worship of one god) are generally known as Muslims. The majority of Muslims are peaceful, law-abiding people. However, some are not.

From the late 1960s onward, radical Islamic fundamentalists have deeply resented oil-motivated American encroachment on the sacred Muslim soil of the Middle East. They view Americans as *infidels,* which means they are nonbelievers in Islam, and hence worthy of contempt. The radicals believe in no separation of church and state and that women should be completely subservient to men. Islam, in their view, could never reconcile with Christianity, Judaism, or any other infidel religion.

Another reason they hate the U.S. is because of American support for Israel, the Jewish nation-state in the Middle East. Islamic fundamentalists loathe Israel for two reasons. First, they believe that Israel exists at the expense of the Palestinians, a neighboring Arab-Muslim group. Second, they just plain hate Jews for religious and racial reasons.

Radical Islamic fundamentalists, hailing from a multitude of countries, have repeatedly attacked Israel and the United States. Their main weapon has been *terrorism,* a tactic of indiscriminate violence, including the wanton butchery of women and children, for some sort of political, religious, or ideological goal. Terrorists generally operate within small, cohesive, shadowy groups of true believers. They thrive on intimidation, bombing crowded places, hijacking airplanes, and randomly killing anyone who doesn't submit to them.

The most dangerous of all radical Islamic terrorists are groups like Al Qaeda, the outfit that unleashed the 9/11 attacks. Al Qaeda wanted to create something called a *caliphate.* This meant they wanted to subject major portions of the planet to an absolute *theocracy* (form of government) under their control. Those who would live in an Al Qaeda–run caliphate would enjoy no semblance of civil liberties, such as freedom of speech, freedom of worship, or freedom of assembly. Women would be treated as mere breeders. Anyone diverging from the dictates of religious authorities would be swiftly punished.

After September 11, 2001, the United States prosecuted a Global War on Terror against these ideological opponents. The invasions of Afghanistan and Iraq were major components of this war against radical Muslims. (Chapter 21 takes a look at these wars.)

Chapter 3

Meeting the Players

. . . .

In This Chapter

▶ Calling the shots

▶ Fighting the wars

▶ Carrying on at home

. . . .

Like any good drama, U.S. military history has a cast of characters. In studying the topic, you find that nearly every American is somehow involved in the story of our wars, from mighty generals to lowly field hands. Almost everyone has had a role to play, whether starring or as an extra. Some did the fighting. Some served in the armed forces but functioned in a support role, never hearing a shot fired in anger. At home, some Americans found prosperous wartime jobs. Others descended into financial ruin, losing homes, farms, and property that could never be replaced. Hovering above the chaotic squall of war were the civilian leaders who set wartime policies and objectives. The best of them, such as Abraham Lincoln and Franklin Roosevelt, provided a steady hand during trying circumstances.

In this chapter, I take a look at the leaders, both civilian and military, who have made key wartime decisions. I explain why Americans have joined the military, who has done the real fighting in wartime, and how the military is set up. Finally, I show you how Americans on the home front have been affected by our wars.

Leading the Charge

Two kinds of leaders call the shots for Americans in time of war: civilian officeholders (politicians) and generals. The job of these high-level leaders is to think about the big picture: Why are we fighting? What do we hope to achieve? What is the best way to coordinate our war effort? How can we fulfill our war aims in the fastest way possible at the least cost in blood and treasure?

In doing their jobs, leaders constantly think about strategy and tactics. There is a distinct difference between the two.

- ✓ **Strategy** has to do with *why* a war is fought. Politicians tend to make strategic decisions.
- ✓ **Tactics** are about *how* a war is fought. Generals and other military leaders lower in the chain of command often make tactical decisions.

For instance, in World War II, when the U.S. fought a two-front war in Europe and the Pacific, American strategy for victory was to defeat Germany first, then deal with Japan. Why? American leaders believed Europe was of primary importance to America's interests, and that Germany was the most dangerous enemy they faced. With that Germany-first strategy in place, the main American tactic for victory was to wear down Germany with a protracted air, sea, and ground campaign. Winning battle after battle, American tactical triumphs eventually produced the strategic aim of defeating Germany first.

Tactical victories in battle don't always equate to strategic victory in war. In other words, one side can consistently defeat its opponent on the battlefield, but not win the war. The American Revolution is a good example of this. The American patriots won very few tactical victories in pitched battles against the British. They didn't have to, though. Over time, simply through their mere ability to avoid total defeat, they wore down the British and eventually fulfilled the patriot side's strategic aim of independence.

Keeping tabs on the generals: Politicians

Americans strongly believe that elected civilian leaders should control the military, not the other way around. The president of the United States functions as the commander-in-chief of the armed forces. That makes the president the superior officer of even the highest-ranking generals. So, the president, congressmen, and other civilian leaders such as Cabinet members set policy, make strategic decisions, and order the soldiers to carry them out. This gives the politicians tremendous responsibility for making life-and-death decisions. The ultimate burden, of course, rests with the president. James Madison, who directed the War of 1812, was the first wartime president. George W. Bush, who presided over invasions of Afghanistan and Iraq, is the most recent.

Setting policies for the forces: Generals

The highest-ranking, most senior officers in the armed forces are generals. The naval equivalent of a general is an admiral. Generals have commanded anywhere from a few thousand soldiers in the Revolutionary Era to hundreds of thousands in the 20th century. These senior leaders do, at times, make

Knowing the different types of generals

In the U.S. military, not all generals are created equal. There are actually several different ranks among generals and admirals.

✔ A one-star general is known as a *brigadier general.* He is the lowest-ranking general officer. He commands, on average, about 10,000 soldiers.

✔ A two-star general is known as a *major general.* He has responsibility for anywhere between 15,000 and 60,000 soldiers.

✔ The next rung up the ladder is a three-star, known as a *lieutenant general.* His responsibilities are vast. Lieutenant generals normally command at least 50,000 troops and sometimes as many as half a million.

✔ A four-star is known as a *full general,* and that's normally as high as an officer can go. A full general may command hundreds of thousands of troops. Or he can serve as *chief of staff,* the highest position in the Army.

The Navy has its own equivalents to these ranks.

✔ A *rear admiral (lower)* is akin to a brigadier general.

✔ A *rear admiral (upper)* is comparable to a major general.

✔ A *vice admiral* is the naval counterpart to a lieutenant general.

✔ And then, of course, there are four-star, *full admirals.*

A few men have earned a special five-star rank that means *general of the Army* or *fleet admiral.* The five-star generals are George Marshall, Dwight Eisenhower, Henry "Hap" Arnold, Douglas MacArthur, and Omar Bradley. The five-star admirals are William Leahy, Ernest King, Chester Nimitz, and William "Bull" Halsey.

strategic decisions, but primarily their job is to implement the strategic policies handed down to them by civilian leaders. To do this, generals devise tactics that they hope will produce victory:

✔ During the Mexican-American War, Gen. Winfield Scott's aim, as given to him by his superior, President James K. Polk, was to persuade Mexico to cede much of the southwest to the United States. Scott chose to do this with an invasion of Mexico itself. By boldly maneuvering his army, employing artillery wisely, and attacking at key moments, he eventually captured Mexico City. The result was the fulfillment of American war aims. (Chapter 10 details Scott's campaign.)

✔ In World War II, Gen. Dwight Eisenhower's civilian masters assigned him the task of invading German-occupied Europe. He put together a massive, multinational, combined arms force of air, land, and sea forces that overwhelmed German defenders in Normandy, France. This hastened the ultimate defeat of Nazi Germany. (Chapter 16 tells of the Normandy invasion.)

✔ During the Gulf War, Gen. Norman Schwarzkopf's mission was to push Iraqi military forces out of Kuwait. To do so, he devised elaborate tactics. For nearly six weeks, he wore down the Iraqi troops with constant air attacks. Then, when he set his ground forces in motion, he surprised the Iraqis by attacking their vulnerable western flank, crushing them, and forcing their retreat from Kuwait. (Chapter 20 has more on Schwarzkopf's tactics.)

American generals have sometimes chosen unsuccessful tactics. During the Vietnam War, America's strategic aim was to prevent non-Communist South Vietnam from being destroyed by Communist North Vietnam and a Communist insurgency known as the *Viet Cong.* To attain the objective of securing South Vietnam, Gen. William Westmoreland built up American troop strength and tried to wear down the enemy through *attrition,* by pursuing large battles in which the U.S. could bring to bear its enormous firepower. The enemy responded with *guerrilla tactics,* avoiding big battles, inflicting losses on the Americans through hit-and-run fighting, drawing out the war, year after year. The U.S. casualties that ensued, along with the lack of tangible results, wore down American political support at home. The Communists ultimately triumphed in South Vietnam. (Chapter 19 covers this largely unpopular war.)

Doing the Grunt Work

Soldiers are the men, and more recently the women, who fight America's wars. The word *soldier* has a dual meaning. In a generic sense, it can refer to all of those who serve in the armed forces. More specifically, the word soldier often means those who serve in the United States Army. Those who serve in the Navy are known as *sailors.* Air Force personnel are called *airmen.* Members of the United States Marine Corps are called *Marines.* (Chapter 4 explains each branch of the service in more detail.) In this section, I'm referring to the larger, more generic term of soldier.

Who are these people called soldiers?

From colonial times through the present, millions of Americans have served in the armed forces, in time of war and in time of peace. That's obviously a big group of folks, so it's impossible to generalize about who they were or are. It's fair to say, though, that young men — sometimes very young — have done the vast majority of the fighting (see Figure 3-1), mainly because women were excluded from the armed forces until only recently.

Almost all warriors in U.S. history have been men. Because of societal beliefs that the military was not for women, few even served in the armed forces before World War II. From World War II through Vietnam, thousands of women served, but always in noncombat jobs. That changed after Vietnam when women began serving as combat aviators, intelligence specialists, and as crewmen aboard warships. Even now, though, women are still excluded from ground combat units and Special Operations forces.

Figure 3-1:
Young Marine recruits are reflective before beginning a grueling three-day exercise, known as the "Crucible," capping their boot camp experience.

© Peter Turnley/Corbis

The military has generally been dominated by Caucasians because, at times, racial prejudice barred African Americans from seeing combat or even serving at all. Beyond these basic facts, you can best understand something about the people who have worn a military uniform by considering the soldiers' backgrounds and why they join the military.

Assembling a mixed bag of just plain folk

In American history, soldiers have come from all over the country. Northerners have fought alongside southerners, westerners with easterners, and so on. Over the broad sweep of American history, no region, ethnic group, or race can claim to have predominantly served more than any other groups in the armed forces. However, at times, some regions or groups have stood out:

✔ Southerners and westerners mostly populated the Army's ranks during the War of 1812. This was because the war was popular in the South and the West, but not in the Northeast.

✔ In the period before the Civil War, service in the armed forces was very unpopular with most Americans. No draft existed. Serving in the Army or the Navy promised a Spartan existence with poor pay in desolate places. Thus, most American men shunned military service. So, who served? From 1815 through 1860, the Army's ranks were dominated by European immigrants who had few other options but the military. At any given time during those years, more than half of all enlisted soldiers were foreign-born.

- In the Civil War, one out of every three white southern men of military age became a casualty. This meant that, in the South, service in the Confederate Army was nearly a universal experience for young men. In the North, though, only about half of all eligible men served in the Army.

- From the Civil War onward, large numbers of African American men served in the armed forces. Some 86,000 black men served in the Union Army during the Civil War. About half of them were ex-slaves, and the other half were free-born men from the North. From the Civil War through World War II, African American soldiers almost always served in segregated, all-black units under the control of white officers.

- In the early 20th century, white southerners dominated the officer ranks of the United States Marine Corps.

- In both world wars, no particular region, race, or demographic group was predominant in the armed forces.

- During both the Korean and Vietnam wars, small-town, working-class white men under the age of 21 were slightly overrepresented in the Army and Marine Corps ranks.

- Officers have tended to come from more educated, affluent backgrounds than enlisted men. This was especially true in the 19th century.

On July 26, 1948, President Harry Truman signed Executive Order 9981, a momentous, long-overdue measure that changed the military forever by mandating desegregation of the armed forces. Specifically, it said that "there shall be equality of treatment and opportunity for all persons in the armed services without regard to race, color, religious or national origin." It took several years to implement this order throughout the vast U.S. armed forces. The last segregated unit was abolished in 1954. Desegregation did more than bring some semblance of social justice to the military. It also led to an infusion of African American manpower into combat units, enhancing the effectiveness of American fighting forces.

Serving their country for a variety of reasons

Americans have joined the armed forces for myriad reasons, from coercion to idealism. In 1917–1918, and from 1940 through 1973, the *draft* was the law of the land. This meant that nearly all able-bodied young men were subject to at least two years of military service. So millions of Americans entered the military because they had to. The only other time in American history that men entered the armed forces against their will was during the Civil War, when both sides employed the draft. In that case, the draft didn't really yield much manpower for either side. The vast majority of those who did the fighting, both North and South, were volunteers.

Indeed, when you take the whole span of U.S. history into account, American military personnel have generally been volunteers. Their motivation for joining, of course, varied by the individual, but there have been some common reasons:

- ✔ **Economics:** The military offered such enticements as a steady job, land, pensions, educational benefits, health benefits, and loans.

- ✔ **Escape:** Some have joined to escape bad family situations, dead-end lives, boring hometowns, or even criminal prosecution.

- ✔ **Idealism:** Many Americans have joined out of sheer patriotism, a desire to serve the country, and in time of war, to fight for freedom. Idealism was a potent motivator during the Revolution, the Civil War, World Wars I and II, Vietnam, and the Global War on Terror.

- ✔ **Peer pressure:** Men often enlisted in the armed services because their buddies were doing it. In some cases, such as the Civil War and World War II, communities exerted great pressure on young men to sign up.

- ✔ **Adventure:** Quite a few Americans have joined the armed forces in hopes of experiencing adventure. This was especially true for those who served in the Indian Wars of the 19th century, along with those who fought in the Spanish-American War and nearly every war since World War II.

Ranking the soldiers

In the U.S. military, there are basically two groupings of rank — commissioned officers and enlisted personnel.

Officers are the leaders and managers. They hold commissions given to them by Congress. They comprise, on average, about 7 to 10 percent of each armed service. Their job is to think, plan, lead, and inspire. Throughout the military's history, they have generally received higher pay, better uniforms, better food, special privileges, and better treatment in general. Officer ranks range from second lieutenants at the very bottom of the scale to full generals at the top.

Enlisted personnel comprise the great majority of the military. They are the doers who carry out the real work, whether that means driving a truck, standing guard, or storming an enemy-held beach. Throughout history, enlisted men have done most of the fighting and dying.

Enlisted ranks vary from private at the bottom to command sergeant major, the highest-ranking enlisted man. The real leaders in the enlisted ranks are the sergeants (the Navy calls them petty officers). These sergeants are like supervisors. They carry out the orders they receive from commissioned officers. In combat, sergeants are usually the real leaders and the best soldiers. An army is only as good as its sergeants.

Supporting the front line

One of the realities of modern war is that well-equipped and well-trained frontline fighting forces require vast amounts of support from those who are behind the lines. Somebody has to take care of administration, keep the records, organize the war effort, cook the food, build the roads, man the ships, and move the supplies. This has especially been true for the U.S. because the American war-making philosophy has been to expend *materiel* (weapons and supplies) rather than manpower. Americans value the importance of the individual, so they are usually reluctant to suffer large numbers of casualties.

What this means is that the majority of American servicemen have functioned in fairly safe, noncombat roles, working to support the minority who did the real fighting. These supporters performed vital jobs, but they didn't see any action. This has particularly been true from World War I onward, when Americans fought overseas and could afford to send fewer men into actual combat.

During that same time, the American aversion to casualties grew, as did the importance of technical services such as the Air Force, which could only function with large numbers of technicians, mechanics, and other specialists to keep a relatively small number of planes and combat aviators in the air. The same was true for the Navy, which required major maintenance, repair, and technical know-how to keep its own ships and aircraft in operation. Even the Army came to be dominated by noncombat soldiers who worked in a variety of jobs such as finance, transportation, administration, civil engineering, and supply. The only exception was the Marine Corps, which remained true to its combat-first ethos. However, the Marines have always been heavily dependent upon other services for logistical support.

In World War II, for every American soldier on the front line, about five were in rear areas, working in support jobs. Quite a few support troops never even deployed overseas. In Vietnam, this "tooth to tail ratio" was at least seven-to-one. During the Gulf War, the ratio grew to almost ten-to-one.

Fighting on the front line

The traditional job of combat troops is to face danger, defeat the enemy, and fulfill America's wartime objectives. From the days of the Revolution to the war in Iraq, this is what American warriors have done. They fly airstrikes, sally forth in submarines or on surface warships, or shoot it out with America's enemies on the ground. Nowadays, the terms we use to describe them are *trigger pullers, grunts,* or those at the *tip of the spear.* In bygone days, they were known by many other monikers such as minutemen, Billy Yanks, Johnny Rebs, doughboys, fighter jocks, and dogfaces. Basically, all these terms simply refer to those who do the actual fighting and dying. Their dangerous jobs have required supreme courage and sacrifice. And, don't forget, they've almost always been the minority of those who serve in uniform. In wartime, everyone in the military and, to some extent, even on the home front, exists to support them.

Here's a quick look at the main combat components that make up each branch of the military:

- ✔ **Air Force:** Bomber crewmen, fighter pilots, reconnaissance pilots, pararescuemen, medics, ground security detachments, and special operations personnel.

- ✔ **Navy:** Crewmen on surface warships and submarines; fighter pilots and other combat aviators; medics; and Special Operations forces such as highly trained SEAL (Sea, Air, and Land) operators.

- ✔ **Marine Corps and Army:** Cavalrymen, artillerymen, engineers, demolitions specialists, helicopter crewmen, medics, tank crewmen, antiaircraft troops, infantrymen, and a variety of highly trained Special Operations forces.

What was it like to be an American ground combat soldier in World War II? In a word, dangerous. Almost two-thirds of the Americans killed in that war were ground combat troops. Over the course of the war, ground units routinely suffered 100 to 200 percent casualty rates. That meant if a soldier was in combat long enough, his chances of getting hit were certain. Combat soldiers lived in the elements, dealing with extreme heat, extreme cold, and everything in between. They ate prepackaged rations rather than hot food. Commonly, they went months without a bath or a shower. A man's existence consisted of going forward into danger, fighting the enemy every day. If he survived, he could only look forward to doing it all over again the next day. Ground troops usually didn't have *tours of duty.* This meant they were on the front lines for the duration of the war. Only life-threatening illnesses, mental breakdown, or wounds offered a way off the front line. Most combat soldiers yearned for safer jobs. Nonetheless, they developed a fierce pride in their status as warriors, as well as a deep disdain for the support troops who were safe and warm, far behind the front lines.

Living on the Home Front

The U.S. military is merely a product of the society it protects. All the supplies, all the monetary support, all the political direction, and even the moral support that military forces require come from civilians on the home front. At times in U.S. history, the home front has been marred by war, as during the French and Indian War, the Revolution, the War of 1812, the Indian Wars, and of course, the Civil War (mainly for the South). More commonly, from the Spanish-American War through the present, the home front has been far away from overseas battle fronts, safely distant from the realities of war.

Audie Murphy — the American warrior

No single person signifies the American warrior more than Audie Murphy, who served in the 3rd Infantry Division during World War II. Born in 1924 to poor sharecroppers in Texas, the baby-faced Murphy volunteered for the Marines when war broke out, but they rejected him on the basis that he was too small and weak. The Army eventually took him but attempted to make him into a cook. He insisted on becoming a combat soldier, though.

From his first battle in Sicily in 1943, to the end of the war in 1945, he demonstrated amazing courage and uncanny talent as a combat infantryman. His bravery and inherent leadership ability earned him a slew of medals and an officer's commission. Murphy even earned the Medal of Honor, the nation's highest military award, for single-handedly disrupting a German counterattack against his unit in January 1945. By the time the war ended, he was the most decorated, and probably the most famous, American soldier.

His extensive combat experiences led to a lifelong struggle with post-traumatic stress disorder, but Murphy built a successful postwar career as a rancher and movie star before dying in a plane crash in 1971. He resonated with the American people because he didn't look the part of a super-soldier. He was an everyman, a small-town kid who made good. Today his name is synonymous with courage and the warrior spirit that all the services attempt to cultivate in their combat troops.

In fact, one can argue that, since the late 19th century, the main mission of the U.S. armed forces has been to shield the home front from the fires of war. Even so, American civilians have inevitably been affected by the wars their country fights, no matter whether those wars have been fought close by or thousands of miles away.

Politicking in the homeland

One of the great myths of U.S. military history is that politics cease in times of war. They don't. If they ever did, the United States would no longer be a free country. Debates about taxes, budgets, national policies, and prospective new laws have always taken place, even in the midst of war. The same is true for elections. Abraham Lincoln was proud, for example, that, even in the middle of the Civil War, the North held a fair presidential election in 1864. No war has ever stopped a congressional or presidential election.

Of course, wartime politics have often been dominated by furious debates over the wisdom, importance, and even morality of whatever war we happened to be fighting at the time. Nearly every war in American history has sparked some level of opposition. In fact, throughout American military history, political debate and bitter disagreements in times of war have been so common as to be routine.

During the Revolution, the Continental Congress was a viper's nest of political infighting. The main bone of contention was the power of the states versus the power of national authorities. Moreover, anywhere from 30 to 40 percent of the American people wanted to remain loyal to Britain. New Englanders stridently opposed the War of 1812, mainly because it hurt their trade with Great Britain. Many northerners were dead set against the Mexican-American War because they believed it was a southern plot to acquire more slave territory. During the Civil War, both Abraham Lincoln in the North and Jefferson Davis in the South dealt with large numbers of serious antiwar political opponents. From 1900 to 1904, members of the Anti-Imperialist League spoke out against the Philippine-American War. One of the most eloquent voices of the League was author Mark Twain. World War I was a popular war, but about 15 percent of the population opposed it. Nearly every post–World War II conflict has led to significant opposition, the most obvious example being Vietnam. As a rule of thumb, the longer an American war drags on, the more unpopular it becomes.

Keeping the home fires burning

Almost all Americans were deeply affected by the early wars in American history, especially the Revolution and the Civil War. While most wanted little more than to be left alone to raise families and tend their farms, they couldn't escape the war. The Revolution pitted neighbor against neighbor, sometimes in guerrilla fighting, as patriot sympathizers battled those who were loyal to the British. Soldiers of both sides stole farmer's crops, burned their homes, and appropriated goods from merchants. The Civil War was a traumatic experience too, felt to the core by most Americans, especially white southerners who lost homes, property, land, and at times, dignity. The war certainly affected one other major group of civilians — slaves. As Union armies overran the South, ex-slaves began new lives as free men and women. Northerners saw their cities grow dramatically, creating a burgeoning industrial world around them.

The wars of the post-20th-century period were not quite as traumatic because they were fought overseas. But, even so, civilians were affected economically, culturally, and politically by all of them, particularly World War II. During that war, civilians dealt with rationing and shortages of such items as sugar, tobacco, and gasoline. The war also led to significant racial reform, almost total employment, decades of subsequent prosperity, and the rise of California as the most populous state. Of course, these wars deeply affect those who have loved ones overseas in the military. Wartime deployments have compelled young lovers to marry, parents to send care packages, and civilians, in general, to rally around their flag.

In order to conserve gasoline and keep tires from wearing out, the national speed limit during World War II was 35 miles per hour.

Chapter 4

Lining Up the Armed Services

● ●

In This Chapter

▶ Understanding the military

▶ Discovering the purpose of each branch of the service

▶ Recognizing each branch's role in history

● ●

*P*eople often refer to the branches of the armed forces as "the military." Actually, this is a pretty vague term, sort of like referring to a carbonated drink as just a "soda" or a "pop." Just as soft drink brands have stories and generate fierce loyalty, the same is true for the armed forces.

Each branch of the armed forces has its unique history, traditions, and distinctive purpose. For much of American history, the branches have been plagued by intense interservice rivalry; the source of the rivalries less visible to the public is competition for congressional budget dollars.

The very visible side of the rivalries comes from sheer pride. The Army and the Navy are big rivals; always have been, always will be. However, the Army and Navy agree that the Air Force is soft. On the other hand, the Marine Corps thinks of itself as the toughest of all. And so it goes.

At times, these rivalries have been so intense that the animosity they generated damaged national security. The best example is Pearl Harbor. Army and Navy intelligence shared little, if any, information on Japanese intentions. Adm. Husband Kimmel, the Navy commander of the Pacific Fleet, and his Army colleague, Lt. Gen. Walter Short, didn't coordinate their efforts well enough at Pearl Harbor. The poor working relationship between the two branches made U.S. forces at Pearl Harbor quite vulnerable and contributed to the disaster that happened on December 7, 1941.

Fortunately, in recent years interservice rivalry is managed with a greater emphasis placed on the need to work together. This new mind-set, often called *jointness,* is the result of greater professionalism, more interservice integration, and a greater realization than ever before that all the services must cooperate for the good of the country. In this chapter, I explain the responsibilities of each branch, important moments in their histories, and what it takes to serve our country.

The Army

Born on June 14, 1775, the Army is the oldest and largest of America's armed services. It's also the most diverse and, by virtue of its size, most closely reflects the population. In combat, the Army is the main land force, although it has an aviation branch as well. The U.S. Army's job is to defend the country's borders and defeat enemy ground forces, wherever they may be.

The Army is made up of many parts, such as aviation, artillery, and infantry, and it's equipped for a variety of missions, both combat and noncombat. Basically, the Army does it all. For example, in World War II, the Army built roads, hauled supplies, and handled administrative duties. Meanwhile, it also did most of the ground fighting that won the war.

As the oldest of the armed services, the Army is deeply proud of its history and traditions. For well over two centuries, the Army has carried the weight of America's wars. From the Revolutionary-era soldier who toted a musket at Bunker Hill to the lavishly equipped GI carrying a Squad Automatic Weapon (SAW) in Iraq, the Army is normally the first line of defense. This elicits great pride among soldiers. Every combat unit fiercely protects its *colors.* This flag, adorned with ribbon-like battle streamers, carries the unique emblem of the unit. For instance, one unit, the 7th Infantry Regiment, traces its heritage all the way back to the War of 1812. Soldiers from this regiment have fought in every American war since, earning more battle streamers than any other American combat formation.

You're in the Army now

Members of the Army are known as *soldiers.* They are sometimes referred to as *GIs* (short for *government issue*), *Joes* (because American men are commonly named Joe), *troops,* or in the case of cavalry units, *troopers.*

Infantry soldiers are the backbone of the Army. These men fight the enemy at close quarters, killing them, capturing objectives, and controlling ground. When war comes, they do most of the fighting. Their job is the essential job of the Army — close with and destroy the enemy. Throughout the history of American wars, they have done most of the dying. In World War II, infantry soldiers comprised about 15 percent of the American armed forces, yet they suffered 70 percent of the casualties. In World War I, they were known as *doughboys.* In World War II, they were commonly called *dogfaces* or just *doughs.* Since Vietnam, they are usually referred to as *grunts.*

The Army features dozens of *military occupational specialties* (MOS), a term that mainly refers to the specific job a soldier performs. Just to cite a few examples, this service is home to doctors, engineers, transportation

---

The Army-Navy Game

The annual Army-Navy football game is the ultimate positive expression of interservice rivalry. Played between the United States Military Academy (West Point) and the United States Naval Academy, the game determines bragging rights each year. The two academies have squared off nearly every year since 1890. Even though the rivalry between Army and Navy is intense, the members of both services enjoy a deep and abiding camaraderie as well. After every Army-Navy game, the players line up and respectfully listen to the alma maters of both schools. On the strength of several victories in recent years, Navy has a 51-49 edge in the all-time series.

---

specialists, linguists, water-treatment experts, public relations specialists, logisticians, and helicopter pilots, as well as, of course, tankers, artillerymen, and infantrymen.

Armies within the Army

From the very beginning, the Army has been divided into distinct subgroups. During the Revolutionary War and well into the 19th century, state militia units made up a significant portion of the Army. These *minutemen,* local volunteers, or militia only took up arms for a short time and usually served close to their homes with friends and neighbors. In contrast, regular Army soldiers served full time, in peace or war, in a variety of places. Regulars accused militia of being lackluster and undisciplined; militiamen didn't understand why anyone would devote his life to the Army full time.

In the 20th century, the Army created a more modern organizational structure that has more or less endured ever since:

- ✔ **The National Guard:** These are state formations mobilized into federal service in times of war or domestic crisis, like after a natural disaster. In normal times, guardsmen train one weekend a month and two weeks over the summer.

- ✔ **Reserves:** These are specialist units, such as engineers, transportation experts, or mechanics. They are called up in time of war. Some of the Reserves are retired soldiers with combat specialties who, in wartime, return to the active-duty regular Army. At any given time, the National Guard and Reserves comprise about half of the Army.

- ✔ **The regular Army:** This is the critical mass of the U.S. Army. These professional, full-time soldiers are on active duty all the time. They perform numerous jobs, but the main combat formations of the Army are regulars.

The modern Army is heavily involved in Special Operations warfare that is carried out by carefully selected, highly trained, elite soldiers. These men serve in Special Forces, Rangers, or in the case of the ultimate warriors, Delta Force.

The Navy

The Navy is the primary maritime service of the United States. Its job is to secure the seas, lend air support, protect America's overseas interests (such as vital shipping lanes), and provide coastal defense here at home.

Naval personnel are known as *sailors*. They perform a dizzying array of jobs in this highly technical, seafaring organization. The Navy includes sailors who specialize in such jobs as avionics, engine repair, nuclear propulsion, flight operations, sonar, medicine, gunnery, missile defense, diving, and communications.

Sailors always use nautical terms, even when they're not at sea or aboard their ships. The floor is always the *deck*. Doors are *hatches*. The bathroom is the *head*. If they misbehave, they are sent to the *brig*, a naval term for jail. Gossip or rumors are called *scuttlebutt*. If something is on the left, it is on the *port* side. If it's on the right, it's referred to as the *starboard* side.

Important roles through history

Like the Army, the Navy's roots trace back to the Revolutionary War. In the summer of 1775, the Continental Congress authorized the creation of a small naval force to defend ports, harass British supply efforts, and fight enemy warships. These early American sailors played a significant role in winning the Revolution.

The Navy also played an important role in the War of 1812 and the Civil War, blunting British seaborne offensives in the former and strangling the Confederacy by controlling vital river and coastal waters in the latter.

The naval service really came into its own in the 20th century. In World War II, the Navy grew to a force of more than 5,000 warships, including 105 aircraft carriers. By 1945, the United States Navy was the largest and most powerful navy the world had ever seen. Since then, it has remained as strong as ever, typically maintaining a fleet of several hundred ships.

The big Navy

Modern ships are basically floating cities. Sailors live, eat, and work aboard their ships for months at a time. The Navy's fleet is basically divided into three kinds of warships:

- ✔ **Surface ships:** This includes destroyers, amphibious warfare ships, frigates, or in an earlier age, cruisers and battleships.

- ✔ **Aviation:** Aircraft carriers are, in the view of some naval strategists, the most important ships in the Navy. They carry airplanes and helicopters that allow the Navy to strike enemies from vast distances.

- ✔ **Submarines:** These underwater craft can destroy enemy ships, scout hostile waters, gather intelligence, land special forces, and since 1960, launch nuclear missiles. Submarine crewmen wear a dolphin insignia on their lapel. They take enormous pride in the danger of their job and their elite status.

Many of the Navy's aircraft carriers and submarines are nuclear propelled. They actually have a nuclear reactor aboard that serves as the engine.

Navy SEALs: Elite units

One of the more recent, but best known, branches of the Navy is Special Operations. Known as *SEALs* (**Se**a, **Ai**r, and **L**and), these men are true warriors. A typical SEAL platoon of about 18 sailors comprises a remarkable set of skills. SEALs can

- ✔ Swim great distances

- ✔ Fight under the water or on the water

- ✔ Seize ships or oil rigs

- ✔ Parachute from airplanes into combat

- ✔ Fight at close quarters

- ✔ Fight as infantrymen

- ✔ Gather intelligence

- ✔ Do just about anything with a variety of weapons

To become a Navy SEAL, you must endure two years of the toughest training in existence. Even then, there's no guarantee that you'll actually end up as a permanent member of a SEAL team and be deployed overseas.

Top Guns

The best known sailors in the Navy are the aviators, especially carrier-borne fighter pilots. They fly high-performance jets, like the F/A-18 Hornet, off the decks of aircraft carriers. Landing on the deck of a carrier is a real challenge, especially at night. Imagine trying to land a 13-ton, $40 million machine precisely onto a bobbing platform of steel, heading into a stiff wind. All of this must be done in such a way that the tailhook of your aircraft catches an arrestor cable perfectly enough to keep you and your aircraft from falling into the sea. That's what naval aviators do routinely.

And that's not even the most dangerous part of their job! Their mission is to engage enemy aircraft, protect the fleet, bomb enemy targets, attack enemy troops with gunfire, and fly close air support for ground troops.

The 1986 movie *Top Gun,* starring Tom Cruise, glamorized these fliers, solidifying the naval fighter jock as an icon in American pop culture. The movie's success spawned documentaries, television specials, books, and articles on naval aviators.

The Marine Corps

The United States Marine Corps is an elite, select group of warriors whose primary mission is amphibious warfare. Those who join the Marines tend to be young, physically fit, and eager for combat. Marines fight on land and in the air, even though they often originate from ships. Marines are primarily trained to fight, so their units rely on the other services for most of their logistical support, including supplies, transportation, and administration. Although the Marine Corps is a separate service, it's under the jurisdiction of the Navy. The Corps is arguably the most famous of the armed services. It's also held in the highest esteem by the average American.

What it takes to be a Marine

Marines argue that their prowess in battle comes from a regimen of tough training combined with a unique fighting spirit that is present only in the ranks of the Corps.

In the modern era, every prospective Marine must first make it through boot camp, a three-month grueling ordeal of physical training, weapons training, occasional humiliation, history lessons, and indoctrination into Marine culture. Only when a recruit completes this training is he or she entitled to be called a Marine. The new Marine can then wear the coveted eagle, globe, and anchor insignia of the Corps (see Figure 4-1).

In the Marine insignia, the eagle represents service to the American republic. The globe symbolizes the Corps' worldwide mission on behalf of that republic. The anchor is an acknowledgment that the Corps is a maritime service.

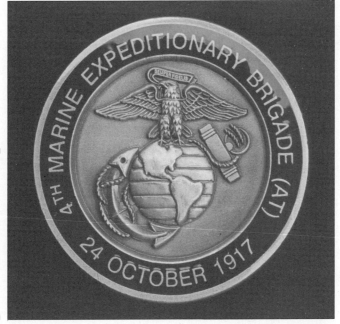

Figure 4-1:
The Marine Corps insignia shown as part of a Marine Corps badge from World War I.

© Jim Sugar/CORBIS

Marine vernacular is liberally spiced with nautical terms, even though many Marines look down on sailors as mere *squids.* Marines are called *leathernecks, jarheads,* or in the old days, *gyrenes* (from a mixture of GI and Marine). A Marine infantryman is called a *grunt,* just like his Army counterpart. But never, *ever* call a Marine a soldier. If you do, be ready to run!

From obscurity to prestige

The Corps cherishes its history and traditions more than any other service, even the lineage-conscious Army. Every Marine knows that the Corps was born on November 10, 1775. In those days of wooden ships and boarding parties that raided enemy ships, Marines served as naval infantry. They guarded U.S. ships, raided enemy ships or enemy coastlines, and protected naval bases. For the first century of its existence, the Corps was a tiny, obscure force of only a few thousand men.

In the 20th century, the Marines really came into their own. During World War I, their dauntless courage in the Battle of Belleau Wood (see Chapter 14) earned them acclaim all over America. A generation later, the Marines saw action all over the Pacific during World War II, invading numerous Japanese-held islands. The best known Marine battle is Iwo Jima (see Chapter 16), where five Marines and a naval corpsman raised a flag atop Mount Suribachi, producing the most famous image in U.S. military history (see Figure 4-2).

Figure 4-2: Marines raise the U.S. flag at Iwo Jima (now renamed to Iwo To) during World War II.

Notable Marine movies

For many Americans, knowledge of military history comes through movies. This is a bit disconcerting to stuffed-shirt military historians (like me) because filmmakers often get things wrong. Overall, though, military movies can be informative and fascinating.

The three best known Marine movies are *Sands of Iwo Jima* (1949), *Full Metal Jacket* (1987), and *Jarhead* (2005). All these films significantly influenced how people view the Corps.

In *Sands of Iwo Jima*, John Wayne is a demanding sergeant who leads a squad of newbies into combat. His men think he is overly harsh until they get to Iwo and find out that he's only looking out for their welfare. The theme is that intense Marine training is designed to help men survive in combat.

The same message resonates in Stanley Kubrick's *Full Metal Jacket*. Actor R. Lee Ermey's portrayal of a sadistic drill instructor is so ingrained in the popular culture that Ermey has often entertained real Marines with this shtick. Ermey served in Vietnam and did a stint as a drill instructor. Originally during the filming of *Full Metal Jacket*, he was only supposed to be Kubrick's expert advisor, but he persuaded the director to let him play the drill instructor. The rest, as they say, is history.

Jarhead depicts the same sense of Spartan discipline, killology mind-set, and commitment to a unique brotherhood among Marines, but with almost psychotic overtones.

There are many more good military movies. In Chapter 24, I tell you my ten favorite military movies.

Since World War II, the Marines have served in every American war, proving themselves time and again to be among the best fighters on earth.

The Coast Guard

The Coast Guard was founded in 1790. Its job is to, well, guard the U.S. coast using smaller ships than you would generally see in the Navy. With 40,000 active-duty personnel, the Coast Guard is the smallest of the services, but it engages in all kinds of missions beyond just guarding the coast. The Coast Guard assists mariners of all types, warning them of approaching storms and generally watching out for them. The service's aircraft and ships also play a vital role in helping to prevent drug cartels from moving their products into the U.S. by air and sea.

One of the primary missions of Coast Guardsmen is search and rescue. If any sort of vessel is in peril in American waters, Coast Guard ships scramble to help, no matter what the weather. During the aftermath of Hurricane Katrina in New Orleans, Coast Guard helicopter crewmen and boat teams roamed the area, searching for people to help.

In spite of the name, the Coast Guard does not serve exclusively at home. During World War II, Coast Guard vessels participated in many amphibious invasions. The most notable Coast Guardsmen were *coxswains* of landing craft. The coxswains navigated their shallow draft boats onto the beach, where their boatloads of soldiers or Marines would then invade, all under fire. Coast Guardsmen also served in Vietnam and Iraq.

Unlike the other services, the Coast Guard is not part of the Department of Defense. It used to be under the Department of Transportation but was made part of the newly created Department of Homeland Security in 2003.

The Air Force

The Air Force is the baby of the services because the technology of flying developed after the other forms of warfare. Instead of being its own branch, the Air Force was part of the Army in both world wars. Only in 1947 did the Air Force, after years of lobbying by its leaders, become an independent service.

The Air Force's mission is to fly and fight in air, space, and today, even in cyberspace against anti-American computer hackers. This is because it's the most technologically advanced of all American armed forces. The Air Force possesses a diverse array of weapons, from high-performance fighters to heavy bombers to missiles. One of the Air Force's most potent assets is its ability to airlift massive amounts of supplies or troops to most anyplace in the world. All told, the Air Force has about 9,000 aircraft.

High-flying airmen and aces

Members of the Air Force are known as *airmen*. This is true even of women, who make up a substantial part of the service. Any pilot who shoots down five or more enemy aircraft is known as an *ace*. The Air Force employs thousands of technicians, computer specialists, air traffic controllers, medics, and weather analysts, to name only a few specialties.

Air Force officers generally face more danger than lower-ranking enlisted personnel, who often perform safer support jobs on the ground. The opposite is usually true in the other branches of the military. But in the Air Force, most aviators are officers, and the aviators do much of the fighting. They fly fighters, helicopters, bombers, fuel tankers, and transports. They rely on many thousands of support airmen who perform vital maintenance and logistical tasks.

The Air Force, like the other services, has highly trained, elite Special Operations warriors. Air Force *pararescuemen* (generally known as parajumpers or PJs) are trained to rescue downed aircrew in any and all environments, whether that's a raging sea or a remote, snow-covered mountain. Their motto is "So that others might live."

Air Force outfits (No, not their shirts and shoes)

Like the Army, the Air Force is divided into three main components:

- ✔ **The active-duty force:** These are the full-time, professional airmen, who serve year-round on active duty. This force consists of about 350,000 airmen.

- ✔ **Air Force National Guard:** They belong to state units that, in time of war, can be called into federal service. These 100,000 airmen serve one weekend per month and two months over the summer.

- ✔ **Air Force Reserves:** These are mostly part-time specialists in finance, administration, and aerospace engineering. The Reserves number some 72,000 airmen.

In a show of interservice cooperation, specialized Air Force units work with Army troops to provide support and protection. The Air Force has tactical air control parties that deploy with Army Special Forces teams to provide them with air support. The same is true of forward air controllers who live and work with the Army's conventional ground combat units.

Ever since the start of World War II, Air Force commanders have sometimes disagreed with their colleagues in the other services over the proper role of the Air Force. Air power is such an awesome weapon that Air Force leaders have often viewed their service as the first line of defense. In World War II, they even argued that they could win the war on their own by bombing Germany and Japan into submission. Since then, some Air Force officers have argued the same thing, most notably during the Kosovo conflict and the Persian Gulf War. Time and again, though, their ideas have been proven wrong, especially in 21st-century Afghanistan and Iraq. Air power is very important, but most wars are won by ground troops, and that will probably never change.

A formidable opponent through history

Even though the Air Force is the newest of the military services, it has a rich history. In World War I, American pilots like Eddie Rickenbacker flew crude biplanes and earned everlasting fame for dueling with German fliers high above the trenches.

In World War II, the Air Force was the most glamorous branch to be a part of. Young men volunteered in droves to become bomber crewmen and fighter pilots. Their jobs were anything but glamorous, though. Bomber crewmen endured *flak* (antiaircraft fire), enemy fighters, and freezing temperatures at great heights while flying deep into enemy-controlled skies. Many were shot down. Fighter pilots grappled with enemy pilots, *strafed* (fired on) ground targets, flew reconnaissance missions, and escorted friendly bombers. In the process, the fighter jocks suffered heavy losses.

In Korea, Air Force fliers were so effective against North Korean, Chinese, and Russian pilots that the U.S. enjoyed mastery of the air. During the Vietnam War, the Air Force suffered heavy losses in bombing raids on North Vietnam. Most Air Force aviators in that war, though, flew in support of ground forces.

During the Gulf War, the Air Force unleashed every nonnuclear weapon in its formidable arsenal, including precision bombs, on Saddam Hussein's over-matched military. The Iraqi air force never even contested the skies, and this has been a pattern for America's enemies ever since. In the late 20th and early 21st centuries, those enemies have fought primarily on the ground, in unconventional warfare. This has relegated the Air Force to flying resupply and close air support for the Army, a prime example of the jointness of the modern military.

Chapter 5

The Changing Experience of Warfare

*T*o understand military history, you must understand how warfare has changed through the decades. The first warfare was most likely hand-to-hand, and it took place on the ground. As more sophisticated weaponry was developed, the distance between combatants grew. River and sea combat also entered the picture. Boats and ships were used to transport fighters and material as well as act as weapons. Finally, air combat was added. Technology has continuously extended the reach of warfare in every way.

Despite the "shock and awe" tactics of the Baghdad airstrikes that opened the war in Iraq, most warfare in U.S. military history has been fought on the ground, and nearly every engagement includes some level of ground combat. Wars are still usually decided by land fighting. And, as it happened in Vietnam and now in Iraq, the battlefield, in many ways, has shrunk.

Although air and sea warfare are grueling in their own ways, ground combat is among the most brutal of all human endeavors. But at its most basic level, all combat means you kill them before they kill you. How this grim reality has played out over the course of U.S. military history has shifted dramatically.

In this chapter, I look at how the battlefields, weaponry, and medical care have changed through military history. I take you into the realities of what it's like to experience combat and tell you what, throughout history, has motivated Americans to fight.

Shifting Battlefields

During the Civil War, soldiers on both sides referred to their first combat as "seeing the elephant," a 19th-century euphemism to describe experiencing danger or adventure. One hundred years later, in Vietnam, American soldiers used less elegant terms to describe the same phenomenon. Essentially these different generations of Americans conveyed the trauma of combat with colorful language.

To the participants, combat is confusing, frightening, chaotic, and terribly exhausting. This is especially true of ground combat. In modern ground combat, even the simplest task becomes difficult. Moving 20 yards, from here to there, can be the most dangerous thing imaginable. Hearing the soldier next to you may be impossible because of the din of weapons. Making a simple radio call, or peering around the next corner, can require great persistence or even superhuman bravery. Just the sheer act of raising your head and taking in the scene around you can be a scary, daunting challenge.

The changing landscape of war

If you were to observe a ground battle scene, what would you see? Well, it depends on the era. Nineteenth-century battles were usually straightforward affairs, often with soldiers out in the open. As an observer, you would see both armies on the same terrain, probably only a few hundred yards apart from one another. The sounds of screaming men, frightened horses, cannon fire, and musket balls would fill the air. Gunpowder smoke would drift everywhere, obscuring everyone, creating what is often called the *fog of war*. You would probably be impressed with the constant motion around you — men running, horses running, wounded men writhing, trees bursting, battle lines careening about in seemingly random sways of movement.

In more-modern times, mainly from World War I onward, you would notice a much emptier, but more destroyed battlefield, pockmarked by craters from artillery and churned up by heavy equipment. As weapons grew deadlier, soldiers sought cover, often below ground level in bunkers and foxholes, to survive. Thus you would have a more difficult time spotting actual soldiers or, sometimes, even knowing what you're looking at. The noise of the battle would be overwhelming — artillery and mortar shells exploding, machine guns chattering, rifles barking, vehicles churning up mud, probably even aircraft streaking overhead. If a bullet barely missed you, you'd hear its supersonic snap in your ears. If a shell scored a near miss, the explosion would momentarily suck the air from around you. The screaming, suffering, and bleeding of soldiers would be the same as at any other time in history.

As the lethality of weapons increased, combatants tended to face one another from greater distances, as across vast no man's land in World Wars I and II and Korea. Even so, modern combatants sometimes have fought at distances of less than 50 yards. This is especially true in the urban jungles of Iraq. For instance, at Fallujah in 2004, American soldiers and Marines sometimes fought their terrorist adversaries at handshake distance.

Modern battlefields have a unique odor. Spent gunpowder produces an acrid, almost sulfuric smell. This odor combines with the smells of burning buildings, vehicle fumes, the coppery smell of fresh blood, and the sickly sweet, rotting-meat smell of dead bodies, producing a powerful and unforgettable stench. The ambient conditions only add to the odors. In Korea and Vietnam, the rice paddies smelled of "night soil," a polite term for human excrement. In Iraq, the nauseating stench of open, raw sewage fermenting in a hot climate is nearly constant.

Ground combat impacts and overloads all the senses, making concentration difficult. Throw in stress, fear, fatigue, many pounds of heavy equipment, as well as a host of other overwhelming factors, and the idea of the "fog of war" begins to make more sense.

Fighting on the water

Throughout American history, naval combat has evolved substantially. In the 18th and early 19th centuries, wooden sailing ships dominated the seas. Opposing vessels usually bombarded one another from distances of less than 2 miles. The ultimate goal was to cripple the enemy ship in such a way that you could close with it, board it, and burn it. From the Civil War onward, iron-clad ships with coal or oil-burning engines and bigger guns forged a greater distance between opposing fleets.

In the 20th century, submarines and aircraft carriers took warfare below the ocean's surface and to the air above the seas. World War II marked the end of substantial surface engagements between fleets. Since then, naval warfare has been dominated by nuclear-powered submarines capable of showering an enemy with nuclear missiles, and aircraft carriers whose planes can strike a slew of targets many hundreds of miles away.

Fleets have always carried troops into battle and continue to do so. No matter the era, when the shells start to fly, sailors have nowhere to run.

The ratio of fire myth

S. L. A. Marshall, one of the greatest American combat historians of World War II, claimed in a shocking series of writings that only 15 to 25 percent of World War II U.S. soldiers ever fired their rifles in battle. He called this the *ratio of fire.* Marshall had conducted many post-battle interviews with combat soldiers, so he based his contention on those conversations. He was so influential among historians and military tacticians that most of them took his ratio of fire claims at face value, without any real evidence on his part.

Only in the 1980s, after Marshall's death, did historians and veterans begin to challenge his contentions. After much investigation of Marshall's research material, they found that he had no evidence for his claims. Thus, most World War II combat historians now view Marshall's ratio of fire as a myth.

Covering from the air

Aerial combat is the newest arena of contest. The earliest combat aviators flew open canopy biplanes that rarely exceeded altitudes of 10,000 feet. Nowadays, fighters pilots fly high-performance jets that are armed with a range of missiles, smart bombs, and cannons, and can fly twice the speed of sound at heights of 30,000 feet. In both world wars, planes locked in combat at such close distances that opposing pilots often could see the expression on their enemy's face. As in ground warfare, enhanced firepower and technology in air weapons eventually forged a greater distance between adversaries. Basically, three kinds of air combat exist:

- **Air-to-air combat (known as *dogfights*) between opposing planes:** Since Vietnam, dogfighting has declined in importance and frequency.

- **Bombing, or *strafing,* targets on the ground:** From World War II onward, this has been the most common form of air combat.

- **Launching missiles or other weaponry at distant targets:** This is a product of the space age.

Evolving Ever Deadlier Weaponry

War is hellish, and the tools of warfare are deadly. Weaponry has changed dramatically over the centuries, with each technological development changing much about how wars are fought.

Even though weapons are more sophisticated and a lot can be accomplished through airstrikes, warfare still requires putting soldiers on the battlefield to fight the enemy. Sometimes the battlefield is actually a field (as in Antietam; see Chapter 11 for more), and other times it's a complex of tunnels (as in Vietnam; read more in Chapter 19) or requires soldiers to go door-to-door (as in Iraq; read more in Chapter 21).

Guns on the ground

Ground combat features three basic types of weaponry, all of which vary in lethality and the range at which they hit their targets.

Very big guns: Artillery

Artillery are the big guns on the ground. In general, there are two types of cannons:

- ✔ **Howitzer cannons:** They fire in an arc at long-range targets.
- ✔ **Rifled cannons:** They fire their shots in a straighter line.

Modern artillery can fire a variety of deadly projectiles as far as 20 miles, and hit within a yard or two of their target. As of the Cold War, artillery could even fire nuclear weapons.

American artillery of the 18th and 19th centuries was horse-drawn. Artillery-men carried ammunition and other supplies in special wagons called *caissons.* From the Revolution through the Civil War, cannons were formidable but not especially accurate. The typical gun fired a cannonball that didn't disperse fragments all that efficiently. Sometimes, soldiers could even dodge a cannon-ball if they saw it in time.

Early 20th-century industrialization made artillery far deadlier than ever before. Two things in particular happened:

- ✔ First, the French figured out a way to minimize the *recoil* (the kick-back action a gun makes when it's fired) of their artillery pieces. This meant they could fire faster and more often.
- ✔ Second, the projectiles themselves grew more dangerous. These modern shells, fired at great distances, sprayed fragments, or *shrapnel,* in a wide arc when they exploded. The inventor's name was Henry Shrapnel.

Because of this new capability, artillery became the deadliest weapon on the battlefield in World Wars I and II, Korea, and Vietnam.

The most dangerous job in an artillery unit is *forward observer*. A forward observer is usually an officer or a senior sergeant, and his job is to find a good spot where he can observe the enemy. Then he radios back to the guns and directs their fire onto the target. Observers, by necessity, must operate close to the enemy, making them prime targets.

Mobile guns: Cavalry and armor

For centuries, *cavalrymen* (soldiers riding atop horses) were the most fearsome weapons on any battlefield. They embodied fast-moving killing power, descending on their enemies, slashing them or shooting them at close range. By the time of the Civil War, cavalry troopers had difficulty surviving the firepower that artillerymen and infantry soldiers could spew forth. So the horsemen turned to scouting and raiding.

The automated age made cavalrymen obsolete. Factories now churned out armored vehicles that possessed the mobility of cavalry but with much greater killing power. The best-known of these vehicles are, of course, tanks. They made their debut in World War I, but played an even greater role in World War II and beyond, solidifying armor as a mainstay on the modern battlefield.

A *tank* is a tracked, armored vehicle that has an artillery-like main gun, plus machine guns. Most tanks are crewed by four or five soldiers who sit packed together inside their formidable beast. A tank is the ultimate mobile land weapon. Good ones are devastating and demoralizing to any enemy.

When the British built the first tanks during World War I, the weapon was so secret that British factory workers were told that they were constructing water tanks. Hence the enduring name *tank*.

Killology

So what does *killology* mean? Well, it refers to the ways in which healthy individuals deal with the awful stress of killing. Lt. Col. Dave Grossman, in a book called *On Killing,* created the word. He argued that most human beings have a serious aversion to killing, even after completing military training.

For those who see battle and must kill, the psychological damage of doing so can be immense. The best ways to prevent such problems are for combat veterans to talk about their experiences with their comrades, understand that killing is a shared responsibility, and believe that the killing was justified by higher authorities, such as commanding officers.

Of all the services, the Marines do the most to understand the psychology of killing in combat. They give their young infantry officers classroom instruction on killology and even order them to visit inner-city emergency rooms to observe the results of shootings, stabbings, beatings, and other violence.

Portable guns: Infantry

Infantry soldiers are the core of any army. They close in on the enemy and destroy him. For most of U.S. history, they've done that grisly job with rifles. In the Revolution, American infantry soldiers mainly used smoothbore muskets of French design. The infantryman loaded his weapon by ramming the musket ball down the *bore* (the gun barrel). A good soldier could fire about four shots per minute, but rarely with any accuracy or distance because the effective range of the musket was 50 yards.

In the Civil War, rifled muskets, like the .57-caliber Enfield, doubled the rate at which a soldier could fire. *Rifling* meant the bullet would spin, enhancing its killing power. Now the soldier could score a hit up to about 300 yards. In World War I, American infantry soldiers were armed with the *breech-loading* (above the trigger) Springfield '03, a *bolt-action* (single-shot) rifle that could kill an enemy soldier within 2,000 yards, but was most effective within 500 yards.

After this came a revolution in American infantry firepower. The M1 Garand rifle, introduced in 1936, fired an eight-round clip to a greater range as fast as the rifleman could pull the trigger. The Garand was the best rifle of World War II and the Korean War. By Vietnam, it was phased out in favor of the M16, which is still in use today.

Infantry soldiers are armed with more than just rifles. To survive, they require a diverse array of weaponry for fire support. Mortars are like mini-artillery. Hand grenades kill in close spaces, as do submachine guns, like the famous Tommy gun. Machine guns are among the deadliest weapons on the modern battlefield because they pour out so many bullets so quickly. American infantry troops also use flamethrowers and special antitank weapons.

Weaponry at sea

For centuries, wooden sailing ships were the primary weapon of the sea. From about the 16th through the 19th centuries, they were armed with the same kinds of cannons that armies used on the ground. After the Civil War, armored ships with engines came to dominate the seas. By the early 20th century, the greatest of these vessels — known as battleships — weighed tens of thousands of tons and bristled with 14-inch guns that could sink opposing ships or bombard enemy shores.

Starting in the 20th century, submarines and aircraft carriers made naval warfare three-dimensional. Now the fighting took place under the sea, on the surface, and in the air. In World Wars I and II, submarines were especially deadly because they could sneak up on opposing fleets undetected, torpedo, and sink their prey. In the atomic era, subs had the capability to launch nuclear missiles at targets that were hundreds of miles away.

Modern navies developed new technology, such as sonar and radar, along with new weapons, such as depth charges and special sub-killing aircraft, to sink subs. Aircraft carriers were also powerful weapons because their planes could hit enemy ships, shoot down hostile planes, or bomb land-based targets many miles away. However, carriers were, and are, vulnerable to surface and submarine attacks.

In World War II, American submarines were so effective that, by 1945, they had sunk two-thirds of Japan's oil tankers and merchant ships. This meant Japan could not rearm, refuel, and resupply its armies. These devastating losses also helped destroy the Japanese economy. The American submariners paid a heavy price for their success, though. Almost one-third of those who went on combat patrols never returned.

Flying into war

Human beings have been fighting in the skies for nearly 100 years. In that time, there have been three basic types of aviation weaponry:

- **Propeller planes:** Prominent from World War I through the Korean War, propeller planes evolved from the biplanes of the early 20th century to single-wing, high-performance fighter aircraft such as the American P-51 Mustang, the German Focke Wulf FW 190, and the British Supermarine Spitfire. Prop planes featured anywhere from a single engine on most fighter planes to four engines on heavy bombers. Planes could drop bombs ranging from 250 to 1,000 pounds. They also bristled with machine guns and even small cannons to destroy enemy aircraft or strafe enemy troops.

- **Jet planes:** The Germans pioneered jet aircraft technology at the tail end of World War II. Since then, the bomber and fighter fleets of the world's modern air forces have generally been dominated by jets, many of which can fly well over the speed of sound. From Korea through the present day, the typical American fighter plane has been armed with conventional bombs, laser-guided bombs, heat-seeking missiles, radar-guided missiles, and cannons. The most successful American fighters of the jet era are the F-86 Sabre, F-4 Phantom, the F-14 Tomcat, the F/A-18 Hornet, the F-15 Eagle, and the F-16 Fighting Falcon. Heavy bombers, such as the venerable B-52 Stratofortress, are capable of dropping nuclear bombs or conventional bombs. The destructive power of modern bombers is literally beyond the imagination of World War II–era airmen.

- **Missiles:** Once again, the Germans led the way in missile technology. Their V1 and V2 rockets terrorized Britain in World War II. After the war, German scientists contributed much to the development of Soviet,

British, and American missile programs, resulting in space flight and, ominously, the creation of nuclear intercontinental ballistic missiles (ICBMs) capable of destroying the planet. Other unmanned air weapons of the modern period include satellites and aerial drones. Both of these weapons are equipped with sophisticated cameras that transmit valuable images to the technicians who control them.

Helicopter technology existed at the time of World War II, but the development of this new type of rotary-winged aircraft really took off (pun intended) after the war. The helicopter is a versatile weapon of war, capable of moving troops, gathering intelligence, and evacuating wounded, to name only a few tasks.

Improving Combat Medical Care

In combat, instant death is actually not all that common. When a soldier gets hit, he's most often wounded, rather than killed. But these wounds can be life threatening, including loss of limbs.

Forget what you've seen in old Hollywood war movies. Wounded soldiers don't fall down in orderly little heaps as they dramatically holler: "They got me!" Powerful modern weapons produce terrible, bloody results. Bodies are spun around, tossed into the air, and ripped apart. Blood, flesh, and bone get spattered in all directions. When a soldier gets hit by a bullet or shrapnel, he often flinches and sags. The usual description of getting shot is that it felt "like getting whacked with a baseball bat." Normally, when a soldier gets hit, it sounds like that same baseball bat just smacked a watermelon — *thwack!*

The most revered member of any American combat unit — ground, air, or sea — is the medic, usually nicknamed "Doc." The job of a combat medic is to save lives. In the Civil War, medical knowledge was very basic. Soldiers could die from any wound. Hospitals were filthy. Doctors performed amputations simply to forestall the spread of gangrene. It was fairly routine to see limbs piled outside of these hospitals. Medics knew nothing about microorganisms and their relationship to disease.

Fortunately medical science improved, especially by World War II. By that time, the Army and the Navy both offered outstanding medical care, with excellent results. Medics in that war saved hundreds of thousands of lives. As an American serviceman, if you were wounded in World War II, you had a two-thirds chance of survival. In Vietnam, that number rose to 81 percent. In Afghanistan and Iraq, the survival rate is over 90 percent.

Throughout U.S. history, infantrymen have generally had the most dangerous job in the military. Air Force bomber crewmen and Navy submariners in World War II also suffered high casualty rates. Overall, though, ground combat soldiers usually experience the most danger and suffer the greatest losses.

The most common cause of death in combat is bleeding to death. Modern American military medics are trained to staunch the bleeding first, then stabilize the patient. They are also taught to make sure their patients have a clear airway.

Why American Soldiers Endure Combat

Because combat is so absolutely awful, why do perfectly rational Americans stand and fight, rather than run away at the first sight of the enemy? Some say that military training and leadership is the answer, but that's only a partial explanation for combat motivation. After studying this question for many years, I believe American soldiers endure combat for these four major reasons.

Love of country

All American soldiers, from colonial militiamen to present-day professionals, love America. The militiaman thought of America as his particular state or hometown. Twentieth- and 21st-century soldiers generally think in broader terms of one national entity.

In the Revolution, American soldiers fought for the dream of self rule. In the Civil War, soldiers North and South fought for their homes. Southerners fought to defend those homes because most of the war was fought on southern soil. Northerners felt that secession and slavery threatened the Constitution and thus the foundation of America. In World War I, soldiers believed their country could make the world safe for democracy. By World War II, American soldiers were embarrassed to speak in such idealistic terms, but underneath a cynical facade, they were deeply patriotic. The same was true of those who fought in Korea and Vietnam, and it's definitely true of the modern all-volunteer force.

Love of comrades

This is a powerful motivator. Combat forges close ties of kinship among comrades. They are united against the enemy, and that isn't limited to opposing soldiers. The enemy can mean high-ranking officers, politicians at home, the weather, bad food, rear-echelon soldiers — anything or anyone who doesn't share in the combat soldier's misery or who may make his existence more difficult. Quite often, combat soldiers love one another with the intensity of those who have shared the most traumatic experiences imaginable.

Noted Civil War historian James McPherson, through extensive research, found that soldiers of both sides fought not just for their cause, but also for their comrades. A powerful bond grew among those who fought together. They would rather die than let down their fellow soldiers.

I and several other historians found this same motivation in World War II American soldiers. I called this phenomenon *the deadly brotherhood* and described it in a book under that title.

Hatred for the enemy

Sometimes combat soldiers are motivated to fight out of sheer hatred for their opponents. This is especially true for those soldiers who have seen their buddies killed or badly wounded. In their eyes, the enemy becomes loathsome and dangerous. In a sense, this dehumanizes the enemy, making it easier to kill him with a clear conscience.

Although some Americans in the Revolution and Civil War fought with such malice, hatred wasn't a major motivator for Americans until well into the 20th century. In World War II, the Japanese fought with unparalleled ruthlessness, and most American combat soldiers absolutely hated them for that (not to mention the color of their skin). The Americans contemptuously called them "Japs" and "Nips."

In Korea and Vietnam, American troops often fought out of similar hatred for their Communist enemies, dehumanizing them with dismissive, racist slurs like "gooks," "slopes," and "zipperheads." In Afghanistan and Iraq, the average American combat soldier despises the hard-core Islamic *jihadists* (holy warriors) who plant improvised explosive devices (IEDs) on roads, carry out suicide bombings, and kill innocent people with bloodthirsty impunity.

Peer pressure

A soldier in combat must be accountable to his comrades. If he doesn't do his job, someone in the unit could die. Combat units are infused with a strong, almost overwhelming peer pressure to perform. Perceptions are everything. If a soldier acquires a reputation as a slacker, a whiner, or a coward, he's in for a rough time from his fellow soldiers. He could be given the cold shoulder, hazed, made fun of, or simply treated with callous disrespect.

Much of this has to do with concepts of masculinity. Combat units have always been male dominated, and they still are, even in today's gender-mixed armed forces. Young men, civilian or military, spend much of their time trying to prove their manhood. This tendency becomes more pronounced in the stress of combat. So, in a dangerous or uncomfortable situation, the average soldier wants to show the others he's every bit as much of a man as they are. This means that he can "hack it." If he doesn't, he loses face among those whose opinions he values most.

For instance, in the Civil War, young men believed that the absence of fear in battle demonstrated manhood. Thousands of them charged into the muzzles of enemy weapons just to show they had no fear. By World War II, American men readily admitted to one another that fear was a natural part of combat. But they believed that a true man mastered his fear and still performed. Thus, most everyone in World War II admitted to experiencing fear in each firefight. In spite of that acute fear, they did their jobs. Nor has this changed in recent years. Popular terms among modern soldiers like "man up" or "cowboy up" refer to this same valued concept of performing to the expectation of one's male peers. They do this by controlling their fear rather than letting it control them.

Part II
Born in War

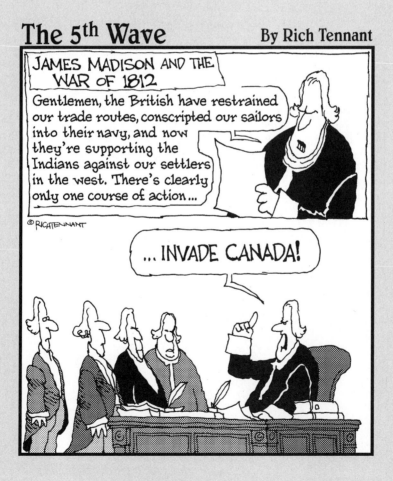

In this part . . .

The United States literally grew out of warfare. In particular, a colonial struggle for empire between Britain and France set in motion a series of events that directly led to the Revolution. After Americans won independence, they fought several wars to maintain it. In this part, you see how these early wars led to the very existence of the United States.

Chapter 6

When the English Were Our Friends: Battling the Indians and the French

*B*ritain and France were the dominant world powers of the 18th century. They had their religious differences — France was Catholic, Britain was Protestant — but, really, their conflict was a struggle for empire. They spent much of the century fighting each other all over the world, including in North America, where Britain and France both had extensive empires. France's empire comprised most of present-day Canada, the Upper Midwest, and the West of the present-day United States. The French also controlled New Orleans, along with much of the Mississippi River basin. Britain's American empire was primarily along the eastern seaboard. The land was divided up into 13 entities that we usually call the *13 colonies*.

By and large, France's American empire was sparsely populated by adventurers, furriers, soldiers, and colonial officials. The French maintained influence by forging alliances with Native American tribes.

Britain's empire was quite different. From the early 17th century to the middle of the 18th, the population of the 13 colonies grew dramatically because many families put down deep roots in America and flourished over time, creating an identity as Americans. By 1750, those Americans were outgrowing the 13 seaboard colonies and had begun migrating westward into French and Indian territory, sparking conflict.

In this chapter, I explain how tensions grew among everyone who wanted to claim land as their own. I discuss the first phase of the conflict, when the British and American war effort verged on disaster. Then I describe how they turned the tables and achieved victory against the French and Indians, along with the dramatic consequences the victory had for Americans.

American historians call this conflict the French and Indian War. Europeans call it the Seven Years War.

The First Fur Flies, 1754–1757

The conflict between the Brits and the French all started in the Ohio River Valley, quite close to present-day Pittsburgh, Pennsylvania. Three rivers — the Allegheny, the Monongahela, and the Ohio — come together at this spot. The Ohio and surrounding river valleys were ideal places to settle, establish farms, and open fur-trading businesses. Throughout the 1740s and early 1750s, French Canadians and colonists from Britain's empire migrated to the area, creating problems.

In 1753, the French built three forts between Lake Erie and the Ohio River to send a not-so-subtle message of French supremacy. Virginia Gov. Robert Dinwiddie and many others in his colony had a lot of money tied up in fur trading in the Ohio River Valley, and French control of that area threatened those investments. In the fall of 1753, Dinwiddie ordered a 21-year-old militia officer, Col. George Washington — yes, *that* George Washington — to take an expedition, meet with the French, and persuade them to leave.

Washington surrenders

When Washington and a small party of men spoke with the French in the fall of 1753, they received a polite kiss-off. Washington returned to Virginia and reported this to Dinwiddie. The governor decided to escalate the situation. With approval from the British government, he sent Washington back to the Ohio River Valley, this time with a small army and orders to remove the French by force if necessary.

The shooting started on May 28, 1754, when Washington's men ambushed a mixed group of Canadian and French soldiers, killing 10 and capturing 21 prisoners. Washington didn't have a large enough force to defeat the French, though. Outgunned and outnumbered, he retreated to the aptly named Fort Necessity. The French surrounded him and forced him to surrender, the only time the proud Virginian would ever do so. Washington's expedition was the first battle in a seven-year world war between Britain and France. Figure 6-1 shows where battles took place when the French were dominating the French and Indian War.

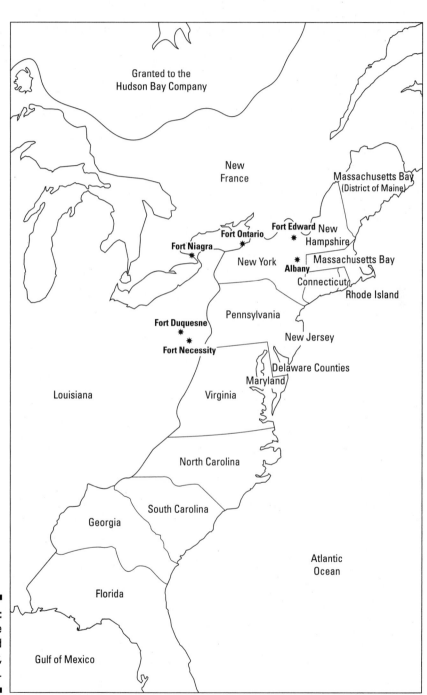

Figure 6-1:
Map of the French and Indian War, 1754–1757.

Braddock's traditional tactics fail

In the wake of Washington's disaster, the British government decided on a forceful response. Realizing that they couldn't rely solely on colonial militiamen to fight the French and their Native American allies, officials in London sent regular British troops under Gen. Edward Braddock to North America. He arrived on February 19, 1755, and spent the next few months building up his supplies, coordinating his efforts with colonial militia commanders, and preparing for the campaign ahead.

When the British and American armies moved west in the summer of 1755, their objective was to sweep away the French forts in all the disputed areas, an ambitious task. Braddock led the main effort against Fort Duquesne, a newly built French rampart located at the site of present-day Pittsburgh.

Braddock's troops crossed the Monongahela River, a day's march away from Duquesne. Here, almost in sight of the enemy, he continued to march his army in a classic European linear formation. This maintained cohesion among his soldiers and allowed him to supply his forces well, but considering the rough terrain his troops were negotiating and his enemies' tactics, Braddock made a poor decision. He would have been better served to spread his troops out, scout Fort Duquesne, and then attempt to surround it.

Instead, on July 9, 1755, the French and Indians ambushed Braddock's soldiers as they walked, in a predictable straight line, down a trail. The French and Indian force of 600 men was hidden by dense foliage on either side of the trail. They shot musket fire into the red-coated British soldiers who couldn't see their enemies. Up and down the line, musket balls smashed into men, provoking screams of pain. The British fired back in confused volleys. Panic set in as men ran for safety, bumped into one another, and got hit by enemy fire. Braddock courageously ran around everywhere, rallying his men, braving the enemy fire, but it was no use. In a matter of three hours, the enemy inflicted 877 casualties, including 456 killed, on the British and drove them back across the river. Braddock himself got shot in the lung and died four days later with the full knowledge that he had suffered a catastrophic defeat.

George Washington was in Braddock's ill-fated battle. The tall Virginian earned a reputation for being cool under fire. Some participants believed that, without Washington's brave leadership, the entire force would have been killed.

Montcalm marches on

The French now had the initiative. Their commander was Gen. Louis-Joseph, Marquis de Montcalm. In the summer of 1756, he led a combined army of

French soldiers and Canadian militiamen into New York and captured Fort Oswego, an important British outpost located near present-day Syracuse. With Oswego in French hands, the British colonies lost their access to rich fishing and trading routes on the Great Lakes.

The next year, Montcalm besieged Fort William Henry on Lake George near present-day Glen Falls, New York. By now, Montcalm's army had swelled to a force of about 8,000 regulars, Canadians, and Native Americans. They outnumbered the British and American colonists by almost four-to-one. The British commander, Lt. Col. George Monro, resisted stubbornly. But in August, when he learned no reinforcements could reach him, he knew he must surrender. With much chivalry, he and Montcalm negotiated a gentleman's *capitulation* (that is, a surrender with conditions attached). Amid great pomp and ceremony, the British and Americans turned the fort over to the French. Thus honorably paroled, Monro's troops began a march toward another British fort.

Montcalm's control over his Native American allies was tenuous at best. To the Indians, the European-style ceremony didn't constitute an honorable end to hostilities. So the Indians pursued Monro's column and, against Montcalm's express wishes, attacked. In the ensuing melee, the Native American fighters killed about 300 people, scalping many of their victims, whether dead or alive. The 2,000 survivors scattered all over the upper New York wilderness, eliminating Monro's army as any kind of effective military organization.

Drawing inspiration from the French and Indian War

The popular novel *The Last of the Mohicans,* published in 1826 by James Fenimore Cooper, immortalized the French and Indian War in American literature. The story is set in 1757, during Gen. Louis-Joseph, Marquis de Montcalm's siege of Fort William Henry. In the book, a small group of Mohican tribesman, plus a British officer, escort Lt. Col. George Monro's fictional daughters through dangerous country to the fort. The leader of the group, and hero of the book, is Hawkeye, a rugged individual who is a symbol of American frontier spirit. Although the book isn't always historically accurate, it does convey the whiff of that time quite well.

In the 20th century, numerous film adaptations of *The Last of the Mohicans* appeared in theaters or on TV. The most recent film portrayal, in 1992, starred Daniel Day-Lewis and Madeleine Stowe. Another less obvious tie to Cooper's book is in the TV show *M*A*S*H.* Benjamin Franklin Pierce, the show's main character, is nicknamed Hawkeye after the character in *The Last of the Mohicans.* Even today, we refer to the book's title to mean the last of a dying breed.

Some Indian tribes put enormous pressure on their fighters to bring home scalps as war trophies. Such was the case for many of Montcalm's allies at Fort William Henry. After the ambush, they were so eager to retrieve scalps that they even dug up corpses to get them. These Indians had no idea that some of the corpses were teeming with smallpox. The infected scalps spread great disease and death in those tribes.

Even as Montcalm's campaigns were unfolding, pro-French Native American tribes launched devastating raids into Pennsylvania, Virginia, and across upstate New York. The Indians crushed colonial farms and villages, burning, scalping, plundering, and generally leaving a trail of destruction in their wake. Needless to say, these raids sent the 13 colonies into a veritable panic. The average American was now deeply worried about the encroaching power of Catholic France and its Native American friends.

The Brits Regroup, 1758–1763

In 1757, with the British war effort in real crisis, William Pitt ascended to the position of secretary of state of Britain, which gave him control over the country's war policies. For more than a generation, the country's leaders had been arguing the merits of two major strategies:

- **Continental:** This group argued that the best way to defeat France and advance British interests was to send large numbers of troops to the European continent.

- **Maritime and colonial:** These men advocated the use of superior British naval power to defeat the French at sea and, on land, fight in colonial areas around the globe.

Pitt was definitely an advocate of the maritime and colonial strategy. He believed that North America was the decisive theater in the war with the French, and he was determined to win there at all costs.

Upon taking office, Pitt implemented three new policies that turned the war in Britain's favor:

- He ordered the Royal Navy to blockade French ports. This cut France off from its North American colonies. Montcalm, for instance, could not be reinforced well enough to follow up on his victories. He was forced to go on the defensive.

- With control of the seas, Pitt shipped more British soldiers to America to carry out a new offensive.

✔ He paid for the arming, equipping, and training of colonial militia. This netted him 42,000 recruits in 1758 and 1759. Pitt's commanders often used these Americans as support troops, freeing up the better-trained British regulars to fight.

Going on the offensive

As Pitt's policies gradually bore fruit, the initiative for offensive operations passed from the French to the British. From 1758 through 1760, the British and their American colonial allies unleashed a series of offensives designed to push the French back from their frontier forts and then take Canada from them. Figure 6-2 shows the battles in the second phase of the French and Indian War.

Louisbourg

The first major British move was at the Fortress of Louisbourg, a French stronghold located in present-day Nova Scotia. In the summer of 1758, a British army numbering some 13,000 soldiers invaded the area and besieged Louisbourg. The siege lasted from June 19 through July 26. For that five-week period, British cannons and ships pounded the fort and sunk several French ships. Finally, the French could take no more and surrendered.

Unlike the year before when Montcalm had afforded Monro all honors of war at Fort William Henry, the British commander, Gen. Jeffrey Amherst, refused to extend the same courtesy to the Louisbourg garrison. He ordered the French to turn in all their arms, equipment, and colors because he didn't want to fight the same units somewhere else. The French were not pleased, but they complied. However, the soldiers of the Cambis Regiment destroyed their muskets and burned their colors rather than hand them over to the victorious British.

Fort Duquesne

A British force under Gen. John Forbes built a road across Pennsylvania in 1758, with the goal to win back Fort Duquesne. Forbes had 6,000 men, including 2,000 Virginia and Pennsylvania militiamen. Once again, George Washington was on hand.

The British were in a better strategic position now than three years before during Braddock's expedition. In 1755, they had consummated an agreement called the Treaty of Easton with the Shawnee and Delaware Indian tribes, former allies of the French. In return for abandoning that alliance, the British promised the Indians a trading post, with no British military presence, at the site of Fort Duquesne. The removal of the Shawnees and Delawares from the war crippled the French in the Ohio River Valley.

When the British neared Fort Duquesne, their leading elements fought a desperate battle with French regulars. In this fight, 100 Pennsylvanians ran away, while the Virginians, with Washington among them, fought well. The French won the battle, though. In so doing, they captured several dozen men from a Scottish regiment. The French decapitated many of the Scotsmen, mounted their bloody heads on stakes, and draped their kilts around the stakes. This shocking incident, along with Amherst's refusal to afford full military honors to his French prisoners at Louisbourg, indicated that the war was becoming steadily more vicious.

Forbes reorganized his men for another push on Duquesne. He expected a serious fight, but instead, the French, knowing they were badly outnumbered, burned the fort and left. In violation of the Treaty of Easton, the British promptly built a new fort and named it Fort Pitt, after William Pitt.

Fort Pitt was situated right at the confluence of the Allegheny, Monongahela, and Ohio rivers. As you may guess, the Delawares and Shawnees were not pleased that the British reneged on their agreement to hand over this vital ground. The Indians besieged the fort in 1763 but never took it. Eventually, in the years leading up to the Revolution, the British abandoned the fort and the Americans took control of it. From this spot, the city of Pittsburgh came into existence. All that remains of the fort today is a house and some of the fort's foundations, all located at Point Park, in downtown Pittsburgh.

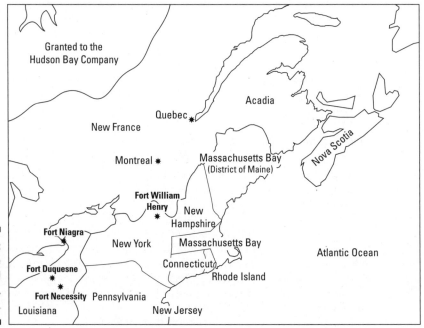

Figure 6-2:
Map of the French and Indian War, 1758–1760.

Quebec and beyond

By 1759, the British were succeeding everywhere in North America. They had pushed the French out of the Ohio River Valley and much of upper New York. The British and American colonials were now in a position to invade Canada, the heart of the French empire in North America.

Using Louisbourg as a jumping-off point, a Royal Navy fleet of about 200 ships carried 7,030 British regular and 1,300 American militiamen up the St. Lawrence River to Quebec. Montcalm was defending the city with about 14,000 French regulars and Canadians. Throughout the summer of 1759, the Royal Navy sailed up and down the waters around Quebec, looking for a good spot to land the troops. Several times the British landed troops, only to be rebuffed by the French, who seemingly had every approach heavily defended.

Out of desperation more than innovation, the British ground commander, Gen. James Wolfe, on September 10, 1759, ordered an elite force to land at the base of some steep cliffs, two miles from Quebec. Wolfe figured that Montcalm would never expect him to land in such a rough spot, and he was correct. Wolfe's troops climbed hand over hand up the cliffs and overwhelmed a surprised Canadian garrison.

This success was just the opening Wolfe had been waiting for all summer. He quickly reinforced his assault troops with 4,500 redcoats. They clashed with the French in a European-style battle on the Plains of Abraham. In a matter of hours, the British routed the French, sending them into full retreat back into the walled city of Quebec. This was the equivalent of checkmate in a game of chess. Cut off from resupply, outnumbered, and outgunned, the French had little choice but to surrender Quebec on September 18, 1759. The next spring, the French attempted, but failed, to recapture Quebec.

The battle at the Plains of Abraham claimed the lives of both commanders. Several musket balls tore through Wolfe. He bled to death, all the while watching the French retreat. Meanwhile, Montcalm also got hit during the retreat. He staggered into Quebec. Seeing the concerned expressions on his men's faces, he assured them he was all right. He wasn't. He died within a day.

The French surrender

For the British, the capture of Quebec meant that they now controlled the St. Lawrence River and could move around Canada at will. In September 1760, they surrounded the last remaining French forces at Montreal. The French governor, Pierre François de Rigaud, surrendered the city and all of Canada to the British. The fighting in North America was finally over.

Cajuns' colorful origins

Everyone knows that Cajuns live in Louisiana. But where did they originally come from? The answer is Acadia, which, nowadays, we call Nova Scotia.

During the French and Indian War, the British uprooted the French-speaking people of Acadia and scattered them throughout parts of the British empire. Some even became slaves in British colonies. Most, though, went to French-controlled Louisiana, especially New Orleans

and its environs. Over the years, the Acadians intermarried with Creoles, French immigrants, Spanish, and Germans. This mixed brew of ancestry created a unique culture that today we think of as Cajun.

Cajuns are known for their distinctive accent which sounds southern but is also replete with French words and phrases. By far, the best known aspect of Cajun culture is spicy food, such as crawfish, jambalaya, and seafood gumbo.

The British conquest of the Ohio River Valley and Canada was a momentous event for the future of North America. British influence in such places as western Pennsylvania, Ohio, and Michigan eventually led rebellious American settlers to claim those lands for themselves after they created their new nation. Control of Canada gave Britain a near-permanent presence in North America, even after the American Revolution. Also, when Britain conquered Canada, it guaranteed a divided ethnic makeup of that country between Anglos and French. Naturally, the conquered French resented — even despised — their Anglo countrymen. Even today, French-speaking Canadians (often called Québécois) chafe at their association with much of the rest of the country, which traces its heritage, institutions, and customs to Britain.

The war officially ended on February 10, 1763, with the signing of the Treaty of Paris. In this agreement, France ceded Canada and all of France's North American empire east of the Mississippi River to Great Britain. Secretary of State Pitt and the British crown had won a huge victory.

What the War Meant to Americans

In one sense, the French and Indian War was the key event of the 18th century in America because it led to the Revolution (see Chapter 7). While the French and Indian War raged, Americans were concerned with the erosion of their rights by the imperial power of France. With the war over, the French enemy defeated, and the British empire dominant in North America, Americans increasingly came to view British imperial power as the main threat to liberty.

Security and growing independence

The defeat of France guaranteed that the 13 colonies would survive. After 1763, none of Britain's imperial rivals even dreamed of infringing on those colonies. This newfound security meant that the American colonists were less and less dependent upon Britain for protection, weakening the ties between colony and home country.

Expansion beyond the Appalachians

To the Americans, the war had partially been about removing the French from the Ohio River Valley. So at the conclusion of hostilities, eager American colonists began crossing the Appalachian Mountains, pouring into the valley. Often they set up homes on land that the British had promised to Native American tribes in return for their assistance during the war. Not surprisingly, this created real problems.

Various Indian tribes attacked frontier posts as far west as Detroit and as far east as Pennsylvania. The British couldn't allow this chaotic situation to continue. Between 1763 and 1765, they squelched Indian resistance in a series of campaigns. Then they set about curbing American expansion.

Unwelcome supervision from London

In 1763, Britain's head of state, King George III, issued the Proclamation Act. The act decreed that no Americans could migrate west of the Appalachian Mountains. The king declared that this land belonged to the Native Americans who had stood with England during the war. Moreover, he ordered his soldiers to forcibly remove American settlers from Indian land.

The colonists viewed this as a betrayal. Some of them had fought in the war, and they believed that land was their just reward. Whenever they could, they simply ignored the king's decree and moved wherever they wanted. The result was conflict with Indians and British regulars, the latter of whom the Americans now began to view as sinister imperial overseers.

Britain won the war, but she was deeply in debt, to the tune of well over £100 million. The need to recoup that debt, more than anything else, led the British government to govern America with more direct supervision than ever before.

The British felt that, to a great extent, they had fought the war to protect the American colonists. With the common enemy defeated, the British then deemed it reasonable that the Americans should pay their fair share of the cost of victory. In the 1760s, the London government implemented a new series of taxes, all of them designed to eat away at the debt.

The Americans were outraged. For more than 100 years they had enjoyed virtual autonomy in their everyday lives. They had seldom, if ever, paid these kinds of direct taxes to London. Many Americans didn't think the British government had the right to arbitrarily impose these taxes, much less restrict the movement of settlers (see the previous section). The stage was now set for a major showdown between the colonials and their ostensible mother country.

Chapter 7

So You Want to Start a Revolution: The War for Independence

In This Chapter

▶ Rebelling against British supervision

▶ Fighting for independence

▶ Arguing among former friends and neighbors

▶ Considering the historical perspectives

*T*he American Revolution made a significant mark in world history. It led to the decline of the British empire in North America, the rise of a new American nation destined to have a global impact, the advent of capitalistic economic ideas for world markets, and the spread of influential ideas about human rights and the legitimacy of governments.

The Revolution started as a skirmish and grew into a full-scale war, both conventional and guerrilla. (A *guerrilla* war or battle is when a small group of irregular, usually volunteer, soldiers uses ambush, trickery, and hit-and-run tactics against the enemy.) By the time the Revolution was over, Britain had found itself once again at war with France, as well as Spain. Nearly every part of "British" America, from the West to the deep South to New England, was touched by the war. Instead of recognizable front lines, there were mostly just hot spots under the control of one side or the other.

Americans themselves were divided over the question of independence, making the Revolution a civil war of sorts. Native Americans were caught in the middle of warring factions, trying to play one against the other, but usually siding with Britain. African Americans fought on both sides. Nearly everyone was affected in some way during eight traumatic years of war.

In this chapter, I explain the causes of the war and describe the important battles. I also tell you what the wartime experience was like for ordinary people. Finally, I explain what historians think about the Revolution.

Taxing Independence to Pay War Debt

The main cause of the Revolution was that the colonists didn't like what they perceived as Britain's increasing threat to their concept of *autonomy,* or their ability to function independently, pursue their own economic interests, and govern themselves. The 13 colonies were unique in the context of most empires, because by the middle of the 18th century, they were largely self-governing with a self-sustaining economy. This was in stark contrast to Britain's usual colonization methods in such places as Ireland, India, and the Caribbean, where the British exploited resources and ruled with an iron fist over the local population.

Most American colonists viewed themselves as loyal British subjects but really had few direct ties to the faraway home island. These Americans pursued their own economic and political interests. They paid their taxes to colonial legislatures and drew political representation from them, not Parliament, the English governing body. When, in the 1760s, Great Britain sought to assert more direct control over the colonies (primarily through taxation), many Americans viewed the government in London as a threat to their economic interests and political liberties.

In the 1760s, the British treasury was deeply in debt. For decades the government had built up that debt through a series of wars and imperial adventures. The costliest such war was the Seven Years War, a conflict known to Americans as the French and Indian War (see Chapter 6). Britain had won this war, in part, because the government had paid to equip colonists for the fight. This expense, and many others, had led to such a serious debt problem that, if Britain didn't do something about it, she faced the possibility of financial ruin.

The British believed that the best way to address the debt issue was for the colonists to pay more taxes than ever before. From the British point of view, this was only fair. After all, the colonists were benefiting from the British empire's protection, so it was only logical that they should pay for their security. So, beginning in 1764, the British government passed a series of laws designed to recoup money from the colonies.

The Sugar Act goes sour

In 1764, the Brits imposed the Sugar Act on the colonists. For years, Americans had imported cheap French molasses and sugar from France's Caribbean colonies. The Sugar Act was an attempt to drive up the prices of those French products in favor of English sugar. The law said that all legal sugar in the colonies must come through Britain first. Moreover, when the colonists bought that sugar, they also had to pay taxes on it. And the law didn't just tax sugar, but wine and cloth, too.

The colonists responded by growing their own sugar in greater quantities and boycotting British sugar. The British hoped that the Sugar Act would generate £100,000 per year for the treasury. Instead, it only yielded £30,000 and, of course, angered the colonists.

The Stamp Act of 1765 gets licked

As unpopular as the Sugar Act was in the colonies, the Stamp Act was even more hated. The law said that, as of November 1765, every legal document, contract, will, pamphlet, letter, and deck of playing cards in America must be affixed with a government tax stamp.

The Americans thought the Stamp Act was absolutely outrageous because it required them to pay the British government in so many ways that affected everyday life. How angry were the Americans? Imagine how you would feel if, all of a sudden, you had to pay taxes on every e-mail and cellphone call. You undoubtedly would not be pleased. So, too, in 1765 Britain was taxing the colonists' main means of communication — paper — and the Americans were angry about it.

Riots broke out. Mobs attacked tax collectors and customs agents who worked for the British government. The harassment of these hapless agents made it hard for England to collect any of the revenues. Americans united as never before. Leading opponents of the act, from all over the colonies, corresponded with one another in clandestine letters, coordinating their resistance efforts. The American colonies had no representation in Parliament and thus no say over the passage of this law. So the colonists claimed that the Stamp Act was illegal because it was "taxation without representation." Some of them felt so strongly about this that they formed a Stamp Act *Congress* (an elected body of representatives similar to Parliament) in New York to protest the law.

In the face of such furious resistance, Parliament repealed the law in March 1766. Nonetheless, the government ominously asserted that, in spite of the repeal, it had the right to pass any future law, including taxes, in the colonies.

The Townshend Duties incite a tea party

Starting in 1766, Parliament passed a new series of taxes on imported items, such as tea, glass, and paper. Named for Charles Townshend, the man who was in charge of the British treasury, the Townshend Duties were designed to reassert Britain's sovereignty over America and ease the war debt.

The taxes did neither. As in the cases of the Sugar and Stamp acts (see previous sections), the American colonists were so displeased with the new taxes that they organized an effective boycott of imported tea, glass, and paper.

The Townshend Duties were a miserable failure. By 1770, they were actually *costing* Britain ₤23,000 per year, as a result of the costly efforts to collect taxes and the American boycott of British goods. Parliament grudgingly repealed all but the tax on tea.

For three years, Americans often avoided the tea tax by smuggling or producing their own tea. But, in 1773, Parliament passed the Tea Act, effectively granting the British East India Company a monopoly on tea in America. Many of the colonists believed that Britain was now forcing them to buy an illegally taxed commodity, so they responded with the usual boycott. Colonial ports refused to unload tea from the East India Company. A radical group of New England colonists, nicknamed the Sons of Liberty, took the issue even further. On December 16, 1773, they dressed up as Mohawk Indians, boarded three of the company's ships in Boston Harbor, and destroyed 342 tons of tea, mostly by dumping it into the harbor. This incident is generally known as the *Boston Tea Party.*

The Coercive Acts are intolerable

The tea party sent shock waves through the British world. Although many colonists didn't approve of such vandalism, they agreed with the cause the Sons of Liberty stood for. King George III and the British government, frustrated from years of colonial mischief, decided to respond forcefully. In 1774, the king and Parliament passed the Boston Port Act, closing the port of Boston until those responsible for the tea party paid for the tea they had destroyed. George III subsequently sent British soldiers to Boston, and he appointed one of his generals as governor of Massachusetts, in so doing dissolving the colonial government.

Parliament also passed the Quartering Act, a hated piece of legislation among the colonists. The Quartering Act required colonists to build or pay for the housing of British soldiers in America. In some cases, Americans were even forced to quarter soldiers in their own homes. Most Americans didn't want the soldiers around in the first place, much less living under their own roofs.

The colonists viewed the Quartering Act as a dangerous threat to their privacy. It hardened an already deep American suspicion of professional soldiers. The colonists called this law, and the others that dissolved the Massachusetts government and closed Boston harbor, the Coercive or Intolerable Acts.

Fighting for Freedom from Taxation

With tension between the British government and the Americans at an all-time high, representatives from all the colonies met in September 1774 at the first

Continental Congress. The Congress included some of the most prominent men in the colonies, such as John Adams of Massachusetts and George Washington of Virginia. The initial purpose of Adams, Washington, and their colleagues wasn't to declare independence, but to find some sort of peaceful solution to the troubles with Britain. Most of the men were still loyal to King George III; they simply felt that Parliament had gotten out of control. Feeling that the king was more reasonable than Parliament, the Continental Congress sent him a personal petition urging him to repeal the Coercive Acts. Needless to say, George III refused.

Spilling blood at Lexington and Concord

By the spring of 1775, British soldiers occupied Boston. The port was still closed. Massachusetts and the other New England colonies were basically in open rebellion. Many of the rebellious colonists, known locally as *minutemen* (because they volunteered to be ready to battle the British at a minute's notice), had begun hoarding weapons for an anticipated fight with the British soldiers. Realizing this, the British sought to find and destroy the weapons.

On April 19, 1775, a column of 700 British soldiers left Boston and marched west toward Concord. Before long, they exchanged shots with minutemen at a town called Lexington, killing eight men. Thousands of other minutemen were converging on the area, though, and the British were fortunate to fight their way back to Boston. Historians generally consider the fighting at Lexington and Concord to be the first battles of the Revolutionary War (see Figure 7-1).

Thinking new thoughts

For many years, American colonists, especially the elite who comprised the Continental Congress, had been heavily influenced by a growing series of new ideas surfacing in Western culture regarding the rights of the individual. An English political philosopher named John Locke wrote that government should only maintain legitimate power through a social contract with the people. This means that the people consent to be governed. If the government behaved in a corrupt or oppressive way, that meant it reneged on its social contract, and so could be overthrown. Freeborn citizens, Locke wrote, enjoyed the in-born, "inalienable" rights of liberty, life, and prosperity.

All these ideas were embodied in what the Americans called *republicanism,* a modern political philosophy that emphasized the importance of free individuals, civic duty, and equality. Belief in these ideas was a major motivation for the Americans in their showdown with Great Britain.

Figure 7-1:
Map of the
Revolutionary
War,
1775–1783
(selected
battle sites).

Declaring independence: Enough is enough

The outbreak of hostilities did not lead to an immediate American declaration of independence. In fact, the official break from Britain didn't happen until more than a year later, on July 4, 1776. For that first year of the war, the majority of the Americans hoped to fight a short, conventional conflict for the limited objectives of repealing the Coercive Acts (see the section, "The Coercive Acts are intolerable," earlier in this chapter for details) and ending taxation without representation. Only after exhausting that possibility did they turn to the more ambitious goal of independence. A rebellion had turned into a revolution.

Thomas Paine's *Common Sense*

Literacy was one of the primary reasons why revolutionary republican ideas spread so quickly through the colonies in 1775 and 1776. Most freeborn colonists, male or female, could read.

In January 1776, Thomas Paine, a pro-independence republican, published a pamphlet called *Common Sense.* In a clear writing style, Paine advocated independence for the colonies and the establishment of a republic that guaranteed equality, civil liberties, and property. Paine's ideas spread like wildfire throughout the 13 colonies. At one time, 120,000 copies of *Common Sense* were in print. Paine's writings helped persuade many of the leading colonists, including George Washington, that independence was the best option for Americans.

After the declaration, Paine devoted his literary talents to pro-revolution writings designed to bolster the morale of the American revolutionaries. Paine's most famous quote is "These are the times that try men's souls," a reference to the enormous sacrifices he believed were necessary to win independence. Another one of his phrases is still with us — he suggested that the new American nation call itself the United States of America.

From Bunker Hill to Saratoga, 1775–1777

In the mid-1770s, Great Britain was the most powerful nation in the world. The British possessed the world's supreme navy, the largest empire, and the wealthiest economy. So, at first glance, the upstart American colonies, with no money, no navy, and an army of ill-trained militia seemed to have no chance of defeating Britain in a war. But the *patriots,* as the American revolutionaries called themselves, did have some real advantages. They outnumbered the British, they were fighting on home ground, and they had the sympathy of most Americans. Plus, in the long run, they could win by wearing down British resolve to fight the war.

When hostilities broke out, the Continental Congress hastily established the United States Army, generally known then as the Continental Army. These soldiers (called *Continentals*), employed by Congress, combined with colonial militiamen to form the patriot ground forces in the Revolutionary War. Congress appointed Gen. George Washington as the commander.

At first, Washington hoped to win a conventional victory in the European model. He quickly learned that his soldiers were a poor match for superbly disciplined and well-trained British regulars. Washington came to understand that to defeat the enemy, he had to

- ✔ Evade the British
- ✔ Keep his army together
- ✔ Fight only when he enjoyed every advantage

Bunker Hill: Who really won?

In the wake of the fighting at Lexington and Concord (see the "Spilling blood at Lexington and Concord" section earlier in this chapter), the British still controlled Boston, but more than 12,000 Massachusetts militiamen appeared, seemingly out of nowhere. They set up fighting positions on the hills around Boston and besieged the British.

At this stage, the British had no respect for the fighting quality of the American troops. They believed that the colonial militiamen would crumble in any sort of serious battle. British commander Gen. William Howe and his officers felt that this blossoming revolution could be crushed by aggressive action. So, on June 17, 1775, they ordered their troops to assault patriot-held hills, particularly Breed's and Bunker hills, at Charlestown. Instead of running away, as the British expected, the patriots stayed put on their higher ground, pouring down fire on the exposed redcoats. Only on the third bloody assault did the British succeed in forcing an American retreat. The British suffered heavy casualties — 226 killed and 828 wounded. The Americans lost 450 men, mostly during the retreat.

Technically, Bunker Hill was a British victory, but it was hollow at best. As one British officer wrote after the battle, "A few more such victories would have surely put an end to British dominion in America." The British had taken the Charlestown Heights, but this didn't break the siege. They eventually had to abandon Boston. Moreover, the battle demonstrated the American resolve to fight. Clearly, only a major British effort could crush this revolution.

Oh, Canada?

The Continental Congress invited French Canadians to join the Americans in their fight against Britain. When they declined, Congress decided to invade Canada in the fall of 1775. The Americans didn't have the manpower or supplies to pull off such an ambitious objective. Half of their army succumbed to disease and the invasion failed, despite the courageous battlefield leadership of Col. Benedict Arnold. The Americans tried another invasion in 1776 but failed again. Canada would remain part of the British empire.

Although this battle is known by the name Bunker Hill, most of the fighting took place at adjacent Breed's Hill.

New York: A Continental rout

Gen. Howe abandoned Boston in the spring of 1776 so he could concentrate all of his efforts on dealing Washington a knockout blow at New York.

The American commander had an army of about 20,000 Continentals and militiamen. He divided them between Long Island and Manhattan. With news of the Declaration of Independence ringing in their ears, they settled in for a fight. On August 27, 1776, Howe landed 22,000 soldiers on Long Island. They quickly pushed the Americans back to Washington Heights. When Gen. Washington evacuated his survivors to Manhattan, the British invaded that island and continued the chase. Eventually, by October, Washington had to order a full retreat from New York rather than risk losing his whole army.

The battered remnants of the patriot army crossed the Delaware River into Pennsylvania. By now, Washington only had 5,000 men left, and many of them were scheduled to be discharged at the end of the year when their enlistments expired.

Trenton and Princeton: Jersey goes to Washington

At this point, the Revolution was on life-support. Congress had even abandoned the capital of Philadelphia. Now was the time for the British to go for the knockout blow, but they were seriously lacking in killer instinct. They decided to hunker down in winter quarters. Their commanders decided that the rebels could be finished off in the spring when the weather was more pleasant.

With the situation bleak and his army melting away, Washington knew he had to make something positive happen or the Revolution might collapse. He decided to unleash a surprise Christmas night attack on Trenton, New Jersey.

The town was garrisoned by *Hessian* soldiers, German professional soldiers whom the British had hired to help them fight the war in America. In the middle of a snowstorm, Washington and his men crossed the Delaware River (see Figure 7-2) and achieved complete surprise on the unwary Hessians. In little more than an hour, the Americans routed the Hessians, killing 23 and capturing 913. American casualties were minimal. Washington followed up this stunning victory with another one at Princeton, New Jersey, a week later.

Figure 7-2: *Washington Crossing the Delaware* depicts Gen. Washington's stealthy approach toward enemy troops on December 25, 1776.

The American victories at Trenton and Princeton proved that patriots could defeat professional soldiers. This strengthened the Revolution, and Congress was able to recruit more troops for the coming year. Plus, these battles awakened patriot sentiment in New Jersey, forcing the British and Hessians to abandon the state.

The Hessians were surprised at Trenton because Washington's troops attacked under the cover of a snowstorm, not, as has been reported in many accounts, because they were drunk from celebrating Christmas.

Pirate patriots

Because Great Britain possessed the world's greatest navy, the new United States could scarcely hope to challenge Britain's maritime might. Congress created the U.S. Navy in October 1775. Each coastal state also commissioned its own vessels to harass the British.

During the Revolution, American naval forces were mainly a hodgepodge of privateers and commerce raiders that sometimes captured vulnerable enemy ships and their cargoes. The most successful American naval commander was John Paul Jones, who actually took the war into British waters when he captured HMS *Drake* on April 24, 1778. Such victories were rare, though. The greatest maritime contribution to the American cause actually came from the French navy that contested British control of American waters off the southern coast.

Philadelphia and Saratoga: A devastating loss, a resounding victory

In 1777, the British launched a two-pronged offensive. In the north, an army under Gen. John Burgoyne attacked from Canada into New York, with the objective of cutting off rebellious New England from the rest of the colonies. The British felt that New Englanders were the main troublemakers. If Burgoyne's troops could cut off and isolate the northern colonies, the rest of the colonists would probably calm down. To the south, another British army under Gen. Howe aimed to take Philadelphia, a great political symbol because it was the capital of the new American nation.

The southern prong succeeded. Howe repeatedly defeated Washington's army, forcing the patriots to retreat from Philadelphia. But in the north, Burgoyne ran into disaster. As he advanced deeper into hostile upstate New York, he ran into serious supply problems. American militia and their Native American allies harassed him at every turn.

The campaign culminated in the fall of 1777 in a series of battles near Saratoga. Each time, Burgoyne's men fought desperately, but they were out-numbered, with little local support. An American army under Gen. Horatio Gates eventually surrounded the British and forced Burgoyne to surrender on October 17. The Americans had won their greatest victory, negating the humiliating loss of Philadelphia.

Refocusing on the South, 1778–1783

The U.S.'s victory at Saratoga, New York, persuaded France to officially recognize the United States as an independent nation and even enter the war. Other British rivals, such as Spain and the Netherlands, also jumped into the war.

From the beginning, the French had been quietly funneling money to the patriots, but only in small amounts. From 1775 to 1777, the international community saw the Revolution as an internal British matter. But when France came forward and recognized American independence, the Revolution turned into an international matter.

It also turned into a world war because France, Spain, and the Netherlands were now involved. No longer could the British concentrate all their efforts on America. They now had bigger things to worry about. Because of this new strategic situation, the Americans now had a much better chance of achieving independence than ever before.

Now that Britain was involved in yet another world war against its imperial rivals (see Chapter 6 for the details of Britain's fight against France in the French and Indian War), the British changed their focus in America. British leaders knew that the southern states, since the beginning of the war, were generally less favorable to the patriot cause than the northern states. Southerners, especially those who owned a large number of slaves, tended to be more loyal to the king because of close economic ties with the mother country and a general uneasiness about revolutionary upheaval. So the British decided to send a large military force to the South. They expected to rally loyal southerners to their cause and establish a permanent foothold in the South. Basically, England was writing off the North in favor of the South. Thus, at the end of 1778, a powerful army under the command of Gen. Sir Henry Clinton boarded ships in New York, set sail, and captured Savannah, Georgia.

A Franco-American force tried, but failed, to retake Savannah in 1779. The next year, the British captured Charleston, South Carolina. A new British commander, Lord Henry Cornwallis — a man of exceptional competence — took charge of the campaign. With control of the South's two largest ports, Cornwallis expanded his operations throughout the Carolinas, defeating the Continental Army time and again. His plan seemed to be unfolding perfectly.

Actually, it wasn't though. A British policy offering freedom to slaves in exchange for service to the king's cause alienated many southern slave owners. Often Cornwallis's soldiers were heavy-handed in their dealings with southerners, even those loyal to the king. Moreover, the mere British presence in the South incited a civil war between patriots and those who remained loyal to London. The countryside was aflame as neighbor fought neighbor in a guerrilla war.

As the campaign wore on for two long years, the patriots adopted hit-and-run ambush tactics to exhaust the British. The revolutionaries even won a pitched battle at Cowpens in South Carolina in early 1781. Try as he might, Cornwallis couldn't annihilate the patriot presence in the South.

Yorktown: Cornwallis gets queasy

Frustrated and with his sources of supply threatened, in July 1781 Cornwallis marched his army to Yorktown, Virginia, to make contact with the Royal Navy. Two months later, a French fleet defeated a British fleet at the Battle of the Chesapeake, cutting off Cornwallis's Yorktown force. Seeing a major opening, Washington deployed troops to Virginia. They hooked up with a French army and besieged Cornwallis's men at Yorktown. The French and Americans had 17,000 soldiers, twice as many as the British. The fighting lasted throughout much of October until finally the British began to run out of food and ammunition. Cornwallis surrendered on October 19, 1781.

Paris: Where people go to negotiate

Throughout history, no fewer than 20 peace treaties, most of which ended major wars, have been signed in Paris. Several of the treaties involved Americans, including the 1763 treaty that ended the French and Indian War, the 1783 treaty that concluded the Revolution, the 1898 accord that concluded the Spanish-American War, the Versailles agreement after World War I, and the Paris Peace Accords that, in 1973, ended the American war in Vietnam.

The British commander was so humiliated by the defeat that he faked illness rather than attend the surrender ceremony.

The defeat at Yorktown broke the will of the British government to continue the war in America. The war had never been popular with the British people. Some sympathized with the colonists' republican ideas. Others thought that keeping the colonies wasn't worth the expenditure of so much blood and treasure. So, with the stunning defeat at Yorktown, the British government began to negotiate an end to the war.

Muddling to the end

Important as Yorktown was, it did not end the war. Hostilities dragged on for two more tense years against the backdrop of negotiations. The British still had 30,000 troops in America, and they still controlled New York and Charleston. But really, they had no more stomach for fighting. At last, the British government and American representatives signed the Treaty of Paris on September 3, 1783. The treaty ended the fighting, established a border between the new United States and Canada, and most importantly, recognized American independence. The dream of the patriots had finally come true.

The People of the Revolution

The war was a defining, traumatic event that affected every American, whether you lived in the Appalachian west, a small New England town, a big coastal city, or on a southern plantation. Although many Americans simply wanted to be left alone, the war put enormous pressure on them to choose sides. Some chose a side out of idealism, others out of sheer economic interests. Some even switched sides when it suited them.

Quite a few colonists chose whichever side seemed to be winning, only to pay a heavy price later when the tables turned. For instance, when the British kicked Washington's army out of New Jersey in 1776, the colony seemed secure for the British, so many residents declared their loyalty to the king. However, when Washington launched his surprise attacks at Trenton and Princeton, the situation changed. New Jersey was no longer safe territory for the British. Those New Jerseyites who had pledged loyalty to Britain were now reviled, and sometimes chased from their homes, by their patriot neighbors.

Patriots from all walks of life

Patriots, of course, were those Americans who sympathized with the Revolution and wanted independence. In general, about half of the American population could be considered patriots. Many of these people were passive supporters who provided intelligence, food, clothing, or liquor to patriot soldiers. Patriots came from all regions, although New England tended to produce more of them than any other place.

The patriot ranks included some of the wealthiest and most prominent men in North America, such as Benjamin Franklin, Thomas Jefferson, John Adams, James Madison, John Hancock, Patrick Henry, and of course, George Washington. However, patriot sentiment cut across all classes. Small farmers, craftsman, importers, fishermen, immigrants, and even the lowliest day laborers all flocked to the patriot cause. Even some African Americans supported the Revolution.

What united all these diverse people was *republicanism* — the cherished ideal of an independent nation free from the heavy-handed rule of a foreign king, where life, liberty, and property would be guaranteed. Many patriots lost their homes, their farms, and even their families in pursuit of their dream.

Loyalists (or Tories) kept the faith

Those who remained loyal to Great Britain were called *Loyalists* or *Tories.* About 15 to 25 percent of the population fit this mold. Tory sentiment tended to be strongest in the South and in seaport states like New York and New Jersey, where merchants had strong ties to Britain. Loyalists were usually wealthier and older than patriots, with more to lose by abandoning allegiance to the king. Some of them were affiliated with Anglicanism, the official Church of England. The most prominent Tories were Thomas Hutchinson, the last royal governor of Massachusetts, and Samuel Seabury, a well-known clergyman.

Loyalist soldiers fought alongside the British during the war, taking an active part in most of the battles. About 50,000 of them served in militia units or the British army. Sometimes, as at King's Mountain in 1780, they fought alone against the patriots. Often small groups of neighbors fought one another in bitter, destructive guerrilla war, especially in the West and the South. A few African American slaves flocked to the Tory cause in exchange for their freedom. Native Americans, fearing the likely expansion of the new United States if the Revolution succeeded, generally sided with the British.

So what happened to the Tories after the war? About 20 percent left the country. Most of them migrated to Canada. A few went to Britain or the West Indies. The vast majority of Loyalists stayed in the new United States, though. Although some had difficulty getting along with their countrymen who had fought on the other side, most blended back into the fabric of American life over time. Who knows? Maybe you even have a Tory ancestor somewhere in your family tree.

Women backed boycotts, patriot ideals

In the 1760s, the colonial boycott of British products wouldn't have been possible without the widespread participation of women. American women bought most of the everyday items like tea, cloth, and sugar for American households. In large numbers, the women improvised, especially for cloth. In 1769 alone, Boston women produced 40,000 skeins of yarn. Another Massachusetts town produced 30,000 yards of cloth in one year. During the war, American women literally clothed the Continental Army and patriot militias.

If women helped the boycotts succeed, they also helped patriot ideas solidify. The Revolution saw the rise of the *republican woman.* This was the notion that a woman's proper role was to espouse revolutionary ideas about liberty to her children, particularly her sons, even as she sewed clothing and prepared food for patriot men.

During the war, out of necessity, many women plowed fields, supervised laborers, and ran large homesteads. Some upper-class women, like Abigail Adams, wife of John Adams, kept up extensive correspondence on current events with other like-minded women. While most Americans didn't go so far as to believe in gender equality, the Revolution did lead to more political and economic opportunities for women.

The American casualties

The Revolutionary War dragged on for eight agonizing years and cost the lives of 5 percent of white men of military age. This was the highest American death rate per capita than any other war except for the Civil War. About 25,000 patriots died in the war, most of disease or in captivity. Another 25,000 were wounded or seriously disabled. These numbers don't even include the casualties suffered by Loyalists, Native Americans, and the British. No reliable statistics have ever been found for those groups

African Americans fought on both sides

Blacks comprised about 20 percent of the colonial population. The majority of blacks were slaves, whether they lived north or south. When war came, black men fought on both sides. About 5,000 served in the Continental Army, and probably at least that many fought alongside the British, who sometimes offered freedom in exchange for military service. Patriot slave owners were reluctant to do the same, and at one point, Congress tried to ban blacks from the Continental Army. But the pressures of war led to a change in that policy. Washington persuaded Congress to accept black soldiers because he needed the manpower so badly.

Overall, the war led to a decline of slavery in America. Republican ideas about inalienable human rights, equality, and individual liberty were obviously at odds with human bondage. The Declaration of Independence said that "all men are created equal" and many patriots, black and white, took this to mean that slavery would be abolished. But to gain colonial unity for the declaration, northern delegates had to agree to leave slavery alone. So in the end, slavery tended to survive in the southern states where it was most economically profitable and where racist ideas were strongest. Within a generation after the end of the war, slavery no longer existed in the northern states, creating a large free black community and a cultural divide that would one day lead to civil war in America.

What Did It All Mean? How Historians View the Revolution

The way we look at the past is always changing, sometimes because of current events, sometimes because of new discoveries, and sometimes because of provocative new arguments. When it comes to the interpretation of historical events, there isn't always a right or wrong answer, just one argument versus another. The way historians have interpreted the meaning of the Revolution is a good example of how history is constantly evolving.

In the 200 years that historians have written about this monumental event, four major arguments, or *schools of thought,* have emerged. Each of them presents a firm argument about what the Revolution really meant and how we should view it. Which school of thought is right and which is wrong? I can't say. Ultimately, it's for you to decide which one you most agree with.

Covered in glory — the first historians

These people actually lived the event. Whether Loyalist or patriot, they wrote colorful, biased accounts espousing the justice and glory of their cause. The Tory Thomas Hutchinson wrote a popular account presenting his side's negative view of the Revolution. This was countered by David Ramsay's *History of the American Revolution,* which portrayed the patriot cause as just and inevitable. Mason Locke Weems wrote the first biography of George Washington, playing loose with the facts, turning him into a folk hero. As you would expect, these first historians had a difficult time being objective about the great events they had experienced.

Later, in the 19th century, a new generation of historians, who had not been alive during the war, compiled the basic documentary history of the war that we use today. To these historians, the Revolution was morally right, a shining, unique turning point in human history. American victory was inevitable so that the nation could fulfill its destiny of freedom.

It was all about economics — the determinists

The *determinists,* writing in the early 20th century, argued that the Revolution was about class conflict. All the rhetoric about republicanism, inalienable rights, and equality was so much window dressing to justify hard-core economic motivations. These historians said that the struggle wasn't just about independence but about empowering an elite ruling class of Americans here at home. They pointed to the wealth of many of the signers of the Declaration of Independence and contended that they merely used the Revolution to further their own grip on power.

Charles Beard, Carl Becker, and Arthur Schlesinger Sr. are the best examples of historians who espoused these ideas. The interesting thing about them is that they wrote at a time when Marxist analyses about class conflict throughout history were quite popular.

The Revolution was conservative — the Neo-Whigs

After World War II, a new school of thought emerged. A group of historians who called themselves *Neo-Whigs* (a term that implied conservatism) argued that the Revolution was neither unique nor radical. Instead, it was simply a conservative reaction to protect American rights and property from Parliament. The republican ideology was real enough, they conceded, but in the end, the patriots were simply conserving rights they already enjoyed. Thus, the American Revolution didn't represent anything brand new or radical beyond one group protecting its interests against another. Great historians like Bernard Bailyn, Daniel Boorstin, and Pauline Maier all subscribed to this point of view.

No, it was radical and ideological — the debate today

In the last couple of decades, the pendulum has swung back in favor of the radicalism and ideological nature of the Revolution. This new group of historians argues that the revolutionaries were motivated by ideology, had much to lose, and that their Revolution was something quite radical by the standards of the age. The Revolution represented a real change in the social life of America, they say, in favor of more equality, more economic opportunity for ordinary people, and greater individual autonomy.

The most important proponent of this view is Gordon Wood who, in 1992, published a classic book called *The Radicalism of the American Revolution*. Wood and many other historians of our time demonstrate their point by including much more detail than ever before about the experiences of common people and minorities.

Chapter 8

War and Peace: Battling Indians, Old Friends, Tax Delinquents, and Pirates

*A*mericans may have won their independence from Great Britain, but that hardly guaranteed them security. In the late 18th and early 19th centuries, a dizzying array of internal and external adversaries threatened the viability of the new United States. Native American tribes stood squarely in the path of a country that aspired to expand its borders far to the west. Bitter arguments flared among Americans as to how the new nation should govern itself. Should the United States have a strong central government, with extensive powers to tax and a standing military force, or would such a powerful government threaten the hard-won liberties Americans so cherished?

European imperial empires such as Britain and France still wielded enormous power in North America, as well as on the world's oceans, threatening the United States' security. To top it all off, North African city-states used organized piracy to extract wealth from international shipping routes in the Mediterranean and Atlantic, calling into question whether the United States could even protect its own ships. It all made for a dangerous, uncertain world.

In this chapter, I discuss the problems the new United States had with Native American tribes in what became known as the Old Northwest. I describe the difficulties the infant republic experienced in collecting taxes from its own citizens, as well as its run-ins with imperial Europe and adversarial Muslim kingdoms on the North African coast.

New Americans versus Native Americans

Nearly every American expected the new United States to expand westward. In fact, Americans had already spread into Kentucky and Tennessee during the Revolutionary War. In the Treaty of Paris, the agreement that ended the Revolutionary War, Britain turned over its American lands east of the Mississippi River to the U.S. In the late 18th century, Americans referred to this area, which comprised much of present-day Illinois, Indiana, Wisconsin, Michigan, and Ohio, as the *Old Northwest* (see Figure 8-1). In 1787, Congress passed the Northwest Ordinance, formally opening up this territory for American settlement.

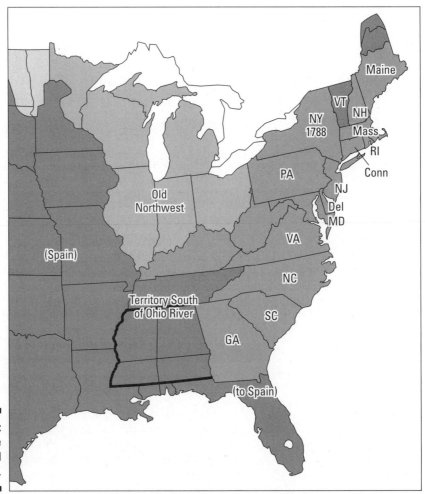

Figure 8-1:
Map of the
Old
Northwest.

Rising tension with Indian tribes

Numerous Native American tribes populated the Old Northwest. Most of them had alliances with the British, and some had even fought on their side during the war. What's more, in spite of what the British had agreed to in the Treaty of Paris, British troops remained in many of their forts and urged their Native American allies to resist U.S. encroachment. The stage was set for conflict.

Throughout the 1780s, American settlers poured across the Ohio River into the Old Northwest. Some of them made homes on sparsely populated land. Others migrated onto Indian land, causing immediate problems. Tension, strife, and bloodshed soon followed. The American government sought to deal with this crisis diplomatically by negotiating treaties with the Indians, but this failed.

A confederation of tribes that included the Shawnees, Miamis, Lenapes, and Ottawas banded together to stop American expansion. This tribal confederation insisted that the boundary line between the United States and themselves must be the Ohio River. The Americans would not accept this. By 1790, the area was in a state of constant warfare and westerners were pleading with their young government for help.

Little battles with big consequences

In June 1790, the federal government responded by sending a mixed force of regular Army soldiers and militiamen to attack the Indians. The Native Americans ambushed them and defeated them. When the government sent yet another militia-dominated column of soldiers, the Indians pinned the column against the Wabash River and inflicted 900 casualties on them.

In the wake of these sobering defeats, George Washington, who was serving as the country's first president, decided to build a truly competent military force. Ever since the Revolution, Americans had been arguing about the need for a professional army. Some thought such armies were instruments of oppression and dictatorship, not to mention ruinously expensive. They believed that a *militia* (an army of citizen soldiers called to fight in times of emergency) could best handle American security. Others, like Washington, believed that a professional army, under proper civilian authority, was an absolute necessity for the republic's survival.

Washington resumed negotiations with the tribal confederation, but he expected that little would come from such talk. So he persuaded Congress to raise a trained army of 5,000 soldiers to fight the tribal confederation. He chose an excellent commander, Gen. Anthony Wayne, to preside over this force. For two years, Wayne trained his men hard, preparing them well for war.

In September 1793, with the Indians still insisting on the Ohio River boundary, Washington ordered Wayne to resume hostilities. In less than a year, Gen. Wayne's disciplined army inflicted a series of devastating defeats on the Native Americans. The tribal confederation turned, in vain, to the British for help. With a world full of obligations, the British were disengaging from the Old Northwest, leaving the confederation vulnerable. This, in combination with Wayne's triumphs, finished off the tribal confederation. The Indians agreed to the Treaty of Greenville, which ceded all of Ohio to the United States. In the years to come, Indiana, Illinois, and Michigan would all eventually come under U.S. control.

New Americans versus the Government

When the 13 colonies defeated Britain in the Revolutionary War, they loosely organized themselves under a new government called the *Articles of Confederation.* Under the Articles, Congress was the highest power in the land. Every state was represented equally in Congress, and the central government was weak, with little power to tax, make war, or regulate trade. Because most Americans believed that strong central authority threatened individual liberty, they initially liked the idea of a weak American government.

The trouble was that this weak government couldn't police the frontier, provide security, negotiate with foreign powers, or establish any sort of coherent interstate economic policy. The resulting chaos awakened a major debate between *nationalists* who advocated a stronger central government and *anti-nationalists* who liked things as they were. All of this played out in several tax-collecting crises that had military implications.

Shays says nay to taxes

One legacy of the Revolution was financial debt. Congress and every state had incurred serious debt during the war years. Just as Britain had sought to recoup war debts by taxing colonists in the 1760s (see Chapter 7), so too state governments in the new American nation taxed their citizens in the 1780s. In Massachusetts, the burden of taxation fell heavily upon farmers in the western part of the state. Many of these farmers were patriot veterans of the war who had not received the land and pensions that Congress had promised them. The farmers believed that the taxation was so great that they would lose their homes and property.

In 1786, a group of these farmers, led by a former Continental Army captain named Daniel Shays, rebelled against the state government. The rebels called themselves *Regulators*. Their rebellion took the shape of a series of demonstrations in Springfield, Massachusetts, and a few other towns. Congress had no power to do anything about the Regulators. Ultimately, the state of Massachusetts had to hire a mercenary militia, under the command of Gen. Benjamin Lincoln, to disperse the rebellion, fortunately with very little violence. Most of the Regulators eventually left Massachusetts or were pardoned by the state authorities.

Shays's Rebellion led many Americans, including prominent leaders like Thomas Jefferson, Alexander Hamilton, James Madison, and Washington, to question the long-term viability of the Articles of Confederation government. This concern, in turn, led many leaders to consider establishing a stronger central government. The ultimate result of all of this was the Constitutional Convention of 1787 in which delegates abolished the Articles in favor of a strong central government and the Constitution under which we live today.

The Constitutional Convention

From May through September 1787, delegates from nearly every state met in Philadelphia to consider changes to the federal government. George Washington presided over the sessions. The delegates included such luminaries as Thomas Jefferson, Benjamin Franklin, and Alexander Hamilton.

After deciding to abandon the Articles government in favor of a brand-new constitution with a stronger central government, the conventioneers spent much of that hot summer arguing over the nature of that new constitution. Those from big states like Virginia and New York wanted a constitution that favored the larger states. Those from small states like Delaware were understandably wary of this. The key was to find a balance between the interests of the many and the few.

In the end, they compromised. They created a *bicameral* (a legislature with two houses) Congress:

✔ The House of Representatives would be determined by population, thus favoring the bigger states.

✔ The Senate would feature equal representation, ensuring that smaller states had a voice in the national government.

The Constitution also set up two other branches of government: the executive, headed up by the president, and the judiciary.

The new government would have the power to tax, coin money, regulate trade, make foreign policy, make war, and use force to ensure domestic security. The president would be the commander-in-chief of the armed forces.

The system was set up in such a way that the Constitution is the highest authority in the land. Every member of the armed forces takes an oath to protect the Constitution, not any particular president, state, or branch of government.

The Whiskey Rebellion

As president, Washington chose Alexander Hamilton to be his secretary of the treasury. Hamilton had served under Washington during the war, and the two had a father-son type of relationship. In addition to being a lawyer, Hamilton possessed a keen mind for finances. He devised an elaborate plan to phase out the serious wartime debt that was eating away at the federal treasury. A key aspect of the plan was a tax on whiskey passed in 1791.

Western farmers who distilled their own liquor were particularly hard hit by Hamilton's whiskey tax. Not only were they taxed at a higher rate than large distillers, they didn't have much cash in the first place because they lived in remote areas. This was especially true for western Pennsylvanians and farmers who lived in the Appalachian Mountains.

Needless to say, these moonshine-making folks didn't react well to the new tax. They believed that the federal tax was just as unjust as Britain's attempts at taxation in the 1760s and 1770s (see Chapter 7). So, just as in those years, they refused to pay. The farmers also engaged in bitter protests and outright rebellion. They assaulted tax collectors. In one instance, a mob caught a collector, cropped his hair, covered him in tar and feathers, and even took his horse.

President Washington was deeply disturbed by this Whiskey Rebellion. He thought it was similar to Shays's Rebellion a few years earlier (see the "Shays says nay to taxes" section earlier in this chapter). Remembering how ineffective the Articles of Confederation government had been during that crisis, Washington was determined to demonstrate federal authority to collect taxes and keep order. He amassed a militia army of 13,000 troops for an expedition to western Pennsylvania. He even rode with them himself. This overwhelming force crushed the rebellion quickly and bloodlessly. Washington pardoned most of the perpetrators.

The Whiskey Rebellion set a precedent. It demonstrated the new constitutional government's willingness and ability to use military force to keep law and order. If an American didn't like a law and wanted to change it, he had to do so through peaceful, constitutional means.

In spite of the federal government's Whiskey Rebellion victory, Congress eventually repealed Hamilton's whiskey tax in 1803. The government never raised much money from the tax anyway.

New Americans versus French "Friends"

In the 1790s, France and Britain were once again at war with each other. France had undergone a revolution that saw the overthrow of the king, the establishment of a republic, and the onset of a war with much of the rest of Europe. Of course, France's main enemy, as usual, was Britain. The two nations were locked in a bitter struggle for control of the Atlantic.

President Washington sought neutrality for the U.S., but this was easier said than done. Overseas trade, particularly with Europe, was a vital part of the American economy. If we traded with the British, the French were angry. If we traded with the French, the British were upset. Even the American people were divided on which side to support. Those who lived in the Northeast and the coastal areas favored Britain because of their commercial ties to the old mother country. Americans in the West and the South preferred France because, in their view, Britain was still the main threat on the frontier. Plus, France was an old ally from revolutionary times.

In 1794, the Washington administration signed a commercial trading agreement with Britain. The French viewed the agreement as equivalent to an alliance with their enemy. French ships began attacking and seizing any American ships that did business with England. The French then cut off diplomatic ties with the U.S., saying they would only restore relations if the Americans paid them a handsome bribe.

All of this inflamed anti-French sentiment in America. A new president, John Adams of Massachusetts, unveiled ambitious plans to build a large navy and army to fight France. Although the two countries never formally declared war on each other, fighting at sea went on from 1796 until 1800 when Napoleon Bonaparte, the French emperor, defused the tension and restored normal diplomatic relations with the U.S. This episode is generally known as the *Quasi-War with France.*

When Washington retired in 1796, he urged his countrymen to "avoid the broils of Europe." But the Quasi-War showed that the United States could easily be drawn into European wars, even if Americans sought to remain neutral. The same issue would arise many more times in the future.

Federalists versus Democratic-Republicans

The Founding Fathers believed that the American republic would not, and should not, have political parties. They had seen political parties rise to prominence in Britain and felt that they had done damage to the country. But, in spite of the founders' intentions, American political parties soon came into being. They grew out of opposing philosophies about national policies and human nature. From the late 1780s through the first two decades of the 19th century, the two major parties were the Federalists and the Democratic-Republicans.

The Federalists believed in a strong central government, a strong national defense, a federal bank, a loose interpretation of the Constitution, the sanctity of private property, a pro-British foreign policy, and rule by the elite. Federalists believed that humans were inherently irrational and foolish. Total democracy, then, was not a good idea. Instead, educated, self-made, sober, responsible leaders who owned property should run the nation. The Federalists were strong in New England and the coastal areas.

Alexander Hamilton, John Adams, and George Washington were all Federalists.

The Democratic-Republicans believed in state's rights, a weaker central government, a strict interpretation of the Constitution, and a pro-French foreign policy. They feared professional armed forces as a threat to liberty. They believed that the core of America was small farmers, not propertied merchants, bankers, and industrialists. Democratic-Republicans felt that human nature was basically good, so ordinary people could be trusted to make societal decisions at the ballot box. Democratic-Republicans were strong in the West and the South. Thomas Jefferson, James Madison, and James Monroe were the leaders of this party.

Both parties opposed and feared the establishment of a European-style aristocracy in America. Both saw themselves as the true guardians of revolutionary republican ideas. Neither of them advocated voting rights or social equality for women and African Americans.

Pirates of the Mediterranean

In 1800, Thomas Jefferson was elected president of the United States. As a Democratic-Republican, he was deeply suspicious of a regular military establishment. He worried that professional officers might turn into a new *aristocracy* (a privileged ruling class). So, too, professional soldiers could threaten or coerce the people, depriving of them of their inalienable human rights.

When Jefferson became president, he initially cut back on the armed forces. For maritime security, he felt that America could be protected by a fleet of small coastal gunboats. He sold off or decommissioned most of the Navy's conventional warships.

Pirate pasha demands payment

In the late 18th century, the Barbary states of North Africa (see Figure 8-2) often captured international ships sailing off their coasts. In return for safe passage through the Mediterranean Sea, they demanded payment from the ship's crews or their government. The Barbary states included Morocco, Algiers, Tunis, and Tripoli. European powers like Great Britain took advantage of this situation by paying the Barbary states to capture their enemies' ships.

American ships sailed these waters quite often. Throughout the last two decades of the 18th century, the American government negotiated treaties with the Barbary states in return for protection of American commerce. These protection treaties only went so far. Sometimes Barbary pirates seized American ships and held the crewmen hostage. The U.S. government didn't always pay the North African rulers as they had pledged in the protection treaties. The result was conflict.

In 1801, Pasha Yusuf Qaramanli, the ruler of Tripoli, demanded payment, or *tribute,* from the American government for the use of his waters. He felt that the Americans had incurred years of debt without paying. To punish the American debtors, he pledged to make war on American ships off the Tripolitan coast.

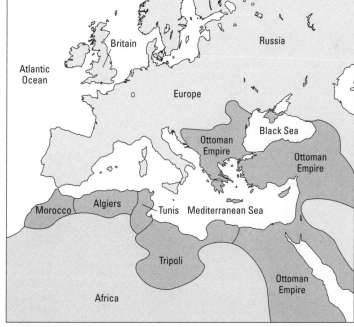

Figure 8-2: Map of the North African coast in the early 1800s.

Jefferson sends in a coalition navy

When the crisis arose with the pasha, Jefferson had only a small navy on hand. Even so, he had no intention of caving in to the pasha, a man he thought of as little more than a glorified robber. Jefferson sent his small navy to the Mediterranean with instructions to coordinate its efforts with a likeminded coalition of ships from Sweden, Sicily, Malta, Portugal, and Morocco. This worked well. The pasha backed off of his demands.

From 1801 to 1803, this small force of American ships, with one frigate and a few supporting ships, sailed the waters off Tripoli. But in October 1803, the frigate USS *Philadelphia* ran aground on the North African coast. The pasha captured the crew of 300 sailors and prepared to ransom them, their ship, and its cargo. A few months later, in February 1804, Lt. Stephen Decatur raided Tripoli harbor with a small group, burning *Philadelphia.* The pasha no longer had the ship to bargain with. In the meantime, the surviving American ships routinely bombarded the harbor.

An intriguing victory in Tripoli

The situation burned with intrigue. William Eaton, the American consul to Tunis, was hatching plans with the pasha's brother to overthrow him. They compiled a force of Arabs, Greeks, and U.S. Marines (hence the line "to the shores of Tripoli" in the *Marines' Hymn*).

Before Eaton's makeshift force had the chance to get rid of the pasha, the Tripolitan ruler and Jefferson struck a deal. Jefferson agreed to pay a ransom for the return of the *Philadelphia's* crew. In exchange, the pasha agreed not to mess with American ships.

Jefferson reaped a nice political windfall from this Mediterranean episode. The country buzzed with poems, books, paintings, and statues commemorating the supposedly great victory over the pasha. However, Jefferson was quite fortunate to have encountered a weak enemy in Tripoli. The United States Navy was so small and weak in Jefferson's time that it would have struggled to defeat an opposing navy of any decent size and training.

If the United States wanted to protect its overseas trade, it would need a formidable navy, not a few gunboats that could barely even cover the American coast.

Chapter 9

We Have Met the Enemy: The War of 1812

*B*y the early 19th century, the brand-new United States was expanding in two directions — overseas in its commerce and westward with its population. Americans of the eastern seaboard states were shipping a range of products, such as fish, timber, sugar, and tobacco, to European markets. At the same time, more and more Americans were migrating to the Northwest Territory (comprising present-day Indiana, Illinois, Wisconsin, Michigan, and Ohio), making new lives for themselves as farmers, shippers, furriers, and craftsmen.

No matter which direction Americans gravitated in pursuit of their economic interests, they were bound to be affected by European events. When war broke out in Europe, the security of American economic interests on that continent was threatened, mainly by the British. The same was true for westerners who were profoundly affected by Britain's close relationship with Native American tribes that stood in the way of American expansion. The result of all this tension was another war between the U.S. and Britain. We usually call this the War of 1812, even though it lasted from that year until early 1815.

In this chapter, I discuss the key events that led to this second war between the British and the Americans. I analyze the main causes of the war. Then I tell you about the battles, some of which were American disasters and some of which were American triumphs. Finally, at the end of the chapter, I tell you the ultimate results of the war.

Overture to the War of 1812

In the first two decades of the 19th century, a world war was raging. Great Britain was locked in a death struggle with Napoleon Bonaparte's France. Almost every country in Europe was involved, in some way, in this war. Great Britain was part of an anti-Napoleon coalition that included Austria, Prussia, and Russia. From 1803 through 1815, fighting periodically raged on land and at sea. The British aimed to use their navy to cut France off from the rest of the world and bring Napoleon to his knees. France wanted to impose the same isolation on Britain.

The United States stayed neutral and tried to do business with both sides because Americans had such vital economic interests in Europe. But staying neutral was easier said than done. Both Britain and France targeted the ships of any country that was trading with their enemies, but Britain was especially aggressive. Thus, the security of American ships and cargoes was constantly in peril — usually from the Royal Navy — throughout the first decade of the 19th century. Over a period of ten years, from 1803 to 1812, American neutrality gradually gave way to war with Britain. Here's how.

Britain or France — pick a side!

In 1806, when Napoleon conquered much of Europe, he imposed his *continental system* on the rest of Europe. Basically, the continental system excluded British trade from Europe. In this way, Napoleon hoped to strangle Great Britain. In response, the Royal Navy blockaded the continent, preventing the French from engaging in overseas trade.

During the war, the mentality of both the British and the French could be summed up as "You're either for us or against us." This war wasn't like the many imperial tilts the two countries had fought during the previous 100 years (see Chapters 7 and 8). This one was a total war of survival. Napoleon planned to invade and conquer Britain. The British wanted to remove him from power and make sure that France could never dominate the European continent.

Americans had trouble finding any middle ground between these powerful adversaries. A major political split existed in America between Federalists, who favored Britain, and Democratic-Republicans, who favored France. The Federalists were prevalent in New England and the coastal areas. They were sympathetic to Britain because of economic and cultural ties.

Democratic-Republicans tended to be stronger in the South and the West, especially the Northwest Territory. They believed that France was America's main ally, dating back to the Revolution when the French had helped

Americans win their independence. Democratic-Republicans despised Britain because they believed that the British incited Indian tribes in the Northwest Territory to attack American settlers. The Democratic-Republicans pointed to the fact that France was a fellow republic (after its own revolution) and thus deserved American support. Finally, Democratic-Republicans didn't like the heavy-handed way in which the Royal Navy infringed on American shipping to enforce the British blockade of Europe.

This tension played out mainly in a regional split that hindered the federal government from choosing sides in the war. The Federalists of the Northeast and east coast lobbied for an alliance with Britain. Westerners and southerners — mainly Democratic-Republicans — wanted to make common cause with France.

Don't try to impress us: Problems at sea

In October 1805, the British Royal Navy defeated the French navy in the decisive battle of Trafalgar, a titanic naval tilt that ensured Royal Navy supremacy for more than a century. In the shorter term, this victory gave the British command of the Atlantic Ocean and, as such, put real teeth into Britain's European blockade. From this point on, the Royal Navy aggressively hunted down, seized, and boarded any European-bound American ships. The British reach even extended to American territorial waters. For instance, in June 1807, the British frigate HMS *Leopard* opened fire on the USS *Chesapeake* in American waters near Norfolk, Virginia, killing or wounding 21 sailors and capturing 4 others.

Besides the invasion of America's waters and the negative impact on trade, what really angered Americans was the British policy of *impressment.* To fight a war on multiple continents and enforce its blockade, the British needed a lot of sailors, more than they were able to enlist. They began to impound American ships and *impress,* or force, American captives into their navy. The British claimed they were only recovering Royal Navy deserters, but this wasn't true. They often impressed naturalized American citizens who had been born in Britain and even, in some cases, impressed natural-born Americans. Very few of these folks wanted to serve in the Royal Navy because the pay and overall treatment were much worse than on American ships. In all, the British seized well over 500 ships and impressed 6,000 sailors into the Royal Navy.

Impressment infuriated Americans because it directly challenged American sovereignty. By forcing American citizens into the Royal Navy, Britain was, in effect, saying that the United States was not a sovereign, independent country. As impressment grew worse each year, anti-British sentiment took hold among more and more Americans.

Passing useless laws to punish Britain

Thomas Jefferson was the president who had to deal with this mounting crisis. He was the standard-bearer for the Democratic-Republicans, and he was fortunate enough to work with a like-minded Congress. Jefferson and his allies thought that the best way to change British behavior was to withhold American products from them. So, in December 1807, they passed the Embargo Act, a heavy-handed law which prohibited American goods from being shipped to foreign ports and even restricted foreign ships from taking on cargo at U.S. ports.

The Embargo Act was a disaster. The law devastated the New England seafaring economy. Sailors were out of work. Merchants went out of business. Shippers went bankrupt. Some people survived only by smuggling products across the Canadian border. Jefferson and his political party had never been popular in New England. After the Embargo Act, though, he couldn't even travel there. Nor did the law have any real effect on the British.

In a 2006 poll, American historians listed the Embargo Act as number seven of the top-ten mistakes American presidents have made. Jefferson's support of the Embargo Act ravaged the American economy like few laws before or since.

Realizing that the Embargo Act was not working, Congress repealed it in March 1809. But they replaced it with the Non-Intercourse Act. No, this was not an attempt to limit sex! The Non-Intercourse Act lifted the American embargo on every nation except Britain and France, the country's two most important trading partners. This law was just as ineffective as the Embargo Act. Plus, it further damaged the reeling New England economy.

In passing these two disastrous laws, the United States was acting like the proverbial child who holds his breath until he gets what he wants. The Americans were only suffocating themselves in the vain hope of influencing British behavior. The British were only too happy to stand aside and watch Uncle Sam's face grow bluer and bluer.

Madison declares war

Jefferson left office in 1809. His successor, James Madison, was a fellow Virginian, founding father, political ally, and protégé. As a southerner and a Democratic-Republican, Madison had an anti-British attitude. As impressment continued (see the "Don't try to impress us: Problems at sea" section earlier in this chapter) and tension with Britain grew worse, Madison contemplated war. New Englanders were, of course, dead set against any such war, but their political power was limited.

The War Hawks eye their prey

A group of young congressmen, mostly from southern and western states, were the main proponents of war with Great Britain. These congressmen had been reared on patriotic tales of the Revolution. They saw Britain as America's main enemy for two major reasons:

✔ They didn't like the Royal Navy's interference with American shipping and commerce on the high seas.

✔ They believed that the British instigated Native American tribes to attack American settlements in western states such as Tennessee, Kentucky, and Ohio.

These congressmen, dubbed *War Hawks* by their colleagues, felt that war was the only honorable way to resolve these problems with Britain.

The War Hawks were led by two of the prominent politicians of the 19th century — Henry Clay of Kentucky and John Calhoun of South Carolina. Clay served as speaker of the House and was known for his brilliant speaking skills. Calhoun was the very embodiment of the southern slaveholding, plantation class. Later, he became a staunch advocate of states' rights and southern pride. Other notable War Hawks were Felix Grundy of Tennessee, George Troup of Georgia, and Richard Johnson of Kentucky. Together, these young men reflected the prevailing attitudes in their states.

A group of powerful young congressmen from the West and South, known as the *War Hawks,* lobbied stridently for war with Britain. As settlers moved farther west, they encountered conflicts with pro-British Indian tribes. This sparked intense anti-British sentiment among Americans in the West.

The War Hawks and other pro-war advocates got their wish. Madison gave a pro-war speech to Congress on June 1, 1812. The House voted 79–49 for war; the Senate 19–13. The West and the South were for the War of 1812. The Northeast was against it.

The Main Movement: The Battles

At the outbreak of war, neither side was particularly well prepared. The British were deeply involved in their war with Napoleon. Most British soldiers were fighting French troops on the European continent, and the bulk of the Royal Navy was busy blockading Europe. Britain had about 6,000 regulars stationed in Canada, but they were augmented by Canadian militiamen and a confederation of friendly Native American tribes that a charismatic chief named Tecumseh had put together. These tribes were, of course, concerned about American expansion onto their lands.

The U.S. Army consisted of 12,000 soldiers. Congress authorized the Army to expand to three times that size, but recruiting was spotty. President Madison assumed that the militia would do most of the fighting for the United States. This method of citizen-soldier warfare was an American tradition dating back to colonial times. The Navy was little more than a collection of small frigates and gunboats. In this war, their role would be to harass British ships in the Atlantic, in hopes of avoiding an enemy blockade of American ports. The Navy also fought on the Great Lakes.

The American offensive, 1812–1813

Because the British were busy dealing with Napoleon, the Americans took the initiative at the beginning of the war. During the first two years of the conflict, the U.S. waged a northern offensive designed to capture Canada.

President Madison believed that because Canada was so thinly defended, American troops could easily seize control of that country. Jefferson, now in retirement, agreed with his protégé Madison. They figured the conquest of Canada would simply be a matter of marching north. With this accomplished, Madison could then negotiate an end to the war on terms advantageous to the U.S.

So, at the beginning of the war, American strategy was to invade Canada in three places (see Figure 9-1):

- In the west, at Lake Erie, roughly along the neck of land between Detroit and Toronto
- At Lake Ontario, opposite upstate New York
- In the east, along the St. Lawrence River and Lake Champlain, south of Montreal

The Lake Erie campaign

On July 12, 1812, Gen. William Hull invaded Canada with an army comprised almost entirely of ill-trained militiamen. Hull's invasion quickly faltered. He lost battles at Brownstown and Monguagon. Soon he had major supply problems. His militiamen did not fight well. They had little discipline nor much enthusiasm for facing a growing number of Indian fighters. In August, Hull turned his army around and retreated to Detroit. A combined force of British regulars, Canadian militiamen, and Indians besieged the Americans at Detroit. Hull surrendered to this enemy force on August 16, 1812.

A year later, the U.S. Navy avenged this humiliating defeat. On September 10, 1813, at the Battle of Lake Erie, a force of nine ships under Capt. Oliver Hazard Perry decisively defeated and captured a British flotilla of six ships. The victory gave the Americans control of Lake Erie, raised U.S. morale, and gave the Yanks a chance to win back Detroit.

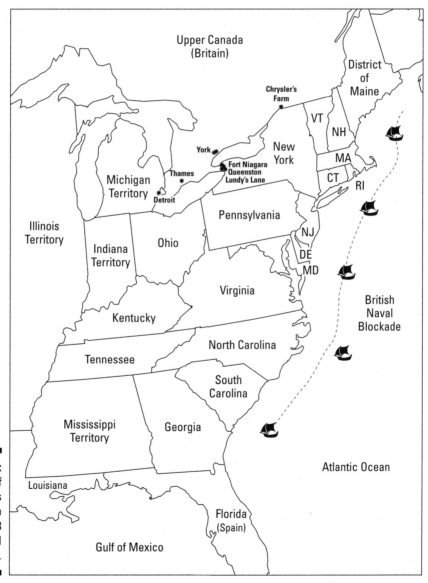

Figure 9-1:
Map of battles fought in 1812–1813 (selected battle sites).

After the battle, Perry sent his Army counterpart, Gen. William Henry Harrison, a jubilant dispatch: "We have met the enemy and they are ours." This was the 19th-century way of saying: "We came, we saw, we kicked some butt!"

In the wake of Perry's victory on Lake Erie, Harrison went on the attack. He recaptured Detroit, pushed the British back into Ontario, and won an engagement called the Battle of the Thames on October 5. The greatest significance of this battle was that Tecumseh was killed in action. His death unraveled the pro-British confederation of Native American tribes that the great chief had assembled. The Americans controlled Lake Erie for the rest of the war, and Detroit, of course, remained part of the U.S. However, U.S. forces weren't able to conquer western Ontario, even though they did sack and burn York, the site of present-day Toronto.

The Lake Ontario campaign

The second prong of the American invasion of Canada was to the east, near the Niagara River. Gen. Steven Van Rensselaer attempted to cross the river on October 13, 1812, with an army of 6,000 soldiers, provoking the Battle of Queenston Heights. Van Rensselaer was a politically well-connected New Yorker who had no experience commanding troops. At Queenston, he was essentially trying to pull off an amphibious invasion, and he didn't have the skill or training to succeed at such a complicated maneuver.

At the Battle of Queenston Heights, American soldiers were packed aboard boats crossing the Niagara River. British soldiers and Mohawk Indians fired on the boats from fortified positions in and around the town of Queenston. British cannon and musket fire swept through the American ranks, tearing into the U.S. soldiers, bloodying them as they tried to get out of their boats. For much of the day on October 13, the Americans struggled to get ashore, find cover, and return fire. Some soldiers — mainly regulars — exhibited great bravery, fighting desperately. Too many soldiers — mainly militiamen — simply cowered under cover and did nothing. By the end of the day, the American force was broken, with most of the men escaping back across the Niagara to New York. In all, 100 Americans were killed, 300 wounded, and 925 taken prisoner.

The defeat at Queenston Heights ended any serious American hope of invading Canada in that area. The war along Lake Ontario settled into an unhappy stalemate.

The St. Lawrence campaign

In the east, Gen. Henry Dearborn was supposed to advance north from Lake Champlain and menace Montreal, but in 1812, this didn't happen. Demoralized by the defeats that Hull and Van Rensselaer had suffered, Dearborn stayed put. In fairness to Dearborn, he was hampered by the fact that his militia refused to cross onto Canadian soil. They would only fight within the borders of their home states. Moreover, he couldn't count on New England militiamen for added force because that section of the country so bitterly opposed the war. These militia-related problems crippled his army. In 1813, a half-hearted American thrust for Montreal failed miserably.

Stuck at an impasse

By 1814, the war had stalemated:

- ✔ The Americans controlled Lake Erie and Detroit, but not western Ontario.

- ✔ Inconclusive naval fighting had occurred on Lake Ontario. The Americans failed to gain a foothold in Canada, but the British couldn't make any headway into upstate New York.

- ✔ In the east, the American invasion of Canada had failed completely.

- ✔ British ships were blockading America's east coast ports.

The British counteroffensive, 1814–1815

By the middle of 1814, the war in Europe had turned in Britain's favor. A strong coalition, consisting of Russia, Austria, Prussia, Spain, and Britain, had defeated Napoleon, forcing him from power in France. With Napoleon out of the way, the British began redeploying soldiers and ships to North America to score a knockout blow against the Americans.

The British planned a three-pronged offensive (see Figure 9-2):

- ✔ In the north, they would push across Lake Champlain and the Niagara River, invade New York, seize control of the Hudson River, and separate sympathetic New England from the rest of America.

- ✔ In the central theater, they would blockade and then invade the Chesapeake area, particularly Maryland, with the purpose of capturing Washington, D.C., and Baltimore.

- ✔ In the South, they would seal off the Gulf of Mexico and seize control of northern Florida, New Orleans, and the Mississippi River.

All in all, the British devised an ambitious plan to score a total victory over the upstart Americans.

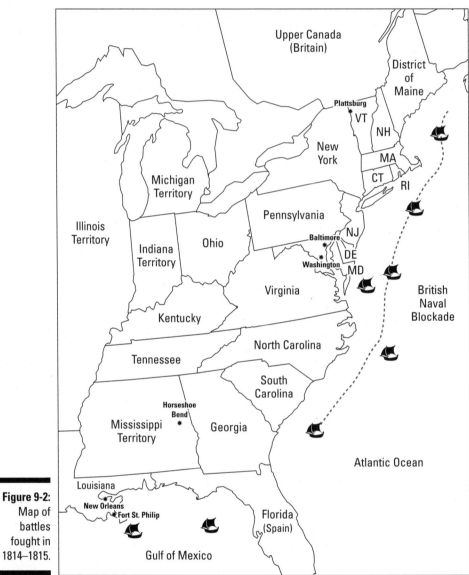

Figure 9-2:
Map of battles fought in 1814–1815.

The British fail in the north

In 1814, the British tried, and failed, to cross the Niagara River into New York. The Americans fought them to a standstill during battles at Lundy's Lane and Chippewa. At the same time, the U.S. Navy defeated the Royal Navy at the

Battle of Plattsburgh, giving the U.S. control of Lake Champlain, ending the British hopes of splitting New England from the rest of the states. In total, the British northern prong was an unmitigated failure.

Disaster in the Chesapeake

Between August 19 and 29, 1814, British ships sailed into Chesapeake Bay and landed soldiers on either side of Washington, D.C. One group landed from the Potomac River, on the Virginia side of the capital. The other group landed in Maryland and approached Washington from the east. On August 24, the Americans tried to save their capital by stopping the British at Bladensburg, Maryland. Some of the American troops fought desperately, but most, including the Maryland militia, ran away at the first sight of the enemy. Washington was now wide open.

President Madison fled to his native Virginia. British soldiers entered Washington against no resistance. In retaliation for the American destruction of York, they proceeded to burn every public building, including the Capitol and the president's home. In the wake of this humiliation, American morale was quite low.

The destruction of Washington was bad for the Americans, but it wasn't decisive. The capital was so small and embryonic that its significance was more symbolic than strategic. For the British, the greater objective was Baltimore, one of the premier ports in America.

After sacking Washington, the British went after Baltimore by land and sea. On land, the Americans stymied them at North Point, even killing Gen. Robert Ross, the British commander. In the wake of this setback, the British tried to barge into Baltimore by sea. To do that, they had to capture Fort McHenry, which guarded Baltimore's harbor. For most of September 13 and 14, the Royal Navy bombarded the fort, but to no avail. Fort McHenry held out, and the British failed to take Baltimore, negating the overall success of their Chesapeake campaign.

The successful defense of Fort McHenry was the inspiration for the American national anthem. Francis Scott Key, a local lawyer, watched the nighttime bombardment and, in the flashes of explosions, noticed that the American flag still flew over McHenry. So he wrote a poem called "The Star-Spangled Banner" with the line "bombs bursting in air, gave proof through the night that our flag was still there." This patriotic poem, later set to music, became the official national anthem in 1931.

The hostess with the mostest: Dolley Madison

One of James Madison's greatest political assets was his vivacious wife, Dolley. The couple had married in 1794. Dolley assumed the hostess duties that Americans would later associate with the "first lady." She was quite comfortable in the company of politicians and statesmen. She enthralled them with her sense of humor, tart opinions, and love of snuff tobacco.

When the British descended on Washington, she demonstrated a cool-headed resolve to keep as many American relics as possible out of enemy hands. She saved state papers, silverware, and a valuable painting of George Washington.

Later, when the British were gone, she helped supervise the rebuilding of the capital. The president's home, having been badly damaged by the British, was later reconstructed from its foundations and given a thick coat of white paint to erase the scorch marks. From that point on, the home was known as the White House.

The southern campaign

In the South, the British wanted to seal off the Gulf Coast from Florida to southern Louisiana. At this point, in Florida and Alabama, the Spanish, British, and Americans all competed for influence with Native American tribes, particularly the Creeks. Louisiana was more settled, dominated as it was by New Orleans, North America's greatest port. The capture of New Orleans was the main objective for the British offensive.

Throughout much of 1814, a rising American leader, Gen. Andrew Jackson, had fought and defeated the Creeks in Florida and Alabama. In the fall of 1814, when he heard that a British armada was heading for New Orleans, he re-deployed his army to defend the city.

Jackson's army was composed of a diverse mixture of troops. He had local militiamen, pirates, free blacks, U.S. Marines, sailors, Kentucky and Tennessee militiamen, Choctaw tribesmen, and U.S. Army regulars. Through force of leadership, he forged this group into a formidable fighting force.

On January 8, 1815, a British army under Gen. Edward Pakenham attacked Jackson's main defensive line at the Chalmette Plantation, just outside of New Orleans. Jackson's men were well entrenched in excellent positions. They had the Mississippi River on their right and an impassable swamp on their left.

When the British attacked, they sent 3,000 redcoated soldiers forward onto open ground — right into the muzzles of American muskets and cannons. The British expected the Americans to run away. Instead, they stayed put and raked the British with wicked fire, slaughtering them in droves. The open ground was littered with enemy corpses, their blood turning the grass red. Pakenham himself was killed, and the remnants of his army retreated. The Americans suffered 71 casualties. The British lost more than 2,000!

The Battle of New Orleans was America's greatest victory in this war. The legacies of the battle were profound:

✔ From that point on, the U.S. controlled New Orleans, leading to massive American economic growth along the entire expanse of the Mississippi River.

✔ The victory solidified American nationalism, leading to more U.S. westward expansion.

✔ Jackson became a national hero, propelling him to an important political career.

✔ The retreat at New Orleans marked the end of most British imperial influence in America.

✔ The victory solidified Madison's Democratic-Republican party as the dominant political party in America.

The Finale: The Treaty of Ghent

The ironic thing about the Battle of New Orleans is that it took place *after* American and British negotiators signed a peace treaty in Ghent, Belgium, on December 24, 1814. Quite simply, the word of the peace treaty hadn't reached New Orleans by the time of the battle.

The treaty restored the status quo. Neither side gained or lost any territory. The Americans also negotiated some new fishing rights. Nothing was said about impressment, but it ended because Britain's war with Napoleon was over and the country no longer needed additional sailors. The British lost about 4,400 soldiers in this war (half at New Orleans). The Americans lost about 20,000, mostly to disease.

Overall, the War of 1812 was a tie, with perhaps a slight edge going to the Americans. The war had the following results:

✔ It solidified American independence.

✔ It led to more American expansion at the expense of Native American tribes.

✔ The Democratic-Republicans were now dominant in politics.

✔ American nationalism grew dramatically.

Part III
Forged in War

"Remember everyone, we're re-enacting the Battle of Chickamauga. Using your cell phones would be totally inappropriate! The Union soldiers would never get service this far south."

In this part . . .

By the middle of the 19th century, Americans understood that the question of independence had been resolved. The question now was what kind of country the United States would be. Would it extend past the Mississippi River? Would it go all the way to the Pacific Ocean? Would slavery or free labor dominate in this new America? As you find out in this part, the sad thing about these questions is that they were answered not by cool-headed statesmen, but on blood-soaked battlefields all over North America in a series of costly wars.

Chapter 10

To the Halls of Montezuma: Fighting Mexico

In This Chapter

▶ Clashing with Mexico over expansion

▶ Fighting in Texas and northern Mexico

▶ Snatching California

▶ Invading the heart of Mexico

As the 1840s began, the United States was growing by leaps and bounds. This hustling, bustling growth was embodied in one word: expansion. Many Americans envisioned a future in which their country would stretch from coast to coast, comprising an "empire of liberty." They believed in the notion of *Manifest Destiny* — the idea that God had bequeathed much of the North American continent for the United States so it could spread its unique culture, liberty, and wealth from the Atlantic to the Pacific, in the process bettering humankind.

Behind the veneer of this idealism, expansion was really motivated by economic interests. The territory west of the Mississippi River contained good farm-land, resources, waterways, and places to build railroads, and the glistening Pacific Coast beckoned as well. Americans dreamed of going west to find wealth, security, and personal independence. As the 1840s unfolded, more and more Americans were migrating west, pursuing their dreams. Inevitably, this led to tension with Mexico, another new nation intent on expansion as well. The ultimate, and sad, result of this tension was war between the two countries.

In this chapter, I explain the key events that led to the Mexican-American War, including the underlying causes of the conflict. I show how diplomacy failed and shooting began. I describe the amazing string of American military victories, explain why they happened, and relate the war's most important consequences.

Clashing Over Expansion

Mexico won its independence from Spain in 1821. In so doing, the new nation inherited much of the sparsely populated, loosely controlled Spanish empire in North America. This empire encompassed the entire west coast and about half of the land west of the Mississippi River, stretching all the way to the Canadian border. Mexico could not hope to control this huge swath of territory, especially when Americans began to migrate westward.

Like the Americans, Mexican settlers had difficulty with Native American tribes (see Chapters 6 through 9). Very few Mexican settlers ventured farther north than present-day California or Texas. In fact, much of northern Mexico was so lightly populated that the Mexican government actually encouraged Americans to settle in such places as Texas (the Spanish government had once done the same thing throughout its North American empire). Eventually, as youthful Mexico and the United States grew and attempted to expand their power over the continent, the two clashed.

The Republic of Texas emerges

Throughout the 1820s and 1830s, American settlers, with the blessing of the Mexican government, migrated to Texas which, at that time, was part of Mexico. The Americans helped stabilize Texas and make it prosperous. They subdued Native American tribes, cultivated farms, and built seaports. They also coexisted peacefully with Spanish-speaking Mexicans. Culturally, the Americans were different, though. They spoke English, worshipped in Protestant churches, and believed strongly that governments should not interfere with individual liberties. Also, most of them were southerners who favored slavery, so they were aghast when, in 1829, the Mexican government abolished slavery.

In the mid-1830s, the Mexican government, under Gen. Santa Anna, sought to centralize power throughout Mexico's northern states. Nearly all these states, including Texas, rebelled against this new supervision. In 1836, Texas fought for and won its independence from Mexico. The United States, Britain, and several other nations recognized the independence of the Texas republic, but Mexico would not do so. The Mexican government never accepted the loss of Texas and considered it a breakaway, rebellious province.

By the early 1840s, the people of Texas wanted the United States to annex their state. Many Americans wanted to welcome Texas into the Union, but this action presented two problems:

✔ The Mexican government would view Texas's addition to the United States as an act of war because it still believed Texas belonged to Mexico.

✔ In the United States, northerners and southerners were divided over slavery, which was legal in the South but not the North. Many northerners didn't want Texas because it would come into the Union as a slave state.

At that time, Texas was larger than the state we know today. The Texas of the 1840s consisted of land that would someday comprise parts of Oklahoma, New Mexico, Colorado, Kansas, and even Wyoming.

Polk's plan to expand

The question of Texas annexation, and expansion in general, was the main issue of the 1844 U.S. presidential election. James K. Polk, the Democratic nominee, was a pro-expansion Tennessean. Believing in Manifest Destiny, Polk wanted to expand America's control all the way to the Pacific Ocean. His expansion plans called for

✔ The annexation of Texas, which southerners wanted

✔ The acquisition from Britain of the Oregon territory in the Pacific Northwest, which northerners liked because slavery wouldn't be legal there

These ideas were popular enough to propel Polk into the White House. Upon taking office in 1845, he immediately went about fulfilling his promises to expand the United States all the way to the Pacific Coast.

Annexing Texas and flirting with war

On March 1, 1845, the U.S. government passed a bill annexing Texas. The Texans eagerly agreed to the annexation, as well as a pro-slavery state constitution. On December 29, 1845, Texas officially became part of the United States.

Mexico considered the annexation to be an act of war. The Mexicans, who had never recognized the legitimacy of Texas independence, argued that the state still belonged to them (see the earlier section, "The Republic of Texas emerges"). Thus, the Mexicans believed that the United States had stolen their land. War fever swept through Mexico. So did political chaos. In 1846 alone, the Mexican presidency changed hands four times. Only politicians who favored war with the U.S. could hope to remain in power.

Americans, by contrast, were divided on the prospect of war. Most southerners were for war because they favored Texas's entry into the Union and believed that Polk's expansion policy would someday produce more slave states. Northerners, especially in the opposition Whig party, tended to oppose the idea of war, mostly because they felt that war would favor southern slave owners.

Trying diplomacy, then baiting for war

In the winter of 1845–1846, Mexico and the United States were close to war. President Polk, committed though he was to expansion, much preferred to achieve his goals through diplomacy rather than war. He sent an emissary, John Slidell, to Mexico City in hopes of defusing the Texas flap and negotiating a purchase of the California and New Mexico territories. Polk authorized Slidell to offer as much as $30 million for this land; Slidell also could forgive $4.5 million in Mexican debts to the U.S.

So *hawkish* (war-minded) was public opinion in Mexico, that when President José Joaquín de Herrera even considered meeting with Slidell, he fell from power. A military, pro-war government replaced Herrera's. The leaders of this new government refused to meet with Slidell. They considered his mere presence in Mexico to be an insult. Thus rebuffed, Slidell left the country and advised Polk that war was the only option.

Polk sent an army of 4,000 soldiers under Gen. Zachary Taylor to south Texas. Ostensibly, they were there to keep an eye on the Mexicans, but most likely, Polk was using them as bait to goad the Mexicans into attacking them. The Americans believed the border with Mexico was the Rio Grande, a river that flows out of the Rocky Mountains to the Gulf of Mexico. The Mexicans thought the border was at the Nueces River, 100 miles to the north of the Rio Grande. When Polk ordered Taylor to move south of the Nueces, toward Corpus Christi, the Mexicans attacked him on April 25, 1846, killing 11 Americans, giving Polk an excuse for war. Actually, by the time of this skirmish, Mexico had already declared a state of "defensive war" with the U.S.

When Polk heard this news, he asked Congress for a declaration of war. The president stated that Mexico had "invaded our territory and shed American blood upon American soil." On May 13, Congress voted for war.

Interestingly enough, one of those who voted against the war was a young Whig congressman from Illinois named Abraham Lincoln. The future president opposed the war because he thought it was nothing more than an immoral land grab to spread slavery.

Favoring the eventual loser

Believe it or not, most European and Mexican military leaders believed that Mexico would win this war quite easily. The Mexican army was nearly four times the size of the U.S. Army, with many professionally trained officers. The Mexicans would be fighting on their own turf, with plenty of food, ammunition, and popular support. Europeans had very little respect for American military prowess. They thought that the Americans wouldn't be able to supply their troops in the far-flung Southwest. Nor, they thought, did they have the maturity to subdue a Mexican fighting force so much larger than their own.

These were shortsighted views. The Americans were indeed outnumbered, but they had better weapons, better training, better military leaders, better soldiers, and a stronger national economy to support them. The U.S. also had a good navy, something the Mexicans lacked.

Gen. Zachary Taylor's Campaign

In the wake of the opening skirmishes with the Mexican army along the Rio Grande, Gen. Zachary Taylor had acute supply problems. Most of his army was in and around Fort Brown, on the river, near the location of present-day Brownsville, Texas. In early May, Taylor left a force of about 600 soldiers at the fort while the rest of his army backtracked to Point Isabel, his main supply port, 28 miles to the northeast, on the Gulf of Mexico (see Figure 10-1). In doing this, Taylor hoped to replenish his army and establish a strong supply line from Point Isabel to Fort Brown. His decision set in motion a series of battles that ultimately led his army into northern Mexico.

Figure 10-1: Map of the Mexican-American War.

"Old Rough and Ready" Taylor

The Mexican-American War made Zachary Taylor a household name and national hero. Born in 1784 to a Virginia plantation family, he was the third of nine children. When he was young, the family moved to Kentucky. In 1808, he decided to join the Army. Using his family's social connections, he secured a first lieutenant's commission in the 7th Infantry Regiment.

For the next 38 years, Taylor fought in several wars and served in a variety of military posts. He was a strict but fair officer with a wry sense of humor. For instance, one day he caught a rowdy soldier using a coffeepot to smuggle whiskey into camp. Taylor ordered the soldier,

Private Charles Gray, to wear the coffeepot on his uniform for the next month. "I had been made a soberer, a wiser, and a better man," Gray later said.

Taylor was promoted to general in 1838. Earning for himself the nickname "Old Rough and Ready" for his rumpled clothing and trademark straw hat, Taylor won several battles against the Mexicans in 1846–1847. These victories propelled him into the national spotlight. With his popularity on the rise, the Whig party recruited him as its presidential candidate in 1848. He won the presidency but died in office on July 9, 1850.

Battles at Palo Alto and Resaca de la Palma

As Taylor's column made its way to Point Isabel, a 6,000-man Mexican army under Gen. Mariano Arista shadowed them. On May 8, 1846, the two forces fought a sharp engagement at Palo Alto.

The fighting raged over the course of four desperate hours. The outnumbered Americans held off several enemy charges, partially because of devastating artillery (a constant American advantage in this war). Arista eventually ordered his troops to retreat. The next day, Taylor caught up with him and attacked at Resaca de la Palma. Taylor's men found a vulnerable flank in the Mexican line, overwhelmed it, and sent the entire Mexican army into a panicked retreat. Resaca de la Palma was an overwhelming American victory. Arista's unnerved survivors retreated, in a total rout, to the Rio Grande. In the two days of fighting, the Americans lost 200 killed and wounded, the Mexicans 600.

The siege of Fort Brown

Even as Taylor fought at Palo Alto and Resaca de la Palma, the Mexicans surrounded Fort Brown. The fort's garrison was under the command of Maj. Jacob Brown, a well-liked, 58-year-old Vermonter who had started his career as an enlisted soldier and earned an officer's commission for his combat bravery in the War of 1812.

Day and night, the Mexicans pounded Brown's men with artillery fire. In the space of one 24-hour period, they fired nearly 1,300 cannonballs at the fort. The Americans dug deep bunkers and hurled artillery back at the Mexicans. In spite of the constant Mexican fire, the U.S. garrison suffered few casualties. The Mexican balls couldn't penetrate the well-constructed American fortifications. The main danger for the U.S. soldiers was a direct hit. One man took a cannonball in the chin that blew his head off. A few days later, an iron ball shattered one of Maj. Brown's legs, forcing an amputation. He later died. The siege lasted a week. For that entire time, the Americans girded themselves for a Mexican attack that never came. The victories at Palo Alto and Resaca de la Palma allowed Taylor to break the siege and save the fort. In all, 2 Americans were killed and 13 wounded during the siege.

The original name for Fort Brown was Fort Texas. However, the men who manned the fort so revered Maj. Brown that, when he died, they renamed the fort for him. Later, the town of Brownsville, Texas, would also be named after him.

Invading northern Mexico

After relieving Fort Brown and winning two major battles, Taylor had the initiative. Arista's army was in total disarray. He asked Taylor for a truce, but Taylor would have none of it. Seizing on his advantage, Taylor crossed the Rio Grande on May 19. Over the course of the summer, his army took the towns of Matamoros and Camargo. Their ultimate objective was Monterrey, a beautiful city at the foot of the Sierra Madre Mountains.

The Battle of Monterrey

The Mexicans fortified the town and many of its key approaches, but not the formidable foothills that brooded over the southern edge of Monterrey. This was a mistake. Thanks to the efforts of his engineers (a real American strength in this war), Taylor discovered he could swing his army around the Mexican defenses to the high ground.

Starting on September 20, 1846, Taylor did just that. Part of his army attacked Monterrey, tying up most of the Mexican defenders. In the meantime, the rest of the army swung around the town, skirmishing with Mexican roadblocks, before capturing the key hills. With this accomplished, the Americans could now attack Monterrey from both sides. What followed was a bitter urban battle, with Americans fighting house-to-house. Small groups would blow holes in a house, assault it, and repeat the process. It was exhausting but effective. Monterrey fell on September 23. The Americans suffered 561 casualties at Monterrey, the Mexicans 367.

With the fall of Monterrey, Gen. Taylor agreed to a two-month *armistice* (a temporary stop to the fighting that all sides agree to) with the Mexicans. This cease-fire allowed the Mexican army to retreat, intact, farther to the south. Taylor agreed to this armistice because his army was overstretched, tired, and deep in enemy country. President Polk, when he found out what Taylor had done, was enraged. He believed that only the president had the power to conclude an armistice, not a general in the field. He also thought that letting the Mexican army escape was a real blunder on Taylor's part.

The Battle of Buena Vista

Amid the political turmoil in Mexico, Gen. Santa Anna maneuvered his way into power (he had ruled Mexico ten years earlier as well). Taking control of the army and the government, he amassed a force of 15,000 soldiers to crush Taylor's army. In early 1847, Taylor entrenched his 4,600 troops at a mountain pass called Buena Vista.

With such an advantage in numbers, Santa Anna called on Taylor to surrender, but the old general refused. On February 22, 1847, Santa Anna launched an attack.

Mexican cavalry and infantry gnawed at the flanks of Taylor's position while another force, consisting mainly of infantry, came forward in a head-on assault. The American soldiers fought ferociously, and so did the Mexicans. Just when it seemed as if the Mexicans might break the U.S. lines and crush Taylor's army, his artillery began to decimate the enemy formations. Devastating, accurate artillery fire sliced through the Mexican ranks, demoralizing them and sending them into a broken retreat. Buena Vista ended in a humiliating defeat for Santa Anna. He retreated back to Mexico City, leaving Taylor in possession of northern Mexico.

The fighting Irish Catholics of St. Patrick's Battalion

At the time of the Mexican-American War, Mexico was predominantly Catholic. The United States was mostly Protestant. Some Protestant Americans didn't exactly welcome Catholic immigrants from places such as Ireland and Germany. Some of those Catholic immigrants, with limited employment opportunities, joined the Army.

When war with Mexico came, about 800 of these men, most of whom were Irish, decided they couldn't fight fellow Catholics. They defected to the Mexican side, forming themselves into the so-called St. Patrick's Battalion.

Men from this battalion fought in many of the major battles of the war. When the Americans captured them, they hanged them for treason. Several dozen met this unhappy fate. Those who survived the war generally went back to Europe or settled in Mexico.

In a classic example of differences in historical interpretation, Americans still view these men as traitors, while Mexicans see them as heroic martyrs. Even today, the St. Patrick's Battalion is commemorated in Mexico each year on — you guessed it — St. Patrick's Day.

Seizing the Southwest

The New Mexico and California territories, comprising much of the present-day American Southwest, were lightly populated, barely defended, and in general, quite difficult for Mexico to control. With the onset of hostilities, President Polk ordered the Army and Navy to conquer New Mexico and California. Even more than Texas, these were the lands Polk wanted for the United States. California, with its long Pacific coastline, favorable climate, and sparse population, was especially valuable.

Invading New Mexico

On June 5, 1846, Col. Stephen Watts Kearny and an army of 1,600 soldiers, most of whom were state volunteers, left Fort Leavenworth, Kansas, for Santa Fe, the main Mexican commercial center in the southwest. In two months, they marched 850 miles and took the town against no opposition. Soon after, Kearny was reinforced by another 1,000 volunteers. He detached 1,200 men and placed them under the command of Col. Alexander Doniphan, with orders to take El Paso.

Doniphan, a volunteer from Missouri, marched to El Paso, defeated a Mexican force, and even occupied the northern Mexican state of Chihuahua. With Doniphan's victory and the bloodless occupation of Santa Fe, the New Mexico territory had fallen to the Americans. Kearny took 300 of his regulars and set out for California, arriving in December 1846.

Bearing down on California

Several months before Kearny left for California, American settlers and a tiny U.S. military force began fighting Mexico. On June 15, 1846, 30 settlers staged a revolt at Sonoma, overwhelmed a small Mexican garrison, and raised a new flag over the town. The flag prominently portrayed a bear, earning the new California the name of the "Bear Flag Republic." Capt. John Fremont and 62 soldiers arrived in Sonoma a week later to guard the new seat of this newborn republic.

At the same time, naval forces under Commodores John Sloat and Robert Stockton reinforced the Americans. Sloat's forces took Monterey on July 7. Stockton captured Los Angeles on August 12. Col. Kearny arrived, after an exhausting desert march, in December. Mexican military opposition to all these moves was practically nonexistent. At this point, the Americans seemed to have won another bloodless victory.

However, Spanish-speaking Mexican settlers, generally known as *Californios,* were determined to remain part of Mexico. Even though they could expect no help from their government in Mexico City, they resisted the American occupation. Throughout the fall of 1846, they fought a series of small battles against the Americans. Dozens died on both sides. In the end, the American military presence was too much for the Californios, who did not have the weapons, resources, or numbers to defeat the U.S.

On January 12, 1847, the last of the Californios surrendered. The next day they signed a peace treaty in Los Angeles with the Americans, yielding control of California to the United States. Most of the Californios then peacefully returned to their California homes.

The agreement that ended the fighting in California was called the Treaty of Cahuenga. Capt. Fremont and Gen. Andres Pico, the Mexican governor of California, signed the treaty on a kitchen table in a comfortable adobe house belonging to Tomas Feliz, in what would someday be North Hollywood.

Gen. Winfield Scott's Incredible Campaign

By early 1847, the United States was clearly winning the war. After all, the Americans had conquered New Mexico and California. They had pushed the Mexicans out of Texas, seized control of Monterrey and northern Mexico, and the Navy was enforcing a partial blockade of the Mexican east coast. President Polk wanted to end the war now. In his view, the Mexicans should bow to reason, agree to end the war, and accept American money for the territory American soldiers had taken in battle. But Santa Anna would have none of this. He still hoped to turn the tables on the Americans and win the war.

Frustrated and angry by Santa Anna's refusal to call it quits, Polk ordered an amphibious force under Gen. Winfield Scott to invade central Mexico and capture the enemy capital. The president hoped that perhaps this invasion would change Santa Anna's attitude and end the war.

Polk chose Scott to lead this expedition for two reasons. First, the president had lost confidence in Gen. Taylor because of the armistice he had negotiated with the Mexicans after the Battle of Monterrey. Second, he knew that Taylor was a Whig and that his battlefield victories had made him a national hero. Sensing this, Polk wanted to eliminate him as a potential political rival. So the president stripped Taylor's army of its best troops and gave them to Scott for his invasion. Ironically enough, this move infuriated Taylor so much that it helped persuade him to get into politics!

Winfield Scott — the embodiment of the Army

By 1847, Winfield Scott was 60 years old and had been in the Army for 40 years. Although he had never attended West Point, he was the consummate military professional. He had fought in the War of 1812, earning a reputation as an excellent combat leader at such battles as Lundy's Lane and Chippewa (see Chapter 9).

In the years that followed, while serving in a variety of posts, Scott emerged as the Army's leading intellectual, not to mention one of its finest officers. He wrote the service's manuals

on infantry tactics, training, and preparation for combat. He brought professionalism and constancy to an army that badly needed it.

Scott had two nicknames. Those who liked him called him the "Grand Old Man of the Army." Those who didn't like him referred to him as "Old Fuss and Feathers" for his stern, overbearing nature. Like him or not, no one was better qualified than Gen. Scott to command the invasion of Mexico.

Invading at Veracruz

Gen. Scott chose to invade at Veracruz, a port city on Mexico's east coast, some 250 miles east of Mexico City. Gen. Scott's invasion force was 12,000 men strong and consisted of volunteers and regulars. Scott worked well with Commodore Matthew Perry, the naval officer whose ships transported the soldiers. The two men coordinated an invasion plan, skirting past Veracruz's considerable coastal guns and landing on March 9, 1847, against little opposition at beaches south of town. Scott had specially requested special surfboats to transport his soldiers from the main ships to the beach. The boats worked well. Each of them could carry between 50 and 80 soldiers. With his army safely ashore, Gen. Scott successfully besieged Veracruz, forcing its surrender on March 28.

Scott's casualties during the siege were light — 80 men killed and wounded. But he was worried. Yellow fever was eating away at his army. Hundreds were sick and the problem would only get worse with warmer spring weather. Using Veracruz as his main supply port, he marched 8,500 soldiers west, to higher, healthier ground, along a new national highway the Mexicans had built. The ultimate objective was, of course, still Mexico City, which Americans called "The Halls of Montezuma" after the famous Aztec ruler. Scott and his army headed straight for this hallowed city.

If you were a soldier in the Mexican-American War, disease was a greater threat to your life than bullets. Of the 13,000 American soldiers who lost their lives in the war, only 1,700 were killed in combat. The rest died of disease or accidents. The ratios were largely the same for the Mexicans.

Battling at Cerro Gordo

Santa Anna reacted to Scott's invasion by raising a new army through *conscription* (a draft) and appeals to patriotism. The Mexican leader intended to stop Scott about 150 miles east of Mexico City in the mountains. He entrenched a considerable force of 12,000 soldiers in the foothills and mountains around a tiny village called Cerro Gordo. Santa Anna knew that to move west on the road to Mexico City, Scott's army had to get through his entrenched army. In Santa Anna's view, this would force the Americans to assault his dug-in troops, leading to a slaughter.

Scott did not oblige him. Thanks to the efforts of a brilliant engineer captain and future Civil War general named Robert E. Lee (see Chapter 11), Scott devised an ingenious plan to flank Santa Anna's defenses. Lee and his colleague, Lt. Pierre Beauregard — another future Civil War general — had found an unguarded trail that offered a way around the main Mexican defenses. Gen. Scott decided to move the bulk of his army along that trail and attack the flank of the Mexican line. In the meantime, a smaller American force would advance toward Santa Anna's main defenses, right where he expected them to attack. This would divert Mexican attention from the main American attack on their flank.

On April 18, 1847, Scott sent his men forward. The plan worked better than the general could have ever imagined. In a matter of hours, the Americans unhinged the entire Mexican line, killing, wounding, or capturing nearly

---

Future generals in the Mexican-American War

Nearly all the generals who earned fame in the Civil War — whether northern or southern — served in the Mexican-American War.

✔ **Robert E. Lee** and **Pierre Beauregard** served as engineer officers on Winfield Scott's staff.

✔ **Ulysses S. Grant** fought in nearly every battle, including the urban combat at Monterrey.

✔ **George B. McClellan** was in the climactic battles in and around Mexico City.

✔ **Thomas "Stonewall" Jackson** was an artillery officer whose guns pounded Mexican lines during the siege at Veracruz and the assault on Mexico City.

✔ **Braxton Bragg** was also an artilleryman, most notably at Fort Brown.

✔ **Ambrose Burnside** served under Bragg for part of the war.

✔ **George Pickett** led assault troops at Mexico City.

✔ **Joe Hooker** and **George Meade** were on the staffs of both Zachary Taylor and Scott.

All these men were West Point–trained military professionals. During the war with Mexico, they were united as Americans, but a decade and a half later, they were mortal enemies when the Civil War broke out. As generals, all of them drew heavily on their Mexican-American War experiences.

one-third of the enemy defenders. Santa Anna and the remnants of his army retreated in disarray all the way to Mexico City. The Americans lost 417 men at Cerro Gordo; the Mexicans lost 4,000.

In the wake of his victory at Cerro Gordo, Scott pushed west to Puebla. Sickness, lack of supplies, and the enlistment expiration of many of his state volunteers forced him to halt at Puebla. The Americans spent much of the summer regaining their strength for the final push to Mexico City. Knowing he was deep in foreign territory and heavily outnumbered, Gen. Scott wisely cultivated good relations with the Mexican people. He made sure his soldiers paid for food, clothing, and other items. He developed friendly relationships with many local leaders. By late summer, many Mexicans were either on his side, neutral, or simply against Santa Anna.

On to Mexico City

In the late summer of 1847, Scott's army marched west with the goal of taking Mexico City. Santa Anna still refused to make peace, so Scott unleashed a new series of flanking maneuvers, swinging his army south of Mexico City. The Americans fought and won battles at Contreras, Churubusco, Molino del Rey, and Chapultepec. Scott's soldiers entered Mexico City itself on September 14, 1847. Santa Anna fell from power and fled.

The End of the War

In his campaign to take Mexico City, Scott lost 3,000 men killed in battle, wounded, and felled by disease. The remnants of his army occupied the city as best they could. Once again, Scott made a point of cultivating good relations with the locals. Mexico was in political chaos. The Americans wanted to end the war, but it was hard to find proper authorities who were willing to negotiate. Throughout the fall of 1847, Scott's victorious army continued to occupy the Mexican capital. Finally, in early 1848, Mexico and the U.S. negotiated a peace treaty.

The Treaty of Guadalupe Hidalgo

The Mexican-American War officially ended on February 2, 1848, with the signing of the Treaty of Guadalupe Hidalgo. The treaty gave the U.S. control of Texas, fixed the Mexican-American boundary at the Rio Grande, and ceded the territories of California and New Mexico to the Americans. In return, the Mexicans received $15 million, less than half of what Polk had originally offered before the war.

The war's legacies

The Mexican-American War was deeply consequential, with lasting legacies:

✔ Stretching all the way to the Pacific Ocean, the U.S. became a truly continental power, winning half a million square miles of land. The states of California, Texas, New Mexico, and Arizona all came at the expense of Mexico, as did parts of Colorado, Nevada, and Utah.

✔ The acquisition of so much territory led to a furious debate in the United States over the potential expansion of slavery, and this was a major cause of the Civil War.

✔ The war solidified the notion of Manifest Destiny in America.

Chapter 11

The Civil War

*T*he Civil War was the main event of 19th-century American history. Lasting four awful years, from 1861 through 1865, the war touched nearly every American who lived at that time. The war claimed the lives of nearly 620,000 Americans, the most of any conflict in the country's history. It led to massive destruction of property, homes, and wealth. The war ended slavery and a distinct way of life in the South. Indeed, the South was so devastated by the Civil War that the region's economy didn't truly recover until World War II. Whether northern or southern, very few Americans were the same — economically, politically, culturally, or emotionally — after the war as before it.

The war was the final, violent resolution to decades of tension between North and South. The deep-rooted causes of the Civil War dated back to colonial times. From the late 18th century onward, the two regions developed differently. A rural, slave-based plantation economy, based upon individual autonomy and racial hierarchy, flourished in the South. The North's development was dominated by small farming, urbanization, industrialization, and entrepreneurial capitalism. These two distinct Americas couldn't reconcile their differences peacefully.

In this chapter, I explain the main causes of the war. I describe the war's most important battles, explain why the North won the war, and convey what the wartime experience was like for northerners and southerners, on and off the battlefield. Americans, of course, still argue today about the meaning of the Civil War. Historians do too. So at the tail end of the chapter, I point out the different interpretations of the war that Civil War scholars still debate. If you want to read even more about the Civil War after you finish this chapter, check out *The Civil War For Dummies* by Keith D. Dickson (Wiley).

Deepening Roots of Conflict

In the summer of 1776, the Continental Congress passed a declaration of independence from Great Britain (see Chapter 7). But the declaration almost didn't happen because of a rift between southerners and northerners. Northerners wanted the declaration to denounce slavery and the Atlantic Ocean trade system that brought slaves to America. Southerners, many of whom owned slaves, refused to agree to this denunciation. If the provision remained, the southern delegates wouldn't sign the declaration. The provision was stricken, and the Declaration of Independence passed, but the incident was a sign that slavery would cause friction again.

After the Revolution, the northern states abolished slavery. The southern states didn't. Two distinct economic systems and ways of life developed in these regions. Northern life was based on free labor; southern life was based on slavery. Northerners tended to believe in strong central government; southerners favored states' rights. As the country expanded west, the two regions often bickered over whose vision would prevail in new states entering the Union, but in the end, they always compromised. However, after the Mexican-American War, the arguments took on an especially harsh, bitter, and even violent tone that eventually led to war.

Arguing over the fruits of the Mexican-American War

Between 1846 and 1848, the United States fought and won a war with Mexico (see Chapter 10). In the peace settlement, Mexico ceded more than half a million square miles of land, comprising much of the Southwest, including Texas, New Mexico, Arizona, California, and Nevada, plus parts of Colorado and Utah. Everyone in the U.S. recognized that someday these newly won territories, known as the *Mexican cession,* would become states. The question was whether those new states would be slave or free. Southerners worried that new free states would upset the delicate balance of power in Congress between North and South in favor of the North. Northerners were concerned that if slavery expanded all the way to the West, black slave labor would undercut free white labor.

With this in mind, David Wilmot, a Pennsylvania congressman, proposed in 1848 that slavery be prohibited in the new territories. This proposal, named the Wilmot Proviso, sparked a furious debate between northerners and southerners. The proviso didn't pass, but the debate grew into an actual secession crisis by 1850.

In 1850, with southerners threatening to *secede* (formally withdraw) from the Union, and civil war a distinct possibility, cooler heads from both the North and South forged a compromise. Senators Henry Clay of Kentucky and Stephen Douglas of Illinois were the main architects of the compromise.

Here's what the compromise did for northerners:

- Admitted California as a free state
- Awarded disputed territory to free-soil New Mexico at slaveholding Texas's expense
- Prohibited the selling of slaves in Washington, D.C.

Here's what the compromise did for southerners:

- Did not place a federal restriction on slavery in the Mexican cession
- Transferred Texas's public debt to the federal government
- Kept slavery legal in Washington, D.C.
- Created a strong fugitive slave law that allowed southerners to apprehend escaped slaves even if they made it to the North

Testing popular sovereignty

When President Millard Fillmore signed the Compromise of 1850 into law, he believed it represented a final peace between North and South. Millions of other Americans shared his optimistic view, but they were wrong.

As the 1850s unfolded, the tension between northerners and southerners grew much worse. The main question was this: Should slavery spread to new territories like Kansas and Nebraska? Southern slaveholders argued that, with no federal restrictions on slavery, they could take their "property" with them wherever they went. Opponents of slavery believed that such unrestricted spread of slavery would undercut the competition of a free-labor market.

To solve this vexing problem, the nation, for a few years, rallied around the idea of *popular sovereignty.* Instead of deciding these issues in Washington, D.C., with federal mandates, the people of each territory would decide the slavery issue themselves, in their own way.

At first glance, this seemed reasonable and democratic. But, in practice, popular sovereignty was a disaster. Extremists from both sides, determined to prevail by force if necessary, gravitated to the new territories. The result was violence. Kansas, for instance, was little more than a bloody, armed caldron of tension by the late 1850s.

Visiting Uncle Tom's Cabin

Added to this was major cultural tension between North and South. In 1852, Harriet Beecher Stowe, the daughter of a northern minister, published an antislavery *(abolitionist)* novel called *Uncle Tom's Cabin.* In the first year alone, the book sold 300,000 copies, almost all in the North. Eventually, the novel became the number-one selling book of the 19th century. The average southerner thought of Stowe's book as a clumsy, unfair attack on southern culture. The average northerner — even the racist white majority who didn't want to abolish slavery — viewed *Uncle Tom's Cabin* as a long overdue indictment of a backward institution. Most historians believe that the book fueled the abolitionist movement of the 1850s, raising tensions to a fever pitch.

During the Civil War, when Harriet Beecher Stowe met President Abraham Lincoln, he allegedly gazed at her and exclaimed: "So you're the little woman who wrote the book that made this great war!"

Raiding Harper's Ferry

In October 1859, an antislavery zealot named John Brown led a raid against the federal armory at Harper's Ferry, Virginia. Brown and his followers — including several of his sons — planned to seize weapons and arm slaves for a general uprising in the South. Brown's little band of abolitionists were no strangers to violence. Several years before, they had killed several proslavery men in Kansas. Their Harper's Ferry raid was poorly planned. Federal soldiers quickly recaptured the armory and took Brown into custody. In two quick months, he was tried and executed.

Even though few northerners agreed with Brown's tactics, many thought of him as a martyr. Southerners despised him as the lowest kind of criminal. Slave owners had for decades worried about potential slave uprisings, and Brown's raid only compounded those fears. Learning of Brown's ties to many prominent northerners, some southerners came to believe that the North was full of many more John Browns, itching for the chance to free the slaves.

The federal troops who took back Harper's Ferry armory and captured John Brown were under the command of Lt. Col. Robert E. Lee, a professional soldier from Virginia who would one day become the most famous southern general.

Electing Abraham Lincoln

By 1860, the mistrust and anger between northerners and southerners were so bad that only one more divisive event would drive the southern states to secede from the union. The presidential election of that year proved to be just such an event. The Democratic Party split along regional lines. John

Breckinridge ran as a proslavery southern candidate. Democrat Stephen Douglas tried to win support in both the North and South, but neither side really trusted him. Abraham Lincoln, from the new Republican Party, advocated the idea of prohibiting slavery's spread to the Mexican cession. Lincoln was so unpopular in the South that he wasn't even on the ballot there. However, he won by sweeping most of the northern states, giving him only 39 percent of the national popular vote but plenty of electoral votes to become president.

In 1860, Lincoln did not yet propose to abolish slavery in the South. He simply wanted to prevent it from spreading west. Thinking of Lincoln as a mere front-man for more John Browns, most southerners viewed his election as an insult and a threat to their way of life. In spite of what Lincoln said, they believed that he would one day abolish slavery everywhere. They also thought that his election represented a new surge toward a northern-dominated central government that would soon threaten southern liberty and the autonomy of states.

Appalled at Lincoln's election, and exasperated with the North in general, several southern states seceded from the Union during the winter of 1860–1861. South Carolina, Florida, Georgia, Alabama, Mississippi, Louisiana, and Texas were all gone by February 1861. These states comprised the deep South, where slavery was strongest. They banded together to form their own country, called the *Confederate States of America* (C.S.A.) or *Confederacy*.

The Most Important Battles, 1861–1862

To Lincoln and the majority of northerners, southern secession was the equivalent of rebellion and even treason. To pro-secession southerners, secession was a right. They were simply leaving a voluntary union to pursue their own freedom from a *despot* (a person who rules with absolute power), much like the patriots during the Revolutionary War period (see Chapter 7).

The seceded southern states quickly established a government with Mississippian Jefferson Davis as president. Initially, the capital was in Montgomery, Alabama, but later they moved it to Richmond, Virginia. The Confederacy armed itself with weapons confiscated from federal armories and purchased from overseas. Attuned to the possibility of war with the North, young southern men flocked to join the new Confederate Army.

Eventually the divergent views between North and South led to war when fighting broke out between Federal soldiers and Confederates at Fort Sumter, South Carolina. The fort was located in Charleston harbor and occupied by Federal troops. Believing that Sumter was part of their new nation, the Confederates besieged it. In April 1861, when Lincoln tried to resupply his men with food, southern leaders decided to open fire on Sumter. Thus began the Civil War. The North was determined to force the seceded states back into the Union, thus quelling the rebellion. The South was equally committed to winning its independence.

After Fort Sumter, the four states of the upper South — generally more moderate than the deep South — finally seceded. Arkansas, Tennessee, North Carolina, and, most notably, Virginia all joined the Confederacy. Lincoln was deeply concerned that every slave state would secede. Much to his relief, though, Maryland, Delaware, Kentucky, and Missouri all stayed in the Union, even though slavery was legal within their borders.

In the spring and summer of 1861, both sides began feverishly mobilizing for war. The North held most of the advantages:

- 22 million people versus 9 million in the South, one-third of whom were slaves

- 97 percent of firearm production; 3 percent for the South

- 71 percent of all railroad mileage; 29 percent for the South

- 91 percent of all factory production; 9 percent for the South

- 75 percent of all farm acreage; 25 percent for the South

The South did have some advantages, though. The Confederacy could win if European nations recognized the legitimacy of the new southern nation. The Europeans would then come to the South's aid or put intense international pressure on Lincoln's government to agree to southern independence. Failing that, the South could simply break the will of northerners to fight and win the war.

Initially, though, both sides hoped for a quick victory. The first major battle occurred outside of Manassas, Virginia, about 25 miles west of Washington, D.C.

The Battle of Bull Run

In July 1861, a Union army of 35,000 soldiers advanced on Manassas with the intention of destroying the main rebel army of 25,000 troops, and then taking Richmond, Virginia, the Confederate capital (see Figure 11-1). The two sides clashed on July 21, 1861, north of Manassas. Both armies were raw and ill-trained. After several hours of bloody struggle, southern soldiers broke through the Union line, prompting a panicked retreat all the way back to Washington, D.C. The battle was a major Confederate victory. Both sides lost about 2,000 men.

During the Civil War, the North and South couldn't even agree on the names of battles! The North named battles after the most prominent geographic feature on the battlefield; the South named them after the nearest town. So, for instance, the North called this first battle "Bull Run." The South called it the "Battle of Manassas." The legacy of these different naming customs continues today, as northerners and southerners still call battles by different names.

Figure 11-1:
Map of
the early
battles of the
Civil War,
1861–1862.

Civil War reenactors

The Civil War is probably the most commemorated, and hallowed, event in American history. Interest in the war has always been intense, from the late 19th century to the present day. One way for Americans to get in touch with their wartime past is to reenact. By some estimates, there are more than 100,000 Civil War reenactors in America. The reenacting craze began in the early 1960s during a wave of 100-year Civil War anniversaries. Since then, it has grown exponentially.

While some reenactors portray civilians, the vast majority of reenactors embrace the soldier's role. They dress up in reproduced Union or Confederate uniforms, arm themselves with the proper reproduced weapons, equip themselves appropriately, and re-fight the battles of that troubled time. Most reenactors depict specific historical units with the intention of reliving, as much as possible, the experiences of their forebears.

Quite commonly, reenactors re-create actual Civil War battles for a public audience, usually on the field where the battle was actually fought. For instance, in 1988, to commemorate the 125th anniversary of the Battle of Gettysburg, 25,000 reenactors brought the battle to life for 150,000 fascinated spectators. Reenactors were vital participants in such grand feature films as *Gettysburg* (1993) and *Gods and Generals* (2003).

Invading the York peninsula

Bull Run was a wakeup call for the North that this war wouldn't be a walkover. Lincoln now recruited tens of thousands of soldiers into federal service and planned for a total war. He also sacked Gen. Irvin McDowell, the commander at Bull Run, in favor of Gen. George B. McClellan (see Figure 11-2), a 34-year-old dynamo who rejuvenated the Union Army in the East (now known as the Army of the Potomac).

Figure 11-2: Gen. George B. McClellan wasn't a very aggressive military leader in battle.

© CORBIS

McClellan excelled at training and building an army, but he suffered from a perpetual lack of aggressiveness. He was the political opposite of Lincoln. Like many of his fellow Democrats, McClellan thought the war should be a limited one, fought simply to sway the South back into the Union, with no change in the status of slavery.

Gen. McClellan spent the entire fall of 1861 training his army, refusing to launch the offensive Lincoln wanted. In spite of the fact that the North held a huge manpower advantage over the South, McClellan believed that the Confederate Army outnumbered his by a margin of two-to-one. He used this as an excuse to drag his feet. Finally, in March 1862, after many months of tension with the president, McClellan made his move.

Instead of attacking the southern army directly in northern Virginia, his army — 100,000 strong now — embarked on boats for an amphibious invasion of the York peninsula, just east of Richmond. He expected to outflank the Confederates, march on their capital, and win the war.

The plan was a good one, causing a real crisis for the rebels, but McClellan let them off the hook by moving very slowly across the York peninsula. As usual, his caution grew from his strong belief that he was outnumbered. By late

June, when his army finally advanced to within 7 miles of Richmond, the Confederates had enough troops in place to stop him. The campaign then climaxed in a series of bloody engagements, often referred to as the Seven Days Battles, fought between June 25 and July 1.

The Union won all but one of the battles fought over those seven days. However, McClellan was deeply troubled by the thousands of casualties his army was suffering, and, convinced as always that he was outnumbered, he didn't order an advance on Richmond. Instead, he retreated in the belief that he was saving his army from total destruction. In late July, a bitterly disappointed Lincoln finally ordered McClellan to bring his army back to Washington. Thus, the Peninsula Campaign ended up as a major defeat for the North, even though the South suffered more casualties.

Another battle at Bull Run

During the Peninsula Campaign, Gen. Robert E. Lee was given command of all Confederate armies in the East. Gentlemanly and polite, he was nonetheless an aggressive, brilliant tactician. With the Union armies in disarray after the Peninsula Campaign and Richmond secure, Lee wanted to hit them with a knockout punch. He marched to northern Virginia with 50,000 soldiers. On August 29–30, outside of Manassas, Virginia, his army clashed with a Union force of equivalent size under the command of Gen. John Pope, an arrogant braggart who was no match for Lee.

Over the course of those two violent days, the Confederates defeated Pope's army in what northerners called the Second Battle of Bull Run (southerners call it Second Manassas). The fighting raged on the same battlefield where the war's first major battle had taken place the year before. Soldiers fought in withering heat made worse by clouds of gunpowder smoke. The volume of firepower was intense, which was bad enough, but this battle featured a special ghoulishness. Many of those who were killed the year before had been buried in shallow graves on the battlefield. Explosions unearthed their remains, spraying decomposed body parts over the living and dead alike.

The North suffered about 15,000 casualties, the South about 9,000 at Second Bull Run. After this defeat, the Union Army was in headlong retreat toward Washington, D.C., but Lee's army was not quite strong enough to take the Federal capital.

Surprise at Shiloh

In the meantime, the war was going better for the Yankees in the West. The key to victory in this region was control of the Mississippi, Tennessee, Ohio, and Cumberland rivers. By the spring of 1862, northern armies controlled major stretches of those rivers. The Federals had captured Nashville and much of Tennessee. They also controlled Kentucky, Missouri, and parts of Arkansas. Their plan was to keep moving south along the Mississippi River with the purpose of cutting the Confederacy in two.

Realizing that the Union was steadily strangling the western states of the Confederacy, Gen. Albert Sidney Johnston, the Confederate commander in the West, decided to counterattack. He scraped together an army of 55,000 soldiers and, on April 6, 1862, launched a surprise attack against 35,000 Union soldiers who were camped along the Cumberland River in southwestern Tennessee, at a place called Pittsburg Landing or Shiloh. Johnston aimed to push this force into the river, annihilating it.

Initially, the Confederate advantage of surprise overwhelmed the northern soldiers. Southern troops swept through Yankee camps, capturing prisoners and war booty alike, prompting panicked survivors to run for their lives. Gradually, though, as the day wore on, Union troops rallied, fought hard, and staved off annihilation. In the midst of the fight, Johnston took a bullet in the thigh, severing his femoral artery. He bled to death in a few short minutes. After Johnston's death, the Confederate advance lost cohesion. Johnston's successor, Gen. Pierre Beauregard, decided to call off the attack, regroup, and finish the Yankees off in the morning. By nightfall, the battle had settled into an uneasy stalemate.

The Union commander at Shiloh was Gen. Ulysses S. Grant, the most successful northern commander of the war. Instead of retreating after a rough day, he decided to attack at sunrise on April 7. Employing newly arrived reinforcements, he did just that, pushing the Confederates back to their original starting points. Rather than lose his army, Beauregard decided to retreat. Thus, Shiloh ended up as a bloody Union victory. In fact, with nearly 24,000 casualties between the two sides, Shiloh was the costliest battle ever fought in North America up to that point.

With the victory at Shiloh, the Union now controlled western Tennessee and northern Mississippi. Plus they soon took New Orleans and Baton Rouge, Louisiana. The Union was definitely winning in the West. However, Vicksburg, Mississippi, still eluded them, leaving the Confederacy in control of a major stretch of the Mississippi River. Plus, in the East, the war was going well for the South.

Ironically, the word *Shiloh* means "place of peace" in Hebrew.

Bloodshed at Antietam

After defeating the Union Army at Second Bull Run, Gen. Lee unleashed a bold plan designed to win the war in 1862. He decided to march his veteran army of 45,000 soldiers north and invade Maryland. The invasion had several strategic purposes:

- ✔ Draw Maryland, a slave state, into the Confederacy.

- ✔ Threaten the security of Washington, D.C.

- ✔ Strengthen peace candidates in the upcoming northern elections. If elected, they would pressure Lincoln's government to end the war on the South's terms.

- ✔ Convince Europeans to recognize the Confederacy as a legitimate nation.

In early September 1862, Lee's army crossed into Maryland. Because his forces were so poorly supplied, they had to live off the land, alienating the very Maryland farmers on whom they counted for support. This ended any hope that Maryland would join the Confederacy. Nonetheless, Lee could still achieve his strategic aims if he could defeat the Union Army in battle. Even now, a powerful force of 87,000 Yankees under the command of George McClellan was moving north, searching for Lee's army. On September 17, 1862, the two sides clashed near Sharpsburg, Maryland, at Antietam Creek.

Several days earlier, McClellan had been the benefactor of some freak luck. Union soldiers found a misplaced envelope containing Lee's entire campaign plan. Even with this knowledge, McClellan moved so slowly that, by the time he launched his main attack on September 17, Lee had ensconced his men into a fairly good defensive position, averting total disaster.

Throughout the day on September 17, the battle raged over the gentle, rolling country around Sharpsburg and Antietam Creek. The sheer violence of the fighting was unprecedented, worse even than at Shiloh. Soldiers had eyes shot out, limbs shattered, and feet crushed. In the middle of the battlefield, at a sunken farm road known forever after as the "Bloody Lane," Confederate soldiers fought desperately to thwart a Union attack. Along an 800-yard stretch of this little dirt road, men fought to the death. "We were shooting them like sheep in a pen," one Union soldier later wrote. More than 5,000 men became casualties. Dead bodies were stacked two and three deep. Blood — Yankee and Rebel — stained the earth.

The fighting went on like this all day, with neither side winning a decisive victory. As the sun set, both armies were crippled, content to lick their wounds in an uneasy stalemate. Eventually, Lee disengaged and retreated back to Virginia, having lost more than one-quarter of his army.

Antietam is the single bloodiest *day* in American history, even surpassing September 11, 2001. At Antietam, more than 6,000 Americans lost their lives in a 24-hour period (see Figure 11-3). The Union suffered 12,401 casualties in the battle; the Confederates, 10,316.

Figure 11-3: Confederate soldiers, killed during the Battle of Antietam, lie along a dirt road.

Even though the actual fighting at Antietam ended in a standoff, the battle was an important Union victory. This is because Lee's strategic purpose failed. He did not persuade Maryland to secede; he did not strengthen peace candidates; he did not threaten Washington; finally, foreign powers like Britain and France thought of Antietam as a Union victory and withheld diplomatic recognition of the Confederacy. Even so, McClellan allowed Lee's army to escape to fight again another day. This was the last straw for Lincoln. He relieved the passive McClellan.

Antietam was important for another reason. For several months, Lincoln had planned to announce the Emancipation Proclamation, freeing all the slaves in the Confederate states (but not border states like Maryland). To give the proclamation some political weight, Lincoln knew he must announce it after a military victory, or else many observers, foreign and domestic, would see it as a desperation move. Antietam was that victory. The proclamation was important for several reasons:

- ✔ The North was not just fighting a war to maintain the Union; it was now fighting a war for the abolition of slavery.

- ✔ The average citizen in Britain and France hated slavery. So they sympathized with the North. Thus, public opinion in both countries was firmly against recognition of the Confederacy.

- The North was now fighting a total war to subdue the South. This meant freeing the slaves, but it also meant training and arming them as soldiers.

- The South was appalled by the proclamation and was determined to fight even harder for independence.

- Many pro-Union northerners, especially in western states like Illinois, Indiana, and Ohio, withdrew their support for the war. They wanted to end secession, not free the slaves.

A Violent Year, 1863

In spite of the victory at Antietam, 1862 ended badly for the North with a bitter defeat at Fredericksburg, Virginia. So, as 1863 began, the North held the advantage in the western theater, while the South was winning in the eastern theater. The two sides now redoubled their efforts to win what had become a total war. This led to a series of ghastly, costly battles fought over the course of the year. This included three of the most important engagements of the Civil War.

Fighting the war at sea

Throughout the Civil War, the North dominated the war at sea. From the beginning of the war, the U.S. Navy blockaded southern ports, slowly strangling the southern economy. The Confederate Navy, consisting only of a few raiding ships that harassed Yankee shipping, could not hope to break the blockade or fight any sizable battle with the Union Navy. Both sides built steam-powered ironclad boats, a harbinger of the future. The Union mass-produced armored gunboats that helped the North control the rivers, shuttle troops on them, and destroy Confederate river traffic. It's fair to say that naval superiority is a major reason why the North won the war.

Lee's great win at Chancellorsville

In the spring of 1863, President Lincoln entrusted the Army of the Potomac to Gen. Joe Hooker, a brash, hard-drinking man who had lobbied hard for the job. Unlike McClellan, Hooker understood that his army was twice as big as Lee's. Hooker had 133,000 men, Lee half that many. With the advantage of numbers, Hooker was determined to move against Lee's forces (now known as the Army of Northern Virginia), destroy them, and then capture Richmond. "May God have mercy on General Lee, for I shall not," Hooker boasted. In late April 1863, Hooker's troops moved south toward Fredericksburg, where Lee's men were still entrenched after their victory there the previous year.

Hooker planned to hit Lee from two sides: In the east, at Fredericksburg, he would feign an attack. Meanwhile, the bulk of his army would bear down on the Confederates from the west, rout them from their fortifications at Fredericksburg, and destroy them. On May 1, 1863, after several days of maneuvering, Hooker was in a position to do exactly that. But he lost his nerve, decided to retreat, and dug his army into defensive positions around an inn called Chancellorsville (see Figure 11-4). This yielded the initiative to Lee, who promptly attacked and defeated the massive Union force in a bloody five-day battle. Hooker and the Federal army fled north. Chancellorsville was Lee's greatest victory.

Crushing Lee at Gettysburg

After his smashing victory at Chancellorsville, Gen. Lee devised a bold plan. He would invade Pennsylvania, a bona fide free state of the North. He hoped to sever Washington, D.C., from all the northeastern states and force Lincoln to end the war on the South's terms. On July 1, 1863, as elements of Lee's army approached an eastern Pennsylvania crossroads town named Gettysburg, they clashed with a smaller Union force. By day's end, both sides had fed in reinforcements.

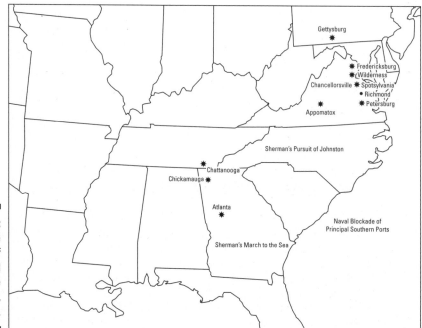

Figure 11-4:
Map of the battles of the second half of the Civil War, 1863–1865.

Civil War battlefields

Over the course of the Civil War, Billy Yank and Johnny Reb fought each other in 10,000 different battles, most of which ended up as forgotten skirmishes. The National Park Service has preserved the war's most significant battlegrounds, and they're great places to visit for anyone interested in the war. Most of these battlefields are well marked with monuments and historical guideposts. You can even hire a park ranger or Civil War expert to give you a guided tour. Historical and visitor information is readily available on the park service Web site (www.nps.gov) or by a simple Google search for whatever battlefield interests you.

Visiting a Civil War battleground is a fun way to learn about U.S. military history. You can walk the ground for yourself, envision the terrible carnage of combat, and begin to understand the war itself. The best battlefields are those that haven't been touched by modern development (builders are constantly squabbling with preservationists over this issue).

So what are my favorite battlefields? In no particular order, they are (drum roll please!): Antietam, Shiloh, Bull Run, Gettysburg, and Spotsylvania.

Believing that he had a chance to crush the Army of the Potomac, Lee decided to mass his forces for a decisive attack. In all, he had 71,000 veteran soldiers. But soon the Union had 94,000 men around Gettysburg, and many of them were deployed along a prominent ridge that dominated the area. For two days, Lee tried, and failed, to overwhelm the Yankees. By the end of the day on July 3, his army had suffered 23,231 casualties. The Army of the Potomac lost a similar number of men but still held the key ground. Lee knew he must retreat. He and his survivors were fortunate to escape back to Virginia.

Gettysburg was the biggest Union victory to this point in the war. After the battle, Lee's army was so crippled that, from here on out, he could only fight a defensive war in hopes of wearing down northern resolve to win.

A surrender at Vicksburg

Gen. Grant, the Union commander in the West, spent much of 1863 trying to take Vicksburg, Mississippi. Taking Vicksburg would give the North control of the whole Mississippi River; plus the Confederacy would be cut in two, with Arkansas, Louisiana, and Texas stranded from the rest of the South. After a sprawling campaign that featured river crossings, cavalry movements, and a series of battles, Grant besieged Vicksburg from May to July 1863. Hungry, desperate, isolated, and filled with despair, the town's 30,000 Confederate defenders were doomed. Their commander, Gen. John Pemberton, surrendered them and the town on July 4, 1863. The Union had now triumphed in the western theater. Vicksburg was every bit as important as Gettysburg in deciding the outcome of the war.

The people of Vicksburg were so scarred by the July 4 surrender of their town that they did not celebrate the Independence Day holiday until World War II, a full 80 years later.

Finishing the War, 1864–1865

By 1864, the South was clearly losing the war, but victory was still possible. War weariness was so great in the North that, if the Confederacy could keep fighting and inflicting major casualties on the Yankees, Lincoln would lose the fall presidential election in favor of a peace government that would agree to southern independence. For the South, this was the last hope. For the North, the key to victory was a swift conclusion to hostilities through the use of overwhelming force.

Bleeding in the East

In the wake of Vicksburg, President Lincoln appointed the victorious Gen. Grant to command of the Union armies. Grant's plan was simple: Attack Lee's Army of Northern Virginia, destroy it, and then take Richmond.

In early May 1864, Grant's army, numbering some 118,000 soldiers, crossed the Rapidan River, west of Fredericksburg. In so doing, the men threatened Lee's supply lines, forcing him to react. Thus began a running series of costly battles fought north and east of Richmond over the course of two months. The most prominent battles were the Wilderness (May 5–7), Spotsylvania (May 8–21), and Cold Harbor (May 31–June 12). Each one of these engagements cost Grant thousands of casualties and ended in stalemate, which, of course, favored the Confederates.

The battle at Cold Harbor, a few miles east of Richmond, was especially horrible. Grant ordered a frontal assault against what he hoped were thinly defended enemy positions. Instead, the rebels had firmly fortified the whole area. As a result, the Union lost 7,000 soldiers killed, wounded, and captured in just one day of fighting. They were pinned down, raked by a deadly crossfire of bullets, shattering their skulls, tearing off arms and legs. Before going forward, many of these veteran soldiers had sensed the danger ahead. Some wrote their names and addresses on slips of paper and pinned them to the inside of their uniforms so their bodies could be identified by burial details.

For Grant, the only good thing about Cold Harbor was that it eventually forced Lee to retreat south to Petersburg, a vital rail junction that he needed to defend Richmond. Here the campaign settled into a trench warfare stalemate for the next nine months. The southern army was in bad shape, but the stalemate at Petersburg, plus the horrendous casualties of Grant's campaign — 66,000 in six weeks — caused northern morale to plummet. By the late summer of 1864, Lincoln was in real danger of losing the election.

Ravaging the South

In the summer of 1864, Gen. William Sherman, one of the North's most ruthless commanders, began a campaign to take Atlanta, a city that was second only to Richmond in political importance for the Confederacy. Starting in Chattanooga, Tennessee, Sherman's men spent the summer steadily fighting their way closer to Atlanta. In late August, Sherman cut the city off, forcing it to surrender on September 2. The jubilant northern commander telegrammed the White House: "Atlanta is ours and fairly won." He ordered the town evacuated and then had it burned to the ground.

The fall of Atlanta was of great importance:

- ✔ Northern morale skyrocketed because a victorious end to the war was now in sight.

- ✔ The surge in morale led to Lincoln's reelection. In November, he easily defeated the pro-peace George McClellan, the general who had once worked for him.

- ✔ Lincoln's reelection ensured the South's defeat because he was committed to total victory. Union victory was now just a matter of time.

- ✔ After Atlanta, Sherman led his army on a "march to the sea" in which he conquered the rest of Georgia, South Carolina, and North Carolina, destroying anything of value to the Confederacy.

The end at Appomattox

By April 1, 1865, Lee's Army of Northern Virginia at Petersburg was under pressure from Grant, whose army was constantly battering the Confederate fortifications, and Sherman, who had knifed through North Carolina to join up with Grant. Casualties, disease, and desertion had whittled Lee's army down to about 35,000 hungry men. They could not hold out against the vastly superior Union armies.

In early April, the Confederate line at Petersburg finally broke, forcing Lee to abandon not just Petersburg but also Richmond. On April 3, the Yankees took the Confederate capital. Meanwhile, Lee and the remnants of his army retreated west to Appomattox, Virginia. Grant's army soon caught up with them. With a heavy heart, Lee now realized that further resistance was futile. On April 9, 1865, he surrendered his army to Grant. The Union general ordered his men to treat the surrendering rebels with respect, like wayward brothers returning home. Within two months of Lee's surrender at Appomattox, all the remaining Confederate military forces laid down their arms. With the war over, the healing could now begin.

The war was the bloodiest in American military history, costing the lives of 360,000 Union soldiers and 258,000 Confederates. The war preserved the Union, abolished slavery, and ensured that the United States would develop along the northern model of industrialization, urbanization, a strong central government, free labor, and entrepreneurial capitalism. But the war didn't resolve the issue of racial equality. In general, African Americans did not enjoy any semblance of equality for at least another century.

Experiencing the Civilian Side of the Civil War

What was the Civil War like for the American people? Mainly an unhappy experience, especially if you were a southerner. Almost everyone, North and South, was affected in some way by the war. People lost homes, property, farms, and loved ones. Some Americans profited from the war. The people of the North generally had an easier time than southerners. During the war years, northerners experienced good economic times; southerners were lucky to eat three meals a day.

Diverging economies

The northern war economy was much stronger than the southern. In the North, jobs were plentiful. The average person ate decent food, earned reasonable wages, and could even afford the entertainment offered by books, newspapers, music, and plays. The war affected them because of the human cost of the casualties, not because of any major personal privations or rationing.

Some northern financiers and entrepreneurs got very rich making war *materiel* (items like weapons and military equipment) for the government, speculating on precious metals, and extending high-interest loans to Uncle Sam. A young Scottish immigrant named Andrew Carnegie got rich from investing in the rising oil industry. He eventually used his earnings to create the world's leading steel company. J. Pierpont Morgan made millions by cornering the gold market. Both Carnegie and Morgan were of military age, but both used their wealth to avoid service in the Union Army.

The Confederate economy was quite weak. The South didn't have the resources, industry, railroads, or farm acreage to provide for its population during the war. Inflation jacked up prices by 9,000 percent during the war. Yankee armies overrunning huge swaths of the South only compounded the miserable situation. As a result of all these problems, hunger and privation dogged southerners. Meat was scarce, especially in the cities. Average southerners often ate meager meals of corn mush and bread, with perhaps some fish or fatty bacon. Some verged on the brink of starvation, particularly rural women with husbands in the Confederate Army.

The food shortages boiled over into actual food riots in the South. In the most famous such riot, Richmond women broke into the stores of merchants who were hoarding meat and flour. The riot got so out of control that Jefferson Davis, the Confederate president, took to the streets to restore order.

Resisting the draft

Hundreds of thousands of Rebels and Yankees volunteered for the armed forces, but the costly battles created a never-ending demand for more troops. Both the North and the South needed military manpower so desperately that they resorted to implementing a draft (or *conscription*). The Confederate Congress passed a conscription law in April 1862. The U.S. Congress passed a similar law two months later. The draft was quite unpopular in both regions, especially because the wealthy could avoid it by hiring a substitute or paying a *commutation fee*.

In New York City, anti-draft sentiment exploded into horrendous violence in July 1863. Working-class Irish immigrants who couldn't afford to pay their way out of the draft rioted when federal officials attempted to conscript them. The Irish were against the war and emancipation because they feared that freed slaves would take their jobs. For several days, the Irish killed or beat up draft officials, blacks, and anyone who favored the abolition of slavery. The rioters looted, burned, and destroyed millions of dollars worth of property. Eventually, Lincoln quelled the riot by sending in troops.

In the long run, the draft didn't raise much manpower for either army. For instance, only 8 percent of Union Army soldiers were draftees. Moreover, most of these draftees were not very good soldiers. Volunteers carried the weight for both sides. Among the white population, about half of military-age northern men served in the armed forces; about four-fifths of young southern men served.

Rousing political rabble

Both Lincoln and Davis dealt with intense opposition. In the North, peace Democrats put constant pressure on Lincoln to end the war. As the war grew ever more terrible, they argued that the goal of reestablishing the Union was unattainable or not worth the cost. They also opposed abolition. Republicans derided these antiwar opponents as *copperheads* (after the poisonous snake).

Lincoln was also under pressure from intensely anti-secession members of his own party. Known as Radical Republicans, they wanted to conquer the South, end slavery, punish Confederates, and establish racial equality. They constantly accused Lincoln of too much leniency against the Rebels. In 1861–1862, they intensely pressured Lincoln to abolish slavery.

In the South, President Davis was plagued with similarly strident opponents. The Confederacy had no political parties, so Davis's main opposition came from states' rights advocates who resented the Confederate government's power in Richmond. After all, many southerners went to war to protect states' rights, so it was natural for them to oppose any strong central government policies, such as the draft, that Davis took in an effort to win the war. In the long run, the South collapsed under the weight of this contradiction — to win the war, the Confederacy needed a strong central government, similar to Lincoln's, but then what would become of states' rights?

Dancing around the race issue

At the outset of the war, both sides denied that the war was about slavery or, by extension, race. Northerners said they were fighting to reestablish the Union. Southerners were fighting for their homes and states' rights.

All of this was true, but slavery was a key issue as well. As Union armies conquered major portions of the South, thousands of slaves fled from their masters (some of whom were away in the service) to the Union lines. Even the most anti-abolition Union commander wouldn't return these fugitives to slavery. Thus, the institution of slavery began to erode as the war dragged on.

After the Emancipation Proclamation, the North was committed to ending slavery (see the "Bloodshed at Antietam" section earlier in this chapter). But the larger question was what would happen to the freed slaves. Would African Americans now enjoy full equality as American citizens? This great question did not just affect the South but also the North. In the North, free blacks didn't enjoy any semblance of equality with whites, and many whites aimed to keep it that way.

Thus, the question of race was a major issue of the Civil War (some historians believe it was *the* major issue). African Americans played a major part in the war's outcome. When slaves escaped, they seriously damaged the Confederate war effort, not just by their absence but also in helping the Union armies. The North mobilized 186,000 African American troops during the war. About half were freed slaves; the other half were free men from the North. Lincoln once commented that without these men, the North would not have won. Most served in support roles, under the control of white officers. Some, like the famous 54th Massachusetts Volunteer Infantry Regiment, did see combat.

The valorous service of units like the 54th created momentum for racial reform in some northern states. Even so, the war didn't result in any kind of long-term racial equality, whether North or South. The issue of race reform festered in America until the civil rights movement of the 20th century. In that sense, the Civil War was incomplete.

What Did It All Mean?

Historians have written, literally, hundreds of thousands of Civil War books. So what do the experts say the war was really about? Opinions vary of course, but some predominant interpretations have emerged over the years:

- ✔ White southern historians of the late 19th and early 20th centuries saw the South's cause as noble, but ultimately doomed by northern material superiority.

- ✔ In that same time period, northern historians saw the war as an abolitionist crusade to end slavery, but not racial inequality.

- ✔ By the middle of the 20th century, many historians saw economics as the real cause of the war.

- ✔ In the last 40 years, quite a few historians have argued that the war was an inevitable clash of distinct cultures — a slave-based society versus a free-labor society.

- ✔ A more recent group of historians emphasizes the importance of racial inequality as the cause of the Civil War.

Chapter 12

The "Indian Wars": The Army Secures the Frontier

*B*etween 1862 and 1900, as Americans expanded westward at an ever increasing rate, they clashed with Native American tribes that controlled significant pockets of territory in the West. This was the final phase of a continuous conflict between settlers and Native American tribes that had been going on since the earliest days of European colonization in America. By now, the vast majority of Native American tribes in North America had been killed off by disease, relocated to reservations, or assimilated into the United States.

The western tribes, then, were the last representatives of ancient Indian civilizations that now stood in the way of U.S. expansion. When Americans moved westward, they inevitably conflicted with Native Americans who were defending their traditional homes. Sometimes the result was violence and outright warfare between the U.S. Army and Native American tribes.

In this chapter, I discuss Native American tribes of the West. I explain how and why they clashed with white settlers and a U.S. Army that attempted to enforce government policy while keeping whites and Indians from killing one another. Finally, I describe some of the most important battles the Army fought with Indian tribes.

Clashing Cultures

In 1862, at the height of the Civil War, the U.S. Congress passed the Homestead Act. This new law guaranteed 160 acres of western land to any family or individual who agreed to live on it for five years. At the end of that time, the citizen would own the land. The idea was to stimulate expansion in the Trans-Mississippi West, an area of the country encompassing present-day Colorado, North Dakota, South Dakota, Minnesota, Montana, Idaho, Oregon, Utah, Nevada, and Wyoming (see Figure 12-1). By 1900, the Homestead Act had led to the establishment of 372,000 farms in the West.

The last quarter of the 19th century saw a clash of cultures in the West as the United States expanded in that direction. Native Americans wanted to live on their tribal lands and hang on to traditional, distinctive cultures that often emphasized

✔ Worship of nature

✔ Community ownership of property

✔ Tribal languages, music, art, and village life

✔ Migratory hunting and gathering rather than sedentary agriculture

✔ Primary loyalty to a chief or tribal entity, not a larger country

By contrast, American culture emphasized very different values:

✔ Christianity, which views humanity as the overseer of nature

✔ Capitalism and private property

✔ The importance of the individual

✔ The use and exploitation of natural resources for financial gain

✔ The establishment of stable, permanent farm communities or cities teeming with industrial growth

✔ Nationalistic allegiance to the United States

In the West, the conflict between these two ways of life was inevitable, especially because both cultures were generally quite warlike. The struggle, of course, had been going on ever since Europeans set foot in North America. It continued throughout early American history (see Chapters 6 and 8 for more) as the United States expanded westward. The late-19th-century West was simply the final phase of this long conflict.

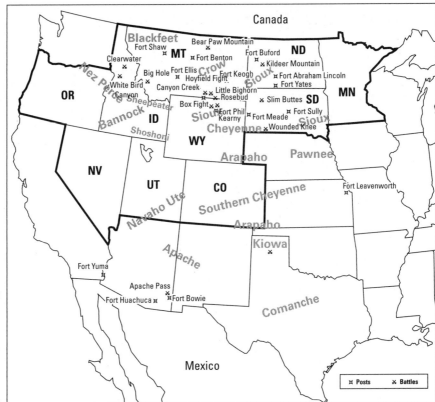

Figure 12-1:
Map of the
Trans-
Mississippi
West,
1860–1890.

The Old West: A pack of myths

No aspect of American history is more mythologized than the West in the late 19th century. People generally call this time period "the Old West." When most people think of this time and place, they conjure up certain images from old movies, TV shows, or bad novels:

✔ Valiant cowboys or soldiers besieged by marauding Indians

✔ The cavalry rushing to the rescue, saving settlers from "savage" Indians

✔ Good guys in white hats engaging in quick-draw gunfights against bad guys in black hats on a dusty street, with sagebrush blowing in the wind

✔ Greedy white men assaulting Indians, stealing from them, and plundering their land

All these things did happen at one time or another, but they have been grossly exaggerated for the entertainment of modern Americans. The truth of the West was far more mundane.

Native American Tribes of the West

As of 1860, myriad Indian tribes populated the West. Some of these tribes were so large that they were known as *nations*. Most Indians lived simple lives, engaging in farming, hunting, and fishing. Their loyalty was usually to their immediate tribe, not any kind of larger consciousness of being an Indian. Warfare among tribes was common and had gone on for many centuries. In fact, the average Indian often thought of his tribe's Native American enemies as the main threat to his survival, not white Americans.

But some tribes, or nations, were especially resistant to *white encroachment* (the taking of Indian land or pressure to sell to the government or settlers). The following sections give you the lowdown on some of the tribes that U.S. settlers and soldiers encountered during the country's expansion west.

The Sioux

The Sioux nation was among the most formidable of all Indian entities. The Sioux lived in Minnesota, the Dakotas, and Nebraska. As whites intruded on their lands, the Sioux pushed west themselves into Montana and Wyoming, displacing the Crows, their bitter enemies. The Sioux were herdsmen, buffalo hunters, and fierce fighters.

The 1990 film *Dances with Wolves* portrayed Sioux Indians at about the time of the Civil War. In the movie, many real Sioux actors played the parts of their ancestors. Throughout the movie, the actors even spoke a modified version of Lakota Sioux, a prominent language among the Sioux.

The Nez Perce

The Nez Perce tribe at one time controlled about 17 million acres of land that would someday be part of Oregon, Washington, and Idaho. They were migratory, constantly moving in pursuit of the buffalo and salmon they relied on to survive.

The Apaches

The Apaches consisted of seven distinct subgroups, each of which spoke its own language. Among them, these tribes dominated much of what would become New Mexico and Arizona. The Apaches were primarily migratory hunters, although they did grow some domesticated plants and were known to trade with other tribes for food. The typical Apache man spent much of his time hunting deer and antelope in the desert Southwest.

The Apaches didn't fight many big battles. They were masters at mounted guerrilla warfare, and they were among the government's most famous and the fiercest opponents.

Geronimo, perhaps the most famous Indian chief of all time, was an Apache (see Figure 12-2). He resisted and defied the U.S. government for nearly 25 years until finally surrendering in 1886. After a period of captivity, he became something of a national celebrity, touring the country, appearing at fairs, telling his stories. He died in 1909, but his very name lives on as a symbol of courage and daring.

Figure 12-2:
Geronimo
was an
Apache
chief.

© Bettmann/CORBIS

Historians often include the Navajos among the Apache peoples because of their similar language and culture. In World War II, many Navajos served as *code talkers.* The code talkers were radiomen who transmitted important orders and other military communications in their native language, making them completely unintelligible to mystified Japanese and German eavesdroppers.

Expanding Relentlessly Westward

After the Civil War, thousands of American settlers, most of whom were white, migrated to the West. Some of these Americans wanted to escape the crowded cities of the Midwest and Northeast. Some wanted adventure. Some wanted land. Others wanted the independent, healthy lifestyle that the West seemed to offer. Some wanted gold, silver, or other marketable resources. Most wanted wealth of one sort or another. No matter what the motivation for going west, the number of whites soon multiplied dramatically. For instance, in 1866, 2 million whites lived in the West. Twenty-five years later, the white population was 8.5 million.

The average American who went west believed in the concept of *Manifest Destiny,* a notion that God had given the North American continent to the United States so it could spread its unique culture, liberty, and wealth from the Atlantic to the Pacific.

Often, settlers and Native Americans coexisted peacefully, respecting each other's land and customs. Too frequently, though, whites encroached on Indian land or pressured the Indians for anything of value. At times, unscrupulous Americans stole from the Indians, sold them liquor and weapons, or bilked them out of their land. The Indians sometimes lashed back by massacring settlers or, in less extreme cases, intimidating them in hopes of getting them to leave.

Developing reservations

The U.S. government was of two minds on these simmering troubles. On the one hand, the government wanted to promote westward expansion and add several new states to the Union. On the other hand, the government hoped to protect Native American lands. The result was an *Indian reservation system* mandated by the federal government. Under this new system, tribes would be confined to clearly definable land known as *reservations.* In this way, the American government hoped to prevent conflict between Indians and whites, while encouraging westward expansion. As an added benefit, American officials hoped that, under the new policy, Indians would convert to Christianity, settle into farming, and assimilate into mainstream American life.

The reservation policy didn't solve the problem because it had many flaws:

- ✔ Native Americans often received the least desirable land that whites didn't want.

- ✔ The federal government sometimes forced tribes away from their traditional lands into places that weren't familiar to them.

- ✔ Many Indians hated the reservations and left them, rebelling against the government. The Army then had to force compliance, by violence if necessary (see the "Policing with Warfare" section later in this chapter).

- ✔ White settlers sometimes defied their own government, poaching or even stealing land or resources from Indian reservations.

- ✔ Consigned to dead-end reservations, Indians had a difficult time assimilating into American life. Most wanted simply to live on their traditional land, in their own culture.

Indian scouts

Between 1866 and 1890, several thousand Native Americans served in the U.S. Army. Commonly called *scouts,* they were a major asset because of their knowledge of terrain, tactics, local customs, local Indian languages, and patrolling. Typically, these young men served three- to six-month enlistments, often when the Army was conducting an operation to apprehend a rebellious tribe and put it back onto its government-approved reservation.

The Navajos, Apaches, Pawnees, and Crows provided the most scouts to the Army. These Indians, and the other tribesmen who served as scouts, joined the Army for many reasons. Some wanted to fight against enemies of their tribe or to settle old scores. Some wanted money. Others had converted to Christianity and fought out of religious conviction. A few believed that the white man offered a better way of life and a better future for their families.

Fellow soldiers didn't always treat the scouts as equals, but most respected them for their toughness, bravery, and uncanny sense of direction. Most Army commanders made liberal use of the scouts. Upon discharge, the scouts and their families received pensions from the U.S. government. Their contributions were essential to the Army's eventual triumph in the West.

Maintaining security

The Army's job was to enforce the government reservation policy, a thankless and tricky task. William T. Sherman, the famous Civil War general, summed up the challenge perfectly. "There are two classes of people," he wrote, "one demanding the utter extinction of the Indians, and the other full of love for their conversion to civilization and Christianity. Unfortunately the army stands between them and gets the cuff from both sides."

Sherman was right. Some Americans (mainly westerners) favored a harsh policy of annihilation against the Indians. Others (generally in the East) urged benevolence toward the Indians, in hopes of assimilating them into American life. Thus, the government's reservation policy represented a compromise between these two opposing views. The Army was in the middle, satisfying neither side. Plus, the Army, of course, had the bloody job of fighting Native Americans who defied the U.S. government. This all added up to a dangerous, frustrating experience for soldiers on the frontier.

Policing with Warfare

The term "Indian Wars" is a bit misleading because it calls to mind images of big battles and national mobilization. Actually, the Army fought very few battles of any size or duration in the Old West. More commonly, soldiers endured months and years of mundane duty, usually at dusty, simple military posts. Every now and again, this monotony was broken by the occasional skirmish against defiant Indians who refused to follow government edicts. For the soldiers, then, serving on the frontier was like being part of a police action, rather than a major conflict like the Civil War or World War II. The U.S. won the frontier mainly through *attrition,* by depriving the Indians of food, water, resources, and comfort, not through combat.

Even so, the Army did, at times, fight significant battles against Native American tribes. The upcoming sections describe some of the most famous such battles.

Paying a stiff price for impulsiveness: Little Bighorn, 1876

In 1868, the U.S. government signed a treaty with the Sioux, requiring them to settle on a large reservation in the Dakotas. The majority of the Sioux complied with the treaty, but powerful groups of dissenters, known as *nontreaty* Sioux, spurned the agreement. Led by charismatic chiefs such as Sitting Bull and Crazy Horse, they moved west into Montana, in an area bordered by the Powder River. Sitting Bull and Crazy Horse, and many others like them, felt total contempt for whites, whom they considered greedy and untrustworthy. Thus, these proud Sioux were determined to defy the government and live wherever they pleased. For several years, the government ignored their lack of compliance.

Things began to change in 1874, though. Prospectors discovered gold in the Black Hills, on the Sioux reservation. The federal government tried to buy the hills from the Indians, but the nontreaty chiefs torpedoed this plan. In response, the government ordered them to report to the reservation by January 1876 or risk war. Naturally, Sitting Bull, Crazy Horse, and their followers refused. The result was a war fought throughout 1876. The Battle of Little Bighorn, fought on June 25, was the main event of that war.

Army commanders correctly believed that the rebellious Indians were at the Little Bighorn valley (see Figure 12-3). Thinking that the Indians only had a few hundred fighters, the commanders planned to converge on them with three separate columns of soldiers, fight a quick battle, and force the survivors onto the reservation.

The plan quickly unraveled. On the way to the valley, one column, under Gen. George Crook, fought a costly battle at Rosebud, Montana, in which 28 soldiers were killed and another 56 wounded. These losses and the ferocity of Indian opposition forced him to turn back. Another column, under 7th Cavalry Regiment commander Lt. Col. George Custer, was significantly ahead of the third column, under Col. John Gibbon. The famous Custer was a flamboyant Civil War veteran with flowing, shoulder-length blond hair. On June 25, 1876, he found the main Indian village at Little Bighorn and decided to attack on his own, before Gibbon could arrive. This was a courageous, but impulsive, decision. Custer stirred up a veritable hornet's nest, because he was outnumbered more than three-to-one. In a frenzied battle, the Sioux overwhelmed Custer, massacring him and 268 of his soldiers. Gibbon's men made it to Little Bighorn the next day, essentially rescuing the 300 7th Cavalry survivors who had held out all night on a ridge against sporadic Sioux attacks.

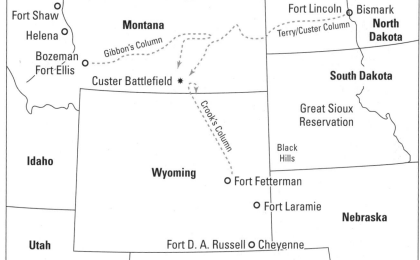

Figure 12-3: Map of the Little Bighorn campaign.

The Buffalo Soldiers

The U.S. Army on the frontier was actually quite diverse. Not only did the Army's ranks include Native American scouts, but African Americans as well. These black soldiers served in segregated Regular Army units, mostly under white officers, in the 9th and 10th Cavalry Regiments, and the 24th and 25th Infantry Regiments. Many were ex-slaves.

Indians called the men of these outfits *Buffalo Soldiers*. The Indians coined the phrase either because the black soldiers' hair reminded them of buffalo hair, or because they felt the African

American troops shared the buffalo's characteristics of stamina, strength, and toughness.

The Buffalo Soldiers served in a variety of posts all over the West and fought in several battles. All the while, they endured occasional racist harassment from white settlers and even, at times, from their white Army comrades. Later, during the Spanish-American War, they earned a reputation for great bravery in battle. Today, monuments at Dodge City and Fort Leavenworth, Kansas, honor the service of these dedicated soldiers.

Romantically remembered as Custer's Last Stand, Little Bighorn was, in reality, a disaster for the U.S. Army. But it didn't lead to victory for the nontreaty Sioux. In the wake of the battle, they celebrated, split up into hunting parties, and acted as if the U.S. government would bother them no more. Instead, the government, stung by the public outcry over Custer's massacre, poured reinforcements into the area. Eventually, by harassing the Indians and depriving them of their food supply, the Army won this war by 1877. Sitting Bull fled to Canada. Crazy Horse surrendered.

The Battle of Big Hole, 1877

Throughout the 1850s and 1860s, as settlers moved into Nez Perce territory in Idaho and Oregon, the government negotiated treaties restricting the tribe onto an Idaho reservation. As newcomers arrived from back east, they hungered for land and gold at the expense of the Nez Perces. These settlers put intense pressure on the federal government to buy more Indian land, especially from those Nez Perces who had not signed the earlier treaties. In the fall of 1876, President Ulysses S. Grant attempted to do so, but the nontreaty Nez Perce refused to sell. In response, Grant gave them an ultimatum: Sell or be forcibly removed to the reservation in Idaho. Some cooperated; others did not.

The result of all this tension was violence. In the summer of 1877, several hundred rebellious, nontreaty Nez Perces began a march to Montana. They believed that if they could make it into Montana, they could find shelter with the Crow tribe, and perhaps eventually go to Canada or maybe negotiate with Washington for a return to their tribal lands. Along the way, they killed about 20 Idaho settlers and skirmished with U.S. Army soldiers. In late July, Chiefs Joseph, Looking Glass, and White Bird led this band of roving Nez Perces past small units of pursuing soldiers and into Montana's Bitterroot Valley.

The Nez Perces didn't fully understand the concept of one nation-state called the United States. They believed that, once they left their white enemies in Idaho and Oregon behind, they would have a clean slate in Montana because, to them, it was a different country. Thus, they didn't comprehend that Montana, Idaho, and Oregon were all part of the same united country and members of a federal union that bonded all Americans together, no matter where they lived. So when the Indians reached Montana, they were surprised that the Army continued to pursue them.

In late July, Col. Gibbon mobilized 149 soldiers from his 7th Infantry Regiment, plus 35 Montana volunteers, and tracked down the Nez Perces. On the morning of August 9, 1877, Gibbon found and attacked the Nez Perce encampment at a fork in the Big Hole River, about 10 miles east of the Idaho border.

The Battle of Big Hole raged all day. At first, the soldiers roamed the village, shooting anyone who offered resistance, even women and children. The well-armed Nez Perces fought back quite effectively, shooting several soldiers to death. In a few hours, they drove Gibbon's forces to a slight rise on the other side of the river from the village. Here, the two sides shot at each other all day. The air was so thick with bullets that dozens of men on both sides were killed or wounded. The bullets shattered bones, knocked out teeth, pierced internal organs, or simply left bleeding flesh wounds. As the hot day wore on, the soldiers suffered from hunger and thirst. Having pinned down the troops, most of the Nez Perces used the cover of nightfall to escape, continuing their exodus.

The Battle of Big Hole cost the lives of 25 soldiers, 6 Montana volunteers, and probably about 80 Nez Perces. In the aftermath of this terrible fight, the Army eventually apprehended the Nez Perces and took them into captivity. Most never returned to their traditional land. A heartbroken Chief Joseph allegedly told his fellow chiefs, "I am tired. My heart is sick and sad. From where the sun now stands, I will fight no more forever."

The end at Wounded Knee, 1890

Many other Native Americans shared Chief Joseph's war weariness. By the 1880s, *pitched battles* (conventional fights like Little Big Horn and Big Hole) were even more rare than before. The Army wore down any rebellious Native American tribes through sheer attrition. In a larger sense, the expanding American nation did the same thing to any tribes that contemplated defying the government's policies. By 1890, most every tribe was on its assigned reservation, resigned to an unhappy fate.

The lone exception was a group of Sioux, known as the Lakota. Trapped on a South Dakota reservation, forced to convert from a hunting lifestyle to farming, they were living dead-end lives. To accommodate new white settlers, the federal government siphoned off Lakota territory, in so doing, reneging on an earlier treaty. The Lakota Sioux was part of the group that had slaughtered Custer in 1876, so they had a long history of conflict with the government.

Simmering with anger and nostalgia, the Lakotas frequently engaged in the ghost dance, a ritual that had warlike connotations. The ghost dance was the brainchild of an influential Sioux religious leader who preached that whites would be banished from the earth, while Lakota Sioux, if wearing certain garments, would be impervious to bullets. The meaning behind the Lakotas' dance caused fear among settlers and soldiers alike.

In response to the growing ghost dance, the 7th Cavalry Regiment surrounded the Lakota Sioux encampment at Wounded Knee, South Dakota, on December 29, 1890. Although the soldiers intended to disarm the Lakotas and take them to Omaha, Nebraska, shooting broke out (accounts still differ as to who fired first). The result was a slaughter in which the troops, with the help of a rapid-firing Gatling gun, killed 300 people, including women and children. The 7th Cavalry lost 25 men killed, mostly by their own crossfire. This sickening massacre ended any remaining Indian resistance to the United States, so most historians see it as the end of the Indian Wars.

Chapter 13

"Remember the Maine!" Fighting Spain and the Filipinos

. . . .

In This Chapter

▶ Quarreling with Spain over Cuba

▶ Going to war with Spain

▶ Inheriting an empire

. . . .

*I*n the 1890s, the United States was entering a new era. In the West, American settlers and the Army had overwhelmed the last resistant Indian tribes (for more details, see Chapter 12). The rest of the country was rapidly modernizing. New technology made new industries like steel, oil, and coal feasible and profitable. This industrial revolution led to massive growth in America's cities, railroads, and economy. With stunning speed, the United States was turning into the world's leading industrial power.

As this happened, Americans began to turn their attention overseas. Some were interested in new markets for American products. Others wanted the U.S. to take its place among the great nations of the world. The most reform-minded wanted to extend the benefits of American democracy around the globe.

At the same time, the old Spanish empire was in its death throes. When Cuban nationalists rose up and fought Spain for their independence, the Spanish responded with brutal force. As the war dragged on, the American people, filled with crusader and imperialist spirits, grew progressively displeased with the Spanish over their repressive war in Cuba. Americans put tremendous pressure on their government to do something about the problem. The ultimate result of this tension was the Spanish-American War.

In this chapter, I look at the key events that led to war between the United States and Spain. I cover the key battles and outline why the United States won the war. Finally, I explain how the ironic result of the Spanish-American War was a new imperialist American empire that led the United States into a bitter, divisive, colonial war of counterinsurgency in the Philippines.

Pressing for War

Americans' new outward-looking mindset led to the rise of two powerful impulses: crusading and imperialism. The crusading impulse was a new form of Manifest Destiny (see Chapters 6, 8 through 10, and 12 for more on this), a belief that America was an empire of liberty, chosen by God to spread its goodness. Americans had used this notion as a motivation to expand coast to coast. Now they hoped to spread American values to the world. The second impulse, imperialism, was not as noble. At a time when European imperial powers dominated most of the world, imperialist Americans hungered for their nation to take its rightful place among the great powers of the earth, by conquest if necessary.

By the late 19th century, Spain's once-great empire was a mere shadow of its former self. Only a few holdover possessions, such as Cuba, Puerto Rico, and the Philippines, remained under Spanish control. The Spanish people wanted to hang onto whatever remained of the old empire. In 1895, when the Cubans began a war for independence from Spain, the Spanish were in no mood to let Cuba go. The United States, growing in power and increasingly concerned with its world status, frowned on the Spanish war in Cuba.

Quarreling over Cuba

In pursuit of their independence, the Cubans fought a *guerilla war* against Spain. This meant destroying anything of value to the Spanish, ambushing their soldiers, harassing them, and killing Spanish sympathizers among the Cuba population. The Spanish responded with harsh tactics of their own. Because the guerillas could simply blend in with the population, the Spanish forcibly moved much of the population into concentration camps to separate the insurgents from the people who supported them. As a result, more than 200,000 Cubans died from malnutrition, disease, and outright executions.

From 1895 to 1898, Americans watched as the war grew increasingly horrible. Most Americans sympathized with the Cubans and wanted them to achieve independence. Anti-Spanish disgust grew in America, to the point where the American people put pressure on their government to intervene in Cuba.

Firing up public opinion

Influential newspapers and magazines stoked anti-Spanish opinion by circulating sensationalized stories of Spanish tyranny in Cuba. For instance, William

Randolph Hearst's *New York Morning Journal* was in the midst of an intense battle for circulation with Joseph Pulitzer's *New York World.* The papers relentlessly competed for readers by printing exaggerated, lurid tales of Spanish atrocities. Both papers reached millions of readers on a daily basis, so their influence was considerable. By 1898, many Americans favored intervention in Cuba.

A more subdued newspaper, *The New York Press,* coined the term *yellow journalism* to condemn the breathless sensationalism so prevalent in the Hearst and Pulitzer papers. The phrase stuck. Even today, critics refer to any media outlet that distorts facts for circulation or viewers as practicing yellow journalism.

Sinking the Maine

In January 1898, the battleship USS *Maine* sailed to Havana on a show-of-force mission designed to protect American economic interests in Cuba. A month later, on February 15, a powerful explosion rocked the *Maine,* sinking the ship and killing 266 sailors. Given the tension between the U.S. and Spain, most Americans immediately blamed the Spanish for the disaster. Some pro-intervention politicians seized upon the sinking of the *Maine* as a justification for war. A naval board of inquiry investigated the tragedy and blamed the explosion on a floating mine, thus implicating the Spanish. Postwar investigations questioned the conclusions of the 1898 naval board of inquiry.

What really sank the *Maine?* Believe it or not, we still don't know for sure. Between 1898 and 1999, four investigations were conducted. Two theories emerged. The 1898 naval board of inquiry and a 1999 *National Geographic* investigation blamed the explosion on an external mine. The other theory, espoused in private investigations conducted in 1911 and 1976, argued that fire in a coal storage bunker caused the fatal explosion.

Declaring war

After the sinking of the *Maine,* public opinion heavily favored war with Spain. Congress put increasing pressure on a reluctant President William McKinley to declare war. McKinley was a Civil War veteran who loathed war. But, in this instance, even though he didn't want war, he knew that he must do something about the situation in Cuba. In April 1898, he asked Congress for authorization to intervene in Cuba. The pro-war Congress was only too happy to agree. The Spanish promptly broke off diplomatic relations and declared war on April 23. The U.S. passed its own war declaration two days later.

The Caribbean Campaign

The Spanish-American War lasted only eight months, from April 1898 to December 1898. The war began over Cuba, so it was only natural that the main theater of operations was the Caribbean (see Figure 13-1). When war broke out, the U.S. immediately planned to invade Cuba and Puerto Rico, another restless Spanish colony. This ambitious plan meant the U.S. needed substantial land and sea forces. The Navy had several modern battleships and was reasonably well prepared. The Army consisted of only 28,000 regular, professional soldiers. The War Department hastily mobilized a force of 125,000 soldiers, some of whom served in the professional Regular Army, others of whom served in state volunteer units (see Chapter 4 to read more on these different types of soldiers).

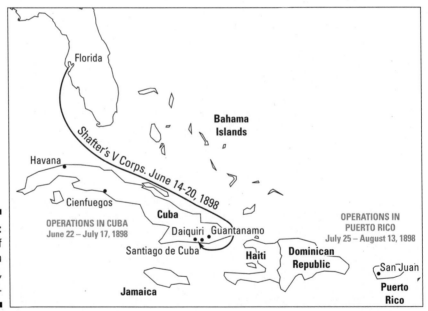

Figure 13-1:
Map of Caribbean operations, 1898.

Invading Cuba

The U.S. Navy held every advantage over the Spanish navy. The Americans had bigger ships, bigger guns with longer range, more-modern technology, and better sailors, too.

Starting in May 1898, the U.S. Navy blockaded Havana harbor, paralyzing Spanish sea movements. The remaining Spanish fleet holed up at Santiago to the southeast, on the opposite portion of the island. The Americans decided to

Scandals and the Dodge Commission

The United States has rarely been well prepared for the wars it fights. The Spanish-American War was no different. Wartime mobilization was disorganized and haphazard. The United States, almost overnight, had to raise an army, train it, feed it, shelter it, and send it overseas.

By and large, the War Department met the challenge well, but not always. Disease, bad food, poor training, and outmoded equipment were persistent problems. In Cuba, American soldiers wore old wool uniforms in the heat of the Cuban summer. Unprepared for the tropical heat, they succumbed in droves to heat exhaustion, yellow fever, malaria, and typhus. In the recollection of one soldier, they ate "tasteless and nauseating" food. In the U.S., soldiers trained in squalid camps, eating lousy food, getting sick in large numbers. For every one soldier killed in combat, the Army lost almost ten others to disease.

Newspapers and magazines reported on these scandalous conditions, prompting action from the government. President McKinley appointed the Dodge Commission which, under the leadership of Maj. Gen. Grenville Dodge, thoroughly investigated the problems and began correcting them, mostly after the war though.

✔ Destroy the Spanish fleet at Santiago

✔ Defeat Spanish ground forces in the area

✔ Capture Santiago harbor

These three objectives were the main focus of the American invasion of Cuba.

Hickory, dickory, landing at Daiquiri

Between June 22 and 24, an amphibious force of 17,000 American soldiers landed at Daiquiri, a few miles east of Santiago. The invasion was amateurish. Soldiers rowed to shore or were towed by Navy steam launches. Pack mules swam to shore. Fortunately, Spanish opposition was minimal; otherwise, the invasion force would have been slaughtered. Instead, Cuban guerilla fighters met up with the Americans, guided them through the jungle, and told them the location of Spanish defenders.

Gen. William Shafter, an old soldier who had won his laurels in the Indian Wars, commanded this force. The 300-pound Shafter had seen better days. He was not well suited to the heat and other unpleasant conditions of a Cuban summer. He planned to push west through the jungle and seize several key hills around Santiago.

In support of the Daiquiri invasion, a detachment of U.S. Marines invaded and seized Guantanamo Bay, about 50 miles to the east. In so doing, they established a long-term base for the United States in Cuba. Even today, the United States has a naval base and detention facility at Guantanamo.

Buffalo Soldiers at San Juan Hill

Until about 1950, African American soldiers generally served in segregated units. This separation of black and white soldiers was, of course, a reflection of racial prejudice. After the Civil War, the Army formed four all-black regiments — the 9th and 10th Cavalry and the 24th and 25th Infantry. Dubbed "Buffalo Soldiers" by the Indians (see Chapter 12), black soldiers served all over the frontier.

In the Spanish-American War, the 9th Cavalry and the 24th Infantry participated in the legendary charge up San Juan Hill on July 1, 1898. In fact, according to many accounts, they were some of the bravest soldiers in the battle. Because of the prevalent racism of the country at that time, these soldiers never quite received the acclaim of the white units that fought at San Juan Hill.

Taking the hills of Santiago

The key to Santiago was the hills that overlooked the seaport town. In particular, anyone who controlled El Caney, San Juan, and Kettle hills would be in position to control Santiago itself. The Spanish had about 10,000 soldiers at Santiago. Fortunately for the Americans, the Spanish didn't concentrate the men on the key hills, but instead stationed them around the perimeter of the city.

By July 1, after a week of arduous jungle marching and a costly battle at Las Guasimas, Gen. Shafter's army was in position east of the hills. The aged commander was battling heat exhaustion and sickness, as were some of his men. Although he had landed with 17,000 men, he had already lost about 2,000 in one week.

In spite of these losses, Shafter decided to attack the Spanish immediately, before they could reinforce their army at Santiago. The general divided his 15,000 men into two strike forces, one of which assaulted El Caney, the other of which attacked San Juan and Kettle hills.

El Caney

Starting at 6:30 a.m., July 1, the Americans hurled themselves at the Spanish El Caney defenses. From the start, the going was rough. The Spanish were armed with modern, German-made Mauser rifles, and they used them well. Clad in blue tunics and doughboy (Smokey Bear) hats, the Americans bent low and moved along El Caney's grassy slopes, under fire all the way.

"The bullets were tearing around us on all sides," Pvt. William Knipes of the 7th Infantry Regiment said. "[It] was a death pit. We were mowed down like sheep." Knipes himself took six hits, but somehow survived. Others died instantly with bullets to the head or heart. The grass around them was stained with blood. Anyone wishing to survive lay prone and fired back. "If one didn't actually 'eat grass,' one kept remarkably close to it," a soldier commented. Eventually, after several grueling hours, the Americans took El Caney, but lost more than 400 men; the Spanish lost about half that many.

San Juan and Kettle

Even as the fighting and dying went on at El Caney, Shafter launched his other attack, to the south, at San Juan Hill. Here the struggle was just as desperate. Fighting with little artillery support, American infantry soldiers and cavalrymen charged straight at formidable Spanish entrenchments. As at El Caney, they were caught in a wickedly accurate crossfire. The air was so thick with bullets that the stooped-over attackers almost looked like they were advancing into a stiff wind. Some soldiers dropped, not from enemy bullets, but from heat exhaustion.

Amazingly, several hundred American soldiers overcame the conditions and enemy fire to capture both San Juan Hill and Kettle Hill, an important neighboring patch of high ground. The cost was steep, though: 124 dead and 817 wounded. The Spanish lost 58 killed in action, 170 wounded, and 39 captured.

The costly charge up these hills quickly became legendary in American popular culture. Several correspondents were right there with the troops and vividly reported the whole event to fascinated readers back home. A 40-year-old lieutenant colonel named Theodore Roosevelt emerged as one of the most unforgettable heroes of the attack. Colorful and eloquent, Roosevelt had once served as assistant secretary of the Navy. When war broke out, Roosevelt resigned that post and formed a unit called the 1st U.S. Volunteer Cavalry Regiment. Nicknamed the "Rough Riders," the unit was composed of western cowboys and eastern socialites. Roosevelt led them so bravely in combat that he became a national hero (see Figure 13-2). He parlayed his fame into a political career, eventually rising to the presidency in 1901.

Young Hamilton Fish

The first member of the Rough Riders to die in battle was 25-year-old Hamilton Fish. The grandson of a secretary of state by the same name, Fish was born into an elite family of wealth and privilege. He graduated from Columbia University. Athletic and adventurous, he eagerly joined the Rough Riders after the declaration of war and quickly rose to the rank of sergeant. "We are going to fight it out like true Americans," he wrote his parents. "We shall win and you shall be proud of me."

At Las Guasimas, Fish was leading the regimental column when an enemy bullet smashed into him, killing him instantly. After the battle, a photographer named Burr McIntosh snapped a picture of Fish's body. In the foreground, the body lies under a poncho. In the background, a group of officers, including Theodore Roosevelt, can be seen talking and laughing.

HISTORIC TRIVIA

Roosevelt is the only president of the United States ever to earn the Medal of Honor, the nation's highest award for valor in combat. He also is one of only two father-son combinations to earn the medal. His son, Ted Roosevelt Jr., received the medal for his heroism during the Normandy invasion in World War II. The other combination is Arthur MacArthur and his more famous son, Douglas.

Figure 13-2:
Theodore
Roosevelt
led his
Rough
Riders in the
charge up
San Juan
Hill.

© Bettmann/CORBIS

Checkmate at Santiago

After the Americans captured the key hills around Santiago, they were in a good position to bombard the town or assault it. However, their casualties had been such that Gen. Shafter preferred a siege. His troops dug trenches all around the city. For two weeks, the hostile armies stared at each other with little fighting.

Meanwhile, on July 3, the outgunned Spanish fleet at Santiago foolishly took on the U.S. fleet in a general engagement. The Americans crushed the Spanish naval forces. After this one-sided battle, the Spanish garrison at Santiago was doomed. Their commander, Gen. Jose Toral, surrendered on July 17. The fighting in Cuba was over.

Grabbing Puerto Rico

On July 25, only a week after the victory in Cuba, the Americans invaded the Spanish colony of Puerto Rico. Gen. Nelson Miles and 3,300 soldiers landed at Guánica. They took the island against almost no resistance. Spanish opposition in the Caribbean had collapsed.

The Philippines

The last remaining Spanish colony in the Pacific was the Philippines, an archipelago consisting of many islands and a diverse array of people. The Spanish had ruled the Philippines since the 16th century, but, as was true elsewhere, their power had greatly diminished by the 19th century. Starting in the spring of 1898, the Americans targeted the Spanish military presence in the Philippines and made common cause with Filipino nationalists who wanted to be free of the Spanish yoke. The result was a major naval engagement followed by a ground campaign (see Figure 13-3).

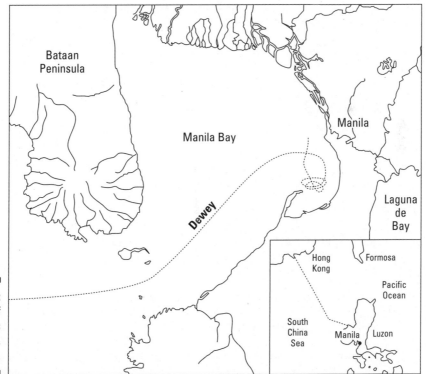

Figure 13-3: Map of Philippines operations, 1898–1903.

Smashing the Spanish fleet

Spanish naval forces in the Philippines were based at Manila Bay, a beautiful natural harbor on the main island of Luzon. As in the Caribbean, Spanish ships were no match for those of the U.S. Navy. Sailing from Hong Kong in late April 1898, an American fleet under Adm. George Dewey trapped the Spanish fleet at Manila Bay on May 1 and destroyed it. The victory had several consequences:

- ✔ The Americans now controlled the waters around the Philippines.

- ✔ Emboldened by the Spanish defeat, Filipino nationalists rose up on Luzon and elsewhere.

- ✔ Adm. Dewey became a national hero.

- ✔ President McKinley became convinced that the Spanish were so weak in the Philippines that the U.S. could take the islands easily.

Getting rid of the Spanish

For two months after his victory, Adm. Dewey blockaded Spanish-controlled Manila and its environs. On land, about 15,000 Filipino nationalists under the command of Emilio Aguinaldo besieged the Spaniards in Manila. In July, nearly 11,000 American soldiers under the command of Gen. Wesley Merritt arrived on Luzon and made common cause with Aguinaldo's men.

Within a month, the Spanish were on the verge of collapse. On August 14, 1898, following some random fighting, the Spanish surrendered all of their forces to the Americans, who afforded them full military honors and prisoner-of-war status. The Filipino nationalists had wanted to overwhelm them, annihilate them, and establish a new independent nation in the Philippines. To prevent this, the Americans took control of Manila and forbade Aguinaldo's men from entering the city. This action indicated that serious conflict was brewing between the Americans and the Filipino nationalists.

Ending the war and making a fateful decision

The collapse of Spanish resistance in the Philippines effectively ended the fighting. On December 10, 1898, Spain and the U.S. signed the Treaty of Paris officially ending the war on the following terms:

- ✔ Cuba received its independence, although the U.S. military occupied the country for three more years and maintained a permanent base at Guantanamo.

> ✔ Spain ceded Puerto Rico, the Philippines, and Guam, another Pacific Ocean colony, to the United States.

> ✔ The United States agreed to pay Spain $20 million for these colonies.

Now that the war with Spain was over, President McKinley faced a decision regarding the Philippines. Should he bow to the wishes of Aguinaldo's movement and agree to Filipino independence, or should he annex the Philippines as a new American colony? After a tremendous amount of soul searching, he decided to annex the Philippines. Here's why:

> ✔ To use the islands as a springboard for economic expansion onto the Asian mainland, especially China

> ✔ To prevent aggressive imperial powers like Germany from conquering a potentially weak new Philippine nation

> ✔ To extend the benefits of American civilization to the Filipinos

The Philippine-American War

McKinley hoped to annex the Philippines with a minimum of conflict and a maximum of benevolence. Embracing the concept of Manifest Destiny, he believed that the United States would bring order, good hygiene, good roads, good hospitals, and prosperity to the impoverished Filipino people.

Aguinaldo and the Filipino nationalists rejected this idealism. They wanted their own independent country, free of outside imperial supervision. They had fought Spain to achieve that goal, and during that war, they had viewed the Americans as liberators. Now, after McKinley's decision, they felt betrayed by the United States. They resolved to fight for their independence.

The conventional war in 1899

On February 4, 1899, fighting broke out between American patrols and Filipino nationalists outside of Manila. This was the first in a series of battles fought throughout the year. In general, the Filipinos were brave fighters but no match for the Americans because of inferior weapons and leadership. By 1900, the Americans controlled almost every major town in the Philippines with a force of about 40,000 soldiers (see Figure 13-4).

Figure 13-4:
American soldiers cross the Tulihan River on patrol in the Philippines.

© CORBIS

The insurgency

Realizing that he couldn't hope to defeat the Americans in a conventional war, Aguinaldo turned to guerilla warfare in 1900. He organized his men into small, irregular groups, and blended them into the *barrios,* or villages, throughout the jungles, mountains, and countryside of the Philippines. The guerillas conducted hit-and-run ambushes against the Americans and anyone who sympathized with them. Although the nationalists were fairly popular with most Filipinos, they resorted to terror tactics against civilians to thwart American attempts to win support in the countryside. Aguinaldo hoped to wear down the Americans and make the war unpopular enough at home that the American people would vote McKinley out of office in 1900.

The guerilla war soon devolved into a brutal struggle. In four short months, the insurgents inflicted more than 500 casualties on the Americans. The guerillas burned crops, butchered soldiers, and terrorized civilians. In an effort to crush the resistance, the Americans unleashed some atrocities of their own. They executed suspected insurgents, burned down entire villages, occasionally tortured prisoners, and interned thousands of Filipinos in squalid concentration camps. The internments, of course, were tragically ironic because, a few years earlier, the Americans had criticized the Spanish for consigning hundreds of thousands of Cubans to similar camps.

HISTORIC TRIVIA

The most common American torture technique in the Philippines was the *water cure treatment*. Several soldiers would hold a prisoner firmly in place while another soldier poured continuous water down his throat. This induced the sensation of drowning even though the victim was only swallowing water. The longer the prisoner refused to cooperate, the more his stomach expanded with water, usually inducing vomiting. Then the process would start all over again. "A man suffers tremendously, there is no doubt about it," one American soldier admitted. "His sufferings must be that of a man who is suffering, but cannot drown."

Widening the war and provoking opposition at home

President McKinley won reelection in November 1900, guaranteeing that the war would widen and continue. Aguinaldo was disappointed in the U.S. election results, but determined to fight on nonetheless. McKinley sent about 80,000 more troops to the Philippines and entrusted them to the command of Gen. Arthur MacArthur, an experienced soldier and Civil War hero. MacArthur expanded the Army's counterinsurgency efforts by crushing guerilla resistance, forging alliances with moderate Filipinos, and dispensing economic aid to barrios that rejected the nationalists. American troops even captured Aguinaldo himself in March 1901. From this point on, the Americans steadily eroded the insurgency, winning the war slowly but steadily.

Even so, the war dragged on indefinitely. American casualties piled up, and atrocities continued on both sides. In reaction to this, and the overall American presence in the Philippines, opposition to the war grew in America. The Anti-Imperialist League included many prominent American voices, such as steel tycoon Andrew Carnegie, writer Mark Twain, and politician William Jennings Bryan, who had opposed McKinley in the 1900 election. These men, and many others like them, believed that the United States was wrong to squelch Filipino independence. They argued that America had gone to war with Spain for good moral reasons but was now acting just like Spain as an exploitative, imperialist power. The atrocity stories only strengthened their viewpoint.

The fighting dies down

By the summer of 1902, the Army had, more or less, squelched opposition, at least enough for the Americans to loosely control the Philippines. Sporadic fighting continued for another ten years, most notably between the Army and Muslim tribesmen in the southern islands of the Philippines. However, the major fighting was over. The United States lost 4,324 soldiers killed and 3,000 wounded. The Filipino nationalists lost 16,000 men killed. At least 250,000 civilians died from disease, malnutrition, exposure, and atrocities perpetrated by both sides.

Really serious consequences

McKinley's decision to annex the Philippines and the war that stemmed from that decision had serious long-term consequences for the U.S.:

- ✔ The international image of the U.S. as a freedom-loving republic was damaged.

- ✔ The American people had difficulty deciding if they really wanted an empire in such places as the Philippines, Hawaii, Samoa, and Guam. This led to bitter debate between imperialists and anti-imperialists.

- ✔ With control of the Philippines, the United States was now committed to maintaining a permanent military, economic, and imperial presence in the Pacific. In the long run, this meant defending the Philippines against a rising imperial Japan.

Part IV
Going Global: The World Wars

"Okay — Mommy's going off now to build a Boeing B-29 Superfortress. You kids behave or I'll bring my rivet gun home with me."

In this part . . .

*I*n the 19th century, the United States was mainly concerned with its own continent. In the 20th century, that outlook completely changed. As this part shows you, America's 20th-century leaders were concerned with protecting American economic interests and exporting American-style democracy overseas. This new American interest in the world beyond our shores was called *internationalism,* and it led to involvement in two world wars.

In the first world war, the United States fought a rising German nation that threatened to dominate Europe. The second world war was much worse. The U.S. once again fought to prevent Germany from conquering Europe, but the country also battled to prevent Japan from overrunning much of Asia and the Pacific. From here on out, Americans fought their wars overseas.

Chapter 14

Over There: The First World War

- -

In This Chapter

▶ A European bloodbath

▶ Joining the Allied coalition

▶ Supporting the war effort here at home

▶ Joining the fight

- -

*I*n the early 20th century, European imperial empires dominated most of the world. The premier empires, France, Britain, Germany, Austria-Hungary, and Russia, had spent years colonizing major portions of Africa, Asia, and the Pacific. As they did so, they competed for influence, resources, and military supremacy.

This mad scramble for empire fueled tension among the great powers. In hopes of guaranteeing their security, several of them banded together into mutual alliances. Britain, France, and Russia were part of an alliance (eventually called the *Allies*) designed for mutual protection against an opposing bloc (which came to be known as the *Central Powers*) led by Germany and Austria-Hungary.

In the summer of 1914, a political assassination in the Balkans ignited the tinderbox of tensions that eventually became a firestorm of war.

The United States initially declared neutrality when the European war broke out. Americans were primarily concerned with their own hemisphere, and they hoped to remain aloof from Europe's troubles. However, in the early 20th century, the American economy depended on trans-Atlantic trade, especially with the Allied countries. By 1917, German submarine attacks threatened that trade, leading ultimately to war between Germany and the U.S.

In this chapter, I examine the causes of World War I and give you a feel for the war's terrible nature. I explain how the United States became involved, how the war affected the folks here at home, and also what kind of impact American soldiers had on the outcome of the conflict.

My Alliance Can Beat Up Your Alliance

On June 28, 1914, in Sarajevo, a 19-year-old Serbian nationalist named Gavrilo Princip assassinated Archduke Franz Ferdinand, the heir to the Austro-Hungarian throne. This murderous act set in motion a series of events that led to World War I.

Austria-Hungary was hoping to expand into the Balkans at the expense of Serbia. Seizing upon the assassination as a pretext for this expansion, Austria-Hungary demanded major concessions from Serbia. Eventually, with Germany's approval, Austria-Hungary declared war on Serbia. However, Russia had an alliance to protect Serbia, so it declared war on Austria-Hungary. This, in turn, led to war between Germany and Russia. Figure 14-1 shows how European countries were aligned at the beginning of World War I.

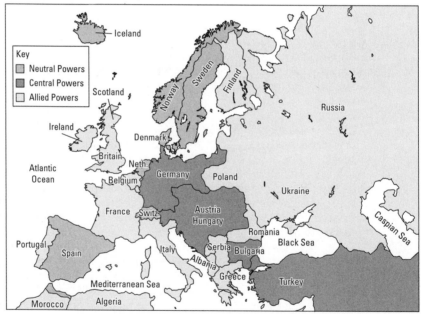

Figure 14-1:
Map of European alliances during World War I.

Because France had an alliance with Russia, it joined the war against Germany, as did Britain. Through conscription, all the belligerents mobilized mass armies and navies consisting of millions of men. Hostilities began in early August 1914. On one side were Austria-Hungary and Germany; on the other were Serbia, Russia, France, and Britain.

The reasons for war

Most historians blame World War I on Germany, claiming Germany failed to reign in its hawkish Austro-Hungarian ally, while at the same time it wanted to conquer major portions of Europe. Although true, the roots of the war go deeper than that. Here are the four main causes of World War I:

- ✔ **Nationalism:** Almost all the belligerents wanted territory they believed was theirs for ethnic and cultural reasons. They also wanted to prove their national greatness.

- ✔ **Imperialism:** Decades of competition for colonies had led to an atmosphere of rivalry, distrust, and fear among the great powers.

- ✔ **The arms race:** For years, European powers had engaged in a bitter, costly *arms race* (a focused effort by countries to build more and bigger weapons than their rivals) that fueled tension and ate up huge sums of money. The best example is Germany's attempt to build a large navy to rival Great Britain's.

- ✔ **Alliances:** The extensive network of alliances among the European powers increased the chances that a small event, like Princip's assassination of the Austrian monarch, could lead to a general war. And it did.

The strategies for war

When war broke out in the summer of 1914, both sides anticipated a quick, victorious conflict. Their strategies reflected that belief. The French Plan XVII called for an offensive into the Ruhr, the industrial heartland of Germany. Deprived of its industry, the French believed Germany would then surrender under certain conditions. At the same time, the Russians planned a major offensive into East Prussia (a province in eastern Germany).

Germany's Schlieffen Plan, however, was the most ambitious strategy of all. Facing a two-front war, the Germans decided to go for a knockout blow against France. German armies would crash through neutral Belgium and Luxembourg, invade northern France, wheel around Paris, and force France to fold, all before Britain could enter the war in any strength. At that point, Germany intended to turn its full attention east and defeat Russia.

None of the strategists on either side imagined that the war would last years, require mass mobilization in each of the warring countries, and claim 10 million lives.

The exploits of war

By August 1914, the battles had begun, with the Russians attacking in the East and both sides tearing into each other in the West.

Russia and Germany square off at Tannenberg

Imperial Russia was ruled by the *tsar,* an aristocratic, almost godlike figure to many Russian peasants. The country was backward and plagued with internal political problems, but its army was formidable for its sheer size.

In August 1914, the Russians mobilized their army and attacked East Prussia much faster than the Germans anticipated. This forced the Germans to reinforce their armies in the East, at the expense of the drive into France. Between August 17 and September 2, the Germans destroyed the Russian attack, capturing 95,000 Russians and inflicting 30,000 more enemy casualties. The battle, known as the Battle of Tannenberg, was an overwhelming German victory, but a costly one because it weakened German armies in the West and helped unravel the Schlieffen Plan.

The Miracle of the Marne

Throughout August, German soldiers overran Belgium and poured into northern France. Belgian and French soldiers fought bravely, but the Germans overwhelmed them with a steady, costly advance. By early September, the Germans were in position for a final drive on Paris. They planned to push west along the Marne, a river that flowed out of the French capital.

Over the course of one week, September 5–12, the French and some newly arrived British troops blunted the German advance, foiling Germany's attempt to conquer Paris and win a quick victory with its Schlieffen Plan. The scale of the fighting was immense and so were the losses. More than 2.5 million troops were involved in the battle. Both sides suffered more than 250,000 casualties. This Allied victory saved Paris and became known as the "Miracle of the Marne."

During this battle, the French abandoned their Plan XVII and redeployed troops from all over their country to plug gaps in the line and stop the German advance. The French even used 600 Paris taxicabs to ferry infantry troops into battle. Some historians still call these troops "The Taxicab Army."

The trench stalemate

After the Miracle of the Marne, neither side could gain a decisive advantage. The war on both fronts soon settled into an uneasy stalemate between antagonists with highly developed industry and technology. The power of industrialization manifested itself in a variety of deadly, cutting-edge weapons. The killing power of new weapons such as point-detonated artillery shells, machine guns, grenades, airplanes, and poison gas made it difficult for attackers to capture objectives. For self-preservation against all of this firepower, soldiers dug deep trench networks that provided some semblance of cover. By the end of 1914, trenches crisscrossed the war's landscape, both east and west.

The trenches were especially extensive in the West, where a continuous line snaked all the way from the English Channel to the neutral Swiss border. Try as they might, neither the Allies nor the Central Powers could break the awful trench stalemate and win the war. Between 1915 and 1917, they fought inconclusive but costly battles at such places as Ypres, Vimy Ridge, Verdun, and the Somme, but the stalemate continued. Hundreds of thousands of men were killed, wounded, captured, or incapacitated psychologically in these futile attacks to break the deadlock.

For the average French, German, British, or Belgian soldier, life in the trenches was miserable. The trenches were usually about 10 feet deep and buttressed with wooden, or perhaps concrete, beams. Floorboards provided some relief from the ever-present mud. The trenches were surrounded by reams of barbed wire. Soldiers ate prepackaged rations or, if they were lucky, the occasional hot meal. The no man's land between enemy trench systems could be as large as 3 miles or as small as 70 yards. No man's land was cratered with sodden shell holes full of rainwater or even dead, decomposing bodies. Soldiers in the trenches were often exposed to the elements, as well as artillery shells, sniper fire, machine gun fire, mortar fire, poison gas, and enemy raids. The trench experience was a hellish industrial war that raged 24 hours a day, seven days a week.

Losing the eastern ally

In 1917, with the war in its fourth year, revolution swept through Russia. The nation's armies had suffered millions of casualties, with little apparent gain or purpose. Bread riots were raging in Russian cities, and the country was in political turmoil. The tsar fell from power, and in late October, the *Bolsheviks,* a group of radical Communist revolutionaries, seized control of the government. The Bolsheviks were against the war, so they immediately negotiated a peace settlement with Germany.

Russia's withdrawal from the war was devastating to the Allies because Germany could now focus its full attention on the western front. It redeployed most of its army to the West. At the same time, Germany unleashed its submarines throughout the Atlantic in an attempt to strangle Great Britain and win the war. In so doing, the Germans began attacks against ostensibly neutral American ships that were carrying food and war *materiel* (military equipment) to Britain.

Facing the worst weapon: Poison gas

In August 1914, the French used tear gas against German attackers. The Germans soon responded in kind. From this point forward, both sides began using progressively worse substances that were usually delivered by artillery shells.

In the spring of 1915, at the Battle of Ypres, the Germans used chlorine gas that attacked and destroyed lung tissue as the victim breathed the fumes. After initial outrage over this chemical warfare, the British embraced the notion of using chlorine and phosgene gas. By the end of 1915, gas attacks were a regular part of life in the trenches. Soldiers were equipped with gas masks that often negated the peril of gas.

In 1917, the Germans introduced mustard gas, the war's worst chemical weapon. Mustard gas burned anyone who came in contact with it. Victims were afflicted with "mustard-coloured blisters, blind eyes, all sticky and stuck together," in the memory of one British nurse. The gas also severely damaged the lungs, sometimes causing suffocation. Heavier than air, it settled into the trenches and shell holes, coating them with an oily, toxic film. The British devised and used their own mustard gas in the fall of 1918.

Although poison gas accounted for only 3 percent of combat deaths in the war, most men feared this weapon above all others. Because of exposure to poison gas, thousands of World War I veterans were plagued with lung problems for the rest of their lives.

Reacting to German Sea Tactics, the U.S. Declares War

For three years, Americans had watched in curious detachment as World War I raged in Europe. Initially, the majority of Americans were glad to stay out of the war. For instance, in 1916, President Woodrow Wilson used the slogan, "He kept us out of the war," to win a tough reelection fight against his Republican opponent Charles Evans Hughes. However, within six months, Wilson led the country into the war. By that time, public opinion was firmly aligned with the Allies. Why? Americans were concerned about the consequences of a potential German-dominated Europe, and Americans were burning with anger over German unrestricted submarine warfare against American ships in the Atlantic.

On April 6, 1917, the United States officially entered the war on the Allied side when Congress declared war on Germany and the other Central Powers nations. This fateful declaration of war stemmed from four causes:

- ✔ Ties to Britain and France
- ✔ Global economics

✔ A sense of global responsibility

✔ Frustration with Germany over neutrality rights

Fighting to support our allies

During World War I, Germany was an *autocracy,* ruled by an elite group of aristocrats, military officers, and bureaucrats. The public face of this regime was Kaiser Wilhelm II, an imperialist monarch who garnered little sympathy in democratic America. By contrast, Britain and France were fellow democracies with leaders who derived their power from elections. The average American thus had a natural sympathy for these democracies in their fight against imperial Germany.

The British exploited this natural sympathy by engaging in a widespread propaganda campaign in America. In hopes of inciting moral outrage and persuading the U.S. to join the Allies, British propagandists circulated stories of German atrocities, some of which weren't true. The campaign did succeed in stoking anti-German sentiment, though.

In January 1917, anti-German opinion increased when the British intercepted a German diplomatic communication and publicized it. This communication, known as the Zimmerman telegram, was a clumsy German attempt to enlist Mexico's help in any potential war with the U.S. Arthur Zimmerman, the German foreign minister, promised Mexico the return of Texas, Colorado, Arizona, New Mexico, Nevada, Utah, and California, all of which Mexico had lost to the U.S. in a war fought between 1846 and 1848 (see Chapter 10 for the lowdown). Although the proposal went nowhere, Americans were outraged at these German schemes.

Fighting for free trade

Americans had a serious economic interest in the Allied cause. Between 1914 and 1916, the U.S. engaged in $3 billion worth of trade with the Allies each year. American bankers lent millions to Allied governments. American farmers were shipping large amounts of food to the Allied countries. Most significantly, the Allies were becoming increasingly dependent on American industrial goods, including armaments, to fight the war. If the Allies lost, many American investors, industrialists, and bankers stood to lose their shirts because a German-dominated Europe would be a less-than-welcoming place for American trade and goods.

Fighting for democracy and a better life

By 1917, many Americans believed that the U.S. must make the world safe for democracy. The prevailing notion was that the United States could and should spread democratic capitalism, self-determination, and freedom to every corner of the globe. To some extent, this was a continuation of *Manifest Destiny,* the popular American notion that the United States was a special empire of liberty destined to dominate the North American continent and spread its ideas far and wide (see Chapters 8, 10, and 12 for more on this concept).

American idealism also stemmed from a series of early 20th-century social reforms, known as *Progressivism,* to alleviate urban decay, poverty, monopolies, and injustice in America. President Wilson was a confirmed Progressive who envisioned the United States as a world leader. The bottom line was that the World War I era was an idealistic time.

Fighting against tyranny

Although the United States professed neutrality, it engaged in extensive trade, commerce, and even arms sales with the Allies, especially the British. The Germans believed that the Americans were neutrals in name only. So, at times, their submarines attacked and sank American ships or vessels with Americans aboard. Perhaps the most notorious example of this was the sinking of the *Lusitania* in May 1915, with the loss of 128 American lives.

In early 1917, the Germans unleashed unrestricted submarine warfare and sank several American ships. American viewed this as outright butchery, and anti-German sentiment swept the country. The Wilson administration severed diplomatic relations with Germany. When Germany refused to end unrestricted submarine warfare, Wilson and Congress saw no other recourse but war.

Wilson sums up America's goals for the war

During World War I, President Wilson was the only war leader who announced a clear set of war aims. In an early 1918 speech, Wilson stated that the United States was fighting for 14 points and stated, point by point, exactly what he meant. The Fourteen Points, as they came to be called, basically stood for the following ideas:

- ✔ An international world of free trade with freedom of the seas and no economic barriers. This would create prosperity and reduce the chances of more wars because nations that do business with one another rarely go to war.

✔ More-open diplomacy because secret deals had contributed to the onset of World War I.

✔ Self-determination for all peoples to create their own autonomous, independent nations.

✔ The establishment of a world peacekeeping body known as the League of Nations.

Preparing the Home Front for War

The United States was not well prepared for World War I. This was a major reason why the Germans had been so belligerent in the months leading up to the American declaration of war. The Germans had little respect for American military prowess because the U.S. Army was small and the U.S. Navy wasn't ready for war. "What can [America] do?" German Gen. Erich Ludendorff dismissively asked a colleague. "She cannot come over here! I don't give a damn about America."

Indeed, when Congress declared war, some American leaders believed that the U.S. would mainly contribute naval and economic support for the Allied war effort. "You're not actually thinking of sending soldiers over there, are you?" one senator naively asked a general in April 1917. Soon reality set in. The only way to win the war was to send large numbers of soldiers to Europe, and this would require a massive mobilization that had a dramatic effect on the country.

Drafting men for war

After the declaration of war, hundreds of thousands of young men flocked to recruiting stations to join the armed forces. Still, the war effort needed more. In May 1917, Congress passed the Selective Service Act, in effect implementing a military draft.

About 10 million men between the ages of 21 and 30 registered for *selective service,* a benign term the Wilson administration used instead of the word *draft* with its coercive connotations. Of these 10 million men, the armed forces took 2.75 million into service. Overall, some 5 million Americans served in the military during World War I, so a little more than half were draftees.

The draft affected young, unmarried men the most — 90 percent of draftees were single. Married men, farmers, and essential war industries workers had a fairly easy time obtaining deferments from the draft.

Expanding the federal government

The wartime mobilization required an expansion in the size of the federal government. In June 1917, Wilson created the important War Industries Board (WIB) under Bernard Baruch, a wealthy financier and longtime supporter of the president. The WIB purchased military equipment, encouraged businesses to adopt mass-production techniques, and made it worthwhile to do so by dispensing lucrative federal contracts. The agency also allocated and rationed vital resources such as rubber, steel, and wood. The WIB was the single-most-important wartime agency.

Wilson created several other important agencies to run the war:

- ✔ The Fuel Administration regulated coal and oil prices as well as consumption of those two fuels. It also implemented daylight saving time, which is, of course, still with us today.

- ✔ The Food Administration oversaw the production and import of food not only to American soldiers but to the entire Allied world. By 1918, the U.S. was providing most of the food that the Allied population ate.

- ✔ The Committee on Public Information (CPI) sold war bonds, spread pro-war propaganda, and circulated anti-German stories, sometimes in Hollywood films. The ultimate goal of CPI was to keep public opinion in favor of the war.

The Food Administration was headed up by Herbert Hoover, a future president. Hoover succeeded in maximizing American food production and feeding America's allies, while avoiding rationing here at home. After the war, he organized food shipments for millions of hungry Europeans. Hoover's success with the Food Administration propelled him into a national political career, all the way to the Oval Office.

Gaining from the war

The American economy did very well during World War I. With the great demand for food, American farm production grew by 25 percent. Farmers made handsome profits by selling their crops to the government. Industrialists also found plenty of markets for such products as bullets, rifles, ships, locomotives, tin cans, and the like. For instance, American factories produced 20 million artillery shells for Allied armies. Overall, industrial production grew by one-third during the war years. All of this growth led to the creation of millions of jobs and a 20 percent rise in wages for the average American worker.

Hiring women to do "man's work"

The wartime mobilization of men into the military created economic opportunities for women. Many found white-collar work as clerks, secretaries, bookkeepers, and typists. Some worked on factory production lines in hard-hat jobs that had traditionally been done by men. A few thousand young women served overseas in relief agencies like the Red Cross. Thousands more served in the Army, mainly as nurses.

Female leaders hoped that the war would lead to greater economic, political, and cultural equality for women. But, when the war ended, so did opportunity for change. Quite commonly, women lost their jobs to returning veterans. The average American, male and female, still believed that a woman's proper place was in the home as a mother. The only significant long-term change that women earned from the war was the right to vote *(suffrage)*. In 1919, under intense pressure from idealist feminist reformers, Congress passed a national suffrage amendment to the Constitution, giving voting rights to American women.

Setting aside differences

During the war, the Committee on Public Information (CPI) made a special effort to reach out to minorities, especially blacks. Using the slogan "We're all in this together," the CPI encouraged all Americans to do their part to win the war. Most black Americans lived as second-class citizens, especially in the South. Racist *Jim Crow laws* prevented them from voting and segregated them from whites in almost every way imaginable.

With CPI's inclusive appeal, African Americans hoped that the war would lead to greater equality and justice. Half a million blacks left the South for the North, mainly in search of war-related jobs. They found greater economic opportunity than ever before. By 1920, 1.5 million blacks were working in northern factories. Although they made more money and earned greater benefits than ever before, they still did not enjoy any semblance of equality with whites.

Some 260,000 black men served in the segregated armed forces, mostly in all-black support units that were commanded by white officers. A few thousand black soldiers saw combat in France, but, reflecting white society's racist, erroneous belief that blacks would not fight, the vast majority of black servicemen worked in menial jobs as laborers, *stevedores* (people who load and unload ships), or *mess stewards* (waiters, kitchen staff, and cooks).

Opposing the war

Although World War I was a popular war, some Americans were against it. Some ethnic Germans felt an affinity for their original homeland and couldn't take up arms against it. They had to be very careful about voicing any opposition, though, or they risked being the targets of anti-German hysteria. During the war, Americans smashed German-language printing presses, eradicated the German language from schools, removed German books from libraries, and, at times, forced German Americans to pledge allegiance to or kiss the American flag to prove their loyalty.

Anti-German sentiment was so strong during the war that Americans came up with a new name for hamburgers because the word sounded too German. Instead they called them "liberty patties."

Socialists, Communists, anarchists, pacifists, and feminists also opposed the war on moral grounds. President Wilson was contemptuous of these dissenters. "What I am opposed to is not [their] feeling . . . but their stupidity. I want peace, but I know how to get it. They do not." The president signed two anti-dissent bills into law, the Espionage Act and the Sedition Amendment, both of which he used to jail about 1,500 antiwar activists. In so doing, he fostered a national mood of intolerance and fear.

Harry Truman in the Great War

Harry Truman was nearly 33 years old when the United States entered World War I. Before the war, he had gone to school part time and attempted to scratch out a living as a farmer in western Missouri. The future president didn't have to go to war, but decided to volunteer out of a sense of patriotism and duty. His eyesight was so poor that he had to memorize the eye chart to meet the physical standards for induction into the Army.

Truman joined the Missouri National Guard, earned an officer's commission, and rose to command of Battery D, 129th Field Artillery, 35th Infantry Division. He served in some of the most ferocious American battles in the fall of 1918. In combat, he commanded 194 soldiers and several artillery pieces. He soon earned a reputation as a steady, courageous commander, and his soldiers looked up to him. At times, his battery *bivouacked* (camped in the open) on battlefields that had been fought over for years. The sensitive Missourian wrote to his sweetheart (later his wife) Bess that he could almost feel the presence of those who had died "holding a sorrowful parade over the ruins" of those tattered battlefields.

The experience of war matured Truman and forever marked his view of humanity. For the rest of his life, he deplored the waste and savagery of war, but firmly believed that righteous wars can bring about a greater good for humanity.

Joining the Fray in Phases

Realistically, the U.S. could provide little significant military help to the Allies for about a year. It took more than 12 months to conscript, train, and send an army overseas. The Americans also had to learn to work with their British allies to counter the German submarine threat in the Atlantic, and that took time as well. Consequently, American soldiers didn't enter combat in any kind of substantial numbers until well into the spring of 1918.

Clearing the seas of German submarines

The German navy maintained a force of 32 to 36 submarines on patrol in the Atlantic. Their job was to sink so many Allied supply and troop ships that Britain would collapse and the United States would be marginalized. As of the spring of 1917, German subs were sinking a staggering 600,000 tons of shipping per month. At this rate, the Allies would lose the war.

At the urging of Adm. William Sims, commander of the U.S. Atlantic fleet, the Allies implemented an elaborate convoy system that was designed to protect the vulnerable, but valuable, ships that carried cargo and troops. Excellent submarine-killing ships, such as destroyers, now escorted the merchant ships across the Atlantic. Over time, the system turned the tide of the war in the Atlantic. Sinkings of merchant ships declined. Sinkings of German submarines increased. This important victory secured Britain's vital sea lanes and allowed the United States to ship a mass army to Europe.

Increasing the American presence in Europe

In a little more than one year, the United States Army expanded from a force of about 100,000 professional soldiers to a mass army of millions. The American presence in Europe in 1917 was a token force of 14,000 soldiers. One year later, that same detachment, known as the American Expeditionary Force (AEF), had ballooned to 1 million men and counting. At that point, 8,000 new American troops were entering France every day. Most still needed more training to be ready for the trenches, but at least they were there. By the fall of 1918, the AEF counted 2 million soldiers in its ranks.

The commander of this enormous army was Gen. John Pershing. He was known throughout the Army as "Black Jack" because he had once served in the 10th Cavalry Regiment, an African American unit. A thoughtful but prickly man, Pershing saw the AEF as the very embodiment of American national sovereignty.

In the spring of 1918, even as the AEF was arriving, the Germans launched a major offensive designed to win the war. They devised effective new tactics to breach the trenches and punched major holes in the Allied lines. French and British commanders desperately needed American manpower to replace their devastating losses. They pressured Pershing to feed his men piecemeal into the trenches wherever they were needed, under British or French commanders. But, even though Pershing was still dependent upon his allies to train and equip his newly arrived units, he refused. To him, the autonomy of his AEF was paramount. If the French and British wanted American help, they would have to deal with the U.S. as equals.

Engaging the enemy on the ground

By May 1918, the Germans had torn a 40- by 80-mile gap in the Allied lines. They were advancing west on a broad front through France, roughly from Arlon in the north to Amiens in the south. Both sides had suffered a quarter-million casualties in just over a month of fighting.

The Germans were engaged in a race against time. Germany was suffering from famine, massive casualties, war weariness, and manpower problems. But, with Russia out of the war, the German army in the West was strong enough to unleash this final push for victory. So the commanders were desperate to administer a knockout blow to the Allies before the Americans could seriously influence the fighting.

Cantigny, Chateau Thierry, and Belleau Wood

As of May, the Americans finally began to enter combat in large numbers (see Figure 14-2). Between May 28 and June 2, the 1st Infantry Division, one of the Army's most famous units, successfully counterattacked and captured the village of Cantigny, helping blunt the German offensive in Picardy province.

The 1st Infantry Division's nickname is the "Big Red One." One of its subunits, the 28th Infantry Regiment, earned the moniker "The Black Lions of Cantigny" for its valor in taking that town. Most unit members shorten the name to "Black Lions."

About 20 miles southwest of Cantigny, the Germans were on the move, attempting to capture Paris. In June, two U.S. Army divisions, the 2nd and 3rd, pushed the Germans back at Chateau Thierry, about 40 miles east of Paris. Nearby, the 5th and 6th Marine Regiments, collectively known as the "Devil Dogs," fought the Germans in a thick forest known as the Belleau Wood. The Marines were outnumbered four-to-one. Like two colliding rams, they attacked east as the Germans attacked west. At times they fought hand-to-hand with bayonets, an extremely rare phenomenon in modern combat. In one attack, Gunnery Sgt. Dan Daly, a man who earned *two* Medals of Honor, urged his men forward with a famous line: "Come on, . . . do you want to live forever?" By the end of June, the Germans were in headlong retreat to the east, away from Belleau Wood.

The Marines earned coast-to-coast headlines for their exploits at the Battle of Belleau Wood. Stories of Marine valor screamed from the front pages of many daily newspapers. Almost overnight, the Marine Corps went from an obscure, tiny force of maritime troops to the most famous and publicly admired of the armed services (see Chapter 4 for more on Marine Corps history). Army soldiers had also fought bravely at Belleau Wood, but they received little of the credit for victory. Soldiers accused the Marines of "cheap advertisement in order to glorify their own cause," and resented that the Marines got most of the glory. Believe it or not, the resentment continues to this day.

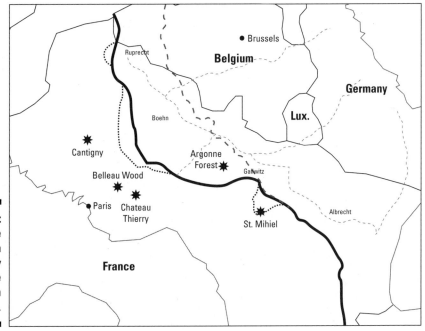

Figure 14-2: Map of the American Expeditionary Force on the western front, 1918.

Holding on at the Marne

After Belleau Wood, time had nearly run out for the Germans. Having suffered hundreds of thousands of casualties, the Germans possessed only enough strength for one last attempt to take Paris. They planned to push across the Marne River (where the French had stopped them four years before), swing west, and take Paris from that direction.

On July 15, at a key point on the Allied Marne River line, the German army launched powerful attacks against the U.S. Army's 3rd Infantry Division. Following a massive artillery bombardment, German soldiers hurled themselves at the 3rd Division trenches. All up and down the line, the Americans fought back with everything they had. They killed hundreds, perhaps even thousands, of enemy soldiers. In one sector, two full platoons (about 50 men to a platoon) literally fought to the last man, inflicting ruinous casualties on the attacking Germans.

By July 17, the German offensive was shattered. The Allies went on the counteroffensive, crossing the Marne River and chasing the Germans north and east, away from Paris. The French capital was saved, and the tide of the war had turned.

The 3rd Infantry Division's epic stand at the Marne River forever earned the unit the nickname "Rock of the Marne." Even today, when you enter the division's post at Fort Stewart, Georgia, the guards, instead of saying hello, greet you with the unit's unique identity: "Rock of the Marne, sir!"

Going on the offensive

After the Marne victory, the Allies were now clearly winning the war. With this new momentum, they began a series of attacks, pushing the Germans steadily east, closer to their border.

Gen. Pershing wanted to continue attacking east, overwhelm a German *salient* (the part of the battle line closest to the Allies) at St. Mihiel, knife into Germany, and take the town of Metz. He saw this as the first step in the ultimate conquest of Germany. However, his French and British colleagues wanted to push the Germans out of France first. They persuaded Pershing to participate in an all-Allied momentous offensive to overwhelm the Germans and kick them off French soil for good. For the AEF, this meant launching an offensive into the Argonne Forest, straight into a formidable network of German trench systems.

The Battle of Argonne Forest began on September 26, 1918, and lasted until November 11 of that same year. About 1.2 million American soldiers participated (see Figure 14-3). For them, the battle was beyond nightmarish. The weather was rainy and chilly. The forest dripped with menace. The ground was muddy and sloppy. For the soldiers, attacking meant venturing into kill zones, being exposed to artillery, mortar, machine gun, and rifle fire, plus some poison gas too. Troops were cold, sick, hungry, dirty, tired, and frightened out of their wits. The Americans steadily gained ground, but casualties were staggering. In one typical example, the 7th Infantry Regiment lost close to 2,300 men, out of an original strength of 3,000, in 28 days on the line. Even so, they were still receiving orders to attack.

Argonne Forest is the costliest battle in American military history. The AEF lost 26,277 men killed, more than 95,000 wounded, and an undetermined number of sick, shell-shocked, and missing men. Horrible though it was, the battle contributed to the eventual defeat of Germany.

Figure 14-3: After capturing a line of German trenches in Argonne Forest, American soldiers take a break from battle.

© CORBIS

The Imperfect Armistice

With the Allies relentlessly attacking and their armies swelling with American manpower, the Central Powers nations began collapsing, one after another. In late October, Austria-Hungary disintegrated, as did Bulgaria. Germany too was at the end of its endurance. Food shortages, political turmoil, and the failure of the 1918 offensives all led to a revolution in early November. Under pressure from a new democratic-style government called the Weimar Republic, the kaiser abdicated and fled to Holland.

The Weimar Republic negotiated an immediate *armistice* (or a truce called in anticipation of a peace treaty) with the Allies. It took effect at exactly 11:11 a.m. on November 11, 1918. This terrible war claimed the lives of 10 million people, including 110,000 Americans.

When the new German government concluded the armistice, it hoped to negotiate a binding peace treaty on the basis of President Wilson's Fourteen Points. Instead, the Allied powers met in 1919 at Versailles, just outside of Paris, and dictated harsh peace terms to a weak Germany that had little choice but to accept them. These terms were known as the Treaty of Versailles. Wilson was against the harsh treaty, but he found himself overruled time and again by his British and French allies, who thought the draconian treaty would prevent Germany from ever threatening its European neighbors again.

The Treaty of Versailles imposed the following terms:

- ✓ Germany was blamed for the outbreak of the war as a justification for its punishment.

- ✓ Germany lost one-tenth of its land and population to France, Poland, and several other European countries.

- ✓ Germany lost all of its colonies. They mostly went to Britain and Japan.

- ✓ Germany would abolish its navy and air force, and cut its army to a mere 100,000 soldiers.

- ✓ Germany would pay $33 billion worth of *reparations* (money paid by a losing country to the victors to offset their economic losses) to the Allies, primarily the French.

The Treaty of Versailles was the kind of peace agreement that could be dictated and enforced only by total victors, but the Allies had earned only a partial victory in this war. They had not conquered Germany. Nor had they even forced the surrender of Germany's armed forces. This meant that, in the long run, they would have difficulty enforcing the treaty's severe provisions. It also guaranteed that a resentful Germany would someday seek to *redress,* or avenge, what Germans perceived as an unjust peace agreement. Thus, the real tragedy of World War I was that it did not solve enough of the issues that had led to war in the first place. Instead, it was only the bloody precursor to a far more terrible war fought by the next generation.

Chapter 15

The Looming Crisis: World War II before American Involvement

*W*orld War II is considered the most devastating war human beings have ever fought. It is probably the most cataclysmic event in the history of humankind. By even the most conservative estimates, it cost the lives of 62 million people. The war affected more than half of the globe's population at that time. World War II included the deliberate fire bombing of cities and civilians, the advent of nuclear weapons, the total mobilization of warring societies, titanic amphibious invasions, the conquest of weak nations, and the systematic extermination of millions of human beings in both Europe and Asia.

In short, World War II is a story of enormous drama and tragedy. So why did it happen? To a great extent, World War II grew from the problems left unresolved after World War I with the Treaty of Versailles (for more details, see Chapter 14). That treaty ended World War I, but it punished Germany severely, creating a great deal of resentment, plus a shaky economy and government in that country. At the same time, a rising industrial Japan, craving resources, wanted to conquer a large empire in Asia and the Pacific, thus challenging a shaky balance of power that the United States hoped to preserve. Britain and France were so devastated by World War I that they had difficulty summoning the strength to enforce the tenuous peace that followed that war. Two other major powers, Soviet Russia and the United States, were deeply preoccupied with their own domestic affairs and thus chose to remain aloof from these growing European problems until it was too late.

In this chapter, I trace the rise of aggressive, conquest-minded Fascist movements in Germany, Italy, and Japan. I explain how those movements directly challenged peace and stability, ultimately plunging the world into a ruinous war. Finally, I outline how the United States became involved in a war that most of its citizens hoped to avoid.

Reacting to Unrest, Fascism Emerges

No one was really happy with the outcome of World War I. In general, the citizens of the Allied countries mourned their millions of dead and vowed to avoid future war at nearly any cost. Some Allied nations even felt betrayed by the Treaty of Versailles. Italy, for instance, felt that it didn't receive the territory its Allied partners promised for entering the war on their side. The United States was deeply disillusioned by its participation in the war, mainly because of the flawed peace that followed. By far, the Germans were the most disaffected of all. The average German hated the Treaty of Versailles that cost Germany one-tenth of its land and population, all of its colonies, and most of its armed forces. Plus, the treaty forced Germany to pay expensive reparations to the Allies, and this stunted German economic growth.

This unhappy situation proved to be an ideal breeding ground for an ideology called *Fascism.* Fascists believed in total government control of society — no freedom of speech, worship, assembly, or dissent — just absolute state control for the common good. To Fascists, the individual meant nothing. The collective was everything, especially the nation-state. Fascists also believed that some races, or ethnic groups, were inherently superior to others. In their view, some people were naturally strong and others were naturally weak. Moreover, the strong must survive at the expense of the weak. Fascism stood for might-makes-right, conquest, and an end to parliamentary democracy, natural human rights, capitalism, and common decency. Fascism appealed to disaffected youths who yearned for security, power, and a sense of belonging to a mass movement.

Difficult economic times helped Fascist parties come to power in Italy in 1922 and Germany in 1933. The German Fascists were known as the Nazis, an acronym for National Socialist German Worker's Party. The Nazi Party originated as a tiny, ultranationalist political group in southern Germany in the early 1920s. By the early 1930s, when a serious economic depression gripped Germany, the Nazis had steadily grown into a large, powerful entity, appealing to millions of Germans at a time of high unemployment and deep anxiety. This was their path to power in 1933. In Europe, the two prominent Fascist leaders were Benito Mussolini in Italy and Adolf Hitler in Germany.

Mussolini rises to power

Mussolini was a World War I veteran and former Socialist, who formed the Italian Fascist Party after the war. In 1922, with civil war a real threat in Italy during a period of deep economic crisis, he came to power because his political rivals viewed his Fascists as a better alternative to Communism. Once in power, Mussolini and his party gradually assumed total control of the government.

Hitler slithers up the career ladder

Adolf Hitler also came to power peacefully. Like Mussolini, he had fought in World War I, although he saw much more combat than Mussolini ever did. An ardent German nationalist, Hitler was devastated by Germany's defeat. He joined the Nazi Party, quickly assumed control of it, and dedicated his life to politics.

In 1923, after an abortive attempt to take over the German government, Hitler decided that he would win power peacefully from within, then destroy democracy once in power. Starting in 1933, when he became chancellor, the number-one post in German government (see Figure 15-1), this was exactly what he did. He and his Nazis ruled Germany with the following popular ideas:

- Restore Germany to its rightful place as a military colossus and leading world power.
- Reject the Treaty of Versailles.
- Use a public works project to rejuvenate the German economy.
- Persecute the Jews. Hitler and the Nazis were deeply hateful anti-Semites. They despised Jews and believed them to be the ultimate enemies of European civilization. These beliefs were widely held in Germany and Europe at that time.
- Conquer a vast German empire in Europe. This was, of course, a secret agenda, but it was Hitler's long-term plan.

Hitler was actually born in Austria, not Germany. As a young man, his greatest ambition in life was to become an artist. He twice applied to and failed to get into the prestigious Academy of Fine Arts in Vienna. Because anyone wanting to become a successful artist in Austria at that time needed this kind of formal training, his career as an artist was over before it started. He ended up on the streets of Vienna, living an aimless life, painting postcards for tourists. His dead-end life only concluded with the start of World War I, when he joined the German army.

Figure 15-1: Adolf Hitler became chancellor of Germany in 1933.

Itching for War, Germany Rearms and Expands

Of the two Fascist dictators, Hitler was by far the more dangerous for two reasons. First, he was much more committed to conquest and repression than Mussolini. Second, Germany was inherently more powerful than Italy because of Germany's industry, economy, military traditions, and educated population. Once in power, Hitler wasted little time in defying the Treaty of Versailles, rearming Germany, and agitating for the return of territory Germany had lost because of the treaty. From 1935 to 1938, Germany grew stronger militarily, and as that happened, Hitler became steadily more provocative:

- **March 1935:** Hitler announced that Germany would begin building an air force and expanding its army.
- **March 1936:** Hitler sent troops into the Rhineland, a western section of Germany that the Treaty of Versailles had demilitarized.
- **August 1936:** Hitler secretly began planning for war.

- **November 1937:** Hitler informed his generals that Germany would soon launch an aggressive war of conquest.
- **March 1938:** Hitler invaded and annexed Austria without firing a shot. Most Austrians didn't resist because they favored the annexation.

The infamous Munich Agreement

As Hitler's Germany made all of these aggressive moves in the 1930s, the British and French were content to stand aside and watch. The political leaders of those countries, most notably Neville Chamberlain of Britain, believed in a policy called *appeasement*. Knowing that the Treaty of Versailles had been unfair, they would not fight to enforce it. They wanted to avoid war at all costs, so they chose to appease Hitler by giving him what he wanted in exchange for peace.

In the summer of 1938, Hitler made new demands that led to a serious war scare in Europe. He demanded that democratic Czechoslovakia, a nation created by the Treaty of Versailles, return a province called the Sudetenland back to Germany. The Sudetenland was primarily composed of ethnic Germans and had once been part of Germany, but the Allies had given it to Czechoslovakia after World War I. Hitler made it very clear that if he did not get the Sudetenland through diplomacy, he would invade it and take it.

The Czechs were determined to hold on to the Sudetenland. Czechoslovakia had an alliance with France so, if the Germans did invade, the French (and probably Britain) would be compelled to declare war on Germany. Wanting to avoid this, Chamberlain and Edouard Daladier, the French premier, engaged in a series of negotiations with Hitler. On September 29, 1938, they met with Hitler in Munich. Over the course of two days, they gave him everything he wanted and more. The Munich Agreement prevented war but at the terrible price of betraying a democratic ally. Hitler had pledged that the Sudetenland would be his last territorial demand, but six months later, he broke the Munich Agreement and swallowed up major portions of Czechoslovakia.

The post-Munich perspectives of three key leaders tell us a lot about the tragedy of what happened there:

- **Neville Chamberlain** returned to England to tell a cheering crowd that the Munich Agreement would mean "peace for our time." He also expressed the opinion that Hitler could be trusted to keep his word.
- **Hitler** was angry at the outcome of the conference because he actually wanted war. He was also deeply contemptuous of Chamberlain, a man he thought of as a weakling "who spoke the ridiculous jargon of an outmoded

democracy." Hitler fantasized about jumping on Chamberlain's stomach in front of photographers.

✔ **Winston Churchill,** the one major politician in Britain who spoke out against the Munich Agreement and appeasement in general, made a gloomy, but chillingly accurate prediction. "We have suffered a total and unmitigated defeat. . . . Czechoslovakia will be engulfed in the Nazi regime. . . . Do not suppose that this is the end. This is only the beginning of the reckoning."

The Nazi-Soviet Pact

In 1939, with the ink hardly dry on the Munich Agreement, Hitler began badgering Poland to return the Danzig Corridor, a slice of territory Germany had lost to Poland because of the Treaty of Versailles. The bitter aftermath of the Munich Conference had finally taught Chamberlain that negotiations with Hitler were pointless. He announced that Britain was preparing for war and would fight alongside Poland if Hitler invaded the Danzig Corridor. France did the same.

Hitler was skeptical that the Western powers would really go to war over Poland. But, just in case, he signed a nonaggression treaty, known as the Nazi-Soviet Pact, with the Soviet Union on August 23. This prevented the Russians from allying themselves with the British and French against Germany, as had happened in World War I (see Chapter 14 for more). Even though Nazi Germany and Communist Russia were bitter ideological enemies, at this point they both found it convenient to remain at peace with each other. In a secret and very cynical clause in the pact, the Germans and Soviets agreed to carve up Poland and the Baltic States between them.

Hitler approved the pact to give himself a free hand to invade Poland and then fight the Western powers without any interference from the Soviets. Josef Stalin, the Soviet leader, signed the pact because his country wasn't prepared for war. Plus, he knew that the pact's secret provisions would give Russia some significant territorial gains.

Bringing the Axis to Bear, War Breaks Out

Bolstered by the Nazi-Soviet Pact, in late August Hitler increased his pressure on Poland to give him the Danzig Corridor. The Poles, knowing what had happened to the Czechs the year before, refused to comply. By now Hitler's appetite for war was considerable. He wanted to make Germany the domi-nant power in Europe (and after that, the world), and he believed Poland was the first step toward that goal. He rejected a new round of peace-minded diplomacy from the Western powers and ordered his troops into Poland on September 1, 1939. Two days later, Britain and France declared war on Germany. As in World War I, their side was known as the *Allies*. The German side in this war was known as the *Axis*. World War II in Europe had begun.

When the war broke out, President Franklin D. Roosevelt immediately declared that the United States would remain neutral. Polls showed that 99 percent of the American people favored this neutrality. A full 70 percent thought that U.S. involvement in World War I had been a mistake. The vast majority of Americans sympathized with the Allies but didn't want to get involved in another European war.

Overrunning Poland

The German army was larger, more mechanized, and better trained than the Polish army. Plus, the Germans possessed a premier air force (known as the *Luftwaffe*) that could bomb Polish cities or *strafe* (fire machine guns or cannon from low-flying planes) Polish troops. Consequently, when the Germans invaded Poland, they overwhelmed the Polish defenders in the border areas and advanced rapidly, deep into Poland.

The Jewish ghettos

The German conquest of Poland took Nazi anti-Semitic policies to a new level when 3 million Polish Jews came under their control. Almost immediately, the Germans began separating Jews from the rest of the population. In some cases, German troops rounded up Jews and shot them.

In 1940, the German authorities began herding hundreds of thousands of Polish Jews into badly crowded ghettos in the country's largest cities. Isolated from the outside world, the ghettos were rife with disease, hunger, and desperation. In this way, the Nazis hoped to gradually kill off the Jews.

By the late spring of 1941, 2,000 Jews a day were dying in the Warsaw Ghetto alone. Not content with this death rate, the Germans built extermina-tion camps in Poland and began deporting Jews to these camps from the ghettos and all over Europe. Knowing the realities of the death camps, in 1943, the Jews of the Warsaw Ghetto rose up. The Nazis crushed the uprising.

Two modern movies, *Schindler's List* and *The Pianist*, portray Jewish ghetto life in Poland quite well.

The Poles fought valiantly but they were overmatched. The British and French were too far away to provide much help to their Polish allies. To make matters worse, on September 17, the Soviets, acting on the secret protocols in the Nazi-Soviet Pact, invaded eastern Poland. By October 1, the Russians and Germans had conquered Poland, beginning a long ordeal of foreign occupation for the Polish people. Proportionally, no population suffered more in World War II. Six million Poles, half of them Jews, were to die in this war.

The German conquest of Europe

After the fighting ended in Poland, nothing much happened in 1939. The British and French were content to build up their forces and wait for the Germans to make the first move in the West. Soldiers on both sides started calling this "The Phony War," but it soon got very real.

In April 1940, the Germans successfully invaded Denmark and Norway. This secured Germany's iron ore lifeline in the Atlantic and gave them numerous naval and air bases. The major blow came on May 10, 1940, when the Germans launched an all-out offensive against the British and the French in the West. The Germans invaded and conquered neutral Holland, Belgium, and Luxembourg (see Figure 15-2). They also plunged into France.

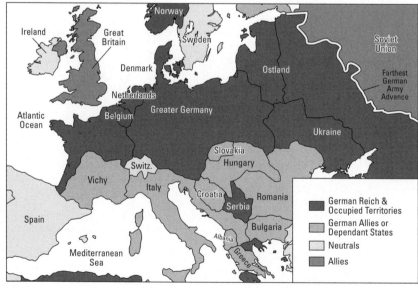

Figure 15-2:
Map showing Germany's occupation of much of Europe in 1940 and 1941.

The Germans devised an elaborate plan to defeat the western Allies. The German army in the West had 3.3 million soldiers divided into three major army groups. One group held fast on the common border with France. To the north, another invaded Belgium and Holland, drawing major Allied reinforcements into that country. A third German army group knifed through the Ardennes Forest, breeched a thinly held section of the French line, and advanced deep into France, all the way to the English Channel in ten days. This cut off all Allied soldiers in Belgium. Rather than lose their whole army, the British evacuated more than 300,000 soldiers from Dunkirk back to England. The Germans followed up this victory by conquering the rest of France, including Paris.

France surrendered on June 25, 1940. Most military analysts had expected another slow-moving, trench-style war in the West, similar to World War I, so the fall of France absolutely stunned the world. Hoping to feast on the spoils of German success, Mussolini's Italy entered the war on the Axis side. Nazi Germany and its allies now dominated most of the European continent.

Flushed with victory, Hitler in the summer of 1940 offered to make peace with Britain, provided the British would acquiesce to German control of Europe. The British refused. By now, Churchill had come to power as prime minister. Defiant and stubborn, he represented a new fighting resolve in the British people. Hitler responded to this defiance by promising to invade Britain.

As a prelude to invasion, Hitler launched major air attacks against Britain's cities and its Royal Air Force. In these air battles, known as the Battle of Britain, the Royal Air Force battled the Luftwaffe to a standstill. This saved Britain from invasion but, in practical terms, the British could do little on their own to challenge German supremacy in Europe. To do that, they would need allies.

Hitler invades the Soviet Union

By the end of 1940, Hitler had decided to betray the Nazi-Soviet Pact and invade the Soviet Union. In early 1941, he massed 3.2 million German soldiers along the common frontier with the Soviets. He enlisted the help of Fascist Romania, Italy, and Hungary for his plan. He also persuaded Finland to join him. Stalin's spies, numerous diplomats, and British intelligence operatives all sniffed out German intentions, but the Soviet dictator refused to believe that Hitler would attack the Soviet Union.

Hitler decided to invade for the following reasons:

- He was concerned that, given time, the Soviets would get stronger and one day attack Germany.

✔ He believed that the British were essentially defeated in the West, freeing him to attack the Soviet Union in the East.

✔ His master plan for Germany was to conquer vast amounts of living space *(lebensraum)* in Russia, at the expense of people he considered racially inferior.

✔ He wanted to eliminate Communism in Russia.

✔ He wanted to fight a racial war of extermination and enslavement against the Russians, Ukrainians, and Jews who populated the western part of the Soviet Union.

On June 22, 1941, the invasion began, thus initiating the largest, most destructive, ruthless war in human history. Throughout the summer and fall of 1941, the German *juggernaut* (a relentless, destructive force) crashed through eastern Poland, Ukraine, and deep into Russia. The Germans battered outclassed Soviet units with a combination of air, armor, and traditional infantry attacks. They encircled and captured hundreds of thousands of Soviet soldiers. By October, Soviet Red Army losses were in the millions, but German losses were heavy too. They suffered 900,000 casualties in 1941 alone.

Hitler believed he was on the verge of conquering Russia but, as fall turned into winter, subzero temperatures, supply problems, and stiffening Soviet resistance stopped the Germans just short of Moscow. The Germans had captured hundreds of miles of territory and had wounded the Russians. However, the Soviet Union was anything but conquered. The war in the East would now turn into a long struggle that favored the Soviets because of their nearly limitless manpower. Moreover, Germany was now facing enemies west and east. Although Churchill was no friend of Communism, he was happy to make common cause with the manpower-rich Soviet Union against Nazi Germany. "If Hitler invaded hell," Churchill said, "I should at least make a favorable reference to the devil in the House of Commons."

When the Germans invaded the Soviet Union, they immediately set in motion Hitler's blueprint for a racial war of extermination. The Germans starved, neglected, tortured, and worked Soviet POWs to death. Any civilians who didn't cooperate with the Germans were enslaved or shot. German army units and special SS death squads rounded up hundreds of thousands of Jews and shot them to death in mass executions. For instance, in September 1941, the Germans, over the course of three days, systematically executed 33,000 Jews at Babi Yar, just outside of Kiev. This kind of thing went on all over German-occupied Russia during that summer and fall of 1941 (see Figure 15-3). Ultimately, the Germans scaled down the executions and instead shipped Jews and other "undesirables" to death camps in Poland, where they were either gassed to death or worked as slaves.

Figure 15-3:
A member of the German SS, Einsatz Gruppen D, prepares to shoot a Polish Jew who is kneeling on the edge of a mass grave almost filled with victims.

© *CORBIS*

Fighting an undeclared war in the Atlantic

The German victories of 1940 and 1941 sent a collective shiver down the American spine. At the outset of war, most Americans complacently counted on the British and French to keep Germany at bay. Hitler's conquest of Europe served as wake-up call of sorts. The American people still didn't want to enter the war, but they now thought it prudent to prepare for war, just in case. President Roosevelt was a great proponent of this "short of war" policy. He had run for and won an unprecedented third term in the White House because he was so deeply concerned with the creeping threat resulting from Axis victories in Europe.

Roosevelt's government implemented the following policies, all designed to help the Allies as much as possible and prepare the U.S. for war:

- ✔ He traded 50 old warships — submarine hunters known as destroyers — to Britain for basing rights in the Caribbean.

- ✔ He and the Congress passed the first peacetime draft in U.S. history.

- ✔ He approved a massive naval rearmament program.

- ✔ He implemented Lend-Lease, a policy of direct military aid to Britain and the Allies.

Heinrich Himmler

One of the war's oddest but most sinister figures was Heinrich Himmler. As head of the *Schutzstaffel* (or SS), Himmler wielded enormous power in the Nazi empire. The SS was made up of the most committed Nazis. They were the concentration camp guards, the secret police, the executioners, the bureaucrats, and the elite soldiers of Hitler's Germany.

Himmler was a slightly built, bespectacled, unimposing figure who had been a chicken farmer before joining the Nazi party in the early 1920s. By 1942, his power was second only to Hitler's.

Himmler and the SS implemented the so-called *Final Solution,* the enslavement and extermination of millions of people in occupied Europe. An amateur astrologist who was fascinated with the occult, he dreamed of creating a German super-race to rule Europe. Himmler even started a breeding program that coupled racially "pure" SS men with similar German women to produce the Nazi demigods of tomorrow.

At the end of the war, Himmler was captured by the British, but succeeded in committing suicide while in custody.

Lend-Lease revealed that the U.S. was neutral in name only, because the Americans were doing everything they could to help the Allies, short of entering the war themselves. By the late spring of 1941, the U.S. Navy was escorting Lend-Lease supplies to British waters. At the same time, German submarines were attempting to strangle Great Britain by cutting off its shipping lifeline to its overseas empire and America.

By summertime, the U.S. Navy was actually fighting an undeclared war with the German navy in the Atlantic. Sometimes the Americans even traded shots with the Germans. The Germans torpedoed several American ships, most notably the USS *Reuben James* which sank on October 31, with the loss of 115 American sailors.

In spite of these naval clashes, neither Germany nor the U.S. declared war in the fall of 1941 because the timing wasn't right. President Roosevelt knew the United States was unprepared. He also understood that, in spite of American Navy casualties, the country was not yet in favor of another war with the Germans. For his part, Hitler was deeply absorbed with his war in Russia at the time and felt that, if and when Russia was conquered, he could take care of the United States in his own good time. Although he had little fear of the United States, he saw no reason to provoke war with the Americans just yet.

Brewing Trouble in Asia and the Pacific

Just as things were heating up in Europe in the 1930s, over in Asia, Japan was at a crossroads. Decades of industrialization had turned the country into a significant military and economic power. But without such resources as oil, rubber, iron ore, tin, and bauxite (needed to make aluminum), Japan would always be dependent on the European colonial empires of Asia and the United States for these resources. In order for Japan to achieve autonomy and first-class status, it had to acquire resources in Asia and the Pacific — probably by conquest — but this might mean war with the Western powers because they all favored the status quo.

The Japanese government was dominated by a ruling clique of military officers, industrialists, and aristocrats who yearned for imperial greatness. Many of them embraced a Fascist belief in Japanese racial superiority and a national destiny of Far Eastern domination. Presiding over this aggressive mix of personalities was Emperor Hirohito, a godlike, distant figure who guided national policies but did not wield everyday power in the same fashion that Hitler did in Germany. Together these leaders undertook an adventurous series of expansionist moves in Asia that eventually led to war with the United States.

Japan starts its own war by invading China

In 1931, Japan, coveting resources, invaded Manchuria, a province that belonged to China. The Chinese had difficulty defending Manchuria because China was behind the Japanese in weaponry, economics, and industry. Also, China was wracked with internal political differences that weakened Chinese military effectiveness. Thus, the Japanese easily conquered Manchuria against little resistance.

Six years later, in July 1937, the Japanese expanded this Sino-Japanese War dramatically by invading the rest of China. The Japanese army conquered major portions of the country, including the key seaports of Shanghai and Canton. Japanese troops generally behaved with ruthlessness and ferocity in an effort to cow the Chinese population into submission.

The main resistance to the Japanese came from the Nationalist Chinese (Kuomintang Party) and the Communist Chinese. The Kuomintang were pro-American and they controlled major portions of the country, but they were corrupt and, at times, militarily inept. The Communists were small in number but formidable and ruthless in battle. The Japanese knew they couldn't hope to beat both of these groups and conquer the whole country. They simply wanted to control the most resource-rich portions of China while keeping their Chinese enemies at bay.

The U.S. drifts steadily toward war

Throughout the 1930s, most Americans disapproved of Japanese actions in China, but they weren't willing to do anything about them. Mired in the Great Depression and disillusioned by the nation's involvement in World War I, the American people wanted no part of any overseas war. President Roosevelt was much more concerned about Japanese actions than the average citizen, but he could do little in the face of such overwhelmingly isolationist sentiment. Indeed, in 1937, when Japanese planes sank an American gunboat in Chinese waters, killing three Americans, the American government settled for a half-hearted apology from the Japanese.

Roosevelt funneled small amounts of military and financial aid to the Chinese, but he was hampered by a series of neutrality laws Congress had passed between 1935 and 1937. These laws were designed to keep the United States out of future wars. They forbade Americans from selling arms to nations at war and also from traveling on their ships.

By 1940, after years of Japanese atrocities in China, relations between the United States and Japan were very tense. American public opinion was quite anti-Japanese, but very few people favored any sort of intervention in China. Still, the U.S. was preparing for war, just in case. The Roosevelt administration was now determined to rein in the Japanese. In a best-case scenario, the president hoped to force a Japanese withdrawal from China. But, at the very least, he wanted to prevent them from expanding anywhere else.

The Rape of Nanking

In December 1937, the Japanese captured Nanking, the Nationalist Chinese capital. In the two months that followed, they engaged in a shockingly barbaric spree of atrocities known to history as the Rape of Nanking.

They beheaded prisoners, buried people up to their necks and watched as wild dogs tore them apart, and stood people up against walls and fired at them with machine guns. They raped many of the city's women, from children to the elderly. In some instances, Japanese soldiers gang raped young women to death and then dismembered their bodies, cooked them, and ate them. Japanese officers competed to see who could chop off the most Chinese heads. Other soldiers nailed their victim's tongues to walls or incinerated them in makeshift bonfires. Some perpetrators even disemboweled pregnant women.

Western diplomats, politicians, missionaries, and businessmen who had lived in Nanking for years saw and documented many of these atrocities. Some of these Westerners offered sanctuary to as many terrified Chinese as they could. The Rape of Nanking, and many other Japanese atrocities in China, left a legacy of bitterness between the two countries that remains to this day.

When the Germans conquered France, they left a pro-German government in place to govern France's overseas colonies. This government, known as the *Vichy French,* was weak and could do little to defend France's colonies in the southeast Asian countries of Laos, Cambodia, and Vietnam. Knowing this, the Japanese forced the Vichy French to allow them basing and transit rights in northern Vietnam. Deeply disturbed by this new Japanese expansion, the Roosevelt administration responded with a formal oil and steel embargo against Japan. From this point forward, the two nations began a steady drift toward war.

Failed negotiations

Roosevelt hoped that his combination of economic sanctions and diplomatic negotiations would force the Japanese to withdraw from China and abandon their plans for empire. The Japanese wanted to force the Americans to end the sanctions and accept Japan's new empire as a reality. Throughout 1940 and 1941, diplomats from both countries held numerous talks, but they accomplished nothing. For either nation to back down would have meant humiliation. The Japanese were determined to upset the balance of power in Asia, and the United States would never agree to this change.

In July 1941, the Japanese took over all of Vietnam. In response, Roosevelt intensified the embargo, depriving Japan of 90 percent of its oil supply. He also froze Japanese assets in the U.S., a course of action that was one or two steps short of declaring war. The U.S. had now effectively pushed the Japanese into a corner. They could either give in to American wishes or they could go to war. Diplomatic negotiations continued throughout the fall of 1941 but, as before, they were totally unproductive.

The Japanese leadership — generals, politicians, and the emperor — held a fateful meeting on September 6, 1941. They decided that, if in two months the United States did not lift its embargo and retreat from its demands, Japan would go to war. They would then launch a daring series of surprise attacks on the Western nations, the most prominent of which would be an air attack against the American Pacific Fleet at Pearl Harbor, Hawaii. The Japanese plan was basic. They would attack the Dutch-controlled East Indies, British-controlled Malaya, the American-controlled Philippines, and Pearl Harbor all at the same time. In the process, the Japanese planned to deliver such devastating blows to the Western powers that they would be hopelessly crippled for the immediate future. Japan then hoped to negotiate peace with a wounded America that would presumably have little stomach for fighting its way across the Pacific in order to deny Japan its empire.

Two months later, nothing had changed so, on November 25, the Japanese leaders decided to go to war and set their plan in motion. For America, World War II was about to begin.

Ever since the Japanese attack on Pearl Harbor, conspiracy theorists have claimed that President Roosevelt knew of the Japanese plans and let them happen in order to mobilize public opinion for American entry into the war. Over the years, no less than half a dozen major books have made this claim, mostly on the basis of circumstantial evidence. Not one conspiracy advocate has ever produced any concrete proof of any conspiracy or any foreknowledge of Pearl Harbor on Roosevelt's part. So what's the verdict of history? In the view of most responsible military historians, Pearl Harbor resulted from American intelligence failures, not from any sort of conspiracy.

Chapter 16

The Greatest War: World War II

*W*orld War II was the biggest, most complex war the United States has ever fought, with Americans fighting all over the world, from remote South Pacific jungles to the North Atlantic. Winning the war required a total mobilization of American resources and manpower, affecting nearly everyone. Servicemen risked their lives in some of the bloodiest battles ever fought. On the home front, civilians experienced rationing and wartime shortages of such valued items as butter, gasoline, sugar, and tobacco. But the folks at home also enjoyed a booming economy. The country was united as never before or since.

The country was also unprepared for the war. For instance, in 1939, two years before the U.S. entered the war, the U.S. Army ranked behind the Romanian army in overall numbers. After Pearl Harbor, Americans began the painful process of mobilizing for war, learning how to fight a modern conflict, and standing up to the most powerful enemies the country had ever faced. Along the way, this massive war changed the country in ways no other event ever has.

In this chapter, I discuss the important battles, in both Europe and the Pacific. I explain what the battles were like, why they turned out the way they did, and their ultimate significance. Finally, I tell you how the war affected Americans at home. And if this chapter heightens your curiosity about the war, pick up *World War II For Dummies* by Keith D. Dickson (Wiley).

Bringing the War Home: Pearl Harbor

The morning of December 7, 1941, appeared to be like most other mornings at Pearl Harbor, Hawaii, home to the U.S. Pacific Fleet. But under strict secrecy, a Japanese fleet of six aircraft carriers sailed to within 300 miles of the Hawaiian Islands. On that sleepy Sunday morning, the fleet launched its planes.

The first wave of these planes achieved complete surprise. In a matter of seconds, their bombs battered the USS *Arizona*. She rolled over and sank, ending the lives of more than 1,000 sailors and Marines. Elsewhere, Japanese planes hit and sank four other American battleships, plus numerous smaller vessels. They also destroyed 164 planes, mostly on the ground. By the time the Japanese onslaught finally subsided, 2,335 Americans were dead and another 1,178 wounded. The attack stunned the American people, but it brought them together as no other event could. The country now burned with war fever and a serious hankering for revenge against Japan.

Sixty-eight of the Americans who died in the Pearl Harbor attack were civilians. Some were killed by Japanese bomb shrapnel or machine gun bullets, but most were killed by American antiaircraft shells fired from the docked ships. As the shells exploded, their fragments cascaded onto land rather than into the open sea, killing the unfortunate bystanders.

When Japan decided to go to war with the U.S. and its allies, the Japanese planned to launch an all-out offensive in so many places that their enemies would be overwhelmed. They expected to conquer such a vast Pacific empire, along with the resources they coveted, such as oil and iron ore, that the U.S. would have to make peace rather than fight a ruinous, long war. So when the war started for America on December 7, 1941, Japanese planes, ships, and troops attacked in the following places:

- ✔ British-controlled Hong Kong, Malaya, and Burma
- ✔ The Dutch East Indies
- ✔ New Guinea and the Solomon Islands in the South Pacific
- ✔ Guam and Wake Island
- ✔ The Philippines
- ✔ The Gilbert and Marshall island chains

On December 8, President Franklin Roosevelt addressed a joint session of Congress. He denounced the Japanese for their surprise attack, referred to December 7 as a "date which will live in infamy," and asked for a declaration of war. Congress was happy to oblige, turning in a nearly unanimous vote. The only dissenter was Congresswoman Jeanette Rankin, a pacifist isolationist from Montana.

A couple days later, Adolf Hitler, Germany's head of state and supreme commander of the armed forces, declared war on the United States. Benito Mussolini, the Fascist Italian prime minister, soon followed. The U.S. was now part of a two-front war. Germany, Japan, and Italy headlined the Axis powers. The United States, Britain, and the Soviet Union led the Allies. Roosevelt and Winston Churchill, Britain's prime minister, agreed that, as the strongest of all the Axis powers, Germany must be defeated first. This was the primary Allied grand strategy vision of World War II.

In the final analysis, the attack on Pearl Harbor was a tactical success, but a strategic failure. Tactics have to do with how a war is fought; strategy encompasses why a war is fought (see Chapter 3 for more). The consequences of Pearl Harbor were:

✔ The Japanese achieved complete surprise. They crippled the U.S. fleet but did not destroy it.

✔ The Japanese failed to destroy the Navy's submarine pens and fuel storage areas, as well as its aircraft carriers, which happened to be elsewhere on the day of the attack.

✔ Pearl Harbor united the American people and ended *isolationism* (America's preoccupation with domestic affairs at the expense of events overseas). A united America is a formidable America, and Americans were determined to win the war. The Japanese would not get their short war and negotiated settlement. Instead, Pearl Harbor guaranteed a long war that was more advantageous to the United States.

Early Battles in the Pacific

After the Japanese attack on Pearl Harbor, the Allies saw disaster after disaster during the first six months of the war in the Pacific. The Japanese were on the attack all over what is referred to as the *Pacific Theater,* from the Asian mainland to the South Pacific (as you can see in Figure 16-1). They even invaded and overran the Philippines. Not until the summer of 1942 did the Americans halt Japanese momentum and begin a slow turning of the tide.

The Philippines

Within a few hours of the Pearl Harbor attack, Japanese planes bombed the Philippines. Amphibious invaders soon followed. Gen. Douglas MacArthur, the American commander in the Philippines, presided over a force that was unique in American history. Because the Philippines was an American colony, he controlled a mixed army of 100,000 Filipinos and 30,000 Americans.

MacArthur had spent years building this army, and he was emotionally attached to it, as well as to the people of the Philippines.

Perhaps MacArthur's emotions clouded his judgment. He thought his army could defend the coastlines against the Japanese invaders, but this coastal force failed utterly. The Japanese easily overran the poorly armed and trained Filipino soldiers. Even worse, the Japanese destroyed half of MacArthur's air force on the ground in the first hours of the war, in spite of the fact that the general knew several hours before the Japanese attack that the U.S. had been drawn into war and such an attack was imminent. This was an inexcusable command screw-up on MacArthur's part. From that point on, the enemy controlled the skies over the Philippines.

MacArthur finally managed to retreat with most of his army to the Bataan Peninsula where he hoped to hold out until help arrived from the States. But that help never came. At this stage, the unprepared U.S. was still staggering under the weight of multiple Japanese blows. For instance, the Navy, in the wake of Pearl Harbor, didn't have the ships, planes, or manpower to save MacArthur. The awful reality was that his army was doomed. They were cut off from the outside world, living in the hills of Bataan, holding off the attacking Japanese. Allied soldiers existed on half rations, then quarter rations, and even ate monkeys and insects. Tropical diseases also ravaged the ranks.

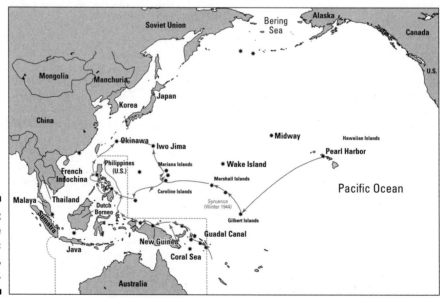

Figure 16-1:
Map of the Pacific Theater, 1942–1945.

The army did well to hold out until April 1942 when finally it could fight no more. By now, however, MacArthur was gone. Roosevelt, mostly for political reasons, ordered him out of the Philippines rather than see him end up a captive of the Japanese. The general escaped to Australia where he vowed, in his famous "I shall return" statement, to some day liberate the Philippines. In the meantime, the sad duty of surrendering the American-Filipino troops at Bataan and elsewhere in the Philippines fell to Maj. Gen. Jonathan Wainwright. "With profound regret and with continued pride in my gallant troops, I go to meet the Japanese commander," Wainwright wrote to Roosevelt. "Good-bye, Mr. President." About 80,000 American and Filipino troops surrendered, the largest single capitulation in American military history.

Coral Sea and Midway

After the Japanese conquered the Philippines, along with much of Asia and the central Pacific, they wanted to solidify the southern and eastern part of their new empire. This meant moving south toward Australia and east toward the Hawaiian Islands. In May 1942, a strong Japanese fleet moved into the Coral Sea, a body of water between Australia and New Guinea. The Japanese planned to take the southern coast of New Guinea and use it as a springboard to invade Australia.

The next month, they sailed an even more powerful fleet to the east, in the direction of the tiny American island base of Midway. The base was about 1,000 miles from Hawaii, close enough that if the Japanese could take Midway, their planes could then bomb Hawaii. These two Japanese thrusts provoked a pair of turning-point naval battles.

Battle in the South Pacific

At Coral Sea, a combined American and Australian fleet fought the Japanese to a standstill in the first great carrier battle in naval history. U.S. Adm. Chester Nimitz used top-secret intelligence, gleaned from broken Japanese codes, to put his forces in position. The American-Australian fleet and the Japanese fleet never actually spotted each other. Instead, carriers launched planes that sought out enemy ships and attacked them.

Almost all the fighting took place on one day, May 8, 1942. The Americans sank *Shoho,* a light aircraft carrier, and damaged another carrier. The Japanese had more success. They sank the USS *Lexington* and heavily damaged USS *Yorktown,* two of the most important carriers in United States' fleet.

Although the Japanese had inflicted significant damage on Nimitz's fleet, they were stunned by the ferocity of Allied resistance. The Japanese commander, Vice Adm. Shigeyoshi Inoue, decided to turn back rather than risk his ships to

Allied land-based air attacks in the narrow waters south of New Guinea. Coral Sea was a costly but vital Allied strategic victory. The vital lifeline to Australia remained open.

Battle in the east Pacific

At Midway, the Japanese amassed a powerful fleet of 145 warships, with a strike force of four major carriers in the lead. Once again, Nimitz's intelligence specialists apprised him of Japanese intentions. Nimitz scraped together his three remaining carriers, including the hastily repaired *Yorktown,* and prepared for a decisive battle.

The fighting took place between June 4 and 7, but the decisive day was June 4, 1942. That day the battle began with a Japanese air raid on Midway. Not long after this, American planes found the Japanese fleet and attacked. The Japanese slaughtered the big, slow torpedo bombers. Out of 41 attacking U.S. planes, only six survived. Then the battle turned. In a matter of minutes, American dive bombers hit three enemy carriers, mortally wounding them. All three eventually sank. In a later attack, they sank the fourth Japanese carrier.

Late in the day on June 4, Japanese planes found the *Yorktown* and damaged her badly. An enemy submarine later finished her off. However, with such uneven losses, the Japanese could not hope to invade Midway. They retreated, never to return, having suffered one of the great defeats in naval history.

Midway turned the tide of the naval war in the Pacific. It bought the Americans vital time to rebuild their Navy and established relative naval parity between the U.S. and Japan.

Bataan Death March

In World War II, the Japanese treated prisoners of war very poorly. This stemmed from two things: their belief that anyone who surrendered had no honor or manhood; and the brutality of the Fascist warlords who controlled Japan. After the fighting was over in the Philippines, the Japanese forced Filipino and American POWs to march 100 miles to their permanent camps in broiling heat, with little food, water, or medical care. This is known as the Bataan Death March.

During the march, Japanese soldiers roamed around, killing anyone who could not maintain the brisk pace they wanted. Many of the prisoners suffered from dysentery, malaria, beriberi, and dehydration. Often the Japanese didn't even allow the men to stop to answer the call of nature. In order to humiliate them, they forced them to soil themselves. The Japanese also executed several thousand Filipinos.

By late April, when the prisoners finally reached their camps, 10,000 had died, including 700 Americans. The survivors had only more torture, deprivation, and degradation to look forward to. Many of them did not survive the war. Thirty-seven percent of American POWs in the Pacific Theater died in captivity.

New Guinea

MacArthur's ultimate goal was a return to the Philippines. To do that, he needed to capture New Guinea as a steppingstone. In the summer of 1942, a combined army of Australian and American soldiers began a long, slow march from the south to the north coast of the island.

Conditions were beyond horrendous — jungles, swamps, mountains, insects, heat, disease, and the like. In December, at Buna and Gona, on the northern coast, the Allies ran into a strongly entrenched Japanese force that held out until well into January. At any given time, one-third of the American soldiers were down with malaria.

The fighting on the northern coast of New Guinea was a victory of sorts because the Allies had blunted the Japanese South Pacific advance. Nearly two more years of tough fighting lay ahead, though, as MacArthur's forces leapfrogged their way along the coast, ever closer to the Philippines.

Guadalcanal

The other turning point came in the Solomon Islands. In July 1942, Allied intelligence discovered that the Japanese were building an airfield on the strategically important island of Guadalcanal. From here, Japanese planes and ships could menace Australia's shipping lifeline to America. The Allies knew they had to take Guadalcanal or risk losing the war. On August 7, 1942, the 1st Marine Division invaded the island against only token resistance, seizing control of the valuable airfield. Realizing the vital importance of Guadalcanal, the Japanese soon reinforced it with strong air, land, and sea forces. The Americans did the same.

The battle turned into a dramatic struggle of wills. From August 1942 until early February 1943, the two sides fought desperately. The Japanese continually bombed the airfield, which the Americans had dubbed Henderson Field after a deceased Marine airman. Offshore, naval battles proliferated, so much so that the waters off Guadalcanal were known as Iron Bottom Sound because of all the sunken ships.

The worst fighting took place amid the jungles and swamps on the island itself. Marines and soldiers engaged in a daily contest for survival against well-trained, tenacious Japanese troops. For instance, the Japanese launched two major attacks in September and October aimed at capturing Henderson Field. They came out of the darkness in screaming human waves. The fighting was hand-to-hand, but the Americans held.

By February 1943, after six months of fighting, the Americans finally triumphed in this battle of attrition. The U.S. lost 1,768 soldiers killed in action, while the Japanese lost 24,600. Guadalcanal was the most important American victory in the first two years of the Pacific War.

Turning Attention to Europe

When the U.S. entered World War II on the Allied side in 1941, the Germans controlled nearly all of Europe, and they were well on the way to conquering the Soviet Union (see Figure 16-2). Without Soviet help, the western Allies could not hope to win the war in Europe. Hitler's Germany was the most powerful of all the Axis nations and thus the most dangerous. He had to be defeated first, before he became too strong. So, in this war, the majority of American resources, supplies, and manpower went to Europe, while the Pacific usually received second priority.

Figure 16-2: Map of the European Theater, 1942–1945.

The Atlantic lifeline

The European Allies had to control the Atlantic. If they didn't, then the United States could never project its manpower, weaponry, food, and industrial might overseas to Europe. The Germans could not compete with the Allies in surface ships, but their submarines were a powerful, potentially war-winning weapon. Churchill wrote that, during World War II, the German submarines (or *U-boats*) frightened him the most because they had the potential to marginalize the United States and strangle Great Britain into submission. They could do this by sinking more ships than the Allies could replace.

Throughout the war, the enemy U-boats roamed the waters of the Atlantic, sometimes operating in packs, savaging vulnerable Allied merchant ships and warships alike. They sank hundreds of ships, some of them right off the east coast of the United States. The heyday for these enemy raiders was 1942–1943 when they sank nearly half a million tons of Allied ships and cargo per month. Had such German success continued, it's likely that the Allies would have lost the war.

But, in the middle of 1943, the Allies began turning the tide in the struggle for their Atlantic lifeline. Using convoy tactics in which submarine-killing warships and airplanes escorted vulnerable merchant ships, the Allied navies sank more and more U-boats, to the point where German shipyards could no longer keep up with the losses. From this point on, the U-boats were more of a deadly nuisance than a mortal threat to America's Atlantic lifeline.

The Allies employed three major weapons to neutralize the U-boats:

- ✔ **Code-breaking**: This was known as *Ultra* (short for Ultra-secret) *intelligence.* The British, and later the Americans, read some of the Germans' secret military traffic during the war. This sometimes included information about the positioning of their submarines.

- ✔ **Escort carriers**: These small aircraft carriers allowed the Allies to protect their convoys with continuous air cover.

- ✔ **Destroyers**: These speedy, versatile ships were ideal submarine hunters and killers. Armed with excellent sonar and radar, along with *depth charges* (bombs that explode under water) and accurate, powerful, 5-inch guns, destroyers sank numerous U-boats.

Hitler's misstep in Stalingrad

Hitler came tantalizingly close to victory over the Soviet Union in 1941, but failed (see Chapter 15 for details). In 1942, he was determined to succeed. He ordered a new offensive in southern Russia aimed at capturing the Caucasus oil fields and cutting the USSR in two. Starting in May 1942, the German army overran huge swaths of Russia and captured hundreds of thousands of Red Army soldiers.

However, in the fall, Hitler decided to refocus his offensive to capture Stalingrad, a city on the Volga River that was more of a political than strategic objective. The result was an urban battle that favored the Russians over the Germans. In several months of bitter urban combat, from September 1942 to February 1943, the Russians steadily turned the tide of battle in their favor. Eventually, they surrounded the Germans and compelled the surrender of about 100,000 freezing, starving survivors. Axis losses at Stalingrad were nearly 750,000 soldiers. This major Soviet victory changed the course of the war in the East. From here on out, the Germans found themselves — with only a few exceptions — fighting a defensive battle to hold what they had already conquered.

Invading North Africa

In the wake of Pearl Harbor and the Philippines, the average American in 1942 wanted to strike back at the Japanese, not the Germans. Thus, President Roosevelt's Germany-first policy was not all that popular. Roosevelt wanted American soldiers in action against the Germans in 1942. He hoped that with U.S. troops fighting the Germans, the American people would inevitably warm to his Germany-first policy. Initially, Roosevelt and his generals wanted a cross-channel invasion of German-occupied France. The British believed, however, that the Allies were not yet ready for such an ambitious, complicated operation. They persuaded their eager American friends to focus on North Africa instead. For two years, the British had been fighting a seesaw war against an Italo-German army in Egypt (a British colony) and Libya (an Italian colony).

Battling the Axis at El Alamein

The most vital artery for the British empire was the Suez Canal in Egypt. In the late summer of 1942, an Axis army under the command of the famous German general, Erwin Rommel, pushed to a dusty railroad town called El Alamein, some 60 miles west of the canal. Rommel had to halt there because he was low on supplies. As he regrouped, Gen. Bernard Montgomery took command of the British Eighth Army. Montgomery received an infusion of reinforcements and equipment, some of it American. He planned a major attack on Rommel and unleashed it on October 23.

In two weeks of costly fighting, Montgomery's soldiers vaulted their way through millions of mines and outfought their Italian and German enemies. This ripped a hole in the Axis front that led to a full-scale retreat. Montgomery pursued them all the way across Libya and eventually into Tunisia by March 1943. Montgomery was overbearing, arrogant, and egomaniacal. But he unquestionably infused his army with a new fighting spirit. Earning for himself the title "Montgomery of Alamein," he became Britain's best known general in World War II.

Together the Allies devised a plan. In Egypt, the British would launch an offensive aimed at pushing the Axis armies out of that colony for good. In the west, the Americans would lead an invasion of the Vichy French colonies Morocco and Algeria. The U.S. hoped the French would not fight. Even if they did, the two Allied armies, converging from the west and east, would catch the enemy armies in a vise, annihilate them, and secure the entire North African coast.

The American-led invasion was code-named Operation Torch. When the invasion force of 65,000 U.S. soldiers went ashore on November 8, 1942, they met with sharp resistance in some spots and little opposition in others. Most of the supposedly French soldiers were actually North African locals under the command of French officers. Some of these officers felt honor-bound to fight, yet few had any special hostility for the Americans. Others were actually eager to convert to the Allied cause. The fighting lasted for about a week and cost about 500 American lives before the Allied commander, Gen. Dwight D. Eisenhower, negotiated a truce with Adm. Jean Darlan, the French commander. Many of Darlan's soldiers joined the British and Americans to form a multinational army in North Africa.

In the weeks that followed, a dizzying series of events took place. Germany occupied the rest of France, ending the Vichy government's existence. Darlan fell to an assassin's bullet on December 24, 1942. The British kicked the Axis out of Egypt, ushering in a mobile campaign in Libya. The Americans raced for Tunisia, but a combination of bad roads, bad weather, lofty mountain peaks, and poor preparation hindered them. At the same time, Hitler decided to send substantial reinforcements, by air and sea, to Tunisia, where they constructed a formidable defensive line that stymied the Allies.

Instead of a lightning victory in North Africa, the Allies were bogged down in a brutal campaign of attrition that raged through the winter of 1942–1943. Gradually, in early 1943, Allied air and sea attacks cut Axis supply lines to Tunisia. Steady ground attacks also increased the pressure. Finally, 275,000 Italian and German soldiers surrendered on May 10, 1943, securing North Africa for the Allies.

Taking Control of the War in Europe, 1943–1944

The Germans were definitely losing the war in Europe now. The tide had turned at such places as Stalingrad and El Alamein. The Germans were powerful and could still win the war, but time was not on their side. Each day the production and manpower capacity of the United States made the Allies stronger. Roosevelt and Churchill announced that hostilities would only cease with the Axis's unconditional surrender, and Stalin concurred.

With North Africa in Allied hands, the question in 1943 was where to strike next. True to form, the gung-ho Americans favored an immediate cross-channel invasion of France. An invasion of France would allow the Allies to return to northern Europe, crush the German army, and overrun the *Third Reich* (a popular term for Hitler's empire).

The British opposed invading France for the same reasons they had in 1942 — the Allies were not ready — and they were right. Among the western powers, only the U.S. had the potential power and resources to successfully accomplish these goals. In 1943, the U.S. was not quite ready for such a significant undertaking, though.

Referring to Italy as "the soft underbelly of the crocodile," Churchill convinced Roosevelt to embark upon an invasion of what was perceived as the weakest of Axis nations. The Allies expected to knock Italy out of the war, thus getting into Europe through the back door.

Invading "the soft underbelly": Sicily and Italy

The invasion of Sicily, code-named Operation Husky, was the second largest in the European war, behind only the Normandy invasion (see the section, "A great moment in history: The D-Day invasion at Normandy," later in this chapter). The invasion force at Sicily consisted of 2,590 ships, hundreds of planes, and 180,000 troops. A mixed bag of Italian and German soldiers defended the island. Many of the Italians were heartily sick of the war and wanted only to surrender. By contrast, the Germans were more than eager to fight.

On July 10, 1943, the Allies struck. The British landed on the southeastern coast of Italy, near Syracuse. The Americans drew the mission of protecting the western flank of their British allies. Three American infantry divisions, the 45th, 1st, and 3rd, landed along a 30-mile front, between Cape Scaramia in the east and Licata in the west. Both the British and the Americans dropped highly trained paratroopers behind the targeted beachheads to secure bridges and harass enemy reinforcements.

Although the landings were a success, the campaign that followed was long and difficult. The British ran into strong German reinforcements around Mount Etna, a peak that dominates the entire eastern half of the island. The Americans also dealt with tough resistance that slowed their advance. It took the Allies five weeks, and almost 24,000 casualties, to secure Sicily. By that time, many of the German soldiers had escaped to fight again another day.

For the Americans, the highlight of the Sicily campaign was the 3rd Division's epic march from the southern to the northern coast. The division commander, Maj. Gen. Lucian Truscott, had trained his men to march long distances in all kinds of weather at a very brisk pace. The men, who were lean, tough, and resilient, called this the "Truscott Trot." Marching in summer heat, through mountainous terrain, they covered 90 miles in three days and took Palermo, one of the main objectives.

With Sicily in hand, the Allies invaded the Italian mainland. By now, Mussolini had fallen from power. The new Italian government secretly negotiated with Gen. Eisenhower to get Italy out of the war. By the time an Anglo-American invasion force went ashore at Salerno on September 9, 1943, Italy had surrendered. The Germans anticipated this whole scenario and simply took over Italy as another occupied country. For Allied soldiers, the occupation meant they were now facing hard-core German soldiers instead of disinterested, war-weary Italian troops.

Over the course of the next two years, the Allies slowly slugged their way up the Italian boot, against fierce resistance, often in terrible weather and mountainous terrain. Far from being a "soft underbelly," as Churchill believed, Italy was a dead end. Only two real positives came out of the Italian campaign:

- ✔ The liberation of Rome on June 4, 1944
- ✔ The capture of air bases from which to bomb Hitler's Europe

Patton's not-so-finest hour

One of the most famous and admired American generals of World War II was George S. Patton, the American commander at Sicily. Patton was a brilliant, dedicated soldier who wanted nothing more than to command troops in battle. But he had a big mouth and a volcanic temper. He also did not believe in the notion of *combat fatigue*, the mental breakdown of soldiers in battle. To him, combat fatigue was nothing more than cowardice.

In Sicily, on two separate occasions, Patton flew into a rage and slapped soldiers who were suffering from combat fatigue. When word of these indiscretions leaked out to the American public, many folks on the home front voiced the opinion that Patton should be fired. The whole episode was a public relations nightmare for the Army. Patton's boss, Gen. Eisenhower, ultimately decided to keep Patton because he was such a fine field commander. If Ike had decided otherwise, Patton might be nothing more than an obscure, scorned figure today.

A great moment in history: The D-Day invasion at Normandy

In the summer of 1944, the Allies were finally ready to invade France. They chose to do so at Normandy on June 6, 1944. The invasion armada consisted of 6,900 ships, with 12,000 aircraft protecting them overhead. More than six divisions, totaling some 90,000 troops, carried out the initial amphibious assault.

The British and Canadians invaded at three code-named beaches — Gold, Juno, and Sword. The Americans went ashore at beaches code-named Utah and Omaha. Three divisions of paratroopers and glider soldiers descended from the nighttime Norman skies to cover the flanks of the invasion. The American paratroopers were scattered all over the Cotentin Peninsula, behind Utah beach. They fought in small groups, hindering the German response to the invasion.

For the Americans, the biggest crisis on *D-Day* (the day on which the invasion occurred) happened at Omaha beach. The sloping, rocky bluffs that overlooked the beach were ideal for defenders. Elements of a first-rate German division — soldiers from Hanover — expertly defended the beach. When the Americans came ashore, they ran into a firestorm of machine gun, rifle, mortar, and artillery fire, plus mines. American soldiers had their heads blown off and their arms, legs, and torsos shattered. The waters ran red with blood. Through sheer courage and tenacity, the Americans prevailed. The film *Saving Private Ryan* graphically and accurately portrays the western edge of Omaha beach on D-Day morning.

The invasion was the culmination of years of planning, and it was a major success. By the end of D-Day, the Allies were firmly ashore in France. For the Americans, the invasion signaled the beginning of superpower status and world leadership. The operation and the campaign that followed could never have happened without American leadership. For instance, over the next year, as the Allies fought to defeat Germany in northern Europe, two-thirds of their supplies, manpower, and weapons were American. This foreshadowed the American world leadership that would follow the war.

Liberating France

As successful as the Normandy invasion was, it didn't guarantee victory. It was actually only the first step in a long, bloody campaign to defeat Germany. In the weeks that followed D-Day, the Germans sent large numbers of reinforcements to Normandy and held the Allied armies in a *stalemate* (or deadlock). Throughout the summer of 1944, the two sides grappled in a terrible death struggle amid the hedgerows of Normandy. Not until August did the

Allies rip through the German lines, break the stalemate, and send Hitler's soldiers into headlong retreat.

On August 25, 1944, French and American soldiers liberated Paris. Raucous celebrations and a parade soon followed. Thousands of American soldiers took a break from the fighting to parade down the Champs-Elysees. Some even found French girlfriends, if only for a night or two.

Elsewhere, the Germans were retreating back to their own country as fast as their legs or vehicles could carry them. In early September, advanced American patrols even crossed the border into Germany. The Allied world buzzed with optimistic talk about the war being over by Christmas, but this didn't happen. Instead, the Germans rallied and set up strong defenses along their western borders. At the same time, the Allies ran into serious supply problems that would plague them for the rest of the war and impede their momentum.

Gambling in Holland

On September 17, 1944, the Allies unleashed a bold gamble designed to win the war in 1944. They dropped three airborne divisions behind enemy lines in Holland — the 101st Airborne at Eindhoven, the 82nd Airborne at Nijmegen, and the British 1st Airborne at Arnhem. Their job was to secure Highway 69 (soon dubbed "Hell's Highway" by the GIs), along with a key series of bridges, including the Arnhem bridge that led over the Rhine. In the next phase of the operation, the British XXX Corps, bristling with tanks, was to hook up with the paratroopers and then drive across the Rhine into Berlin and win the war. The code name for the operation was Operation Market-Garden.

The plan soon went awry. German resistance was much more potent than Allied intelligence officers had estimated. In fact, the British landed right in the midst of elite Nazi SS armored units. These Germans annihilated the British 1st Airborne Division. The Americans lost 3,664 killed in action. In the end, the Allies gained some ground but failed to cross the Rhine into Germany. They instead endured a rainy stalemate in Holland that fall.

Kaput! The End for Hitler and His Cronies

Hitler's Reich was strong enough to hold out for the rest of 1944, but defeat was now inevitable. Germany was surrounded on all sides. The western Allies were preparing to breach Germany's western borders while the Soviets were doing the same in the east. Germany was running low on fuel and manpower. Allied fighters and bombers, in a round-the-clock offensive, had swept German planes from the skies. Hitler himself was in bad shape. He had survived an assassination attempt in July 1944 that left him shaky and frail. Like a cornered but dangerous animal, he decided to lash out one more time.

The Battle of the Bulge

On December 16, 1944, Hitler gambled everything in one last-ditch offensive. Under the cover of bad winter weather that negated Allied air power, 300,000 German soldiers attacked the American lines along a thinly held, 80-mile sector in the Ardennes Forest. These forces included Germany's best remaining armored formations. The German objective was to cross the Meuse River, capture Antwerp, Belgium, the most vital supply port in northern Europe, and split the Allied armies in two. Hitler hoped he could negotiate an end to hostilities in the West at that point and turn his full attention to fighting the Russians in the East.

Hitler's plan was heavily dependent on surprise, which he achieved, but also speed. Although the Americans were shocked by the bold offensive, they fought well. Small, isolated groups fought ferociously, costing the Germans valuable time, men, and equipment. The Germans drove a bulge in the American lines — earning the battle its famous nickname, "Battle of the Bulge" — but never even crossed the Meuse. By Christmastime, the attack had lost all momentum, and American reinforcements had begun to turn the tide. The Americans spent the next month on the offensive, recapturing the Ardennes ground they had lost, all in bitterly cold winter weather.

The Bulge was the second-costliest battle in U.S. military history, behind only the Argonne Forest in World War I (see Chapter 14). In the Bulge, the Americans suffered nearly 90,000 casualties: 19,276 killed, 23,218 captured or missing in action, and more than 47,000 wounded.

Invading Germany

With the failure of his Ardennes offensive, and another lesser one in Lorraine, Hitler's defeat was now just a matter of time. In the early months of 1945, Allied armies, from east and west, overran Germany. The fighting was fierce. In fact, American casualty rates were on par with the bloodlettings they had suffered in the fall of 1944. But victory was imminent. Hitler took to his Berlin bunker. On April 30, 1945, with Soviet troops only a few blocks away, Hitler took his own life. Nazi Germany unconditionally surrendered a week later on May 7, 1945.

As Allied soldiers conquered Germany, they liberated hundreds of concentration camps, thus discovering the terrible results of Nazi tyranny. The emaciated, diseased survivors of these camps greeted their liberators with tears and hugs. In all, the Nazi Germany regime killed 10 million people, including 6 million Jews, through a systematic policy of cruelty, exploitation, and genocide. This is generally known as the *Holocaust.*

For the Americans, the greatest prize in Germany was to capture Hitler's lavish alpine home in Berchtesgaden. In the war's final days, many units were vying to get there first. Because of a mistake in the book and miniseries *Band of Brothers,* most Americans believe that the 101st Airborne Division was the first unit into Hitler's home. In reality, the 7th Infantry Regiment of the 3rd Infantry Division got there first, at roughly 4 p.m. on May 4, well before the paratroopers ever reached the area.

Island Hopping in the Pacific

On the Pacific front, throughout 1943 and early 1944, the Americans gradually ate away at the Japanese empire by *island hopping.* In other words, they chose several Japanese-held islands to assault, outflanked others, and left their *garrisons* (or troops) to starve. The most intense of these selective invasions took place at tiny Tarawa, where 4,500 Japanese soldiers mostly fought to the death in three brutal days of combat November 20–23, 1943. The battle cost the 2nd Marine Division 1,009 men killed.

In 1944, hard-earned victories like Tarawa put the Americans in a position to pierce the inner ring of Japanese defenses. Gen. MacArthur, who was finishing up a long campaign in New Guinea, focused on liberating the Philippines. In the meantime, Adm. Chester Nimitz, commander of the U.S. Navy's Pacific Fleet, planned to liberate the Mariana Islands.

Invading the Marianas

Nimitz made his first move at the Japanese colony of Saipan, on June 15, 1944, when two divisions of U.S. Marines hit the beach. Japanese resistance was desperate, even fanatical. The Japanese carried out *banzai* (suicide) *attacks* on foot, emerging from the cover of darkness, screaming and hurling themselves at the Americans, attempting to bayonet Marines in their foxholes. The Americans held fast and slaughtered the Japanese in droves. A combined force of soldiers and Marines needed a little over three weeks to capture the island. Rather than surrender, some of the Japanese hurled themselves off cliffs into the sea or blew themselves up with grenades. In July and August, at Guam and Tinian, the Japanese fought with similar ferocity, but lost in the end.

Meanwhile, at sea, Nimitz's fleet won a great victory. In two days of fighting on June 19–20, 1944, the Americans sank three Japanese aircraft carriers and shot down 600 planes. The U.S. Navy lost 123 planes, mostly because aviators ran out of fuel and had to ditch them into the Philippine Sea. The vast majority of the American fliers survived. This naval battle was so one-sided that the Americans called it "The Great Marianas Turkey Shoot." The official name of the battle, though, is the Battle of the Philippine Sea.

The Marianas campaign was the pivotal moment of the Pacific War. With the Marianas under control, the U.S., for the first time, had ideal bases from which to bomb Japan. They had breached the vital inner ring of Japanese defenses and could now use the Marianas as a perfect jumping-off point for a final push on Japan itself. The Marianas campaign was to the Pacific War what Normandy was to the war in Europe — a vital pivot point that decided the outcome of the war. (See "A great moment in history: The D-Day invasion at Normandy" earlier in the chapter for more about the Normandy invasion.)

Returning to the Philippines

On October 20, 1944, Gen. MacArthur's forces finally returned to his beloved Philippines with an invasion of Leyte. The campaign on land was a deadly slugging match. The Americans fought two months before liberating the island. They killed 49,000 Japanese soldiers and suffered about 15,000 casualties.

At sea, the two sides fought the largest naval battle in modern history. The Japanese converged on Leyte with two major fleets, nearly overwhelming the American fleet and mauling the invasion beaches. However, the U.S. Navy battled them to a bloody standstill. In the end, the Japanese failed in their mission to thwart the invasion. From now on, the U.S. Navy controlled the waters around the Philippines. Realizing this, the Japanese began launching suicide *kamikaze attacks* by deliberately crashing their planes onto the American ships.

MacArthur followed up the Leyte operation with an invasion of Luzon, the main island. There, and at other smaller islands throughout the archipelago, his troops fought some 380,000 Japanese soldiers under the command of Lt. Gen. Tomoyuki Yamashita. The Japanese commander sprinkled his die-hard soldiers throughout the Philippines's rugged mountains and ridges, forcing MacArthur to come to him. The result was a slow, costly campaign of attrition. The worst fighting took place in Manila, where elements of three American divisions liberated the city in close-quarter, intense urban combat.

MacArthur liberated most of the Philippines but never completely defeated Yamashita in the Philippines, because Yamashita was still holding out at the end of the war. American losses were considerable. One out of every three American casualties in the Pacific War occurred in the Philippines campaign of 1944–1945.

A Horrible Climax: The Close of the War

The Pacific War became progressively worse with every American victory as the Japanese grew more desperate. After the Americans took the Philippines and the Marianas, their next move was to take some final steppingstones to Japan and then the home islands themselves. Japanese resolve did not falter. They were determined to inflict such terrible losses on the Americans that the U.S. would make peace before winning a total victory in this war.

Destruction from above and at sea

By the end of 1944, the United States was employing two major weapons to bring Japan to its knees: airpower and sea power. On November 24, 1944, America's newest heavy bombers, B-29s, began flying missions from the Marianas to bomb Japan. At the same time, American submarines were sailing in the waters off China and around Japan, inflicting catastrophic damage to Japanese shipping. Together these air and sea attacks crippled Japanese industry, resources, shipping, and mobility.

The Air Force started out by bombing very specific targets in Japan, but soon gave this tactic up in favor of all-out raids:

- Beginning in late February 1945, the B-29s flew low-altitude, fire-bombing raids on Japan's cities. These were devastating because traditional Japanese construction employed heavy use of paper and wood as opposed to concrete and steel.

- These raids killed hundreds of thousands of civilians and rendered millions of others homeless in such cities as Tokyo, Nagoya, Kawasaki, and Yokohama.

- By mid-summer of 1945, the bombers were running out of worthwhile targets.

The U.S. also waged successful sea attacks against Japan. Armed with new-generation boats and torpedoes, U.S. submariners achieved in the Pacific what German subs attempted to accomplish against the United States in the Atlantic — they destroyed Japan's economy.

- By the middle of 1945, American subs had sunk two-thirds of Japan's oil tankers and nearly her entire merchant fleet — 3 million tons of ships in all.

- Submariners comprised only 1.6 percent of the Navy, but sank, in Europe and the Pacific, 5.3 million tons of enemy ships and cargo, including eight carriers.

✔ Overall, in both theaters, the Navy lost 52 subs during the war and 3,505 submarine sailors, a 22 percent casualty rate.

The atomic end of the war

In 1945, the Americans fought climactic battles at Iwo Jima and Okinawa, Japan. As usual, the Japanese fought to the finish. Iwo Jima was the costliest battle in the history of the Marine Corps, ending the lives of more than 5,000 Marines. At Okinawa, the Japanese turned the kamikaze attack into a veritable art form, sinking 38 ships and killing more than 5,000 American sailors. In spite of these devastating losses, the Americans prevailed in both battles and were on the doorstep to Japan. U.S. commanders planned for an invasion of Kyushu in November 1945, to be followed by an all-out assault on Honshu in March 1946.

In recent years, historians have begun to debate whether the invasion of Iwo Jima was necessary. The main reasons commanders gave for the invasion was to win an emergency landing field for B-29 crewmen and eliminate a significant Japanese airbase that was a thorn in the side to the bombers. For years, World War II historians bought this argument, assuming that, though Iwo was costly, it saved the lives of many airmen. However, recent research, especially a book by a Marine captain named Robert Burrell, has shown otherwise, prompting a lively and emotional debate.

On July 20, 1945, the United States became the world's first nuclear power with a successful atomic bomb test at Alamogordo, New Mexico. President Harry S. Truman, who had succeeded FDR upon the latter's death, decided to use the new weapon against Japan. Truman was hoping to forestall a costly invasion. He viewed the atomic bomb as simply another weapon in the strategic bombing campaign against Japan.

On August 6, 1945, a B-29 dropped the atomic bomb on Hiroshima. Three days later, an American bomber dropped another one on Nagasaki. Both of these bombings inflicted serious damage and hundreds of thousands of casualties. In the wake of this nuclear onslaught, the Japanese surrendered on August 14, 1945, ending the greatest of all wars. The war cost the lives of 62 million human beings.

Life on the Home Front

World War II profoundly affected the American people and led to significant changes in the country. Americans were unified as never before or since. Nearly everyone agreed that the war needed to be fought and won. Most

Americans, from the very young to the very old, wanted to do their part to win the war:

- ✔ Children collected scrap metal for war industries.

- ✔ Housewives donated blood.

- ✔ Older men served as air raid wardens.

- ✔ Young men volunteered for the military in droves.

Mobilizing for war

The United States transitioned to a wartime economy, creating 17 million war-related jobs, many of which went to women and African Americans. Unemployment declined dramatically, to less than 2 percent. The government doled out healthy profits to industries for producing war materiel. A large government agency, the War Production Board, allocated raw materials, oversaw production of civilian and military items, and distributed defense contracts. Hundreds of other agencies dealt with everything from price controls to weapons research and housing shortages. The results of this mobilization were dramatic:

- ✔ The United States produced more war materiel than all the Axis nations *combined.*

- ✔ American shipyards constructed more than 90,000 ships.

- ✔ 45 percent of the federal budget went to defense.

So how did we pay for all of this? Federal income taxes were very high, up to 90 percent in some cases. The government sold low-interest, secure war bonds to finance its wartime spending. Bankers loaned Uncle Sam money. When all that was still not enough, the government embraced *deficit spending* (spending more money than you bring in). The budget deficit was $259 billion by 1945.

Changing the face of society

Unlike the citizens of most World War II belligerents, Americans lived in a secure environment, free of bombings, combat, or even serious deprivation. *Rationing,* a limit placed on how much a person could purchase of certain products, was one of the most obvious ways the war affected average people. The needs of the war fronts, combined with a decline in the availability of consumer goods, produced shortages. The government mandated strict rationing of such valued items as nylon stockings (because nylon could be used to make a range of military items), eggs, butter, tobacco, and gasoline.

Americans were constantly on the move during the war years. Young men left home and entered military service. Six million women entered the workplace, sometimes in traditionally male jobs like shipbuilding or welding. In the process, these working women traveled the country and achieved some level of economic independence, thus challenging the accepted gender role of women as homemakers. The West Coast grew exponentially. For instance, 2 million people moved to California during the war. Six million Americans, attracted by wartime jobs, left farms to go to cities. African Americans migrated from the South to the upper Midwest and the West Coast.

All of this mobility led to dramatic changes in America. Sun Belt states like California, Arizona, and Florida rose in population and importance. The national economy that grew from the war was the strongest in world history. African Americans yearned for racial justice and equality in a country where segregation and second-class status for "coloreds" was often the norm. As black Americans migrated all over the country, race became a national issue, not just a southern concern. Thus, a major civil rights movement grew out of World War II.

Racial injustice was a serious problem in wartime America. In 1943, in Detroit, tension between blacks and whites boiled over into riots that cost the lives of 34 people. Harlem, New York, also experienced race riots, as did numerous military bases in the South. In Los Angeles, white servicemen clashed with Latino youths in what became known as the Zoot Suit Riots. The federal government was worried that Japanese Americans would spy for Japan, so troops rounded them up and placed them in internment camps during the war. Many Japanese Americans lost homes and property, not to mention civil liberties.

About 900,000 African Americans served in the military in World War II. At that time, the armed forces were still segregated, a bitter irony while the U.S. was fighting such intensely racist regimes. The vast majority of black servicemen worked in noncombat jobs under white officers. During the war, it was not at all unusual for whites-only restaurants to feed German and Italian POWs (on lunch breaks from paying jobs outside their camps) but turn away black servicemen.

Part V

Bearing Any Burden: The Cold War and the Unpaid Peace Dividend

The 5th Wave   By Rich Tennant

STOP THE WAR IN VIETNAM SUPER STORE   A&P

★Picket Signs ★T-Shirts   ★Bumper Stickers Posters Buttons

"The antiwar movement seems to be gaining some mainstream acceptance."

In this part . . .

World War II created as many problems as it solved. Even as Germany, Japan, and Italy transitioned into peaceful democracies, a major showdown emerged between the United States and the Soviet Union. This confrontation is often called the *Cold War*. It lasted until 1991 when the Soviet Union collapsed under the weight of its own economic incompetence and lack of social justice. Americans then hoped for a peace dividend. Instead, they found themselves enmeshed in the troubled Middle East, at first fighting a war with Saddam Hussein's Iraq, then dealing with the rise of extremist Islamic terrorism, plus another war in Iraq.

In a sense, you can think of the years since World War II as an age of terror. For almost 50 years, in the age of Cold War terror, the world faced the very real possibility of nuclear annihilation. That phase gave way to Islamic extremist terror, with the events of September 11, 2001, being the ultimate manifestation, prompting an American Global War on Terror.

Chapter 17

Toying with Nuclear Armageddon: The Cold War Years

*W*orld War II did not usher in a new era of peace and understanding for humankind. The war's greatest and most tragic legacy was a protracted conflict known as the *Cold War.* The Cold War lasted roughly from 1945 to 1991. Nearly every person on the planet was affected by it, so it's important to understand what it was, why it happened, and how it turned out the way it did. The Cold War was an ideological, diplomatic, cultural, economic, and military struggle between the diametrically opposed ideologies of Communism and anti-Communism.

The Cold War deeply affected the American people who lived through it. Out of fear of Communism, the United States armed itself to the teeth, grew intimately involved in small and large countries around the globe, and assumed defense of the non-Communist, or free, world. Sometimes opposition to Communism led Americans into real shooting wars, as in Korea and Vietnam (see Chapters 18 and 19 for more).

But, fortunately, the Cold War never led to an all-out war between the United States and the Soviet Union, the country primarily responsible for promoting Communism. Instead, the superpowers duked it out in nearly every other arena imaginable, from propaganda rhetoric to nuclear brinksmanship, to athletics and economics. In this chapter, I discuss many of the key events of the Cold War, from its beginning in the days that followed World War II through its end in the late 1980s. You get a feel for why the Cold War happened and see how it affected modern American history. Finally, this chapter describes and explains the demise of Communism, which led to the end of the Cold War.

Igniting the Cold War: The 1940s

The first phase of the Cold War lasted from 1945 through 1949 and focused mainly on Europe. During this time, relations between the United States and the Soviet Union steadily deteriorated, mainly because of serious disagreements over the future of post–World War II Europe. The Americans envisioned an economically revitalized, democratic Europe. The Soviets wanted a stable Europe with authoritarian regimes. This fundamental disagreement led to a divided Europe.

By 1949, the United States put together a military alliance of like-minded western European states to deter potential Soviet aggression. The Soviet Union did the same with eastern European countries. By the end of the decade, these two hostile blocs glowered at each other. This chasm between East and West was an enduring aspect of the Cold War.

Trying tough love with the Soviets

At the end of World War II, Soviet troops occupied eastern Germany, Poland, Romania, Hungary, Bulgaria, and parts of Czechoslovakia, while U.S., British, and French troops occupied western Germany and much of the rest of western Europe. The western powers naturally favored democratic, capitalist governments in their area of occupation, while the Soviets preferred Communist regimes in theirs.

Communism versus capitalism

The Communist world, led by the Soviet Union, stood for total economic equality and fairness in society (no rich and no poor), no organized religion, no private property, and very few civil liberties for the individual. Basically, Communist governments were totalitarian, meaning they exercised total control over their population, with no free elections, no legal opposition, and no freedom of speech. Such Communist countries as the Soviet Union, Cuba, North Korea, and Poland all experienced major economic problems and extensive poverty, mainly because people had no incentive to work hard to create wealth or jobs. The anti-Communist world, led by the United States, stood for private property, entrepreneurial capitalism, personal liberty, freedom of worship, free elections, disparity between haves and have-nots, and, in some countries, authoritarianism as a means of stamping out Communism. In general, non-Communist countries experienced significant economic growth and prosperity during the Cold War. Even so, poverty among some segments of the population was a serious problem in all non-Communist nations, including the United States.

The Iron Curtain speech

During the 1930s, as Hitler's Nazi Germany grew more powerful and more aggressive, Winston Churchill was the one major British politician who warned of the Nazi threat and urged a firm response. He was proven right at every turn so, when the war began, he ascended to the office of prime minister of Great Britain.

By the spring of 1946, with the war over, he was no longer in power. Instead, he was touring the United States, making speeches. On March 5, 1946, he traveled with President Truman to Fulton, Missouri, to deliver a speech he called "The Sinews of Peace."

With the president on the podium behind him, Churchill warned of the gathering Soviet threat to the peace and security of the West. He decried the division of Europe between East and West, and blamed this on the Soviets. In the most memorable part of his speech, he declared that "from Stettin in the Baltic to Trieste in the Adriatic, an 'iron curtain' has descended across the continent" of Europe. Churchill called for an Anglo-American alliance to counter this new and sinister threat.

The iron curtain image proved to be vivid and enduring. From that point on, Americans referred to nations in the Soviet sphere as being "behind the Iron Curtain." The speech solidified the notion of the Cold War in the mind of the average American, in part, because Churchill had been so correct about the Nazi threat a decade earlier.

The Soviet leader, Josef Stalin, wanted to establish a protective buffer zone in Europe for his devastated country. His nation had been invaded by Germany twice in the 20th century, and he wanted to make sure this could never happen again. Only by establishing pro-Soviet, Communist, authoritarian regimes in eastern Europe could he accomplish this goal. The American president, Harry Truman, believed those countries should have free elections. Truman's predecessor, Franklin Roosevelt, thought he had secured an agreement from Stalin to hold those elections. When the elections never happened, the Americans grew to distrust and fear Stalin's Soviet Union.

These erstwhile elections led to a stormy Oval Office meeting between Truman and Soviet Foreign Minister Vyacheslav Molotov in the spring of 1945. During the meeting, the president chastised Stalin and the Soviet government for going back on their agreement to hold elections in Poland. Truman and Molotov bickered for a bit and then, in exasperation, Molotov said, "I have never been talked to like that in my life." Unimpressed, Truman replied, "Carry out your agreements and you won't get talked to like that." It was only the first exchange in a long war of words between the Russians and the Americans.

Truman was determined to deal with the Soviets firmly and toughly. He knew that the war had damaged the Soviet economy and that the Russians needed American aid, so he decided to use this as a weapon to shape Soviet behavior in eastern Europe. In May 1945, he ended Lend-Lease, an extensive American aid program to its wartime allies, including the Soviets. But the move backfired. The ensuing outcry among the Allies, most notably the British, forced Truman to relent and re-implement the program. This incident hardened Soviet distrust of Truman and the U.S. Eventually, after the end of the war in the Pacific, the United States did discontinue its aid.

Keeping the dominoes from falling in Greece

By early 1947, Truman had decided that America's main strategy to curtail Communism would be *containment*. In essence, this was a defensive policy. Truman recognized that he could not roll back Communism in eastern Europe and Russia without fighting World War III. Instead, he decided to contain Communism wherever it threatened to spread. The proving ground for this new policy was Greece.

During World War II, the Germans conquered Greece. Two resistance movements, one Communist, the other non-Communist, fought the Germans, and each other, during the war. When the war ended, the Communists and anti-Communists engaged in full-fledged civil war. The Greek Communists received help from Yugoslavian Communist leader Josef Broz Tito. The non-Communists drew aid from the British who had a detachment of soldiers in the country, but could no longer maintain this presence by 1947. Feeling that Greece could soon fall to Communism if the U.S. did nothing, Truman decided that he must send aid to the anti-Communists.

Truman and most of his trusted advisors believed in the *domino theory*. They feared that if Communism prevailed in one country, it was likely to spread, one after the other, to neighboring countries, similar to the sequential fall of a row of dominoes. To them, Greece was merely the first domino. If it "got knocked over," then Turkey would be next, with most of Europe likely to follow. Thus, they were determined to prevent that crucial first domino (Greece) from falling. A decade and a half later, American policymakers applied this same domino theory to Asia. In part, this led to American intervention in Vietnam (see Chapter 19).

In a speech generally known as the Truman Doctrine, the president addressed Congress on March 12, 1947, and asked for the legislature's approval of his Greek aid program. Outlining the fundamentals of containment, he said that the United States must now help "free peoples who are resisting attempted subjugation by armed minorities or outside pressures." The American people rallied around his speech, and Congress approved his plan. In the space of one afternoon, Truman had outlined American Cold War foreign policy for a generation or more.

The aid program worked. By 1949, the non-Communists had prevailed, solidifying Greece as a staunch American ally during the Cold War.

Marshalling a new plan to help Europe rebuild

Postwar economic recovery in Europe was slow. The war had been absolutely ruinous. Cities were choked with rubble. Railroads were in disrepair. Businesses were defunct. Millions of refugees were still in limbo, congregating in displaced-persons camps or eking out a living in foreign countries. For Europeans, the economic outlook was grim. In the summer of 1947, the Truman administration decided that, for three reasons, the United States must implement a program of massive economic aid to Europe:

✔ It would help the U.S. economy because most American exports went to Europe.

✔ Only with strong economies could Europeans maintain enough military strength to deter the Soviets.

✔ Economic aid was a key component of containment.

In June 1947, during a Harvard commencement speech, George C. Marshall, the secretary of state, announced the plan that would eventually bear his name. In the weeks that followed, the European nations eagerly voiced their needs, asking for $22 billion in aid. Truman considered this but cut the number to $17 billion in the final plan he sent to Congress for approval.

The debate over the Marshall Plan was intense. Some Republicans opposed the Marshall Plan as nothing more than welfare for Europe. Because of this opposition, the plan might not have passed if not for a Communist coup that toppled a democratic government in Czechoslovakia. This event melted away opposition to the Marshall Plan, and after much debate, Congress passed it in early 1948.

The Marshall Plan was the economic aspect of containment. Between 1948 and 1952, the United States pumped almost $13 billion into non-Communist Europe. The result was a major rebirth of the European economies. By 1951, they experienced a remarkable 32.5 percent increase in their gross domestic products, a key indicator of economic growth.

The United States actually invited the Soviet Union and Russian-occupied eastern Europe to participate in the Marshall Plan. Although the Americans hoped the Communists would decline, the Soviets did briefly consider accepting the aid. But they couldn't agree to the preconditions set forth by the Americans, namely that they submit to independent scrutiny of their economy and integrate it into a general European market-oriented, capitalist economy. In the end, the Soviet Union and its eastern European partners refused participation in the Marshall Plan.

Flying aid to locked-in West Berlin

In 1948, with antagonism between the Soviet-led East and the American-led West deepening, a major crisis erupted in Berlin. The city was deep inside Soviet-occupied eastern Germany. Even so, four major powers still occupied the city. The Soviets were in East Berlin. The British, French, and Americans occupied the other half of the city in what became known as West Berlin. Because the western countries couldn't agree with the Soviets on any sort of postwar vision for Germany, Stalin decided to force them out of Berlin. Starting on June 24, 1948, the Soviets blocked all railroad and road access to West Berlin. This event is generally known as the Berlin Blockade.

This blockade was a hostile, perhaps even warlike, act. Still, President Truman didn't want to risk war over Berlin. Nor did he want to retreat from the city, abandon West Berliners to a Communist future, and suffer a defeat in the Cold War. So he decided to thwart the blockade with an airlift operation. Almost immediately, the United States Air Force and Britain's Royal Air Force began flying supplies into West Berlin.

Western pilots soon were flying round-the-clock, hauling everything that a modern city could need, including milk, flour, coal, construction material, medicine, machinery, and even candy. The airlift lasted for a year, and at its height, a British or American plane was taking off or landing every minute of the day. The western countries even built a new airport, Tempelhof, to handle many of the flights. The Soviets didn't attempt to shoot down any of the planes, but they did, at times, harass them with their own planes. Thirty-nine British and 31 American pilots lost their lives during the airlift. Throughout 1948–1949, the airmen made about 278,000 flights and hauled more than 2 million tons of supplies to a grateful West Berlin population. Knowing that the blockade had not worked, Stalin lifted it on May 11, 1949.

West Berlin would remain non-Communist, and from that point on, the city would be on the very front lines of the Cold War. In 1961, the Communists actually built a wall between East and West Berlin. With the exception of prisons, it was the first wall built in modern history to keep people in rather than out. It stood for 28 years as the iconic symbol of Cold War tension. In November 1989, the whole world watched as the two Berlins were reunited and the wall "fell."

Facing off with opposing alliances

Even as the Berlin Airlift unfolded, the United States and its western European allies were putting together a military alliance for mutual defense in case of a Soviet attack. Founded on April 4, 1949, the *North Atlantic Treaty Organization* (NATO) included Britain, Belgium, Holland, Luxembourg, France, Italy, Greece, Turkey, Portugal, Spain, Norway, Iceland, Denmark,

Canada, and, of course, the United States. A new non-Communist West Germany, cobbled together out of the old western allied occupation zones in that country, eventually became part of NATO by the mid-1950s.

Stalin responded by creating the *Warsaw Pact,* a Soviet-led alliance of eastern European Communist states. This alliance included Poland, Bulgaria, Hungary, Czechoslovakia, Romania, and, of course, East Germany, a country the Soviets created out of their zone of occupation. Figure 17-1 shows which European countries belonged to which organization.

Figure 17-1:
Map of Europe divided — NATO and Warsaw Pact countries, 1949–1989.

Cold War 1945-1990 Military Alliances
- Founding members of the North Atlantic Alliance (NATO) 1949
- Entry: Greece and Turkey 1952, West Germany 1955, Spain 1982
- Founding members of the Warsaw Pact 1955
- Entry: East Germany 1956
- Withdrawal: Albania 1968
- Neutrals

Joining NATO was a landmark event in American history. It was the first time the United States ever agreed to become part of a military alliance in peacetime. The Americans knew that, for the alliance to have any viability, they would have to provide the bulk of the manpower and firepower. In practice, this meant assuming responsibility for the defense of Europe. Membership in NATO also guaranteed a continued and major American cultural presence in Europe, from 1949 until today, because the alliance still exists.

Expanding the Cold War Globally: The 1950s and 1960s

Starting in the 1950s and continuing into the 1960s, the Cold War became a truly global struggle, with particular focus on Asia. China became a Communist country in 1949, greatly expanding the scope of the Cold War. Aided by China, Communist nationalist movements struggled for power in such countries as Korea, Vietnam, Laos, Malaya, and the Philippines. The United States, imbued with an intense anti-Communist mood, expended significant resources to contain Communism in all of those countries. But the major American focus was still against the Soviet Union that, by now, had nuclear weapons on par with America's weapons. Stalin died in 1953 and was eventually succeeded by Nikita Kruschev, a Ukrainian peasant and loyal Communist Party man. Kruschev was not as repressive or murderous as Stalin, but he was a committed Communist, determined to prevail in the Cold War. Thus, the 1950s and early 1960s were a time of major nuclear tension between the superpowers, when any crisis, large or small, could have led to all-out war.

Taking a "New Look" with Ike

In 1952, as the Cold War was hardening into a long-term struggle, the American people elected Dwight Eisenhower, a World War II hero, to the presidency. He had enjoyed a long and successful career in the Army, commanding Allied forces in the Normandy invasion (for more, see Chapter 16). Americans liked Eisenhower ("Ike") and trusted him to defend the nation during this time of Cold War peril. When Ike took office in early 1953, his first priority was to end a war the United States was fighting against Communism in Korea (for more, see Chapter 18). With that accomplished, he set about the task of keeping the peace in the wider world.

Eisenhower believed that small, containment-oriented conventional wars around the globe would drain the federal treasury and eventually ruin the American economy. In a larger sense, he believed that federal spending was too high and that budget deficits were very bad. He knew that the United States could never achieve equality in conventional military forces with the larger

Soviet Union, so he decided to save money by paring down conventional U.S. forces while employing airpower and nuclear weapons as the main deterrent to the Russians. This strategy was known as the *New Look*. He cut the Army from 3.5 million soldiers to 2.47 million, essentially gutting the combat readiness of America's ground forces. He even cut the Navy by 300 ships. The lion's share of defense resources went to the rapidly expanding United States Air Force, the main delivery source of nuclear weapons in the 1950s.

The New Look rested entirely on the threat of massive retaliation against any aggressive Soviet moves. The policy depended "upon a great capacity to retaliate, instantly, by means and at places of our own choosing," in the opinion of Secretary of State John Foster Dulles, one of its greatest proponents. Essentially, the New Look was a bluff designed to deter the Soviets with the threat that the United States would use nuclear weapons against them in response to any sort of Russian aggression. Eisenhower stayed with this policy through eight years in office. He retired in 1961.

Filling the SAC with nukes

The centerpiece of Ike's New Look strategy was the Air Force, specifically the Strategic Air Command (SAC). Consisting of nearly 2,000 heavy bombers capable of delivering nuclear weapons on Soviet targets, the SAC was a powerful weapon. Gen. Curtis LeMay, a cigar-chomping World War II hero and hawkish innovator, commanded SAC. LeMay and his aviators pioneered the use of jet bombers and in-air refueling techniques.

By the mid-1950s, nuclear-armed SAC bombers were on runways or in the air at all times, constantly on the alert for orders to hit the Soviet Union. Fortunately those orders never came. In that sense, SAC fulfilled its main mission of deterring the Soviets.

By the end of the '50s, the American and Soviet nuclear arsenals diversified to include intercontinental nuclear ballistic missiles (ICBMs), nuclear-armed and -propelled submarines, and even nuclear artillery shells. By 1960, the two superpowers were in the middle of a full-fledged arms race for newer, bigger, and better doomsday weapons.

Going to the brink: The Cuban Missile Crisis

In 1959, Fidel Castro came to power in Cuba on the wings of a revolution. He soon implemented policies that greatly damaged American economic interests in that country. More ominously, he pursued a strong friendship with the Soviet Union. In April 1961, a group of amateurish Cuban expatriates, with the help of the CIA, attempted to invade Cuba at the Bay of Pigs and overthrow Castro, but they failed miserably. This clumsy disaster only strengthened Castro as an anti-American tyrant, a Communist, and an ally of the Soviet Union.

John F. Kennedy succeeded Eisenhower as president after a narrow electoral victory over Richard Nixon in 1960. By 1962, Kennedy was deeply concerned with Castro's Cuba as a potential threat to American security. These fears hardened that October when American U2 spy planes revealed the existence of Soviet nuclear missiles and extensive launch facilities in Cuba.

Kennedy announced the presence of these missiles to the world and demanded that the Soviets remove them. He even contemplated a U.S. invasion of Cuba if the Soviets refused. This began an extremely tense two-week standoff in which the two superpowers edged steadily closer to a nuclear war. At last, after protracted negotiations, the Soviet Union and United States resolved the crisis on the following basis:

- The United States agreed to remove its nuclear missiles from Turkey. Unbeknown to the Russians, Kennedy had planned to do this anyway because the missiles were antiquated and the Turks wanted them out.

- The United States pledged not to invade Cuba.

- The Soviets agreed to permanently remove all nuclear weapons from Cuba.

The Cuban Missile Crisis was so frightening that it actually brought the Soviets and the Americans closer to each other. They established a hot line between Washington and Moscow to facilitate communication during any future crisis. In 1963, they also agreed to a nuclear test ban treaty, the first attempt to limit the proliferation of nuclear weapons.

The crisis was the closest the world ever came to nuclear war during the Cold War years. Thanks to personal interviews with Soviet commanders and the post–Cold War release of key documents, historians now know that, if the U.S. had invaded Cuba during the crisis, the Soviet military commanders actually had some leeway to launch their missiles against the east coast, with or without Moscow's permission.

Calming the Cold War with Détente: The 1970s

During the 1960s, the greatest Cold War hot spot was Vietnam, where the United States fought a protracted, costly, and unpopular war to contain Communism (for more, see Chapter 19). However, as the 1970s began, the United States was scaling back its operations in Vietnam with the intention of eventually withdrawing its troops from the country. At the same time, the two major Communist powers, China and the Soviet Union, were on poor terms with each other. They clashed over border issues, differing Communist philosophies, and traditional nationalist tension. By 1970, they were actually on the verge of an armed conflict.

Richard Nixon, elected to the presidency in 1968, sought to exploit this deep split in the Communist world. He initiated triangular diplomacy, reaching out to both Communist powers, hoping to gain an advantage by playing one off against the other. He also hoped that they would help him end the war in Vietnam. Commentators called his new Cold War policy *détente,* a French word that means "defusing tension."

Globetrotting with Nixon

In February 1972, Nixon stunned the world by visiting Communist China (see Figure 17-2), a country the United States had fought in the Korean War (for more, see Chapter 18) and had treated as a veritable enemy ever since. For their part, the Chinese wanted better relations with the Americans for economic reasons and diplomatic too — they sought to end their U.S.-imposed isolation in the United Nations. Nixon's dramatic visit began a process that resulted in the re-establishment of diplomatic relations between the two countries in 1979 and a tremendous amount of economic activity as well.

Figure 17-2: President Richard Nixon inspects Chinese troops during his historic visit to Communist China in 1972.

© CORBIS

Then, in May 1972, Nixon visited the Soviet Union and met with Leonid Brezhnev, the Russian leader who had succeeded Kruschev in 1964. Brezhnev decided to accept Nixon's détente for two reasons:

- ✔ His country was in bad shape economically. Believe it or not, the Soviets needed American grain imports to feed their people.

- ✔ Brezhnev was concerned that Nixon's China visit could lead to an anti-Soviet alliance between the U.S. and China, so he hoped to prevent that by growing closer with the U.S.

Nixon had the political strength to cozy up to the Communist powers because he possessed such staunch anti-Communist credentials. He had made his political career on fierce opposition to Communism from his days as a young congressman and senator in the 1940s, to his term as Eisenhower's vice president. Thus, when he visited China and Russia to pursue détente, he received very little criticism at home. Most commentators lauded these visits and painted Nixon as a peace-minded statesman.

Limiting nukes with SALT

Both superpowers were tired of the considerable cost of building nuclear arms, so they wanted to place some sort of limit on them. The result was the *Strategic Arms Limitation Treaty* (SALT), a major effort to slow down the superpower arms race. SALT was the centerpiece of Nixon's détente. He signed this treaty with the Soviets in 1972.

Although SALT didn't require the USSR and U.S. to destroy any actual weapons in their arsenals, it did limit how many offensive nuclear missiles they could build in the future. The same was true for SALT II, a follow-up treaty that another American president, Jimmy Carter, signed with the Soviets in 1979. The SALT treaties represented a rare moment of cooperation between the main Cold War antagonists.

Invading Afghanistan deflates détente

Détente came to a screeching halt in December 1979, when the Soviet Union invaded its neighbor Afghanistan. The Soviets did so to support a pro-Communist Afghan government in its struggle against fundamentalist Muslim insurgents. Although Brezhnev expected a quick war, Afghanistan turned into a Soviet quagmire, lasting nine years, ending in defeat, and costing more than 13,800 Russian lives. The Soviet invasion of Afghanistan also led to a major decline in relations with the United States. The Americans viewed the invasion as a troubling example of Russian expansionism and worried that the Soviets would soon make a grab for Middle Eastern oil.

President Carter was an enthusiastic proponent of détente, but he felt betrayed and troubled by Afghanistan, an invasion he called "the most serious threat to the peace since the Second World War." In 1980, Carter adopted a new hard-line stance against the USSR. He issued an embargo on détente-inspired exports of U.S. grain and technology to the Soviet Union. He condemned the Soviet invasion of Afghanistan in the strongest possible terms. He boycotted the 1980 Summer Olympics in Moscow (the Soviets retaliated by boycotting the 1984 Olympics in Los Angeles). Carter announced that any further Russian expansion into the Middle East would be regarded as an attack on the vital interests of the U.S. In other words, it would mean World War III.

Watching Communism Crumble: The 1980s and 1990s

By 1980, the United States was in the midst of what Carter called a severe "malaise." The country was filled with pessimism and apprehension for the future, and this stemmed from several events. The war in Vietnam (for more, see Chapter 19) had ended in catastrophic defeat in 1975. Détente had unraveled. The Soviets were on the offensive, seemingly winning the Cold War. In November 1979, Iranian fundamentalist Muslim terrorists had overrun the U.S. embassy in Tehran and taken 66 Americans hostage. American military forces were in a poor state of readiness. To top it off, the economy was in the throes of a serious recession.

Carter's inability to negotiate the release of the hostages, combined with his failure to solve these other major problems, contributed to his defeat in the 1980 presidential election. His Republican opponent, Ronald Reagan, swept into power on his promise to rejuvenate the military, get tough with the Soviets, fix the economy, and win the release of the hostages. More than anything, he wanted Americans to feel pride in their country again. The new president's impact on the Cold War, and American history, was so profound that it is sometimes referred to as the *Reagan Revolution.*

Rebuilding the military — a martial renaissance

In order to have the strength to confront America's enemies, Reagan knew he had to rebuild America's armed forces. Congress had ended the draft in 1973, creating an all-volunteer force. Lack of funding, poor recruiting standards, and low public esteem for the armed forces eroded the quality of the all-volunteer military by the early 1980s. To combat this problem, President Reagan dramatically increased defense spending, leading to budget deficits.

When he took over in 1981, the defense budget was $140 billion. When he left office in 1989, it was $300 billion. This spending, combined with advances in weapons technology, innovative recruiting campaigns, and a pro-military upsurge in American public opinion, transformed the American military into a powerful, formidable force.

Many Americans blamed the military for the ill-fated war in Vietnam. Thus, in the early 1970s, anti-military sentiment was at an all-time high. For instance, a 1973 Harris Poll of the American people revealed that the military was the second-least respected occupation, ranking only above garbage collectors.

The poor state of the armed forces in the 1970s contributed to its soiled reputation at that time. The Army was in especially bad shape. Forty percent of American soldiers in Europe used drugs. Seven percent were addicted to heroin. Forty percent of soldiers had no high school diploma, and a like number scored in the lowest mental category on standardized tests. By the end of the 1980s, the Army had undergone a dramatic change. More than 98 percent of soldiers now had high school diplomas, 75 percent tested in the highest mental category, discipline problems were at an all-time low, and only 1 percent of soldiers tested positive for drugs. The result of this transformation was a volunteer army of well-trained, upwardly mobile soldiers who excelled in combat. The Navy, Air Force, and Marines also transformed for the better during this time, but the Army's renaissance was the most remarkable.

Hostile armies in Europe

Throughout the 1980s, as Cold War tension worsened due to Afghanistan, the potential for Soviet expansion in the Middle East, and the ascension to power of a new group of hard-line, anti-American Communists in Russia, the NATO and Warsaw Pact armies manned their positions on either side of the Iron Curtain and prepared for the possibility of war. Reagan beefed up NATO forces by sending American Pershing II nuclear cruise missiles to West Germany. This move provoked widespread protests by peace activists in Europe, but it caused the Soviets much consternation. In the meantime, tens of thousands of American soldiers served under the NATO mantle in Europe, training for a war that never came.

Fighting proxy wars

From 1980 to 1986, relations between the two superpowers were as poor as they had ever been. Détente was only a distant memory. Leonid Brezhnev died in 1982, giving way to Yuri Andropov and Konstantin Chernenko, two hard-line Communist expansionists. The Soviet war in Afghanistan continued unabated. The Russian armed forces were the largest in the world, and the Soviets were sponsoring Communist movements or insurgencies all over the globe.

The Star Wars defense

"Wouldn't it be better to protect the American people than avenge them?" With that simple question, President Reagan, in March 1983, embarked upon the *Strategic Defense Initiative.* Known to its supporters as SDI and its detractors as "Star Wars," the program envisioned the creation of a ballistic missile defense shield that would protect the United States against any Soviet nuclear attack. Essentially, the Strategic Defense Initiative raised the stakes of the Cold War. The program was quite costly and years away from fruition.

Nonetheless, if the United States could make itself impervious to Russian nuclear attacks, its Cold War position would be greatly strengthened. This meant the Soviets had to take the Strategic Defense Initiative seriously and prepare a costly response of their own, something they could not afford by the 1980s.

Reagan was a hard-liner himself. Describing the Soviet Union as an "evil empire" and "the focus of evil in the modern world," he labored tenaciously to contain Communism. His Reagan Doctrine sought to eliminate Communism in third-world countries. Bolstered by a strengthening military and a steadily growing economy, Reagan fought small, largely successful, proxy wars against Communists in a variety of places:

✔ He aided right-wing paramilitary forces against Marxist revolutionaries in El Salvador.

✔ In Nicaragua, he sent weapons, money, and even some troops to support the Contras, an anti-Communist group who opposed the Soviet-sponsored, leftist Sandinistas who had won power there in 1979.

✔ In 1983, Communist revolutionaries took over the tiny Caribbean island of Grenada, home to several hundred American medical students. In response, Reagan invaded and took over the island, saving the students and crushing the budding Communist movement.

✔ Reagan sent extensive aid to the *Mujahideen,* the Islamic fundamentalists who were fighting the Soviets in Afghanistan. The Americans helped train the Mujahideen, but most notably, they provided them with Stinger missiles that could shoot down Soviet helicopters.

Ending the Cold War

By 1985, the Soviet Union was in deep economic and political crisis. Years of backward, inefficient Communist economic policies, plus Cold War military spending, had led to societal stagnation. Economic growth was close to zero percent. Consumer items were scarce. The average citizen's standard of living was poor. A tiny Communist elite enjoyed a wealthy lifestyle while ordinary people had little access to opportunity. The system was on the verge of total collapse.

In March 1985, Chernenko died. A young, reform-minded leader, Mikhail Gorbachev, succeeded him. Mindful of the dismal state of the country, Gorbachev knew that the Soviet Union must reform economically and politically. His reforms were known as *perestroika*. In essence, perestroika meant more free-market capitalism, more personal freedoms, ending the arms race, and less Cold War tension with the United States.

Beginning in 1985, Gorbachev met with Reagan in a series of summits. Sensing a change in the Soviets, and reacting to major Gorbachev military and political concessions, Reagan softened his own stance. The two leaders, through laborious negotiations over several summits, agreed to new arms limitation treaties that defused Cold War tension. A new détente now ruled, and the United States clearly had the upper hand.

Unable to sustain its commitments abroad, the Soviets reigned in their support for third-world Communist movements. They also withdrew from Afghanistan. Having unleashed the forces of change, Gorbachev found that he could not control them. The new freedoms greatly weakened the Communist Party's hold on power in Russia and eastern Europe. In the fall of 1989, Communist regimes collapsed, one by one, under pressure from anti-Communist reformers in Poland, East Germany, Romania, Hungary, and Czechoslovakia. In Berlin, jubilant crowds demolished the infamous wall that had separated East and West for 28 years. The Soviet Union did nothing to stop them.

Germany reunited in 1990 under a democratic government. Democracy also spread to the rest of eastern Europe. Soon these reforms spread to Russia. In 1991, the Communist Party fell from power, bringing a final end to the Cold War.

The rapid collapse of Communism in Europe and Russia was stunning to most Americans. During the Cold War, the vast majority of Americans believed that the Cold War would rage for their entire lives. Instead, in the blink of an eye, the United States had prevailed. The dramatic end to so many decades of tension and conflict convinced many jubilant Americans that the country was now entering a new era of perpetual peace and security. To borrow a popular phrase from the time, Americans believed they could now enjoy the "peace dividend" they had earned through so many years of vigilance.

Chapter 18

Hot War in Asia: The Korean War

• •

In This Chapter

▶ Containing the North Korean onslaught

▶ Crossing the 38th parallel

▶ Dealing with a wider war

▶ Negotiating a status quo ending

• •

A significant consequence of World War II was the disintegration of colonial empires, such as the Imperial Japanese empire. Between 1904 and 1945, the Japanese controlled Korea, a peninsular country in east Asia. With Japan's defeat, Soviet and American troops occupied Korea with the Soviets in the north, above the 38th parallel, and the Americans below it in the south. Their job was to disarm the Japanese and then, together, create a new Korea.

However, as the *Cold War* (a period of intense conflict between the U.S. and the Soviet Union without actual warfare; see Chapter 17 for more) solidified between 1945 and 1949, the ensuing tension between the Soviets and the Americans led to the creation of two Koreas:

✔ North Korea was a hard-line Communist state in the Russian model.

✔ South Korea was a non-Communist, but not necessarily democratic state that emerged under American support.

In 1949, when Communists under Mao Tse-tung won power in China after several years of civil war, Cold War tensions in Korea grew even worse. By 1950, Soviet and U.S. troops were gone. Both Koreas wanted to unite the peninsula under their control. That summer, when the Communist North attempted to do just that, President Harry Truman decided to send American troops to stop them and save South Korea from Communism. This was the beginning of a three-year war fought from 1950 to 1953 that claimed more than 33,000 American lives.

In this chapter, I outline why the war happened and give you a feel for how close the North Koreans came to winning in 1950. I describe the seesaw battles of 1950–1951 and explain the overriding politics that dictated much of what happened on the battlefield. Finally, I cover how, why, and when the war ended, and provide you with a sense of its enduring legacy that still affects us today.

Conspiring for Conquest in Korea

In 1949, Kim Il-Sung, the Communist leader of North Korea, conceived of a plan to conquer South Korea. To go forward with his plan, he needed Chinese and Soviet approval because he would be dependent upon these two premier Communist nations for supplies and protection in case the U.S. intervened in Korea.

Contrasting Koreas

The two Koreas were a study in contrasts. The North was clearly stronger than the South. This imbalance was what prompted Kim Il-Sung to contemplate his invasion in the first place. Needless to say, comparing the two Koreas' military and geopolitical strength did not bode well for South Korea:

North Korea had

- A hard-line, absolutist, Communist regime in total control of the country
- Control of most of Korea's industry and water resources
- A well-trained army of 133,000 soldiers, many of whom had fought in the Chinese civil war
- Soviet-made tanks, artillery, warplanes, and small arms

South Korea had

- A shaky, repressive, non-Communist government, headed by Syngman Rhee, an aged former political exile who had won a mildly corrupt election in 1948.
- An insurgent Communist movement that used terrorism in an attempt to overthrow Rhee.
- Very little industry or natural resources.

✔ An army of 95,000 militia soldiers who were poorly armed, poorly trained, and were not prepared for conventional warfare. They had almost no American military support.

By April 1950, after months of secret meetings with the Russians and Chinese, Kim Il-Sung had secured the approval of his two Communist allies to invade South Korea. The Soviets would supply him with weapons and technology, while the Chinese planned to send troops. On June 25, 1950, North Korean troops and tanks crashed across the border into South Korea (see Figure 18-1). The Korean War had begun.

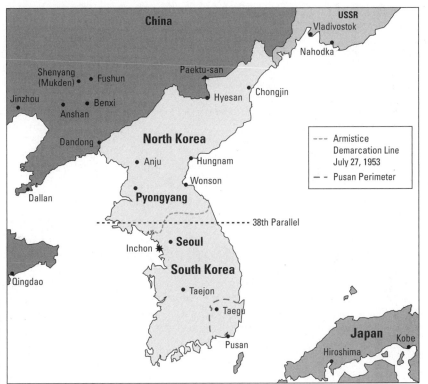

Figure 18-1:
Map of the Korean War, 1950–1953.

Slicing into the South

Not surprisingly, when the North Koreans invaded in June 1950, they sliced through South Korean defenders like the proverbial hot knife through butter.

They captured Seoul, the South Korean capital, in three days. They continued their advance along the three major north–south roads that spanned South Korea. South Korean resistance was spotty at best. Wherever the South Koreans did resist, their North Korean enemies crushed them.

At this point, the South had nothing with which to hold back the North Korean juggernaut. The Rhee government fled south, rather than surrender. Their days were clearly numbered, though, unless they received help from the United States.

Getting U.S. and UN Political Ducks in a Row

President Truman believed that the United States must contain Communism wherever it threatened to spread. He knew that the American people were deeply worried about the threat of Communism to America's security and liberty. Indeed, as committed as he was to opposing the Communists, some of his political opponents, such as Sen. Joseph McCarthy, repeatedly accused him of being too soft on Communism. Thus, when he heard about the North Korean invasion of South Korea, he felt strongly that the United States must intervene. He immediately ordered American troops, planes, and ships to Korea. Congress overwhelmingly supported this decision.

Stemming the tide of Communism

The ironic thing about Truman's commitment to the war in Korea is that most American policymakers didn't consider the country to be of vital interest to the United States. Truman's secretary of state, Dean Acheson, had even given a highly publicized speech in January 1950 omitting Korea from the Asian/Pacific countries America planned to defend in the event of Communist aggression.

So why the change of heart? Two reasons:

- The United States was committed to a policy of *containment* of Communism, no matter where it threatened to spread.

- Truman and other American leaders were convinced — correctly as it turned out — that the North Koreans could never invade South Korea without Soviet and Chinese approval.

Truman and his advisors feared that, if the United States did nothing in Korea, their inaction would embolden other Communist invasions, perhaps against western Europe or Japan.

Calling on the UN

At the end of World War II, the Allies had created the United Nations (UN) as a world peacekeeping body that would enforce collective security. President Truman was determined to enlist the support of the UN to check North Korean aggression.

Working with his allies, Truman succeeded in getting the UN to adopt a resolution that mandated North Korean withdrawal from South Korea. Under the mandate, multinational military forces would be deployed to Korea, fight together with UN support, eject the North Koreans from South Korea, and restore the prewar status quo. Eventually, 16 non-Communist countries sent troops to fight in Korea, including Turkey, Greece, Philippines, Canada, Britain, Belgium, Luxembourg, and, of course, the United States.

The United States succeeded in winning UN approval to intercede in Korea partially because of a stroke of luck. The Soviet Union was absent from the proceedings of the powerful UN Security Council whose approval was necessary for UN troops to be sent to South Korea. The council consisted of five permanent members: the U.S., Britain, France, China, and the Soviet Union. In late June 1950, the Soviets were boycotting the Security Council meetings because the non-Communist countries on the council had not allowed the new Communist Chinese government to assume control of that country's council seat. The Soviet Union's absence was a lucky break for Truman and a bad mistake by the Soviets.

Implementing NSC-68

The war in Korea created a favorable political climate for Truman to implement a National Security Council policy paper called NSC-68. The paper was the product of a top-secret meeting of Truman's national security team in January 1950. At the meeting, the team analyzed the Soviet and Chinese threat in dire terms. To counter the growing threat, they called for three major courses of action:

  ✔ The U.S. and its allies had to begin an immediate conventional military buildup.

✔ For containment to succeed, the United States should now assume the defense of the non-Communist world.

✔ These new defense responsibilities would mean spending between $35 billion and $50 billion per year and 20 percent of the gross domestic product on national defense.

The authors of NSC-68 envisioned a new military draft and higher taxes to support their program. Truman agreed with NSC-68. However, he knew it would be controversial because of its call for larger armed forces, more military spending, and higher taxes. So he kept the plan secret until the North Korean invasion created a more receptive political environment. From that point on, one of Truman's key wartime objectives was to implement NSC-68.

Clashing with the Titans

The United States was ill-prepared to fight in Korea. The closest American ground combat formations were on occupation duty in Japan. These units were undermanned, ill-equipped, and poorly trained for war. Nonetheless, the desperate circumstances in Korea meant that these men had to be thrown into battle against the North Koreans. Throughout the summer of 1950, these Americans, along with their hard-pressed South Korean allies, clung to a small perimeter, anchored by their main supply port of Pusan. This little perimeter was all that stood between the North Koreans and the total conquest of South Korea. Day after day, the North Koreans attacked, putting maximum pressure on their enemies before reinforcements could arrive to help them.

Holding the Pusan Perimeter

For the unfortunate American soldiers in the Pusan Perimeter, the summer of 1950 was a terrifying, difficult time. They had little tank support. They were not in good enough physical condition to deal with the suffocating heat. Their weapons were inferior to the Communist weapons. Some of the Americans had never even been trained to fire their weapons, particularly the recoilless rifles that were their only defense against North Korean tanks. Numerous American soldiers died because they couldn't figure out how to use the weapon against enemy tanks. By August 1, American ground forces had suffered more than 6,000 casualties, including 901 taken prisoner. The North Koreans simply executed many of their American captives.

As bad as the situation at Pusan was, the Americans did have complete control of the air. Within days of American entry into the war, Navy, Air Force, and Marine aircraft swept the North Korean air force from the skies. With unchallenged mastery of the skies, American planes repeatedly strafed and bombed North Korean supply columns and troop concentrations. Before long, the planes were doing so much damage that the enemy could only move at night. Soon supply problems were slowing down North Korean attacks. In the final analysis, this air support helped save the Pusan Perimeter from total annihilation.

Calling on MacArthur

Seventy-year-old Gen. Douglas MacArthur was the supreme UN commander. During World War II, MacArthur had earned a hero's reputation for his exploits in the Pacific Theater (for details, see Chapter 16). Since then, he had presided over the American occupation of Japan.

By early September, he knew that North Korean attacks on the Pusan Perimeter were losing momentum and that his forces there were getting stronger by the day, thanks to reinforcements. He now had 500 tanks and 180,000 troops in the perimeter, plus complete control of the air and sea. To MacArthur, the time had come to unleash a bold counterattack and turn the tide of the war.

Invading at Inchon

Instead of attacking from within the Pusan Perimeter, MacArthur proposed an amphibious invasion at Inchon, South Korea, near Seoul, far behind the North Korean lines. The idea was to unhinge the whole North Korean army, outflank them, force them back from the Pusan Perimeter, and then cut them off before they could retreat from South Korea. The plan was so risky that many of the military service chiefs in Washington, D.C., initially opposed it.

The main problem was Inchon itself. The tides and winds were tricky and unpredictable. The area didn't have beaches so much as wide-open tidal flats that forced invaders to reveal themselves. Only MacArthur's reputation swayed Truman and the generals in Washington to approve his invasion plan.

On September 15, 1950, the 1st Marine Division led the way into Inchon against almost no opposition. The invasion succeeded beyond anyone's wildest expectations. Within two weeks, the North Koreans were in full retreat, UN forces had liberated Seoul, and the troops were in a position to cross the 38th parallel into North Korea. The military situation had completely reversed. Now the North Koreans were on the verge of losing the war.

Mao Tse-tung, the Chinese Communist leader, actually warned the North Koreans in late August 1950 that the Americans might make an amphibious invasion at Inchon. From the start, Mao had been planning to enter this war, so he was massing troops along his common border with North Korea, and he was studying the situation in South Korea intently. His intelligence reports, combined with what he knew of American amphibious capability, made him believe an invasion was coming. Alas, the North Koreans didn't heed his warning.

Crossing the line: The 38th parallel

Crossing the 38th parallel into North Korea was a political, not a military decision. The UN mandate had only called for the return to the status quo in Korea. Moreover, the status quo was in line with Truman's policy to contain, but not necessarily roll back, Communism. Invading North Korea would mean embracing a more ambitious policy of rolling back Communism, not just containing it. Taking this into consideration, Truman decided, for several reasons, to send his troops into Korea:

- He had a good chance of eliminating the Communist regime in North Korea and uniting the whole country under Rhee's anti-Communist government.

- He was concerned that if he stopped at the parallel, the North Koreans would regroup and invade the South again.

- Many of his UN partners favored invading North Korea.

- In a moral sense, Truman liked the idea of liberating the North Korean people from Communism.

With UN approval, Truman gave the go-ahead to invade North Korea. American troops crossed the parallel on October 7, 1950. In the next few weeks, they took the North Korean capital of Pyongyang and overran much of the country.

Thinking wrong about China

In crossing the parallel, the main concern now for UN forces was the possibility of Chinese entry into the war. China was just across the Yalu River border from North Korea. The Communist Chinese might not like the idea of an American-dominated army marching all the way to their border. The Central Intelligence Agency (CIA) advised Truman that the Chinese, after their long civil war, were in no position to intervene in Korea. MacArthur told the president the same thing during a brief meeting at Wake Island on October 15, 1950. They could not have been more wrong.

Thanks to recently released Chinese government documents, we now know that the Chinese intended to enter this war from the beginning, even before U.S. involvement. After American entry into the war, and with the great reversal of fortune that occurred in the UN's favor in the fall of 1950, the Chinese were even more determined to get into the war. For months they had been massing troops on the North Korean border.

In late October, Mao ordered a quarter million of those soldiers to cross the Yalu into Korea. Immediately, they clashed with American and South Korean soldiers. When MacArthur's commanders on the ground told him that they were now facing Chinese soldiers, the general refused to believe it. Aloof from the situation on the front lines and surrounded by a skeptical staff of mediocre sycophants in his Tokyo headquarters, he couldn't bring himself to face the truth of Chinese involvement.

Hawkeye, Hot Lips, Radar, and the rest of the gang

The long-running television program *M*A*S*H* is, in American popular culture, the most enduring image of the Korean War. Based on a movie and novel of the same title, the TV show portrayed an American medical unit in Korea (the acronym *MASH* stands for mobile army surgical hospital). Alan Alda (Capt. "Hawkeye" Pierce) headlined a cast that included Loretta Swit (Maj. Margaret "Hot Lips" Houlihan), Jamie Farr (Cpl. Max Klinger), Gary Burghoff (Cpl. "Radar" O'Reilly), Harry Morgan (Col. Sherman Potter), Mike Farrell (Capt. B. J. Hunnicut), and Larry Linville (Maj. Frank Burns). The program aired between 1972 and 1983 on CBS. What made the show unique was that it successfully mixed comedy and drama to show both the lighter side and stark realities of the Korean War. Many of the story lines were inspired by interviews with doctors who had actually served in MASH units during the war. This gave the show a gritty, cutting-edge mood.

But, in reality, how historically accurate was *M*A*S*H?* The answer is, reasonably accurate.

The show beautifully conveyed the dedication and competence of Army medics in Korea, as well as the overwhelming, demoralizing nature of their constant duel with death. As the program indicated, the real MASH units did generally operate a few miles behind the lines. If need be, they could pick up and move at short notice. *M*A*S*H* accurately poked fun at the silliness and foolishness of military bureaucracy.

The program did have some problems, though. Weapons and uniforms were sometimes incorrect for the time period. *M*A*S*H* also exaggerated the role of helicopters in ferrying wounded to the hospital. The vast majority of wounded patients arrived via ambulances or jeeps, not by helicopter. *M*A*S*H* had an unabashedly antiwar and liberal message that sometimes led to naively inaccurate images of enemy soldiers, as well as unfair portrayals of American war policies, Regular Army soldiers, and leaders. Overall, though, *M*A*S*H* was a great show that brought the Korean War to life.

Changing the face of the war

Like phantoms in the night, the Chinese, by early November, melted away almost as quickly as they had arrived. Feeling vindicated, MacArthur breathed a sigh of relief and initiated his final push to the Yalu River. However, the Chinese had simply retreated to lick their wounds. Mao was amassing an even larger force of more than half a million soldiers. MacArthur had about 250,000, many of whom were advancing piecemeal, separated from one another, in the mountain gaps so prevalent in North Korea. In late November, the Chinese attacked them in force, forcing a major retreat, changing the whole nature of the war.

In the East, the 1st Marine Division, the U.S. Army's 3rd and 7th Divisions, plus South Korean troops bitterly fought their way back to evacuation ports in Hungnam and Wonsan. The U.S. Navy evacuated to South Korea 105,000 American and South Korean troops, along with about 100,000 North Korean civilians who wanted to escape Communism. This desperate struggle is generally known as the Battle of Chosin Reservoir. In the West, UN forces retreated overland, back across the parallel, with the Chinese threatening to annihilate them every step of the way.

The fighting around Chosin Reservoir was some of the worst that American soldiers have ever experienced. Temperatures were below zero. The wind was howling. Snow and ice covered the cold hills that permeated the area. The Chinese attacked, usually at night, in human waves, sometimes outnumbering the Americans ten-to-one. Soldiers or Marines manned perimeters, usually designed to keep control of key road nets or bridges. When the Chinese attacked them, they would blow bugles and then charge. The average Chinese soldier fought with suicidal fanaticism. The Americans would mow row after row of enemy soldiers down, and still they would keep coming. Their screams as they charged were bloodcurdling. Only firepower and the courageous resolve of American combat soldiers kept Chosin from ending in complete disaster.

Gaining and losing ground

"We face an entirely new war," MacArthur now admitted to the president. The general was absolutely right. With China in the war (and plenty of covert Soviet support), the Communists had great momentum. While UN forces were in headlong retreat, the Communists recaptured Seoul. But eventually, supply problems and horrendous casualties forced the enemy to halt. In February and March, the UN counterattacked and liberated Seoul for good. For much of the rest of 1951, the front lines ebbed and flowed as both sides launched limited offensives. The fighting was fierce, but neither side could gain a decisive advantage.

Truman didn't want this war to turn into World War III. After the failed rollback experience in North Korea, he sought to limit the war to the smaller objectives of preserving the status quo and implementing NSC-68. Even so, in January 1951, he and Congress approved the following emergency wartime measures:

✔ Reintroduced *selective service* (the draft)

✔ Put together a $50 billion defense budget

✔ Increased the size of the Army, including the deployment of tens of thousands more troops to Europe to deter the Soviets

✔ Doubled the size of the Air Force

Replacing a rebellious MacArthur

In the spring of 1951, the war turned in the UN's favor and, once again, American troops were in a position to cross the 38th parallel. Not wanting to invade North Korea again, Truman intended to halt at the parallel, negotiate a *cease-fire* (a mutual agreement to stop fighting) with the Communists, and end the war on the original UN mandate of preserving the status quo.

MacArthur vehemently disagreed. He wanted to push across the parallel, overrun North Korea, and even continue into China if necessary. In essence, Truman was sticking with containment while MacArthur favored rollback. Instead of keeping his opinions to himself, MacArthur went public with them, undercutting Truman's plans and ending any hope of a quick end to the war. MacArthur then wrote a public letter to a Republican congressman declaring that there was "no substitute for victory."

MacArthur and Truman never liked each other. They were very different individuals with radically divergent backgrounds. MacArthur was the son of a general and a West Pointer who had spent all of his adult life in the Army. He was aristocratic, egotistical, and politically ambitious. The son of a Missouri small farmer, Truman's origins were humble. His family was too poor to send him to college. In World War I, he had served in combat as an artillery officer (for more, see Chapter 14). Truman spent much of his life barely scraping by before going into politics. He disliked arrogant people, and he had a near-reverence for the common man. So, to him, MacArthur was nothing more than an overblown "brass hat." To MacArthur, Truman was a little man who was out of his depth as president.

Truman was furious with MacArthur for deliberately disobeying his commander-in-chief. The president felt that MacArthur's actions threatened the traditional American principle of civilian control over the military. Even though MacArthur was popular with the American people, Truman relieved him on April 11, 1951, ending his 50-year career.

MacArthur returned home to a tumultuous reception. He even addressed a joint session of Congress and rode in ticker tape parades in his honor. Over time, the excitement waned, and the American people grew less enamored of the old general. He hoped to launch a bid for the Republican presidential nomination in 1952, but his candidacy went nowhere. Truman later summed up the disagreement between the two men quite succinctly. "General MacArthur was ready to risk general war. I was not." Gen. Matthew Ridgway succeeded MacArthur as commander of UN forces in Korea.

Stalemate and Armistice

From the fall of 1951 until the end of the war in July 1953, the front lines stalemated while on-and-off peace negotiations proceeded. Each side now understood that total victory was no longer possible without a larger war that no one really wanted. Both hoped to end the war advantageously but not at great cost. So they were content to construct extensive front-line defenses along the ubiquitous Korean hills on either side of the parallel and engage in stationary warfare.

In the meantime, the Communist North Koreans and Chinese engaged in a dizzying series of negotiations with UN military leaders. The main sticking point in the negotiations was the exchange of prisoners of war (POWs). Because many North Korean and Chinese POWs didn't want to return to their Communist homes, the UN didn't want to force them. Enraged, the Communist negotiators threatened not to return UN POWs until all of their men were returned. It took nearly two tortuous years of peace talks for negotiators to finally hammer out a POW exchange agreement and sign an armistice to end the war.

Enduring on the main line of resistance

For the last two years of the war, the average American combat soldier served in static positions along the *main line of resistance,* or MLR. The MLR consisted of a long series of mutually supporting bunkers, trenches, observation posts, minefields, and listening posts that snaked along Korea's considerable hills, all the way across the peninsula.

Standing ground against the Chinese

One of the greatest American heroes of the Korean War was Cpl. Hiroshi Miyamura, who earned the Medal of Honor for his valor in fighting a massive Chinese attack on April 25, 1951.

Born to Japanese immigrants in Gallup, New Mexico, Miyamura served in World War II but never saw combat. When the Korean War started, he eagerly joined H Company, 7th Infantry Regiment, 3rd Infantry Division, as a machine gunner.

When the Chinese attacked on the evening of April 25, Miyamura refused to retreat. He remained at his machine gun, mowing down droves of Chinese soldiers. When his ammunition ran low, he killed ten soldiers in hand-to-hand combat. With enemy soldiers all around his position and his gun running out of ammunition, he turned to his comrades and said, "Take off. I'll cover you." They left, and he manned the gun alone, until he fired all of his bullets. "I still don't know why I did that," he said 50 years later. Regardless of why, he fought at close quarters with the enemy attackers before they eventually captured him the next morning.

Over the next two years of torturous captivity, he lost 50 pounds and constantly worried that the Chinese would shoot him if they ever discovered how many of their men he had killed. Most likely they never knew. The Chinese released him in August 1953, right after the war ended. Miyamura was shocked to find out that he had earned the Medal of Honor. Truman himself presented him with the medal.

Soldiers generally spent two months on the MLR for every month off the line. Most of the men were draftees serving a tour of duty that often lasted for one year. They were exposed to the freezing cold of the Korean winter and the heat of the country's summer. They ate prepackaged rations or hastily cooked food. They spent their days on watch for enemy attacks, patrolled at night, and often endured intense artillery and mortar bombardments. Periodically, one side or the other would make a limited attack that was usually designed to garner some advantage at the negotiating table. Some of these battles were among the fiercest of the war.

Ending the war: Eisenhower finishes what Truman began

As the war dragged on into the fall of 1952, Harry Truman decided to retire rather than run for reelection. He was succeeded by Dwight Eisenhower ("Ike"), a World War II hero and Republican who promised to go to Korea and break the stalemate. The American people elected Ike, in part, because they had great confidence in his ability to deal with the war in Korea.

True to his promise, Eisenhower visited Korea in late November 1952, sized up the situation, came home, and concocted a plan of action. He shared Truman's war objectives and had no wish to flirt with World War III. However, he thought the best way to end the war was to threaten to widen it. In the ongoing peace negotiations, he conveyed this threat to the Communists and even hinted darkly that he was considering using nuclear weapons.

Eisenhower's tough rhetoric produced the desired effect. In the spring and summer of 1953, the peace negotiations gathered momentum. The Communists were concerned about Ike's hawkish intentions, but they also wanted peace for two other reasons:

✔ Josef Stalin had died in March 1953, throwing the Soviet hierarchy into disarray. The turmoil diminished Russian interest in Korea, weakening the Communist position there.

✔ Chinese leaders now saw Korea as a dead end, and because they were involved in a burgeoning war in Vietnam (for more, see Chapter 19), they wanted to make peace in Korea.

On July 27, 1953, the two sides signed an armistice, creating a cease-fire, with the two Koreas intact. They created a tense *demilitarized zone* (or DMZ), a heavily fortified no man's land at the 38th parallel that both sides were to patrol in the years to come.

Technically, the two Koreas are still at war, and over the years, plenty of fighting has taken place along the DMZ, with some loss of life. The worst bloodshed, of course, took place between 1950 and 1953, when 5 million people, most of whom were Korean, died in the three terrible years of conventional war.

Lasting Legacies and Entrenched Contrasts

For the United States, the Korean War was a limited, albeit difficult, victory. The Americans succeeded in saving South Korea from Communism. South Korea even gained some North Korean territory in the final armistice agreement. In the years after the war, the United States extended and strengthened alliances with non-Communist states in both Europe and Asia. The war left several other legacies:

✔ Total victory was not always desirable or attainable in the nuclear age because it could stem from nuclear war.

✔ American power was not unlimited.

✔ Containment would be costly, and it would sometimes be bloody.

✔ From now on, America would maintain a large and costly but powerful military to contain Communism.

✔ The United States would keep a permanent military presence in South Korea that continues to this day.

The war led to many significant legacies for the two Koreas. North Korea became one of the Soviet Union's closest allies and hardened into a repressive, heavily militarized state in which Kim Il-Sung, and later his son Kim Jong-Il, wielded absolute power. After a period of industrial growth, North Korea's economy collapsed in the 1980s. The result was famine and more repression. Since the 1990s, North Korea's attempts to build a nuclear weapon have led to major tension with South Korea and the United States.

South Korea grew into a staunch American ally after the war. The country was not a true democracy until the late 1980s, when the authoritarian, military government gave way to free elections and political parties. By that time, South Korea had grown into a powerful capitalist economy and a significant military power. Today, South Korea is a rebellious but reasonably stable democracy. Many Koreans, North and South, hope their nation will one day be reunited peacefully.

Integrating the military (finally)

In 1948, President Truman signed Executive Order 9981, declaring that the United States military must integrate racially. In reality, very little integration took place until the Korean War, though.

In the three years that the war lasted, all the armed services implemented integration. From then on, black soldiers, sailors, airmen, and Marines served in the same units with their white peers. This strengthened the quality of American fighting forces immeasurably, not just for reasons of social justice, but because integration made the best use of American manpower.

By the 1960s, the military offered more career and advancement opportunities for blacks than nearly any other institution in American life.

Chapter 19

The Very Long War: Vietnam

The Vietnam War was the longest, and probably most controversial, conflict in American history. American involvement in Vietnam began during World War II, continued at a very small level in the 1950s, but then exploded into direct intervention during the 1960s before finally ending with a total withdrawal in 1975.

In 1960, the vast majority of Americans had either not heard of Vietnam or could not locate it on a map. Three years later, the U.S. was spending $400 million per year in Vietnam. Moreover, several thousand American servicemen were there. But polls showed that 63 percent of Americans were paying little or no attention to the situation in Vietnam. However, by 1969, with more than half a million American troops in country, the war in Vietnam had become the central issue in American life, affecting the economy, the political environment, the culture, the government's Cold War policy, the health of the armed forces, and even the way Americans felt about their country.

The Vietnam War was a complex war that doesn't lend itself to easy explanation. Nonetheless, in this chapter I demystify it for you. I explain how a strong Vietnamese Communist nationalist movement challenged and overcame French colonial authority in the 1950s. I give you a sense of how and why America entered the war in Vietnam, what the war was like for those who fought it, and why it became unpopular here at home. The chapter describes the tragic end to the war and its enduring place in the American psyche. Decades later, the war and its legacy still generate controversy, especially among historians, who stridently debate nearly every aspect of the war. I outline how these debates have evolved into three main explanations of the war and its ultimate significance.

If this chapter piques your interest, pick up a copy of *The Vietnam War For Dummies* by Ronald B. Frankum Jr. and Stephen F. Maxner (Wiley).

Conflicting Agendas Churn into War

So what was the Vietnam War about? It stemmed from a complicated mix of conflicts:

- ✔ It was a Cold War confrontation between the United States and its Communist Chinese and Soviet antagonists.
- ✔ It was a counterinsurgency war to contain Communism in Southeast Asia.
- ✔ It was a cultural war for the hearts and minds of Asians.
- ✔ It was a conventional war against a determined, dedicated Vietnamese Communist foe.
- ✔ It was a Vietnamese civil war.

The greatest legacy of World War II was the Cold War, an enduring struggle between the non-Communist world, led by the United States, and the Communist world, led by China and the Soviet Union (for more, see Chapter 17). In the 1950s, Asia was at the forefront of the Cold War. From 1950 to 1953, a bloody war raged in Korea between Communist North Korea and China on one side and a United Nations coalition consisting of non-Communist South Korea, the United States, Britain, and at least a dozen other countries (for more, see Chapter 18).

In 1953, the Korean War ended in stalemate but, at the same time, another Cold War confrontation was brewing in Vietnam, a country that had been a French colony since the early 19th century. This war pitted the colonial French against a Vietnamese nationalist Communist movement that was fighting for independence from France. Because of intense opposition to Communism, the United States sent aid to the French for their war in Vietnam. When the French faltered, the U.S. eventually inherited the war from their erstwhile allies, beginning a long and unhappy struggle in a faraway place.

Growing nationalism lifts Ho Chi Minh

French rule of Vietnam declined during World War II. With their homeland conquered by the Germans (for more, see Chapter 15), the French found it difficult to control their distant colony in Vietnam. Sensing French weakness, the Japanese promptly took over the country. Soon Vietnamese nationalists began fighting a *guerilla war* (an unconventional, hit-and-run war of ambush and harassment) against their Japanese occupiers.

When World War II ended with Japanese defeat, Vietnam's future was in doubt. By this time, Ho Chi Minh, a former schoolteacher and hard-core Communist, had emerged as the most powerful Vietnamese nationalist leader. He had considerable popular support among the Vietnamese people. His followers were known as the *Viet Minh*.

In September 1945, Ho attempted to declare independence for Vietnam under his Communist leadership. Instead, he found his country jointly occupied by the Chinese and British for a short time, mainly to disarm the defeated Japanese. No sooner did the Chinese and British leave, when the colonial French returned. Rather than submit to the renewal of French imperial authority, Ho and his Viet Minh unleashed a guerilla war of independence against the French.

The United States supported and worked with Ho Chi Minh during World War II because he was fighting the Japanese. They sent him supplies and weapons. American agents from the Office of Strategic Services (the precursor to the Central Intelligence Agency) even helped train Ho's men. In his postwar independence speech, Ho borrowed heavily from the American Declaration of Independence.

Annoying the French and drawing in the U.S.

Between 1946 and 1954, the French battled the Viet Minh in a frustrating, demoralizing *war of attrition* (a war that hopes to wear down the opponents until their resolve and supplies are spent). The French knew that their troops were better armed, with more firepower at their fingertips than their Viet Minh enemies. They yearned for a decisive, conventional battle to destroy the Viet Minh once and for all. Instead, Ho's troops, fighting with whatever weapons they could scrounge, avoided major combat. They harassed the French with booby traps, mines, snipers, hit-and-run ambushes, and anti-imperialist propaganda. Even though the French were using only volunteers in Vietnam, the war was unpopular in France.

Ho and the Viet Minh were totally committed to the ultimate goal of driving the French from Vietnam, regardless of the cost in time and lives. Their strategy was to wear down the French. Ho willingly suffered heavy casualties in exchange for inflicting enough losses on the French to empower the antiwar opposition back home. He told one Frenchman, "You can kill ten of my men for every one I kill of yours, but even at those odds, you will lose and I will win." Even with this kind of determination, the Viet Minh couldn't have fought the war without substantial aid, weapons, and military training from two powerful Communist allies, China and the Soviet Union.

President Harry Truman had mixed emotions about the French war in Vietnam. On the one hand, he wanted old-style colonial empires to go away in favor of newly independent countries in such places as Vietnam. On the other hand, he didn't want to see Communism spread. Indeed, his official administration policy was to contain Communism. Truman's ambivalence reflected American public opinion, but as the president, he had to decide on an American course of action in Vietnam. By 1950, he decided to support the French because, in his estimation, Communism was the greater evil than colonialism. Within four years, the U.S. was paying 80 percent of the cost of France's war in Vietnam, to the tune of $1 billion.

Dividing Vietnam

In 1954, after years of struggle, the Viet Minh finally engaged the French in an all-out battle at Dien Bien Phu (see Figure 19-1) and defeated them. In effect, this victory won the war for the Viet Minh.

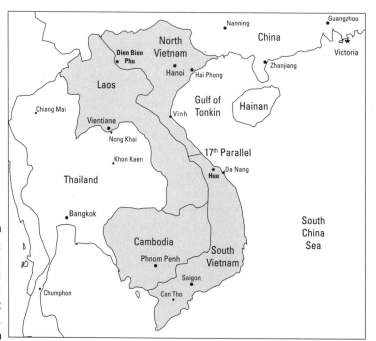

Figure 19-1: Map of the Vietnam War and Southeast Asia.

Even as the fighting raged, representatives of the warring parties were in Geneva, Switzerland, attempting to negotiate an end to the war. China, the Soviet Union, the U.S., and Britain were all present at the conference, putting pressure on their combatant allies to conclude an agreement. The negotiations resulted in the Geneva Accords signed by France and the Viet Minh on July 21, 1954. The accords did the following:

✔ Ended the fighting in Vietnam.

✔ Created provisions for a French exit from Vietnam.

✔ Temporarily partitioned the country. Ho Chi Minh's new Communist government would rule north of the 17th parallel in what became known as North Vietnam. Below the 17th parallel, in South Vietnam, Bao Dai, the Vietnamese emperor who had worked with the French, was in charge.

✔ In 1956, the Vietnamese would vote to decide if Vietnam would unify under Ho Chi Minh, Bao Dai, or some other leader.

The Geneva Accords led to France's withdrawal from Vietnam, the solidification of North Vietnam as a Communist country under Ho, and the establishment, with major American assistance, of a non-Communist South Vietnam. The elections never happened. Fearing a possible Ho Chi Minh victory, the United States helped thwart them in favor of solidifying the new non-Communist South Vietnam with its capital in Saigon. By the end of the 1950s, Ho and his comrades were determined to unify the whole country under their control, even if it meant war with South Vietnam.

After the accords, close to 1 million North Vietnamese migrated south, mainly to escape Communism. The CIA aided and abetted this exodus. These migrants formed the critical mass of support for the new non-Communist South Vietnamese government.

Creating the Viet Cong insurgency

Bao Dai appointed an anti-Communist nationalist named Ngo Dinh Diem as his prime minister. Within two years, Diem was the real leader of the country, grabbing power from a range of political enemies, including Communists. Diem had bitterly opposed the French even though he was a Roman Catholic just like them. He was personally hardworking and honest, so, at first glance, he was the perfect person around whom to build a viable South Vietnamese government. But, far too often, he repressed his political opponents. Moreover, many officials in his government were corrupt and dishonest. Overall, Diem's government depended on the support of urban Catholics, professionals, and rural landowners. It struggled to win the support of rural peasants, the majority group in the country. Diem's tyrannical tendencies eventually exasperated his American supporters.

In 1960, Diem's opponents created the *National Liberation Front,* an insurgent, largely Communist organization dedicated to overthrowing him and uniting the country under Ho. These insurgents, mainly from the South, were generally known as the *Viet Cong,* or VC. Their strategy for victory was guerilla war, similar to the way the Viet Minh had fought the French. From 1960 to 1963, the VC plagued the Diem regime with ambushes, terrorism, and general harassment. The insurgents operated at the grassroots level, dominating villages, stirring up opposition to Diem. By the end of 1963, the Viet Cong controlled well over one-third of the countryside.

The VC was supported, authorized, supplied, and, to a great extent, created by the North Vietnamese government. By 1960, the North Vietnamese had decided to unleash a "war of liberation" against the South Vietnamese. In other words, they wanted to unite the country under their control, and the VC was one of their primary weapons to make that happen. The North Vietnamese infiltrated men, weapons, and supplies through rough terrain into South Vietnam via a network of supply routes that became known as the *Ho Chi Minh Trail.*

South Vietnam's army falters

Diem's army was called the Army of the Republic of Vietnam, or ARVN. The Americans heavily subsidized ARVN, paying 98 percent of its costs and supplying the South Vietnamese soldiers with equipment and weapons. In the early 1960s, in response to the growth of the VC, the U.S. president, John F. Kennedy, sent several thousand American soldiers to South Vietnam. Their job was to train ARVN soldiers and help them defeat the VC.

In spite of American assistance, ARVN had major problems with corruption, poor leadership, political infighting, and a lack of fighting spirit in some of the soldiers. A disconcerting pattern soon emerged. The Viet Cong usually outfought and out-thought ARVN. The most infamous example was the Battle of Ap Bac in January 1963 when the VC soundly defeated ARVN. By the fall of that year, ARVN was struggling mightily to contain a growing VC presence in South Vietnam.

On November 1, 1963, a group of ARVN officers, with American consent, overthrew Diem. The Americans hoped this would salvage the situation in Vietnam, but it didn't. The war raged into 1964, with the Communists steadily gaining the upper hand.

Torpedoing the U.S. in the Tonkin Gulf

On November 22, 1963, President Kennedy was assassinated. His successor, Lyndon B. Johnson, thus inherited the mounting crisis in Vietnam. Like Kennedy before him, Johnson wanted to contain Communism and maintain South Vietnam's security. In an effort to help the South Vietnamese, he sent more American troops, planes, and ships to the country. In response, the North Vietnamese increased their aid to the VC.

On August 2, 1964, this festering situation boiled over in the Gulf of Tonkin. That evening, North Vietnamese torpedo boats attacked the USS *Maddox,* a destroyer that was operating several miles off the coast of North Vietnam in international waters. The *Maddox* shot back, but the engagement was inconclusive. Two nights later, a different American warship, the USS *C. Turner Joy* reported another such bloodless attack. Collectively, these two skirmishes are known as the Gulf of Tonkin incident.

The August 4 "attack" on *C. Turner Joy* probably never happened. Journalists and historians have thoroughly investigated the events of that evening and determined that no North Vietnamese boats were in the area. However, the first attack, on August 2, definitely did occur. Even though the Gulf of Tonkin incident was relatively minor, Johnson used it as a justification to expand American involvement in Vietnam.

On August 7, Johnson persuaded Congress to pass the Gulf of Tonkin Resolution, granting him broad war powers and empowering him to dramatically increase American troop strength in Vietnam. In essence, the resolution authorized a vast American war in Vietnam. The House voted 416-0 in favor of it. The Senate vote was 88-2.

The Gulf of Tonkin Resolution, and the growing American involvement in Vietnam, flowed naturally from two prominent beliefs among U.S. policymakers. First, many believed in the *domino theory,* which argued that if Communism triumphed in one country, it would soon spread to neighboring countries, like a row of dominoes tumbling over. The goal, then, was to keep that first domino from falling. Second, nearly all Americans thought that Communism must be contained wherever it threatened to spread, even in a remote place like Vietnam.

Raising U.S. Stakes through Escalation

The passage of the Gulf of Tonkin Resolution began a long period of American escalation in Vietnam. From 1964 until the end of 1968, Johnson steadily increased the American military presence, until more than 500,000 troops were in country. By that time, the Americans were basically fighting the war for the South Vietnamese. Even so, Johnson didn't mobilize America for war, or call up the Reserves and National Guard to fight in Vietnam. To him, Vietnam was a limited war for the limited objective of saving South Vietnam from Communism. He sought to do "what will be enough, but not too much."

From 1964 to 1968, both sides in Vietnam gradually upped their commitment to the war. The North Vietnamese, augmented by extensive Soviet and Chinese aid, infiltrated thousands of soldiers down the Ho Chi Minh Trail into South Vietnam. These North Vietnamese Army (NVA) soldiers joined with the Viet Cong to fight an increasingly intense war against ARVN and U.S. soldiers. At the same time, the Americans began bombing North Vietnam in hopes of persuading the North Vietnamese to abandon their goal of overrunning South Vietnam. When bombing and escalation didn't work and casualties began to rise, the American people grew impatient with the war. As the war widened and grew more unpopular, it ultimately destroyed Johnson's presidency.

Bombing backfires

Starting on March 2, 1965, the United States Air Force and Navy began an intensive bombing campaign against North Vietnam. In ordering the bombing, named Operation Rolling Thunder, Johnson hoped to achieve several objectives:

- Halt NVA infiltration on the Ho Chi Minh trail
- Boost South Vietnamese morale
- Persuade the North Vietnamese to stop the war

Over the course of the next three and a half years, American planes bombed myriad targets in North Vietnam, including power plants, bridges, oil storage facilities, steel mills, and factories. The bombing significantly damaged North Vietnam, but it was largely a failure. It didn't halt infiltration — in fact it had doubled by 1967. Nor did the bombs break the will of the North Vietnamese to win. If anything, it hardened their resolve and fueled their anger against the Americans. Plus, the propaganda-minded North Vietnamese used the inevitable collateral damage that bombing raids inflicted upon homes, schools, and innocent people to depict the Americans as indiscriminate butchers and bullies. This helped turn world opinion against the Americans.

In fact, the Americans tried very hard to minimize civilian casualties, but the perception around the world was otherwise, thus eroding international support for the American war effort. Worst of all, the raids were costly to the Americans who flew them. Over three and a half years of Rolling Thunder, the Air Force and Navy lost 700 planes and a like number of aviators either killed or taken prisoner. For American pilots in Vietnam, flying missions over North Vietnam was the most dangerous duty of all.

Johnson kept strict control over Operation Rolling Thunder, mainly because he didn't want errant bombs to draw China or the Soviet Union into the war. His rules of engagement were tight. Aviators could only fly in certain corridors and drop certain kinds of conventional bombs on their targets. Johnson even picked those targets himself at weekly lunch meetings with his secretary of defense, Robert McNamara.

Using attrition as a tactic

Vietnam was not a war with fixed front lines. The enemy could pop up nearly anywhere at any point in time. Gen. William Westmoreland was the American commander in Vietnam during the escalation period of the war. His aim was to find the enemy, force them to fight on American terms, and annihilate them with massive American firepower. He believed that the best way to do that was to wear them down by patrolling the rice paddies, jungles, and coastlines of Vietnam with large units of American soldiers. He assigned ARVN a support role of protecting the villages while American troops went out and destroyed the VC and NVA. To do this, he requested hundreds of thousands of American troops, and he got them. By 1967, he had about 400,000 American servicemen at his disposal.

Westmoreland's strategy for victory was attrition. He would have liked to invade North Vietnam, but Johnson forbade this for fear of provoking a larger war with China and the Soviet Union. Confined to fighting the enemy in South Vietnam, the general felt the best way to defeat them was to bleed them. He decided to fight them with large formations of American soldiers, inflicting such devastating losses on the VC and the NVA that they would have to quit. He called this "reaching the crossover point," which meant the point at which Communist losses would be so great that they could no longer replace their casualties. Westmoreland's attrition strategy put enormous pressure on his commanders to produce large body-count estimates of enemy fighters killed. As a result, American estimates of enemy casualties were sometimes absurdly inaccurate.

From 1965 to 1967, Westmoreland launched dozens of operations with code names such as Masher/Whitewing, Davy Crockett, and Hastings. All of these operations were designed to find large VC or NVA formations, bring them to battle on American terms, and destroy them. Without question, Westmoreland's operations did serious damage to the enemy. But his strategy ultimately failed because of several major problems:

- ✔ With sanctuaries in the ostensibly neutral neighboring countries of Cambodia and Laos, the Communists could retreat, lick their wounds, and fight again another day. Cambodia and Laos were generally off-limits to American soldiers. This meant the Communists could control the rate of their losses, undercutting the attrition strategy.

- ✔ Big unit operations took American soldiers away from the South Vietnamese villages, allowing the VC to control many of them, eroding the average villager's confidence in the U.S. and the South Vietnamese government.

- ✔ Because of the intense pressure to produce large body counts, the numbers were often inflated, creating false optimism among the Americans.

- ✔ Attrition took time to bear fruit, so it depended on strong political support at home. However, Johnson didn't enjoy such support from an increasingly impatient American public.

Growing opposition at home

The longer the war dragged on, the more the public's support for it diminished. People lost their belief in the war for many reasons. Some were discouraged by the lack of clear-cut, traditional battlefield victories, or even demonstrable progress. Some thought the war wasn't worth fighting unless Johnson would approve an invasion of North Vietnam for total victory.

Others disliked the military draft, which was netting 30,000 men per month by 1966. Many of these draftees ended up in Vietnam, and some got killed there. By 1967, the U.S. had already lost close to 7,000 dead, and a rising number of Americans felt that Vietnam wasn't worth this price.

By that same time, a growing, vocal group of antiwar activists espoused the belief that the war was morally wrong. They felt that the United States, for imperialist reasons, had injected itself into a Vietnamese civil war. They believed that the U.S. was in the wrong and should leave Vietnam. Some of these activists claimed that American troops were routinely perpetrating atrocities on the Vietnamese or slaughtering them with the heavy-handed use of firepower.

The Vietnam soldier's vocabulary

The Vietnam War gave rise to a unique set of slang terms. These words were so common, and casual conversations were so spiced with them, that the Americans who served in Vietnam almost spoke their own language. So what were some of the most popular words?

✔ A *grunt* was an infantry soldier.

✔ *Beaucoup* (pronounced "boo coo") meant a large amount of something.

✔ If you did not like something, you derided it as "Number Ten."

✔ If something was good, you called it "Number One."

✔ A *Kit Carson scout* was a former Viet Cong who was working with the Americans as a guide.

✔ An *AO* meant an area of operations.

✔ An *LZ* was a helicopter landing zone.

✔ A *pogue* was a contemptuous term that combat soldiers used to describe rear area personnel.

✔ A *hootch* referred to any simple Vietnamese dwelling.

✔ When Americans soldiers talked about *The world* or *The Land of the Big PX,* they were referring to the United States.

✔ The enemy was known as *Charlie* or *Nathaniel Victor.*

✔ If someone called you an *FNG,* it meant you were a bleeping New Guy or replacement.

✔ If you were *short,* it meant your year of service in country was almost over.

✔ Soldiers called military policemen (MPs) *mommas and the poppas* after a popular singing group of the time.

✔ Finally, most soldiers longingly looked forward to their *DEROS,* which meant "Date of Expected (or Estimated) Return from Overseas," the magical date when they finally got to go home.

Antiwar protestors staged demonstrations on college campuses, in Washington, D.C. (even outside the White House), in major cities all over the country, and near military bases. Young men who were opposed to the war burned their draft cards or jumped the border into Canada. Many simply evaded the draft through *student deferments* (postponing their military service until after they completed their college education) or contrived physical problems. A few thousand chose *conscientious objector status,* refusing to serve for religious or moral reasons. The most famous conscientious objector was heavyweight boxing champion Muhammad Ali.

As of 1968, the majority of Americans still supported the war, but the antiwar minority was growing. Antiwar organizations drew their support from two major demographic groups:

✔ Young men who wanted to avoid military service

✔ Americans over the age of 50, many of whom felt the war was morally wrong or a hopeless struggle

The growing antiwar restlessness forced Johnson to react. He responded with official optimism, claiming that the war was going well and would soon be won.

Contrasting experiences for grunts

In Vietnam, only about 15 percent of American soldiers were in the infantry, but they suffered 83 percent of the casualties. These infantry soldiers, known as *grunts,* were the guys with rifles and machine guns in their hands, carrying the fight to the enemy. Their job was to go out, find the enemy, and kill them.

The grunts spent much of their time out in the jungles, swamps, rice paddies, mountains, and border areas of Vietnam (see Figure 19-2), amid mosquitoes, ants, leeches, and other nasty creatures. Infantrymen carried, on average, 60 pounds of gear, including weapons, ammo, water, grenades, a shovel, a steel helmet, and rations.

Figure 19-2:
A U.S. Army grunt patrols as a Viet Cong base camp burns nearby.

Source: US Archiv ARCWEB ARC Identifier: 530621

What was a typical day like for a grunt? Starting very early in the morning, he would patrol, in temperatures that often exceeded 100 degrees, constantly on the alert for booby traps or the enemy's actual presence. After a full and very tense day of this, his unit would find a campsite, set up a perimeter, dig protective foxholes, set up their weapons, get re-supplied by helicopters, eat, and then keep watch for the enemy. During the night, he slept two hours at a time, alternating guard shifts with his foxhole buddy. Then, in the morning, he would get up and do it all over again.

In the Vietnam War, most patrols resulted in no contact with the enemy. When fighting did break out, the nature of the combat varied significantly. Sometimes grunts fought bloody pitched battles with regular NVA formations as at Hue, Ia Drang, Dak To, and Hamburger Hill. They also, on occasion, fought big battles with the VC as well. But, most of the time, combat consisted of, in one typical description, "hours of tedium followed by a few moments of sheer terror." This meant short, often inconclusive engagements with small groups of enemy soldiers. In Vietnam, a grunt could go months without firing his weapon. Or he could find himself fighting in an intense, bloody battle for a week straight. Experiences varied that dramatically.

In Vietnam, the Communists made extensive use of booby traps and mines. Throughout the war, 20 percent of all American casualties resulted from these anonymous, demoralizing weapons, which were more likely to cause serious wounds than outright death. In Vietnam, amputations or crippling wounds to the lower extremities were 300 percent higher than World War II and 70 percent higher than Korea.

Kicking off the new year with the Tet Offensive of 1968

1968 marked the fourth year of major American involvement in Vietnam. President Johnson, in the face of growing national impatience, hinted that the U.S. was on the verge of victory and the war would soon begin winding down. Westmoreland did the same. However, the fighting and dying was only beginning. In 1968, the war entered a new and bloodier phase as the Communists chose to widen the war.

Even though the Communists were determined to fight an open-ended war to achieve their goal of uniting Vietnam under their control, they decided to try for a quick victory in early 1968. In the final months of 1967, they amassed regular NVA formations in remote areas, drawing American troops away from South Vietnam's cities. In the meantime, VC and NVA operatives, blending in with the population, infiltrated the cities. On January 30, 1968, during the revered Vietnamese New Year, a holiday called *Tet,* the operatives launched major attacks all over the country, in nearly every city of consequence. Their goal was to overwhelm ARVN units that were guarding urban areas and inspire a pro-VC uprising among the South Vietnamese people to overthrow the Saigon government. This would then force the checkmated Americans to leave the country.

The Communist offensive was powerful and well planned. Seemingly in the blink of an eye, South Vietnam boiled over with violence. A special squad of Viet Cong *sappers* (soldiers who lay mines and dig trenches toward enemy lines) attacked the American embassy in Saigon. Another group overran the South Vietnamese government's radio station. Larger formations took control of Cholon, Saigon's western suburbs. To the north, large NVA units captured Hue and put serious pressure on a Marine base called Khe Sanh.

Throughout February and March, American and ARVN soldiers fought back with equal aplomb, retaking everything from the Communists. In battle after battle, they defeated the NVA and VC, killing nearly 40,000 of them. To make matters worse for the Communists, the South Vietnamese people didn't join them. What's more, ARVN resisted as never before, probably because many South Vietnamese soldiers were home on leave during Tet and thus defending their own families from the NVA and VC.

Militarily, the Tet Offensive was a dismal failure for the Communists. The best soldiers the VC had died in the fighting. From here on out, the NVA carried the war. Politically, Tet had the unintended effect of actually strengthening the Saigon government because its soldiers fought well and its citizens rejected the Communists. But these weren't the only important considerations. Tet's effect on the American political environment was far more advantageous to the Communists.

Losing politically after winning militarily

The Tet Offensive was the beginning of the end of Johnson's presidency. After months of sunny government pronouncements about the demise of the enemy and the imminence of victory in Vietnam, the American people were shocked by the ferocity and extensiveness of the enemy attacks. The mere fact that the VC and NVA could pull off such an elaborate offensive cast serious doubt on Johnson and his administration, creating a credibility gap for him. When Westmoreland and Johnson pointed out that Tet was a military victory, most Americans reacted with skepticism. Indeed, during the Tet offensive, one out of every five pro-war Americans turned against the war.

Students for a Democratic Society

One of the leading antiwar groups during the Vietnam War was Students for a Democratic Society, or SDS. Originally founded in 1960 as a pro-labor union organization, SDS morphed into a significant antiwar mouthpiece during its heyday from 1965 to 1969. It was especially prevalent on larger college campuses like California-Berkley, Michigan, and Wisconsin.

The leaders of SDS rejected capitalism, organized religion, and the traditional family in favor of a society rooted in love and creativity. To them, the Vietnam War revealed the United States as a racist, imperial bully, fighting an immoral war for its own bloodthirsty power.

At its height in 1968, SDS had more than 400 chapters around the country. Members protested the war, resisted the draft, and urged Americans to embrace grassroots left-wing reforms to eliminate poverty, racism, and injustice. The organization drew most of its support from two sources: youthful college students who were morally opposed to the war, and young men who hoped to avoid the draft.

As the war wound down, SDS disintegrated. By 1972, it was fully defunct. However, in 2006, in response to the Iraq War, a new generation of activists re-founded SDS.

Tet also widened a growing chasm between pro-war and antiwar members of Johnson's Democratic Party during that presidential election year of 1968. In the New Hampshire primary, Sen. Eugene McCarthy, a peace candidate, nearly defeated the president. A stunned Johnson now knew that he had little chance of being reelected. On March 31, in a nationally televised speech, he announced that he would not run. He also called for immediate peace talks with North Vietnam and promised to suspend the bombing of that country.

The ultimate significance of the Tet Offensive was that it broke the will of the American people to continue the war indefinitely. After Tet, the majority of Americans wanted to begin the process of withdrawing from Vietnam, even though they didn't necessarily want to abandon the South Vietnamese to Communist domination. Instead, they hoped that the United States could steadily turn responsibility for the war over to its South Vietnamese allies.

Winding down the war

The implosion of the Democratic Party in 1968 over the war created an opening for the Republicans. That year, Richard Nixon won a close race for the presidency.

Reacting to the new post-Tet political environment, Nixon promised a "secret plan" to end the war. This plan entailed turning the war over to the South Vietnamese, while negotiating with the North Vietnamese to stop the fighting. Nixon knew that North Vietnam was dependent on Chinese and Soviet aid, so he hoped to approach the Communist superpowers, reduce Cold War tensions with them, and appeal for their help in negotiating some sort of face-saving peace in Vietnam.

Meanwhile, as of 1970, he began withdrawing American troops from Vietnam, mainly to assuage public opinion here at home. Thus, 1969 to 1973 is generally known as the de-escalation phase of the war.

Floundering at the peace talks

On May 19, 1968, representatives from North Vietnam and the United States met in Paris to begin peace talks. Xuan Thuy headed up the North Vietnamese delegation while Averill Harriman, a veteran diplomat, led the U.S. side. For many months thereafter, the two sides negotiated but accomplished very little, establishing a pattern that would plague the peace talks for years to come. The main sticking points were

- ✔ A North Vietnamese demand for the Viet Cong's legitimate inclusion in the peace talks
- ✔ North Vietnam's insistence that the U.S. dismantle the non-Communist Saigon government
- ✔ The presence of North Vietnamese troops in South Vietnam
- ✔ The potential return of American prisoners of war
- ✔ The American refusal to confer any legitimacy on the VC
- ✔ A North Vietnamese demand that the U.S. cease all bombing of their country

The peace talks were, by and large, fruitless. From 1968 to 1973, they ebbed and flowed, more or less in reaction to events in Vietnam. When Nixon became president, he actually bypassed the official Paris talks in favor of secret back-channel negotiations between Henry Kissinger, his national security advisor, and Le Duc Tho, a powerful member of North Vietnam's ruling Politburo. He also reached out to the Chinese and Soviets in major peace initiatives, warming relations with them and urging them to pressure the North Vietnamese to end the war.

Reinventing a strategy to secure South Vietnam

In the wake of Tet, Westmoreland lost his job as commander in Vietnam. He was promoted to a new job as Army chief of staff, but this was tantamount to being "kicked upstairs" because Westmoreland didn't want to relinquish command. The new commander, Gen. Creighton Abrams, knew that, with impending troop withdrawals and eroding support for the war at home, he couldn't fight the same kind of big unit, attrition war that Westmoreland had favored.

In line with Nixon's Vietnamization policy, Abrams heaped more responsibility on ARVN for fighting the war. He emphasized counterinsurgent tactics to negate Communist influence in the villages. He significantly enhanced the security of many villages, broke up VC supply and base networks, and fought NVA formations wherever they appeared. Abrams felt strongly that the way to win the war wasn't necessarily to go out and destroy the enemy in remote areas near Cambodia and Laos, but to secure the populated areas of South Vietnam. Abrams called his strategy *One War,* meaning it was a blend among Vietnamization, counterinsurgency, and conventional battles.

Stepping over the line into Cambodia

Abrams's One War approach brought immediate, but unspectacular, results. Even as his troops steadily enhanced security for the South Vietnamese people, Nixon was growing frustrated with the dead-end peace negotiations. The longer the war dragged on, the more unpopular it grew with the American people.

In dealing with the North Vietnamese, Nixon employed a carrot-and-stick approach. The carrot was U.S. withdrawal from Vietnam. The stick was greater military force, in the form of aerial bombing or ground operations. Abrams, like Westmoreland before him, wanted to cross the border into Cambodia to destroy Communist base camps there. By and large, American commanders had been prohibited from doing so because, technically, Cambodia was neutral, so a U.S. invasion could well lead to a backlash in world opinion. Hoping to score a major victory that would force the Communists into a pro-American peace agreement, Nixon in 1970 ordered U.S. and ARVN troops into Cambodia.

Nixon had actually begun secretly bombing Cambodia in 1969, so the ground invasion was simply an extension of this policy. Throughout May and June

1970, American and South Vietnamese troops captured several Communist base complexes and killed thousands of enemy troops. However, the invasion of Cambodia ended up as a dismal failure for two major reasons:

- ✔ NVA troops simply withdrew deeper into the country, where U.S. troops couldn't get them. After this, they joined forces with Cambodian Communists known as the *Khmer Rouge*. This helped the Khmer Rouge eventually come to power in Cambodia.

- ✔ The invasion of Cambodia led to a massive wave of antiwar protest in the United States, especially on college campuses. Nixon had promised to de-escalate the war, but in Cambodia, he seemed to be doing the exact opposite, alienating many Americans. Reacting to public opinion, Congress passed bills forcing the president to withdraw troops from Cambodia.

Ending with a bitter aftertaste

In the wake of the failed invasion of Cambodia, Nixon stepped up troop withdrawals. By 1972, the U.S. only had about 60,000 soldiers left in Vietnam. When the North Vietnamese attempted a major offensive to win the war that year, Nixon dramatically increased bombing raids on North Vietnam and NVA troop concentrations in the South. These bombings, in addition to ARVN resistance, defeated the Communist offensive. Finally, on January 23, 1973, North Vietnam, South Vietnam, and the United States signed the Paris Peace Accords, ending the war on the following terms:

- ✔ American troops would withdraw from Vietnam.

- ✔ U.S. prisoners of war would be returned.

- ✔ The Saigon government remained in place, as did NVA troops in South Vietnam.

- ✔ Vietnam could only be unified peacefully, not by war.

Nixon called this agreement "peace with honor" but it was essentially a capitulation. Within a year, the North Vietnamese violated the agreement, renewing hostilities against the South with an all-out conventional war. By that time, Nixon was so weakened by the Watergate scandal that he couldn't persuade a hostile Congress to provide desperately needed U.S. aid to South Vietnam. On April 30, 1975, the North Vietnamese overran Saigon, securing total control of South Vietnam. The Vietnam War thus ended in defeat for the United States.

More than 58,000 Americans lost their lives in the war, yet the U.S. failed in its goal of securing a permanent non-Communist South Vietnam.

Viewing the Vietnam War Three Ways

The Vietnam War is one of the most controversial and traumatic events in American history. In the 21st century, Americans still bitterly argue about the war. For instance, in the 2004 presidential election, the Vietnam-era military service of both major candidates turned into a serious campaign issue. Like everyone else, historians continue to debate the war. Among those historians who study the war, three distinct schools of thought exist on Vietnam.

Making a tragic mistake — the liberal realists

This group agrees that the war was wrong, but on pragmatic, not moral grounds. They argue that, from the start, the war wasn't winnable for the United States. The U.S., they believe, fought the good fight against Communism, but would have been better served to expend its resources elsewhere in more vital areas of the world. To the liberal realists, Vietnam was not worth the loss of so much American life and treasure. The most prominent liberal realists are George Herring, Neal Sheehan, and Stanley Karnow.

Seeing America as the real villain — the New Left

These historians, mainly left-wing radicals known as "New Leftists," argue that the United States was morally wrong to fight the war in Vietnam. They view America as an imperialist power that was intent on dominating the third world, mainly for economic reasons. The United States, they argue, was the true aggressor, injecting itself into a civil war, slaughtering innocent people, behaving like an imperial bully. The most enduring New Left Vietnam War historian is Gabriel Kolko, who wrote that Vietnam resulted from an attempt by the American ruling class to control capitalist markets in Asia.

Losing a noble war that politicians screwed up — conservative revisionists

This group of historians believes that the war was morally right, a noble crusade against ruthless Communism, but that American political and military leaders committed terrible blunders that undercut this worthy cause. They maintain that the war was quite winnable but that the limited war policy prevented the soldiers from securing victory. Many of these historians even argue that the U.S. side was winning in the early 1970s, only to be undone by antiwar politicians here at home. Harry Summers, Lewis Sorley, Bruce Palmer, Phil Davidson, and Andrew Krepinevich are examples of conservative revisionists.

Chapter 20

A War with Allies: The Persian Gulf War

*O*ne of the major subplots of the Cold War was the rise of the Middle East in strategic importance to the United States. Before and during World War II, European colonial empires controlled much of that part of the world. After the war, as those empires dissolved, new Arab nations, rich in oil, rose in importance. Increasingly, the United States was dependent upon the rich vein of oil prevalent in many of these countries. To a great extent, oil drove the modern American economy. Basically, this meant that American security depended upon the free flow of oil at world market prices.

When Saddam Hussein, a bloodthirsty dictator in control of Iraq, invaded Kuwait, an oil-rich nation, in August 1990, the United States saw this as a major threat to world stability.

In less than two days, the Iraqi army overran overmatched Kuwait (see Figure 20-1). The Iraqis seized control of Kuwait's oil fields, its financial markets, and its capital of Kuwait City. With the fighting over, Saddam Hussein announced that he would now officially annex Kuwait as a province of Iraq. Indeed, he had justified the invasion by arguing that Kuwait was a "lost province" that should, by all rights, become part of Iraq again.

In this chapter, I discuss why Iraq invaded Kuwait and explain how the world reacted to Saddam's aggression. I take a look at how America's mighty new armed forces triumphed in the air and on land, throwing Iraq out of Kuwait. Finally, this chapter examines the uneasy legacy of the Gulf War — unfinished business with Saddam Hussein that contributed to a more ambitious American-led war 12 years later.

Operation Desert Shield

In the 1980s, Iraqi dictator Saddam Hussein had incurred considerable debts during a ruinous war with his neighbor, Iran. To him, oil-rich Kuwait was an artificial country that, by all rights, belonged to Iraq. Possession of Kuwait would recoup many of his debts and turn Iraq into a major regional power. He would then be in a position to threaten the security of neighboring Saudi Arabia, a backward, insular country that was slathered in oil wealth.

On August 2, 1990, the Iraqi army invaded little Kuwait, a helmet-shaped country on the edge of the Persian Gulf. The Kuwaitis were no match for the Iraqi army, which was the fourth largest in the world at the time. The Iraqis were equipped with a wide range of Soviet-made tanks, planes, missiles, and small-arms weapons.

In order to thwart Saddam, President George Herbert Walker Bush (father of George W. Bush) sent American military forces to Saudi Arabia. In the diplomatic arena, he put together a vast multinational coalition of nations committed to defend Saudi Arabia and eject Iraq from Kuwait. Through the United Nations, the coalition demanded that Saddam withdraw from Kuwait. When he didn't, Bush authorized, in January 1991, the use of force, thus beginning the Persian Gulf War.

The occupation was harsh. Iraqi soldiers mercilessly looted the country. Some engaged in rape and torture, particularly against Kuwaitis who spoke out against Saddam or resisted the occupation. Saddam appointed his cousin Ali Al-Majid as the new governor of Kuwait. The infamous Al-Majid had unleashed poison gas against thousands of Iraqi Kurds in 1988. His reputation for cruelty, along with a growing chorus of Iraqi atrocity stories in Kuwait, rallied support for the tiny country around the world.

Some of the stories about Iraqi atrocities in Kuwait were not true. The Kuwaiti government-in-exile hired a public relations firm, bought advertising, and lobbied congressmen to influence American public opinion to free their country from Saddam. To suit their purposes, they fabricated some outright lies. In one instance, a woman who claimed to be a nurse in a Kuwait City hospital said she witnessed Iraqi soldiers pulling babies from incubators, leaving them to die. As it turned out, this story was a complete fabrication. The "nurse" was actually a Paris-based member of the Kuwait royal family who couldn't have witnessed atrocities because she wasn't in Kuwait City.

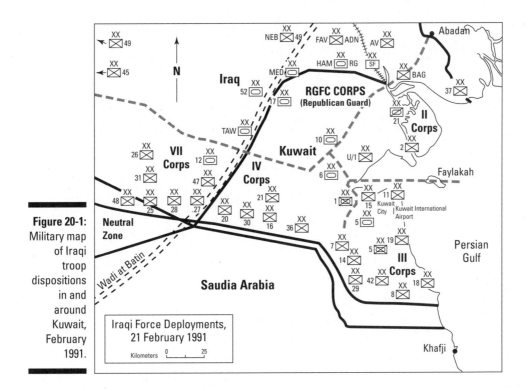

Figure 20-1: Military map of Iraqi troop dispositions in and around Kuwait, February 1991.

Putting together a broad anti-Saddam coalition

After Saddam easily took over Kuwait, the Saudis were deeply worried that their country would be next. So, for protection, they allowed a major American military buildup in their kingdom.

Throughout the fall of 1990, at Saudi invitation, President Bush built up American forces in Saudi Arabia to prevent Iraq from invading it. He also put together a large anti-Saddam coalition. Eventually, the Americans in Saudi Arabia were joined by troops from the host country, Egypt, Britain, France, and numerous other nations. Dubbed Operation Desert Shield, the American goal was to deter Saddam Hussein from invading Saudi Arabia and then force him to leave Kuwait. Bush also lined up support at home and in the UN for the use of force to remove Iraq from Kuwait, but only if diplomacy failed to fulfill this objective.

Be all you can be! The new, all-volunteer American military

The long, unpopular war in Vietnam had eroded the readiness and effectiveness of the American military, especially the Army, because it had done the bulk of the fighting in Vietnam. Because compulsory military service was unpopular, Congress ended the draft in 1974, at the tail end of the Vietnam War. From this point forward, everyone who served in the U.S. armed forces was a volunteer. Even so, every branch of the military needed dramatic improvement by the end of the 1970s.

During the 1980s, President Ronald Reagan invested enormous amounts of money and attention to rejuvenate the armed forces (for more, see Chapter 17). During his time in office, he doubled the defense budget to pay for new weapons and technology.

Most importantly, the money helped attract quality volunteers to the armed services by offering them enlistment bonuses, medical care, college benefits, and decent pay. A new Army advertising slogan, "Be all you can be," challenged young people to make the most of themselves while serving their country.

By 1990, this new emphasis on building an excellent, all-volunteer military was producing good results. The Air Force and Navy were both at a high state of readiness for war. The Marine Corps, as always, featured some of the country's best-trained combat troops.

The Army had undergone the most remarkable transition, though. More than 98 percent of soldiers had a high school diploma. Seventy-five percent scored in the highest mental category on aptitude tests. New weapons such as the M1 Abrams main battle tank, the M2 Bradley Infantry Fighting Vehicle, and the Apache attack helicopter enhanced the lethality and combat readiness of Army units. All of these machines were ideally suited for desert warfare. They were also vastly superior to the Soviet-made tanks, armored personnel carriers, and helicopters of the Iraqi army.

President Bush pursued this buildup for two major reasons:

- Iraq's takeover of Kuwait threatened the free flow of the world's oil supply. Because oil was so vital to the American economy, the United States couldn't allow this.

- Bush didn't want to set the precedent that one country in the Middle East could simply erase another one off the map with no consequences.

In August, Bush sent the 82nd Airborne Division to the Saudi desert, soon to be followed by a major influx of American land, sea, and air forces. Through able diplomacy and plenty of eager persuasion, Bush built a large anti-Saddam coalition of nations from all over the world. Quite a few Arab states, including Algeria, Egypt, Syria, Bahrain, Oman, Qatar, and United Arab Emirates, joined the coalition. So did Cold War–era American allies such as Britain, Canada, Australia, France, Germany, South Korea, Japan, Portugal, Turkey, Greece, and Spain. In all, 34 countries joined the coalition. Most sent only token military forces or just money. American soldiers comprised 74 percent of coalition forces, with substantial troop contributions from Egypt, Kuwait, Saudi Arabia, Canada, Britain, France, and Italy.

In the diplomatic realm, this large number of like-minded nations wielded a powerful influence. On August 3, 1990, the Council of the Arab League condemned Iraq and demanded its withdrawal from Kuwait. At nearly the same time, the United Nations Security Council voted 14-0 for a similar resolution. Within three months, the UN resolutions (suggestions) turned into imperatives (orders). On November 29, 1990, the UN Security Council authorized the coalition to use "all necessary means," including military force, to expel Iraq from Kuwait if Iraq did not leave by January 15, 1991. This was known as UN Resolution 660. Throughout the fall of 1990, coalition nations built up their military forces in Saudi Arabia, while diplomats frantically negotiated for a peaceful resolution to the crisis.

Reviewing the military buildup — Iraq versus the coalition

Throughout the fall of 1990, as the standoff between Saddam and the coalition unfolded, both sides built up their forces on either side of the Iraq, Kuwait, and Saudi border areas. On one side, huge numbers of Iraqi soldiers set up what they hoped would be an impregnable defensive line. On the other side, American, British, French, Egyptian, Saudi, and Kuwaiti soldiers constructed their own defenses while training for the possibility of war. By the end of the year, the buildup on both sides was impressive:

Iraq

- 43 infantry and armor divisions, consisting of some 500,000 soldiers.
- 3,475 main battle tanks.
- 3,080 armored personnel carriers and other armored vehicles.
- 2,475 artillery pieces.
- 950 combat aircraft.
- 3,000 missiles, including "Scuds" that could be fired from mobile launchers, to a range of about 300 miles. The Scuds could also carry chemical and biological weapons.
- A few gunboats, but otherwise no major naval forces.

Living in the barren Saudi desert

During Operation Desert Shield, thousands of American soldiers were introduced to the Saudi desert, a foreboding, seemingly endless wasteland close to the Kuwaiti and Iraqi borders. There were no trees. There was no greenery of any kind, just an endless expanse of sand, all the way to the horizon.

The troops dealt with the brutal, unforgiving heat of the desert in the daytime and the chill of evening. Daytime temperatures sometimes exceeded 120 degrees. At night during the fall, the temperature could plummet to 30 or 40 degrees.

Soldiers and Marines drank copious amounts of bottled water, but this alien environment took its toll. "It was like being inside a dryer," one soldier recalled. "It's just so dry. It's so hot. You could drench yourself, and literally ten minutes later, your uniform would be dry. It's like living in a dryer." Armored vehicles were often so hot that soldiers could, and sometimes did, fry food on them. Sand got into everything — boots, food, tents, blankets, helmets, engines, and even drinking water.

Hygiene was makeshift. Soldiers took impromptu showers by standing under buckets draped over tank gun tubes, but the troops rarely ever got clean. Nor did they have any ice to cool their water so, with typical soldierly improvisation, they developed a cooling technique. They would drench a sock in water, put a water bottle inside the sock, tie it to their vehicles, and drive around. This cooled the water bottle temperature so much that it seemed like it had been sitting in ice.

Some troops, particularly those from the 82nd Airborne Division and the 24th Infantry Division (Mechanized), spent five months in the desert before the war even started.

Coalition

- About 15 infantry and armor divisions, comprising nearly 700,000 troops, including 527,000 Americans.

- 2,430 combat aircraft, including 1,800 American planes.

- 1,700 American helicopters.

- 2,846 tanks and other armored vehicles, 2,000 of which were American.

- 6 major aircraft carrier groups and 2 battleship groups. The U.S. Navy had 110 ships in theater.

Winning political support at home

It was one thing to deploy American forces to Saudi Arabia to deter an Iraqi invasion. It was quite another to order them into battle to throw the Iraqis out of Kuwait. To do this, President Bush needed the support of Congress.

In the fall of 1990, politicians and millions of Americans debated the wisdom of going to war. Radio talk shows buzzed with debate. Newspaper editorialists wrote millions of words on the topic. Representatives and senators argued back and forth through the news media and on the Capitol floor.

The UN's endorsement of the use of force, Saddam's obvious transgressions, and the vital importance of Kuwaiti oil all helped sway Congress to vote for war. The Senate voted 52-47 in favor of the authorization to use force. The House tally was 250-183.

Bush and his UN colleagues imposed January 15, 1991, as the deadline for Saddam's forces to leave Kuwait. If they did not, the coalition could then remove them by force.

Diplomacy comes up short

In the weeks leading up to the deadline, coalition representatives engaged in negotiations with Iraq. The leading personalities in these 11th-hour talks were Tariq Aziz, Iraq's foreign minister, and Secretary of State James Baker, a close Bush associate.

Aziz and Baker met at Geneva, Switzerland, on January 9, 1991, for marathon talks. In the end, they couldn't reach any sort of agreement. Saddam was determined to remain in Kuwait. Bush was just as determined to remove him. Thus, the deadline came and went with tensions at a fever pitch.

Finally, on January 17, Bush, with the full support of his coalition partners, gave the order to eject Iraq from Kuwait by force. The war had begun.

Operation Desert Storm

On the evening of January 17, 1991, presidential press secretary Marlin Fitzwater strode into the White House briefing room and told reporters: "The liberation of Kuwait has begun." The military campaign, he explained, would be code-named Operation Desert Storm. The moniker stuck, so much so that some Americans still refer to this war by that title.

In its initial phase, lasting almost six weeks, Desert Storm consisted almost entirely of an air campaign, while hundreds of coalition planes pounded enemy targets in Kuwait and Iraq (see Figure 20-2). In the second phase, beginning on February 24 and lasting until March 1, the coalition launched a massive ground campaign that kicked Saddam out of Kuwait once and for all.

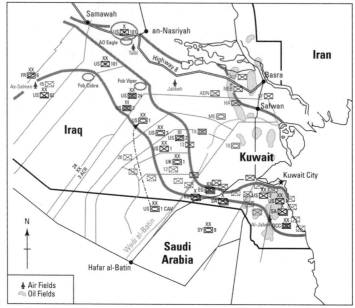

Figure 20-2:
Military map
of Operation
Desert
Storm,
January
17–March 1,
1991.

Pounding Saddam from the air

The commander of coalition forces was Gen. H. Norman Schwarzkopf, a West Point graduate, Vietnam veteran, and career Army officer. He had vast military forces at his fingertips, but he knew that Iraqi defenses were formidable. In addition to hundreds of thousands of soldiers, the Iraqis had sown millions of mines, constructed thousands of bunkers, and filled ditches with oil that could be set afire at any time. They also had dug in many of their tanks, antiaircraft guns, missile launchers, and machine guns. Thus, Gen. Schwarzkopf was determined to inflict as much damage as possible on them with his air forces before attacking them with his ground forces.

Beginning on the first night of the war, American helicopters, F4 "Wild Weasel" fighters, and F15 Strike Eagle fighters did major damage to Iraq's radar warning facilities. In essence, this blinded the Iraqi air defense controllers and made Iraq itself quite vulnerable to bombing raids. Other coalition aircraft bombed Baghdad, the Iraqi capital, enemy air bases, and troop concentrations. At the same time, cruise missiles, launched from U.S. ships, showered a variety of targets. All of these attacks did major damage to the power grid in Iraq, plunging much of the country into darkness.

The Allied technological advantage was considerable. Led by the Americans, they flew better aircraft, used better radar, could unleash superior bombs and other weaponry, and enjoyed better equipment too. They also were much better trained than their Iraqi counterparts. Even so, a defiant Saddam announced on state radio his intention to fight and prevail. "The mother of all battles has begun," he told his people. "The dawn of victory nears as this great showdown begins."

During the aerial phase of Desert Storm, Schwarzkopf's aviators took off from bases all over the Middle East, from aircraft carriers in the Persian Gulf, and even from the continental United States. They averaged about 1,000 *sorties* — or missions — per day. In-air refueling made this amazing operational pace possible.

Iraqi pilots proved to be no match for their coalition enemies. American, British, and Saudi fighter pilots shot down dozens of enemy planes during the first week of the war. They destroyed many others on the ground with cluster bombs and bunker-busting, precision-guided munitions that most people called *smart bombs*. By late January, the Iraqi air force had ceased to exist. Enemy radar operators were afraid to turn on their sets for fear of attracting the attention of sophisticated coalition radar-sniffing equipment. Iraqi planes remained grounded. Some pilots hopped into their planes and fled to neighboring Iran rather than fight the Americans. In all, 112 planes of the Iraqi air force ended up in Iran. With complete command of the air, coalition planes were free to savage Iraqi positions, day after day, week after week. They destroyed 1,385 enemy tanks, 1,155 artillery pieces, 930 armored vehicles, and an untold number of enemy soldiers.

Although Saddam yielded control of the air to his enemies, he did unleash a strategic terror weapon with the power to do political damage to the coalition. Using mobile launchers, he fired conventional Scud missiles against Saudi Arabian cities and, most ominously, Israel. The Scuds were inaccurate and unpredictable, but they could, and did, kill people and destroy buildings. Saddam fired missiles into Israel in hopes of drawing that country into the war. Why? Because he knew that few, if any, Arab nations would fight on the same side as the Jewish nation state, so this was Saddam's attempt to unravel the coalition.

The Bush administration placated Israeli passions for revenge by promising to destroy the Scuds. Publicly, the Americans claimed that their Patriot antiaircraft missile batteries could knock down the Scuds. But the real results came from other sources. From late January onward, the Americans flew thousands of anti-Scud sorties. They also infiltrated highly trained Special Operations soldiers into western Iraq, where most of the launches originated. These men sowed mines, gathered intelligence, and assisted the Air Force in their strikes against the Scud launchers. As a result, Scud launchings declined from five per day in mid-January to one a day by February. Most importantly, Israel stayed out of the war, and the coalition held together.

Nonstop war coverage on CNN

The Gulf War was the first war to be televised 24 hours a day, in full color, almost in real time. The undisputed leader in coverage was the Cable News Network (CNN). Founded in 1980 by Ted Turner, the network was devoted completely to news and was thus ideally suited to the dramatic, continually unfolding story of a modern war.

Throughout the 1980s, CNN had grown steadily as cable television had grown. But the Gulf War thrust the network into a position of supremacy in news broadcasting. When the war began, CNN was the only network with the ability to broadcast from within Iraq. It aired dramatic images of coalition bombing raids on Baghdad as they were happening. CNN also broadcast large numbers of Scud raids and jarring images of coalition POWs in Iraqi hands.

As the war unfolded, all of these images came to represent the conflict in the minds of millions of people all over the world. These breathless reports made household names out of such correspondents as Bernard Shaw, Peter Arnett, and Christiane Amanpour. Some policymakers, by their own admission, even tuned into CNN to find out what was going on. For six weeks, as the Gulf War raged, CNN bristled with images of exploding smart bombs, precision bombing raids, and high-tech warfare, almost creating a pseudo-intimate video game feel.

CNN emerged from the war as a true giant in the news business and remains so today. The ironic thing about all this was that Gulf War news coverage was actually very restricted. The military greatly limited media access to the aviators and soldiers who did most of the fighting. So, even though viewers seemed to have unprecedented access to the realities of war, they really did not.

Gen. Schwarzkopf's secret plan

Schwarzkopf was a strong-willed man with a penchant for belittling subordinates with volcanic temper tantrums. He was also a meticulous planner and an excellent communicator who cared deeply for his troops. Even though his air campaign inflicted tremendous damage on the Iraqis, he knew he must eventually launch a ground campaign to expel them from Kuwait. So he devised an ingenious plan for victory.

The general's goal was to fix the Iraqi army in place, sweep to its left, inflict a devastating blow to its best units, known as the Republican Guards, and either destroy all enemy units in Kuwait or force them to retreat. In the weeks leading up to the ground campaign, Schwarzkopf maneuvered his ships off the coast of Kuwait to make it seem as if an amphibious invasion was imminent. This drew Iraqi attention to the east. In February, he also seemingly massed his forces along the main route of advance to Kuwait, right where the Iraqis expected the coalition to attack. In reality, he was secretly moving strong armored units west, preparing to hit the enemy with a surprise "left hook" along its lightly defended western flank. This clever and well-executed plan is generally known to historians as *the left hook*.

Launching the ground war

Schwarzkopf intended to set his plan into motion when his air campaign had degraded Iraqi strength and capability by at least 50 percent. By February 24, 1991, he felt that the time was right. On that day, he ordered, with Bush's permission, half a million coalition troops into motion, unleashing a massive ground offensive into Kuwait and Iraq. Under cover of supporting helicopters and jets, the ground units rolled into enemy territory. Coalition forces moved along three main axes of advance:

- In the east, the I Marine Expeditionary Force and an all-Arab corps of Egyptians and Saudis knifed straight through an extensive enemy minefield, into Kuwait. Their objective was Kuwait City.

- To the west, Schwarzkopf unleashed his left hook, with the armor-heavy VII Corps smashing into the vulnerable flank of the Iraqi line, right at the convergence of the Kuwaiti and Iraqi borders. The mission of the VII Corps Abrams tanks and Bradleys was to liberate northern Kuwait, destroy the Republican Guard, and cut off the route of retreat for the Iraqi army in Kuwait.

- On the extreme western flank, the mobile XVIII Airborne Corps, consisting of the 82nd Airborne Division, the 101st Air Mobile Division, the 24th Infantry Division (Mechanized), and the French 6th Light Armored Division, slashed into southern Iraq, pushing all the way to the Euphrates River. Their mission was to protect the flank of Schwarzkopf's whole army.

Gorby's last-ditch bid for peace

In the days leading up to the ground war, Mikhail Gorbachev, leader of the Soviet Union, attempted to broker a peace agreement between the Iraqis and the coalition. By now, the Cold War had ended. The Soviet Union was in decline economically, militarily, and politically. Indeed, it was actually on the verge of a democratic revolution. But before that, in February, Gorbachev, whom westerners called "Gorby," repeatedly tried to prevent a ground campaign.

On February 21, he met with Tariq Aziz in Moscow. He succeeded in getting Aziz — but not Saddam — to agree to an eventual Iraqi withdrawal from Kuwait. However, the Iraqis would not agree to any sort of timetable for their withdrawal. The coalition wanted them out in four days.

In the end, Gorby's efforts came to nothing. Some in Washington saw him as a well-intentioned peacemaker. Others believed he had an ulterior motive for thwarting a ground campaign. He knew that the Soviet weapons with which the Iraqis were armed would prove to be inferior to the American weapons in a ground war. The Soviet Union would then be humiliated before the world.

From the beginning, the ground campaign was a major success. The rate of advance was well beyond what planners expected, even in their most optimistic scenarios. Some units advanced against little or no resistance. Others ran into resistance but annihilated enemy formations in one-sided battles. On February 26, just two days into the campaign, Marines and Kuwaiti soldiers liberated Kuwait City. At the same time, VII Corps advanced deep into northern Kuwait and southern Iraq, overrunning enemy resistance. On February 27, VII Corps tanks crushed the better part of two Republican Guard divisions at the Battle of Medina Ridge. The Iraqi army was soon in headlong retreat out of Kuwait. At the same time, the XVIII Airborne Corps raced east, all the way to the edge of Basra, a southern Iraqi metropolis. In so doing, they blocked an avenue of retreat for many fleeing enemy soldiers.

All along the front, thousands of Iraqi soldiers, many of whom were ill-trained *conscripts* (men drafted to fight), surrendered to Allied troops. In all, 86,000 Iraqis surrendered, nearly overwhelming the ability of coalition military policemen to take care of them. Coalition casualties were stunningly low. In the entire war, they lost 378 killed and another 1,000 wounded. Friendly fire incidents were responsible for many of these casualties. Coalition commanders were worried that Saddam would use chemical or biological weapons, but this never happened.

The Gulf War ground campaign was a one-sided victory, but this didn't mean that American soldiers experienced a carefree joyride. For the ground troops, the war was an exhausting, stressful experience. Packed into armored vehicles that were constantly on the move, most soldiers got very little sleep. The best they could do was catnap in their tank turrets or troop compartments. They ate prepackaged rations and drank bottled water. The pace of movement was so fast that soldiers sometimes didn't have time to stop and relieve themselves. They did their business in empty water bottles or ration boxes and threw the refuse into the desert. The contours of the desert bounced them around in their vehicles in an endless series of kidney-stabbing lurches. The weather was actually cold and rainy for most of the ground war, so that added to the misery. Combat consisted of terrifying exchanges of gunfire with enemy vehicles or dismounted groups of determined Iraqi soldiers, usually at distances of more than 200 yards. The noise of these firefights was immense. The stench of burning vehicles, fuel, hair, and flesh permeated the leaden desert air. The sight of destroyed enemy tanks and dismembered enemy bodies was sickening in the extreme, an unforgettable image that remains deeply embedded in the mind of nearly every soldier who witnessed this destruction.

When Saddam realized that his forces were losing badly and that he must abandon Kuwait, he vindictively sought to create an oil-induced ecological disaster. He ordered the burning of Kuwaiti oil wells and even told his minions to dump hundreds of thousands of gallons of oil into the Persian Gulf. It took years to clean up these oil spills. Meanwhile, the flaming wells spewed black, oily fumes that bathed much of Kuwait and southern Iraq in an eerie, shadowy blackness, even at the height of the day. These fumes gave the air an oily smell and feel. In the shadow of the burning wells, every breath of air actually tasted like oil.

Bush calls off the dogs

On February 26, just two days into the ground war, the Iraqi government announced that they would comply with UN Resolution 660 and withdraw from Kuwait. Actually, this was already happening on the battlefield. Thousands of Iraqi soldiers were fleeing for their lives. Many of them were moving north, by vehicle or by foot, on Highway 80, the main road from Kuwait City to southern Iraq (see Figure 20-3). American planes repeatedly attacked this long column of retreating Iraqis, inflicting massive destruction upon them. Mile after mile, the highway was strewn with the wreckage of these attacks — burning buses, armored personnel carriers, tanks, cars, and equipment. Here and there, roasted bodies smoldered in vehicles and alongside the road. The destruction was so staggering that, since 1991, this stretch of road has been known as the *Highway of Death.*

Figure 20-3: Iraqi forces retreating during Operation Desert Storm fled along Highway 80, also known as the Highway of Death.

Source: Department of Defense

Knowing that coalition forces had accomplished the mission of evicting Iraq from Kuwait, Bush decided to order a cease-fire that would take effect February 28. Three days later, Schwarzkopf met with his Iraqi counterparts and dictated what he considered to be surrender terms. According to these terms, Iraq would fully comply with UN Resolution 660. In another meeting a month later, Iraq agreed to abide by all UN resolutions, including those that required *reparations payments* (money paid to make up for the war) to Kuwait, economic sanctions against Iraq, disarmament, and international inspections of potential nuclear, biological, and chemical weapons facilities in Iraq.

Saddam loses Kuwait and half of his army, but he stays in power

Bush's decision to halt hostilities before his troops could annihilate the Iraqi army, in effect, meant that Saddam would remain in power. Instead of pressing on to Baghdad and toppling Saddam, the coalition countries were committed simply to removing him from Kuwait. Bush knew that if he had widened the war to conquer all of Iraq, the coalition would have fallen apart, and the war would have dragged on, costing more American lives.

Bush's decision was later controversial in America. Some argued that Bush had failed to push on to full victory when it was within his grasp. Others supported Bush, though, arguing that he had done all he could within the UN mandate.

Whatever the wisdom of Bush's decision to end the war, by April 1991 thousands of victorious American troops were already returning home from the Middle East. The president hoped that with Saddam so clearly defeated in Kuwait, the Iraqi people would overthrow him in favor of a more benevolent, responsible government.

Iraq is composed of three mutually hostile groups — Sunni Muslims, Shiite Muslims, and Kurds. The Kurds live in the north. The Sunnis dominate the west and northwest. The Shiites are the majority and control much of the rest of the country. As a Sunni, Saddam appealed predominantly to those of the same religious faith. Using propaganda broadcasts during the war, the Americans hoped to stir up an uprising among Kurds and Shiites against Saddam.

In the wake of the cease-fire that ended the war, the Iraqi dictator had lost about half of his combat forces, including thousands of his loyal Republican Guards. But he was still strong enough to maintain control of the country. He ruthlessly crushed a Kurdish uprising in the north and Shiite uprisings in the south. The Americans provided some humanitarian assistance to these rebellious Iraqis, but otherwise abandoned them to their unhappy fate. Battered but resilient, Saddam remained in power.

The Uneasy Aftermath

The Gulf War was clearly an American-led coalition victory. As the UN mandate required, Iraq was out of Kuwait. That country's security was guaranteed by a permanent American military presence there that continues today. Eventually, Kuwait would evolve into a democracy of sorts. The free flow of oil resumed in a stable market. Saddam's power to menace his Middle Eastern neighbors was curtailed. Americans celebrated the Gulf War victory with parades, speeches, and delirious welcome-home ceremonies for the returning troops.

Even so, the aftermath of the war was uneasy, with troubling signs. As the 1990s unfolded, Saddam gradually grew stronger, militarily and politically. He remained a considerable thorn in the United States' side. He turned away UN weapons inspectors, shot at Allied planes that tried to enforce no-fly zones over portions of his country, and funded terrorists. He even plundered a UN humanitarian "oil for food" program designed to help feed the Iraqi people, instead using the funds to buy weapons and line his own pockets. Eventually, in 2003, the U.S. began another, much costlier, showdown with Saddam (see Chapter 21).

The happy homecoming — parades and plaudits

The American people were immensely relieved at the war's relatively low cost in casualties and buoyed by the victory over Saddam. They welcomed the troops home with gusto. Throughout the spring and summer of 1991, returning soldiers, Marines, sailors, and airmen participated in parades all over the country. Adoring crowds lined up by the thousands to thank the returning servicemen and women. Fittingly, Gen. Schwarzkopf led the largest of all the victory parades in Washington, D.C.

President Bush declared that the country had once and for all kicked the *Vietnam syndrome,* a crisis of confidence that had deflated Americans in the wake of that difficult war (for more, see Chapter 19). Knowing that returning Vietnam veterans had often received shabby treatment, Americans bent over backwards to convey their gratitude to Gulf War veterans. In the minds of most Americans, Saddam was defeated and he would simply fade away, like a losing movie villain. The country turned to other concerns, such as a looming recession. This economic downturn was such a serious issue that it cost Bush reelection in 1992.

The unhappy legacy — unfinished business with Saddam

Saddam did not fade away, though. In 1993, he tried unsuccessfully to assassinate Bush during the ex-president's visit to Kuwait. Five years later, Saddam once again had the largest army in the Middle East. His repression continued with a wave of cruelty and atrocities, many of which were perpetrated by his psychopathic sons, Uday and Qusay.

The most ominous aspect of Saddam's regime was its potential possession of nuclear, biological, and chemical weapons. Contrary to UN mandates, he was less than forthcoming with UN inspectors, repeatedly kicking them out of his country. By the end of the 1990s, American policymakers and most U.S. allies believed Saddam had such weapons. They worried that he might attack his neighbors or sell the weapons to fanatical Islamic fundamentalist terrorists. In the wake of the September 11, 2001, attacks by such terrorists on the United States, President George W. Bush (son of George H. W. Bush) decided to eliminate Saddam once and for all. In March 2003, he launched a preemptive invasion of Iraq, prompting a long and difficult war. The Persian Gulf War, then, was only the first round in a long struggle against Saddam Hussein's regime.

Chapter 21

The Long War Ahead: Terrorism, Afghanistan, and Iraq

....

In This Chapter

▶ Absorbing a devastating attack at home

▶ Invading Afghanistan

▶ Taking down Saddam Hussein

▶ Struggling for stability in Iraq

....

The September 11, 2001, terrorist attacks on the United States (9/11 as the attacks are generally known) ushered in a new and deadlier phase to a long-festering and escalating struggle against terrorism. Led by President George W. Bush, the United States government launched a "Global War on Terror" against Islamic radicalism. The first manifestation of the war on terrorism came in October 2001 with the invasion of Afghanistan, home to *Al Qaeda* and the *Taliban,* two extremist organizations that were responsible for the 9/11 attacks. Subsequently, in 2003, Bush widened the global struggle, invading Iraq to remove his father's old adversary, Saddam Hussein, from power.

In this chapter, I trace the long conflict between Muslim terrorists and the United States. I take a look at the invasion of Afghanistan and how an American-led coalition removed the Taliban from power, but then found itself involved in a long-term occupation of the country to build a new democracy in hopes of preventing the Taliban from taking over again. In the second half of the chapter, I explore why the United States invaded Iraq and outline how a lightning military campaign toppled Saddam. Finally, I explain how Saddam's removal led to a long, controversial, and bloody American occupation of Iraq.

A New War against an Old Enemy

In the early 19th century, the United States fought North African Barbary pirates for access to Mediterranean Sea routes (for more, see Chapter 8). These pirates just happened to be Muslims. The conflict was really fueled more by economics than religious ideals. At the end of the 19th century and the beginning of the 20th, American soldiers fought against the *Moros,* a group of Muslim Filipinos who, for religious and nationalistic reasons, opposed the U.S. occupation of the Philippines (for more, see Chapter 13).

But the trouble between America and Islamic fundamentalists really began after World War II, when the American presence in the Middle East — home to millions of devout Muslims — increased because of the growing American dependence on the region's oil. Many Muslims didn't like how the American culture, language, and economic influence were creeping into their respective homelands. Moreover, the United States generally supported the Jewish nation-state of Israel, a country that most Middle Eastern Arab Muslims hated because of their own latent anti-Semitism and their belief that the Jews, with American support, created Israel by stealing land from Palestinian Arabs. In the early 1970s, this seething conflict boiled over, as Islamic radicals began to employ terrorism against the Israelis, the Americans, and anyone else they perceived as an opponent of their fundamentalist views.

Terrorism is a tactic of indiscriminate violence used for some sort of political, religious, or ideological goal. Terrorists believe that there is no such thing as a noncombatant. Any member of an enemy group is fair game, from highly trained soldiers to infants and the elderly. Terrorists generally operate within small, cohesive, shadowy groups of true believers. Terrorist networks are multinational. They can, and do, exist in nearly every country in the world. Terrorists specialize in hit-and-run, wanton violence and the threat of the same. Examples of terrorist tactics include the bombing of crowded places such as restaurants, airports, sporting events, and bars; hijacking aircraft; taking hostages; stealing weapons; assassinating prominent political leaders; and blowing up buildings. Some terrorists, particularly Islamic radicals, engage in suicide attacks. Terrorists rely on vast networks of surreptitious financial and political support from like-minded, but more "respectable," cohorts. Ultimately, the greatest terrorist weapon is fear and intimidation. Osama bin Laden, who masterminded the 9/11 attacks, is the most famous example of a terrorist.

Sleeping through terrorism's rise

Throughout the 1970s and 1980s, instances of Islamic fundamentalist terrorism grew, with a litany of attacks against Israel and the United States:

- At the 1972 Summer Olympics in Munich, Germany, Palestinian terrorists abducted and killed 11 Israeli athletes.

- In 1977, Muslim terrorists took control of several buildings in Washington, D.C., and held 123 hostages. They killed a reporter and wounded several other people before surrendering to authorities.

- On November 4, 1979, a mob of Iranian fundamentalists overran the U.S. embassy in Tehran and took 52 Americans hostage, holding them for more than a year. This crisis prompted a failed rescued mission in April 1980 by United States military forces. It also was one of the reasons why President Jimmy Carter failed to win reelection in the fall of 1980.

- On April 18, 1983, Islamic terrorists packed 1,000 pounds of explosives into a pickup truck and bombed the U.S. embassy in Lebanon, killing 63 people, including 17 Americans.

- On October 23, 1983, a suicide bomber rammed a truck with 1,500 pounds of explosives into the Marine barracks in Beirut, Lebanon, killing 241 Marines and wounding 100 others.

- On December 21, 1988, Libyan terrorists blew up a Pan American passenger plane over Lockerbie, Scotland, killing 281 people.

Preoccupied with the Cold War (see Chapter 17 for more), American leaders did little to combat Islamic terrorism in the 1970s and 1980s.

Pushing the snooze button — more Islamic terrorism in the 1990s

In 1992, the Cold War had ended, an American-led coalition had defeated Saddam Hussein in the Gulf War (for more, see Chapter 20), and most Americans turned their attention to domestic issues. Thinking that the United States had defeated all of its significant enemies, people spoke of a peace dividend. Politicians mirrored this "all is well" mentality. President Bill Clinton and Congress teamed up to cut the defense budget and the size of the armed forces.

Unfortunately, Islamic radicals continued to make war on the United States with a series of bloody attacks:

- On February 26, 1993, Al Qaeda–linked terrorists detonated a powerful car bomb in the parking garage of the World Trade Center in New York City. The blast killed 6 people and injured 1,042 others, but it didn't collapse the Trade Center towers as the terrorists had hoped.

- Later that same year, Saddam Hussein tried to assassinate former President George H. W. Bush while Bush was visiting Kuwait.

- On June 26, 1996, Al Qaeda terrorists detonated a car bomb at the Khobar Towers, a U.S. military housing complex in Saudi Arabia. The blast killed 19 Americans and wounded 372 people.

- On August 7, 1998, Al Qaeda operatives bombed U.S. embassies in Kenya and Tanzania, killing 12 Americans, plus numerous local embassy employees in both countries.

- Al Qaeda struck again on October 12, 2000, in the Yemeni port of Aden. That morning two suicide bombers sailed a small, explosive-laden craft into the USS *Cole,* touching off an explosion that killed 17 American sailors.

The American response to these attacks was tepid. Shocking as these events were, none of them touched off any kind of political consensus among the American people to retaliate against Al Qaeda in any meaningful way. It took the bloody tragedy of 9/11 to finally change that political climate.

Jarring awake to an ominous reality

The sight was strange, almost surreal. On September 11, 2001, as millions watched on television or on the ground, an airliner slammed into one of the World Trade Center towers in New York City. Was this some sort of dreadful navigation error? Perhaps the pilots had died? Weather couldn't be a factor because the day was clear and bright. Then, in the next instant, a second airliner hit the Trade Center's other tower. Soon thereafter, a third plane crashed into the Pentagon, near Washington, D.C. Yet another airliner mysteriously crashed in a Pennsylvania field.

As the Trade Center towers collapsed and the Pentagon smoldered, the awful reality of what had happened began to sink in. The United States had been attacked by a group of dedicated, cunning, and suicidal terrorists headed by Osama bin Laden. These 19 terrorists were Islamic fundamentalist radicals who hated the United States and everything it stood for. On September 11, they butchered 2,973 people. This heinous attack was just the latest event in a 30-year struggle between the United States and Islamic extremists around the world. But it finally made Americans aware that the nation was not immune from people who would go to any extreme to express their venom toward the United States.

Osama bin Laden was born into a wealthy family in Saudi Arabia. A devout Muslim, he fought against the Soviet Union in Afghanistan during the 1980s (for more on that war, see Chapter 17). Bin Laden didn't approve of the American presence in Saudi Arabia during the Gulf War (that war is covered in Chapter 20). To him, the presence of American *infidels* (nonbelievers) on sacred Islamic soil was an abomination that must be avenged. Thus began his long "holy war" against the United States. After 9/11, the United States government offered a $25 million reward for bin Laden.

Invading Afghanistan

Within days of 9/11, American intelligence analysts and policymakers knew that bin Laden's Al Qaeda and its close ally, the Taliban, were responsible for the attacks. The *Taliban* was a hard-line group of Muslim fundamentalists who had come to power in Afghanistan several years after the Soviet withdrawal from that country in 1989. With Taliban approval, Al Qaeda was using Afghanistan as a base from which to launch terrorist operations. As dedicated, violent Muslim fundamentalists, the two groups were basically ideological bedfellows and made common cause with each other. Knowing this, President George W. Bush, after 9/11, demanded that the Taliban turn over custody of bin Laden and anyone else responsible for the killings. The Taliban government refused to comply with these demands. So, in October 2001, the United States and its allies in the North Atlantic Treaty Organization (NATO) invaded Afghanistan with the goals of toppling the Taliban, destroying Al Qaeda, and apprehending bin Laden.

Taking down the Taliban

Afghanistan is a highly factionalized country with myriad warring tribes and interest groups. The country's harsh climate and rugged mountains make mere existence a struggle for many Afghans. American and NATO planners knew that it made no sense to invade the country with large conventional military forces or great numbers of soldiers. Instead, the U.S. and its partners infiltrated the country with small, highly trained Special Forces teams that made common cause with the Taliban's many enemies to create a powerful fighting bloc known as the Northern Alliance. Special Forces soldiers helped train, equip, and arm the Afghan members of the Northern Alliance.

In combat, the Americans made liberal use of airpower to support Northern Alliance attacks and batter Taliban positions. In a lightning two-month campaign, the Northern Alliance and the Americans drove the Taliban from power. Taliban and Al Qaeda survivors generally did not surrender, though.

Instead they retreated east, across the rough, mountainous border areas, into western Pakistan (see Figure 21-1), a fertile place for them because of the large number of Muslim fundamentalists in that country. There the survivors licked their wounds, evaded Pakistani government troops, and prepared to fight the American-led coalition in Afghanistan another day. For fear of provoking a revolution by Muslim radicals, the military junta that controlled the Pakistani government did little to apprehend the Taliban and Al Qaeda. In the meantime, Gen. Tommy Franks, the American commander, reinforced his Special Forces teams with regular troops specially trained for mountain warfare, such as the 10th Mountain Division.

The Taliban regime was highly repressive. As hard-line Islamic radicals, they believed in no separation of church and state. In their case, the Muslim faith was the state, and they were the keepers of that faith. Everyone was to comply with *shariah,* or Muslim, laws. Needless to say, infidels such as Christians, Jews, Buddhists, or atheists were highly unwelcome. The Taliban's greatest repression was against women. They forced women to wear heavy, robe-like *burqas* that covered their entire bodies. Women were allowed no education after the age of 8 years old. Before that, their only schooling would be in the *Koran,* the holy book of Islam. Women couldn't work, travel alone, drive, sing, dance, or even be photographed. Adultery was punishable by death. Religious police hunted down violators and imposed severe punishments, which ranged from public floggings to facial disfigurement and even outright executions.

Figure 21-1:
Map of
Afghanistan.

Striking with Operation Anaconda

Even though the initial military campaign in Afghanistan had been a big success for the U.S. and its allies, thousands of enemy fighters, including bin Laden, were still at large. In an effort to cut them off and round them up, the Allies, in March 2002, launched Operation Anaconda in Paktia province. The attacking forces, numbering about 2,000 soldiers, consisted of a multinational blend of regular and irregular troops:

- ✔ Elements of the U.S. Army's 10th Mountain Division and the 101st Air Assault Division

- ✔ Army Rangers, Special Forces teams, Navy SEAL (Sea, Air, and Land) teams, and British Royal Marines

- ✔ Afghan fighters

- ✔ Soldiers from the 3rd Battalion, Princess Patricia's Canadian Light Infantry

- ✔ Special Forces teams from Germany, New Zealand, and Australia

Taliban and Al Qaeda fighters were extensively dug into caves, ridges, and mountainsides. They laid down withering fire on Allied soldiers who assaulted from helicopters and from the valleys.

Perhaps the most intense fighting of this operation took place at Taku Ghar on March 3–4, 2002, when two SEAL teams engaged in a vicious close-quarters firefight with several hundred Taliban and Al Qaeda fighters. The enemy fighters then shot down a helicopter carrying a Ranger quick-reaction force that was coming to the aid of the SEALs. Thus ensued a 24-hour battle in which the Americans fought the enemy troops to a standstill with the help of deadly airstrikes. Rescue forces eventually extracted the Americans who had killed 200 enemy fighters, at the cost of 7 of their own dead comrades.

Operation Anaconda cost the enemy between 500 and 800 dead, but it was not decisive. Osama bin Laden got away, probably into Pakistan, and remained a thorn in the American side. From here on out, the Taliban and Al Qaeda rested, replenished, and trained new fighters along the lawless border between Afghanistan and Pakistan. Using these areas as bases, they forayed into Afghanistan to fight coalition forces.

Rick Rescorla — Vietnam and 9/11 hero

Rick Rescorla was definitely not your average Joe. Born in Cornwall, England, in 1939, Rescorla's childhood was heavily influenced by the presence of World War II–era American GIs in his town. Wanting to be like them, he enlisted in the British army in 1957 at age 18. Trained as a paratrooper, he served stints in Cyprus and Rhodesia.

When his hitch in the British army was done, he decided, at the urging of an American soldier friend named Daniel Hill, to join the U.S. Army in 1963. After basic training, he attended Officer Candidate School and graduated as a second lieutenant. He became a platoon leader in the 2nd Battalion, 7th Cavalry Regiment. With this unit he fought in the famous Battle of Ia Drang, portrayed in the book and movie *We Were Soldiers.* Rescorla was such a brave soldier that his men called him "Hard Core." Gen. Hal Moore, author of *We Were Soldiers Once . . . And Young,* once referred to him as "the best platoon leader I ever saw."

After Vietnam, Rescorla earned a college degree in criminal justice, got married, and ended up as director of security for Dean Witter/Morgan Stanley at the World Trade Center in New York. Consulting with his old buddy Hill, Rescorla warned the New York Port Authority that terrorists could detonate a truck bomb in the parking garage of the Trade Center. When that exact thing happened in 1993, Rescorla oversaw the evacuation of the buildings.

In the aftermath, he and Hill co-wrote a report warning that terrorists would next attack the towers with airplanes. Those warnings fell on deaf ears. On 9/11, when that nightmare scenario came to fruition, he evacuated almost 2,800 Morgan Stanley employees. He repeatedly went back into the burning towers to help more people out. He simply would not leave until "I make sure everyone else is out." He was last seen on the tenth floor of Tower No. 2 right before it collapsed. His remains were never recovered.

A new Afghanistan government and a counterinsurgency struggle

After ejecting the Taliban from power, the U.S., in conjunction with its NATO partners and the United Nations (UN), installed a new democratic government in Afghanistan. Afghans voted in elections for the first time in decades, electing Hamid Karzai, a close U.S. ally, as their president. With extensive American aid, the new government created its own military, known as the Afghan National Army (ANA). American and NATO soldiers worked closely with ANA troops, training them, arming them, equipping them, and teaching them how to defeat the Taliban. Afghanistan became a moderately stable country, but with some serious economic and security problems that required a continued NATO presence.

From the summer of 2002 onward, Afghanistan became a counterinsurgency struggle. Taliban and Al Qaeda fighters conducted guerrilla warfare against the ANA and NATO throughout Afghanistan. The main enemy tactics were improvised explosive devices (IEDs) on roads, ambushes in mountain passes, and periodic efforts to take over villages in the country's many remote areas. To contain the insurgency, the U.S. and its allies maintained about 10,000 soldiers in Afghanistan. Their counterinsurgency struggle continued into 2007 and beyond.

Although the counterinsurgent war in Afghanistan was basically successful, two serious, long-term problems vexed the Americans:

- Western Pakistan was a sanctuary for the Taliban and Al Qaeda. These terrorist organizations recruited young Muslims in Pakistan, indoctrinated them at schools known as *madrasahs,* and sent them into Afghanistan to make trouble. Osama bin Laden himself probably took refuge in Pakistan.

- Opium was the main cash crop of Afghanistan. For the Americans, cutting off the opium trade risked destroying the fledgling Afghan economy. However, keeping it in place would support the world drug trade.

Resuming the fight with Saddam: The Iraq War

On January 29, 2002, President George W. Bush, during his State of the Union Address, described several terrorist-sponsoring nations as the "axis of evil." One of those nations was Saddam Hussein's Iraq. In 1991, Saddam had taken over neighboring Kuwait (for more, see Chapter 20). In response, the United States and a vast coalition fought a successful war to force Saddam out of Kuwait. However, he kept control of power in Iraq, partly through the ruthless suppression of war-inspired uprisings in his country. He had agreed, though, to verifiably destroy any nuclear, chemical, and biological *weapons of mass destruction* (WMD) in his possession.

Instead, throughout the 1990s, Saddam flouted UN mandates, shot at U.S. and British planes that tried to enforce a no-fly zone over parts of Iraq, and concealed information about Iraq's WMD program. These weapons were a major concern to American leaders partially because of Saddam's aggressive and tyrannical nature, but also because he had actually used chemical weapons to kill rebellious Iraqis in 1988.

By 2002, Bush, and many intelligence analysts from a variety of nations believed that, contrary to UN mandates, Saddam secretly possessed weapons of mass destruction. Saddam's less-than-forthright dealings with UN weapons inspectors during their visits to Iraq in 1998 and 2002 only added to these suspicions. Bush and other world leaders, like British Prime Minister Tony Blair, also thought that Saddam had strong ties with terrorist organizations such as Al Qaeda. The president worried that Saddam would sell nuclear or chemical weapons to terrorists, who could then use the weapons to kill millions of Americans. Feeling, in the wake of 9/11, that he had to prevent such a situation from ever developing, Bush came to believe that the United States must invade Iraq to remove Saddam from power unless he honestly proved he had no WMDs.

The controversial decision for war

Saddam never proved whether or not he had weapons of mass destruction. So, in the fall of 2002 and the early months of 2003, the Bush administration prepared for war with Iraq. Bush had little trouble lining up the necessary war mandate from Congress. But he had a much more difficult time gaining UN approval for his prospective invasion of Iraq.

Led by France and Russia, the UN Security Council opposed an American-sponsored resolution for war. A detailed pro-war presentation by Secretary of State Colin Powell, who had earned universal acclaim for his service as chairman of the Joint Chiefs of Staff during the Gulf War, did little to persuade the UN. In the end, enough Security Council members opposed military action that the UN would not approve of Bush's war resolution. In defiance of the UN, the president decided to go to war anyway.

Over time, the decision process for the invasion of Iraq grew into one of the most controversial in U.S. military history because

- ✔ UN leaders viewed the war in Iraq as illegal.

- ✔ After overrunning Iraq, U.S. forces never found any WMDs, undermining one of the administration's major justifications for war.

- ✔ Saddam's ties with Al Qaeda and other terrorist organizations weren't as extensive as Bush had argued.

Bush called his national security policy *preemption*. He argued that, after 9/11, the United States could no longer afford to simply react to security threats. Rather, it must now preempt such threats — in places like Iraq — before they cost American lives. Prior to the Iraq War, most Americans agreed with preemption. However, when the war grew into a long and difficult struggle with thousands of American casualties, support for preemption diminished dramatically. Opponents of the policy argued that it probably cost more American lives in military campaigns than it saved at home. Plus, they argued, it stimulated as much bloodshed and terror around the world as it prevented.

Even without UN approval, Bush still put together an anti-Saddam alliance, but it was nowhere near as vast as the coalition his father had built in 1990 to repel Saddam from Kuwait. In 2003, the Americans built an alliance that George W. Bush called "the coalition of the willing." This coalition included more than 40 countries, most of which simply supported the invasion politically or provided some sort of aid. Only a few sent troops. Ninety-eight percent of the invading troops in 2003 were either British or American. Only Poland, Australia, and Denmark contributed troops to the invasion force. Several other countries, including Spain, Italy, Ukraine, and Japan, sent troops for the occupation that followed the invasion. However, by 2006, nearly all of these countries had withdrawn their soldiers from Iraq.

"On to Baghdad!" The invasion of Iraq

In late 2002 and early 2003, U.S. and British forces massed along the Kuwait-Iraq border (see Figure 21-2). By March, about 248,000 American troops and 45,000 British soldiers were in place. Iraq had about 390,000 regular soldiers, 45,000 Fedayeen Saddam paramilitary fighters, and roughly 120,000 Republican Guard troops, who were among Saddam's best, most loyal men. On March 17, 2003, Bush issued an ultimatum to Saddam. He and his sons were to leave Iraq within two days or face invasion. The ultimatum passed with no response. So, on March 20, Bush gave the order to invade.

Gen. Tommy Franks, the coalition commander, devised a bold invasion plan that depended upon speed, firepower, technology, and the lethality of American weapons. His objective was to reach Baghdad and destroy Saddam's regime as quickly as possible. He made liberal use of devastating American airstrikes — what reporters called "shock and awe." On the ground, he intended to seize and control all northerly roads that led to the capital, dash north, bypass other major cities, and avoid costly urban combat. He only had enough ground forces for a two-pronged advance. In the east, the British 1st Armored Division's mission was to seize Basrah, the second-largest city in Iraq. He ordered the 1st Marine Division, plus other supporting Marine units, to advance north, with the intention of entering Baghdad from the east. To the west of the Marines, the Army's 3rd Infantry Division was to advance along the western side of the Euphrates River, cross that river, and enter Baghdad from the west. Follow-up units from the 101st Air Assault Division and the 82nd Airborne Division drew the mission of mopping up any resistance that the heavily mechanized 3rd Division bypassed. Gen. Franks planned to stage another major unit, the 4th Infantry Division, in Turkey and order them to invade Iraq from the north. But the Turkish government wouldn't agree to this. Instead, Franks dropped the 173rd Airborne Brigade and Special Forces teams into northern Iraq, where they linked up with friendly Kurdish militia units to tie down substantial Iraqi forces.

In 21 days, coalition forces overran Iraq and captured Baghdad. Saddam's regime collapsed like a house of cards. Iraqi resistance to the invasion was mixed. Some units surrendered in droves. Others simply vanished as soldiers threw away their uniforms and went home. Other formations, particularly Fedayeen Saddam and Republican Guards, fought desperately, even in suicidal fashion. Plus, thousands of foreign fighters from all over the Middle East filtered into Iraq to fight the coalition. These men were usually poorly trained but fanatical Muslims who didn't like the idea of an Anglo-American army conquering Islamic soil.

The invasion succeeded, but it was no walkover. American troops had fought bitter, costly battles at such places as An Nasiriyah, An Najaf, Baghdad International Airport, and in Baghdad itself. By the end of April 2003, the fighting in Iraq had mostly died down. Even though no formal surrender of Saddam or his regime had taken place, to most Americans the war seemed to be over.

Figure 21-2:
Map of Iraq.

Atrocities at Abu Ghraib

Although the vast majority of American troops in Iraq comported themselves with discipline, honor, and decency, a few behaved abysmally. In 2003, as the insurgency grew, the Army apprehended thousands of guerrilla suspects, many of whom ended up in the Abu Ghraib prison on the northwestern outskirts of Baghdad.

Abu Ghraib had once been one of Saddam's most infamous torture sites. Under the Americans in 2003, it was overcrowded with suspects, the majority of whom were not involved with insurgent groups (at least not yet). The prison was poorly run by an understaffed, ill-trained group of Army military policemen and women. Prisoners didn't receive adequate food, clothing, water, medical care, or shelter. But those weren't the worst problems.

Under pressure to get information from prisoners to prevent future attacks against Americans, some soldiers, primarily from the Army's 372nd Military Police Company, abused, humiliated, mistreated, and even tortured prisoners. Some of the soldiers routinely took pictures of themselves abusing the prisoners.

In April 2004, the *New Yorker* magazine and the television program *60 Minutes* broke the story of these abuses, touching off an international outcry. The nauseating photographs and tales of abuse did serious damage to the moral credibility of the American war effort in Iraq. The Army later court-martialed seven of the offending soldiers.

A long, grim struggle: The counterinsurgency phase

Franks's war plan was well designed for the limited objective of overthrowing Saddam's government and destroying the conventional Iraqi armed forces. But the larger issue was the fate of post-Saddam Iraq during the ensuing coalition occupation. Franks and his superiors in the Pentagon and the White House made few concrete plans for this more complicated mission. This was a fatal oversight. With an invasion force of only about 250,000 troops, the coalition couldn't hope to maintain security and keep control over the whole country. Even before the war, a host of media, military, and political critics had said the invasion would require a much larger force. But Defense Secretary Donald Rumsfeld believed that large armies were a thing of the past. He argued that American swiftness and technology, especially airpower, would allow a moderately sized army to subdue and occupy Iraq.

As it turned out, he was dead wrong. Throughout 2003, American ground forces in Iraq struggled to maintain order in a country that seethed with ethnic, religious, and economic tensions. When the Americans killed Saddam's sons in July and captured the dictator himself in December, it hardly affected the situation in Iraq. Almost overnight, a variety of violent insurgent groups came into being, waging guerrilla war against the Americans, who were shocked and unprepared for this kind of war. Soon, the number of U.S. casualties exceeded those suffered during the invasion phase. Sadly, that trend would only get worse in the months and years to come. As the violence grew worse and the casualties mounted, the war grew increasingly unpopular with the American people. As of 2007, more than 3,700 Americans had died in the Iraq War.

The failure of Rumsfeld's 2003 Iraq invasion plan can, to some extent, be attributed to numbers. For instance, during Desert Storm, the anti-Saddam coalition employed a force of nearly 700,000 soldiers for the limited objective of expelling Iraqi forces from Kuwait. In 2003, the smaller "coalition of the willing" drew on less than half that number for the much more ambitious objective of destroying Saddam's regime, occupying Iraq, and converting it into a model democracy. Rumsfeld's biggest mistake was his failure to understand the historical importance of ground combat power in winning wars.

Struggling for security

By 2004, the Americans were focused on creating a new Iraqi government and army, to further the goal of a strong, peaceful, economically stable Iraq. But this would take time. In the meantime, American soldiers struggled mightily to maintain order and quell the daily violence that plagued the country. Thus the conflict raged on, year after year, into 2008. A dizzying variety of insurgent groups engaged in daily attacks, sometimes against one another, often against American soldiers.

Iraq is home to three major groups, none of whom particularly like one another. Sunni Arab Muslims comprise about 20 percent of the population, mostly in the western part of the country. They were traditionally the ruling class, especially under Saddam. Non-Arab Kurds comprise another 20 percent, and they live primarily in the north. The Kurds tend to be pro-American, but some want their own country, separate from Iraq. About 60 percent of Iraqis are Shiite Arab Muslims. They dominate the south and Baghdad. Sunnis and Shiites despise each other passionately because of theological and political hatreds that go back hundreds of years.

Anti-American Islamic groups in neighboring Syria, Iran, and Saudi Arabia exacerbated the problems in Iraq by sending weapons, money, and plenty of committed fighters across the borders into Iraq. The insurgent opposition to the coalition, though diverse, can be boiled down into three categories:

- ✔ Sunnis who want to evict the Americans and return to prominence in the country.

- ✔ Shiites who hate Americans as invaders and infidels. As representatives of the majority group in Iraq, these Shiites feel control of the country should rightfully be theirs. They also yearn to settle old scores with their former Sunni oppressors.

- ✔ Foreign fighters, particularly anti-American Al Qaeda insurgents whose goal is to create a world-dominating Islamic fundamentalist empire.

For the volunteer, professional American troops who served in Iraq, the war was a seemingly never-ending commitment. Soldiers, Marines, sailors, and airmen served tours of duty ranging from 7 to 15 months. Many served multiple tours. For the soldiers on the ground, the war consisted of a range of experiences. Sometimes they fought pitched battles with insurgents as at Fallujah in 2004 or Tal Afar in 2005. More commonly, the enemy avoided such conventional battles. So soldiers and Marines patrolled an area of operations, trying to help the locals, provide for their security, and hunt down insurgents. All the while they had to be wary of insurgent ambushes, deadly improvised explosive devices on the roads, suicide bombers, and sniping. Soldiers and Marines patrolled in vehicles and on foot, in temperatures that often exceeded 115 degrees Fahrenheit. Those who served in Iraq could never forget the shimmering waves of heat, the pungent stench of raw sewage that pervaded much of the country, or the grinding poverty of many Iraqis. The soldiers also couldn't forget the strange duality of serving in Iraq. One minute they could be handing out candy to children or chatting amiably with local folks. The next minute they could be in grave danger from an insurgent attack. In Iraq, an American never can be sure where and when such danger may lurk.

Part VI
The Part of Tens

The 5th Wave — By Rich Tennant

One of the great battles of the Civil War...
The Battle of Ft. Stuckey

©RICHTENNANT

"The Union Army's cut off our supply line, Sir. All we have left are these crates of pecans. Hey – what if we chopped up the pecans, mixed them with a caramel-like substance, and rolled them into a log shape? We could then hurl them at the Unionists and hopefully knock a few teeth out."

In this part . . .

Every Dummies book includes a Part of Tens section. This is a group of chapters that include top-ten lists of interesting, thought-provoking, even controversial information. What makes each of the lists so fun is that they are both arbitrary and subjective. Some might agree with what they read. Others might disagree to the point of fisticuffs. Like military history itself, the questions will never be completely be settled, but the debates sure are fun. In this part, I've prepared top-ten lists of the greatest and worst generals in U.S. military history, along with a special list of the top ten films on the subject. So take a few moments to check out these lists and get ready to experience U.S. military history from some new points of view.

Chapter 22

The Ten Best Generals in U.S. Military History

*F*or every general on this list, there are half a dozen others who deserve recognition. But this is a short list. It's only for the best of the best, the greatest of the great. I base these selections on several criteria: the difficulty of their respective missions; their ability to think, plan, and strategize to achieve national wartime objectives; and, as much as anything else, their personal combat leadership. To avoid sparking needless controversy, I have listed the generals alphabetically.

Dwight Eisenhower (1890–1969)

The amazing thing about Eisenhower is that he never actually led soldiers in combat, yet he became a great general. In World War I, when he was a young officer, he never got the opportunity to serve overseas. During World War II, he was too high ranking to actually fight in battle. Eisenhower's great strengths of generalship were personal character, approachability, wisdom, level-headedness, and diplomacy.

A vast coalition of nations comprised the Allied armed forces in World War II. As supreme commander, Eisenhower's task was to unite all the divergent, multinational egos around the task of defeating Germany, and he succeeded mightily. He made friends easily and worked well with practically everyone from Winston Churchill to George Patton. Eisenhower was a paragon of reason, good humor, and steadiness. His low-key demeanor and passion for meeting his men firsthand endeared him to hundreds of thousands of Allied soldiers.

In commanding the Normandy invasion, Eisenhower was under more pressure than any other American general in history. Failure would have jeopardized Western civilization for generations. Basically, he had to succeed. Working with a broad array of Allied soldiers, he devised a winning invasion plan. Then, in the months after the invasion, he successfully led the largest, most complicated ground campaign in modern history. After the war, he presided over the denazification of Germany, sowing the seeds of democracy in that country. Later, during the Cold War, he was the first commander of NATO military forces. Oh, and as if that wasn't enough, he spent eight good years in the Oval Office, too. . . .

James Gavin (1907–1990)

Gavin was the very essence of a fighting general. He dressed like an ordinary soldier, talked like one, and fought like one, too. At 36 years old, he was the youngest two-star general in the U.S. Army in World War II. He was an airborne pioneer, helping to create America's paratrooper units in 1942 and 1943. He started his combat career as a regimental commander but, because of his brilliant leadership, eventually was promoted to divisional command. At Sicily, Normandy, and Holland, he jumped into combat alongside his troopers in the 82nd Airborne Division, earning the nickname "Jumping Jim." Many of the division's admiring troopers also called him "Slim Jim" because of his athletic build and youthful appearance.

His leadership philosophy was that officers "should be first out the door [on a combat jump] and last in the chow line." On the ground, Gavin was an inspirational figure, planning attacks, figuring out the enemy's weak points, risking his neck in firefights. At La Fiere, Normandy, on June 9, 1944, he personally led an almost-suicidal attack to capture a vital causeway from the Germans. Time and again, whether in Normandy, Holland, or the Battle of the Bulge, he was in the middle of the fighting. In so doing, he helped make the 82nd Airborne Division a premier fighting unit.

Nor was he just a warrior. He was a leader in desegregating the armed forces. An African American soldier once referred to him as the most colorblind officer in the U.S. Army. After World War II, while serving as a lieutenant general, he restructured the Army's ground forces and pushed for the use of helicopters, the wave of the future. In the 1950s, he correctly denounced America's over-reliance on airpower at the expense of ground combat forces. After retiring from the Army in 1958, he served as U.S. ambassador to France, fostering good relations. He was an early opponent of the war in Vietnam, mainly because he thought it would require a massive influx of American troops. As usual, Gavin was proved right.

Thomas Jackson (1824–1863)

"Stonewall" Jackson never lost a battle. During the Civil War, he was the most competent, audacious commander in the Confederate Army. He was a devout Christian and an introvert who nonetheless drove his men mercilessly. His performances in several Civil War battles, such as both Bull Runs, the 1862 Valley campaign, Fredericksburg, and especially Chancellorsville, were among the best of all time. Chancellorsville was particularly impressive. He devised a surprise attack that stunned the Yankees. But his ingenuity cost him his life. After this surprise attack, while scouting at night to plan a follow-up attack, one of his own soldiers mistook him for a Union commander and shot him. Jackson died eight days later. The South could never replace him.

Robert E. Lee (1807–1870)

The man's very name is still hallowed throughout the South. He was no mere symbol, though. He was a truly great commander. Lee was the consummate military professional, who understood strategy, tactics, and everything in between. The Virginian was blessed with an amazing feel for terrain. He was personally courageous, and he had an uncanny ability to judge the essential character of friend and foe alike. He was offensive-minded, aggressive even to a fault. This was a product of his quiet, cool self-confidence. More than any of that, Lee was well-mannered, polite, kind, and incorruptible.

These qualities made him an inspirational leader for Confederate soldiers, most of whom would have followed him into hell itself. As commander of the Army of North Virginia, the South's main military force, he won victory after victory at such battles as Second Bull Run, Fredericksburg, and Chancellorsville. Many Civil War historians believe that, without Lee, the South would not have lasted more than two years. He almost single-handedly held his army together through years of adversity. By the end of the war, he was the most revered commander on both divides of the Civil War. Northerners respected him. Southerners loved him. He may have lost the war, but he earned an enduring place as a legend in U.S. military history.

George Marshall (1880–1959)

Winston Churchill aptly called him the "organizer of victory" in World War II. Marshall was chief of staff of the U.S. Army during the war, which was, more or less, the top job in the military at that time. Although Marshall would rather have been leading troops in combat, he fought the war from a desk in Washington, D.C., directing the grand strategy. More than anyone else, he harnessed the enormous power of the wartime United States for victory. Marshall had a major impact on nearly every aspect of the Allied war effort. As a first-rate strategic thinker, he was a principal architect of the "Germany First" policy, the cross-channel invasion of France, the strategic air campaign in Europe and the Pacific, and the island-hopping campaign that defeated Japan.

Like his protégé Eisenhower, Marshall's greatest leadership asset was his personal character. He was austere, honest, hardworking, and reasonable in his dealings with everyone from the president to congressmen, high-ranking Allied leaders, and his own subordinates.

Universally respected by the end of the war, he retired from the Army. During the Cold War, he subsequently served as secretary of state and defense. He also authored, in 1948, the European Recovery Plan to help Europeans rebuild their shattered countries. We generally know that program as the Marshall Plan.

George Patton (1885–1945)

Like Lee, the very name of Patton is legendary, and with good reason. He was the most effective American ground combat general in World War II. Flamboyant, foul-mouthed, tempestuous, and brave, Patton was a hard-charging, aggressive commander who never lost a battle. More than anyone else in the U.S. Army, he understood the potency of combined arms — tanks, infantry, planes, and so on — working together on the battlefield. A warrior to the core, he yearned for action. Mystical and maudlin, he believed he had lived many previous lives as a soldier, from ancient times through the Civil War.

In Tunisia, he defeated the Germans at the Battle of El Guettar. In so doing, he made a major contribution to Allied victory in North Africa. A few months later, he led American soldiers to victory in Sicily. The 1944 campaign in France and the Battle of the Bulge were his greatest moments. Under Patton's driving leadership, his Third Army fought across Europe, killed thousands of enemy soldiers, and contributed mightily to Allied victory. Patton was mortally wounded in a car accident after the war.

Matthew Ridgway (1895–1993)

Born on a military post to a soldier father, Ridgway was the embodiment of a military professional. As commander of the 82nd Airborne Division at Sicily and Normandy, he earned a reputation as the best two-star general in the Army. In fact, he was such an effective leader that, by the fall of 1944, he was promoted to corps command of several airborne divisions. Ridgway's leadership style was hands-on. He was steely, hard-nosed, and ruthless. Two things mattered to him: victory and his soldiers. He took care of both in World War II.

Ridgway's greatest achievements came after World War II, though. In December 1950, the American/United Nations war effort in Korea was at a low point. Communist forces were on the offensive, threatening to win the war. At this point, Ridgway assumed command. In just a few weeks, he authored an amazing turnaround in the military situation, pushing the Communists back across the 38th parallel, in effect saving the non-Communist government of South Korea. Later, after the war in Korea stabilized, he served as Army chief of staff. When the Eisenhower administration contemplated intervening to help the French fight a war in Vietnam, Ridgway persuaded his old friend Eisenhower not to intervene, delaying U.S. entry in Vietnam by a decade.

Norman Schwarzkopf Jr. (1934–)

In spite of a tendency toward volcanic, even abusive, temper tantrums, Schwarzkopf became one of the great generals in U.S. military history. The son of a general and a successful combat leader in the Vietnam War, Schwarzkopf had a deep reverence for the Army and its fighting soldiers. He strongly believed that training them to ultimate fighting efficiency would prevent casualties and win wars. During the Army's post-Vietnam malaise, he helped rejuvenate the Army into a potent all-volunteer fighting force. Then, during the Gulf War, 1990–1991, he put that force to the test.

As the supreme commander of multinational coalition military forces with the mission of expelling Saddam Hussein's Iraq from Kuwait, his role was similar to Eisenhower's in World War II. Though he lacked Eisenhower's charm, he drew upon years of experience in the Middle East, and was no less successful in keeping the coalition together. When it came time to fight the war, he and his staff devised a brilliant offensive plan that brought victory, with minimal casualties, after only four days of ground fighting. In terms of strategizing and fulfilling the nation's wartime objectives at the least possible cost, Schwarzkopf has no peer among post–World War II American generals.

Winfield Scott (1786–1866)

Scott had it all. He was a first-rate combat leader. He was a professional soldier to the core. Moreover, he was an excellent strategic thinker who knew how to accomplish wartime objectives. He served in the Army from 1808 to 1861, longer than any soldier, before or since. He led troops in the War of 1812 as a 27-year-old general in the battles of Chippewa and Lundy's Lane, both American victories. Scott was badly wounded at Lundy's Lane, and it took him many months to recuperate. For several decades after the war, he *was* the Army. He rose to major general, the highest rank at that time. He wrote the field manuals, devised the doctrine, and oversaw the education of cadets at West Point. Basically, he ran every aspect of the Army.

His shining moment came in 1847–1848 during the Mexican War. Working closely with his Navy colleagues, Scott oversaw the first major amphibious invasion in U.S. military history, at Veracruz, Mexico. Using a combination of dash, boldness, imagination, maneuver, firepower, and diplomacy, he advanced some 300 miles, conquered Mexico City, and won the war. He did this in spite of the fact that he was heavily outnumbered and poorly supplied. Plus, he was deep inside enemy country, with about one-third of his army down with disease at any given time. Scott's campaign was one of the most brilliant in American military history.

After an abortive run for the presidency in 1852, he returned to his post in charge of the Army. When the Civil War broke out, he was very old but still nominally in charge. He suggested blockading southern ports and seizing control of the river systems. Policymakers and subordinates initially ridiculed his plan, so he retired in November 1861. However, the North's victory resulted, in part, from Scott's blueprint.

George Washington (1732–1799)

Washington won very few battles, presided over a ragged, ill-trained army, and did not regularly perform great feats of courage. So why was he great? He was an adept planner, a first-rate organizer, a charismatic personality, and a brave combat leader when he needed to be. More than anyone else in his time, he understood that the Revolution was a mindset, not necessarily a mass movement. His main goal was to mobilize public opinion, not vast armies, for the Revolution. For him, this meant that he must keep his army intact, wearing down the British over time, demonstrating to the American people that independence was possible and desirable. He did this superbly, over the course of seven long years of up-and-down warfare. In that time, he earned a reputation as an honest, patriotic American, a giant among men.

His leadership was characterized by personal modesty, self-restraint, and a broad vision about what was best for the country at any given time. He was the ultimate big-picture thinker. By 1783, when the war ended and the United States earned its independence, he was the very symbol of American nationhood. He took that status very seriously, setting strong precedents for every future American military leader. He did the same, from 1789–1797, as the new American republic's first president.

Chapter 23

The Ten Worst Generals in U.S. Military History

In This Chapter

▶ Promoting poor combat leaders

▶ Making foolish mistakes

▶ Putting up with narrow-minded egotists

*B*ad generals are dangerous. They make poor decisions, give in to their egos, harass subordinates, waste resources, and worst of all, get people killed. A commanding general literally has the power of life and death in his hands. That means if he's unfit to command, the consequences of his failure can be pretty dramatic. Every general on this list of failed in some significant way that hurt the country and the troops under his command. My selections are based on each general's persistently poor leadership qualities, the negative views of his subordinates, and the overall damage he did to his soldiers and his cause. Not all of these guys were bad people. Some were solid military professionals who made poor choices or simply got promoted too high up the chain of command into jobs they couldn't handle. I list the generals alphabetically instead of ranking them.

Braxton Bragg (1817–1876)

Bragg just could not work and play well with others. He was a competent enough professional soldier, but his personality was a disaster. He was rude, abrupt, and humorless. He was such a tyrannical disciplinarian that, early in his career, his men tried to kill him. During the Civil War, Bragg was one of only eight full generals in the Confederacy, so he had a lot of responsibility. As commander of the Army of the Mississippi and the Army of the Tennessee, he controlled large numbers of Rebel soldiers in the key battles of Shiloh, Perryville, Murfreesboro, Chickamauga, and Chattanooga. He didn't perform well in any of these fights.

To a man, his subordinate commanders hated him with a passion. After the Battle of Chickamauga, they revolted in an effort to get him relieved. Nathan Bedford Forrest, perhaps the South's greatest tactician, refused to serve under him again, and even threatened to kill him. But Bragg had one powerful friend in President Jefferson Davis. The president rebuked Bragg's commanders and left his buddy in charge, with predictably poor results. In November 1863, Bragg came up short again in the Battle of Chattanooga, opening the way for Union forces to advance on Atlanta. Davis finally removed Bragg from command, but the southern cause never recovered from the damage he did.

Ambrose Burnside (1824–1881)

This Rhode Islander is the classic example of a good man who got promoted way beyond his capabilities. In the early days of the Civil War, he started well, commanding a brigade at First Bull Run, and presiding over a successful amphibious invasion that bottled up North Carolina's Tidewater region.

These successes earned Burnside promotion to major general and command of a corps (roughly 15,000 Union soldiers). Here's where the trouble began. At the Battle of Antietam in 1862, he was in charge of the whole right wing of the Union Army. Instead of fording the shallow Antietam Creek and attacking the Rebel defenders in several places, he funneled all of his troops into a costly attack across a well-defended stone bridge. This cost him thousands of casualties and precious hours when time was of the essence. Instead of achieving an overwhelming victory, the North had to settle for a favorable stalemate.

Two months later, President Abraham Lincoln inexplicably promoted Burnside to command of the Army of the Potomac, a large military force that consisted of more than 100,000 men. To his credit, Burnside knew he wasn't fit for this assignment and tried to turn it down, but to no avail. He then proceeded to lead his army into disaster at Fredericksburg, where he sent his whole army into an uphill attack, straight into Robert E. Lee's strongest fortifications. The result was one of the worst slaughters of the Civil War. Lincoln sacked him a month later.

Burnside sported a unique mutton-chop look with strips of facial hair extending from his mustache to the sides of his head, giving us the term *sideburns*.

Mark Clark (1896–1984)

First, you need to understand something. Clark was a courageous man and an excellent soldier. In World War I, he was wounded in combat. In the years leading up to World War II, he masterminded an important U.S. Army modernization and reorganization plan. In 1942, he risked his life in North Africa on a clandestine spy mission.

So, why is he on this list? Because, when he became a commander, he made disastrous, glory-seeking decisions that cost many American lives. The publicity-hungry Clark never saw a camera he didn't like. From 1943 to 1945, Clark was in charge of the U.S. Fifth Army in Italy. In January 1944, he ordered the 36th Infantry Division to launch a series of ill-conceived attacks across the well-defended Rapido River. The result was a bloody disaster.

At almost the same time, another part of his army landed at Anzio, behind enemy lines. Instead of pushing forward to seize the high ground that overlooked the beachhead, he stayed put, allowing the Germans to take the initiative, pen the Allies into a perilous perimeter, and stalemate them for five months. Later, in May and June 1944, when his forces finally broke out of the perimeter, he had a chance to trap the retreating German army and annihilate it, thus winning the campaign in Italy. But, giving in to his glory-seeking vanity, Clark chose instead to advance on Rome and enter the great city as a conquering hero. On June 4, 1944, while Clark basked in his Roman parade, most of the Germans escaped to set up a new defensive line, stalemate the war in Italy, and kill many more Allied soldiers. In spite of this inexcusable decision, Clark's subsequent military career prospered, mainly because of his close friendship with Dwight Eisenhower.

Lloyd Fredendall (1883–1963)

Pound for pound, Fredendall was the worst high-level American field general in World War II. In 1943, he commanded the II Corps, about 50,000 soldiers, in North Africa. He was incompetent, aloof, rash, and cowardly. He used his engineers to build an enormous, bomb-proof headquarters for himself in a cave 70 miles behind the lines. Eisenhower once visited the place and was shocked, saying he had never seen a headquarters so obsessed with its own safety. Fredendall rarely visited his subordinate commanders or went anywhere near the front.

At Kasserine Pass, in February 1943, the Germans nearly overwhelmed Fredendall's II Corps. The Allies staved off disaster, but not because of anything Fredendall did. By all accounts, he was a complete nonentity during the battle. In the wake of this close call, Eisenhower relieved Fredendall and replaced him with George Patton (see Chapter 22).

John Lucas (1890–1949)

As commander of VI Corps at Anzio, Lucas served under Mark Clark. After invading Anzio behind German lines in Italy, Lucas's mission was to thrust inland, cut the main road to Rome, capture the crossroads town of Cisterna, outflank the Germans, and take a patch of high ground known as the Alban

Hills. This was a difficult task for even the best commander. But Lucas was weak-willed and passive. His invasion was a complete success, catching the Germans by surprise.

However, Lucas was frightened of what reinforcements the Germans might have near Rome, so instead of advancing inland, he consolidated his forces into a small perimeter around Anzio and lost the initiative. When the Germans counterattacked him, they had the advantage of controlling the Alban Hills and other key terrain. Anzio turned into a pointless, arduous five-month stalemate with great loss of life on both sides. On February 22, 1944, Clark relieved Lucas, partly to find a scapegoat for his own failures. Lucas went home and never commanded troops in combat again.

George McClellan (1826–1885)

Some officers are good at preparing troops for battle. Others excel at leading them into combat. McClellan was definitely in the first category. When Lincoln appointed the 34-year-old general to command of the Union's Army of the Potomac in 1861, the "Young Napoleon" turned it into a first-class fighting army. McClellan excelled at training, organizing, and instilling good morale. For the most part, his soldiers loved him. McClellan had an enormous ego, though. He thought of the president as nothing more than "a well-meaning baboon," and spoke of himself as the savior of the country. He also had ill-concealed presidential ambitions.

McClellan's worst problem was that he was a complete washout as a battlefield commander. He could train the army and devise good plans. But he simply could not lead his army into battle. He was cautious and timid. To justify his inaction, he chronically overestimated enemy numbers, even though the Union Army had twice as many soldiers as the Confederate Army. In the bloody battles that were so common to the Civil War, he couldn't stand to see his soldiers suffering and dying. His tentativeness dearly cost the Union and extended the war he so hated.

He blamed everyone but himself for his failures. In voluminous letters, telegrams, and reports, he raged against everyone from the president to his fellow generals. Blinded by ego, he never understood that he failed because of his own shortcomings. In the wake of the Battle of Antietam, when McClellan failed to annihilate Lee's Army of Northern Virginia, Lincoln fired him.

William Rupertus (1889–1945)

Rupertus commanded the 1st Marine Division, one of the finest American fighting units, during the Battle of Peleliu in World War II. He quickly proved himself to be unworthy. He was a poor communicator who seldom conversed meaningfully with his staff, much less the riflemen who did the real fighting. He rarely visited the front lines. He was prickly, unapproachable, and narrow-minded. On the eve of the invasion of Peleliu, he declared publicly that the battle would only take three days. When Japanese resistance turned out to be much more difficult than he or anyone else expected, he stuck to his unrealistic timetable, pushing his Marines into hurry-up attacks, straight into fortified Japanese ridges and caves.

The fighting raged on for weeks. His casualties were disastrous. For instance, the 1st Marine Regiment, one of his main attacking units, suffered 54 percent losses. Still, he kept attacking with the few survivors he had on hand while the Army's entire 81st Infantry Division was in reserve, at his disposal, waiting to help. But Rupertus was a prisoner to interservice rivalry. He hated the Army and looked down upon the fighting qualities of soldiers. So he refused the Army's help, preferring to let his men suffer and die, when they clearly needed reinforcements. Finally, Rupertus's superior, another Marine general named Roy Geiger, ordered him to accept reinforcements from the Army. After Peleliu, Rupertus was quietly "promoted" to a desk job at home where he died of a heart attack in 1945.

Stephen Van Rensselaer III (1764–1839)

During the War of 1812, Van Rensselaer received an appointment as a militia general because he was from one of New York's wealthiest, most politically connected landowning families. He had no training, no experience, and basically, no clue what he was doing. No matter. In the fall of 1812, he devised a plan to invade British-controlled Canada. Unfortunately, his invasion was poorly planned, with little appreciation for how to cross the Niagara River, how to control high ground, and how to outflank British defenders in Queenstown. The result was the Battle of Queenstown Heights on October 13, an unmitigated American defeat that kept Canada under British control. After the battle, Van Rensselaer resigned his commission and returned to politics.

William Westmoreland (1914–2005)

Westmoreland was a fine man and a good soldier. He's on this list only because of the catastrophic consequences of choosing the wrong strategy in Vietnam. In 1964, upon taking command of Allied forces, Westmoreland decided to escalate the American troop presence, fight a big-unit, conventional war against the Communists, and wear them down through attrition. He planned to inflict so many casualties on them that they would have to give up the war.

On the surface, Westmoreland's strategy made sense because the U.S. had distinct advantages in mobility and firepower. The problem was that the Communists chose to fight a guerrilla war at the grassroots level. This meant that large American units had great difficulty finding enemy fighters. Enemy commanders could often control the rate of their losses, thus undercutting Westmoreland's attrition strategy. Moreover, his lavish use of firepower killed thousands of innocent Vietnamese, alienating some of the population. Equally as bad, the strategy failed to protect South Vietnam from the Communists and led to large numbers of U.S. casualties, undercutting support for the war at home.

Westmoreland never quite understood that in a guerrilla war like Vietnam, success came from providing security for the average villager, not from defeating large enemy units in an attempt to refight World War II.

James Wilkinson (1757–1825)

Wilkinson never met a corrupt scheme or traitorous plan he did not like. As a young general, he fought in the Revolution but spent much of his time trying to sabotage George Washington. After the war, he continued his military service.

While in uniform, he was involved in a dizzying array of corrupt deals and under-the-table conspiracies usually designed to enhance his own power or wealth. He was especially beholden to the king of Spain, who paid him to betray American state secrets. In exchange for a promise of 60,000 acres of land from Spain, Wilkinson offered to give the Spanish control of the Mississippi River, along with huge swaths of western land that Americans hoped to settle. Another time he conspired with the notorious Aaron Burr to lop off a major tract of western land to create their own country. Wilkinson even handed over the secret battle plans of a fellow American officer to the Spanish. Yet somehow, he remained in the Army as a major general until the War of 1812, when he suffered several defeats at the hands of the British and was finally dismissed from the service.

Chapter 24

The Ten Best Movies on U.S. Military History

*N*othing brings history to life like movies. In movies, the people we read about in our history books become actual living, breathing, flesh-and-blood human beings. War and military history contain so much human drama that they are irresistible topics for filmmakers. I'm a big believer in the power of film to teach U.S. military history, and I use movies all the time in my classes. In this chapter, I've prepared my list of the ten very best films on U.S. military history. My biggest criterion for excellence is historical accuracy, followed by the overall quality of the filmmaking and the actors' performances. No doubt this list will provoke some disagreement and debate.

1. Saving Private Ryan (1998)

Quite simply, *Saving Private Ryan* is the greatest movie ever made. Steven Spielberg's World War II blockbuster is about a small group of U.S. Army Rangers whose mission is to find Pvt. James Ryan (Matt Damon), a young 101st Airborne Division paratrooper somewhere in Normandy. Ryan is to be removed from combat because his family has already lost three sons to the war. From D-Day at Omaha beach to the fictional Norman town of Romelle, Capt. John Miller (Tom Hanks) leads his Rangers in combat and on their search for Ryan. Hanks's performance is, in my view, the greatest of his legendary career. Before the filming of this movie, Dale Dye, the ex-Marine who has made a career as a military advisor for dozens of war films, worked his magic again, putting the principal actors through an intense boot camp. By the time the cameras rolled, Hanks and his guys knew their weapons, their jobs, and one another.

Spielberg succeeds in bringing the smell, sights, and overall feel of 1944 Normandy to life. While not every historical detail in *Saving Private Ryan* is perfect, Spielberg's commitment to realism is obvious. The movie portrays World War II combat more accurately and powerfully than any other film before or since. The opening scenes at Omaha beach are some of the most intense ever put on film. The same holds true for the small-town combat scenes in Neuville-au-Plain and Romelle, which are often overlooked.

Saving Private Ryan hit theaters in 1998 like a proverbial bombshell. The film was so powerful, so realistic, and such a cultural sensation that it was the subject of dozens of newspaper and magazine articles. It almost single-handedly sparked a renewed interest in World War II and those Americans who fought the war. If you watch any war movie made after 1998, you'll immediately notice the profound influence of Spielberg's movie.

2. Black Hawk Down (2001)

Based on Mark Bowden's excellent book, *Black Hawk Down* is the story of a bloody urban battle in October 1993 between U.S. Army Special Operations soldiers and Somali militiamen in Mogadishu. The battle was an American victory, but it cost the lives of 19 Americans, mostly U.S. Army Rangers, and prompted an American withdrawal from Somalia. It also created an earnest wish among Americans to never get involved in such urban combat again.

The movie is so authentic that it nearly has a documentary feel. Director Ridley Scott gets the little things right, including the soldier's weapons, the slang terms they use, the real conversations they had, the tactics they employ in combat, and even the proper sequence of events in the actual battle. *Black Hawk Down* is shocking, graphic, and disturbing, as any good war film must be. It's also confusing, dirty, messy, and chaotic. Just like war. In terms of wall-to-wall combat action, the movie has no equal. It is relentless and evocative.

Black Hawk Down was filmed right before the terrorist attacks of September 11, 2001, and released not long after them. What makes the movie truly significant is that it anticipated the exact kind of fighting American soldiers eventually would face in Iraq.

3. Glory (1989)

Glory portrays the trials and tribulations of the African American 54th Massachusetts Volunteer Infantry Regiment in the Civil War, from recruitment to its assault on Fort Wagner in 1863. The film is a wonderful blend of great acting, good storytelling, and accurate history. Matthew Broderick stars as

Col. Robert Gould Shaw, who commanded the 54th. Morgan Freeman plays Sgt. Maj. John Rawlins. Denzel Washington is Pvt. Trip, an escaped slave who is itching to lash back at the white power structure, North and South.

Glory manages to intelligently touch on most of the war's major issues, including race relations, slavery, property rights, states' rights, and differing conceptions of freedom. It's also a first-rate combat chronicle, graphically portraying such battles as Antietam and the assault on Fort Wagner. By and large, director Edward Zwick went to great pains to make his movie historically accurate, and it shows. Throughout the film, we see this small group of young black soldiers evolve as a group, committing themselves not just to the cause they're fighting for, but also to one another. By the end of the movie, they are molded as one, fighting to prove themselves as men and to ensure a better future for their families. In that sense, their story transcends race. It's really about the struggles of all Americans in combat throughout U.S. military history.

4. Platoon (1986)

In making this film, director Oliver Stone drew on his own Vietnam War experiences as a grunt in the 25th Infantry Division. The movie portrays a platoon of soldiers from that division in 1967–1968. To put the actors into a realistic mindset, military advisor Dale Dye put them through an uncompromising boot camp. The authenticity shows in their performances. They eat, walk, talk, dress, and even spit like real grunts. As a Vietnam vet, Stone makes sure to get all the little things right. For instance, the jungle patrol scenes are the best ever recorded on film. Every bit of the soldier's experience is in these scenes — the heat, the bugs, the foliage, the fatigue, and even the sense of isolation.

For well or ill, *Platoon* was really the first movie to address the Vietnam War honestly. Sensing this, Vietnam veterans flocked to the theaters to see it. Stone conveys in *Platoon* an obvious antiwar message but with a disarming passion for depicting the moral ambiguities of guerrilla war. From one scene to the next, the Americans might be heroes or villains, depending on the circumstances. Stone's ultimate purpose is not just to criticize America's involvement in Vietnam, but to counsel us to learn from the Vietnam experience to produce a better future.

5. Hamburger Hill (1987)

In terms of pure combat realism and an accurate portrayal of American soldiers in Vietnam, this film has few equals. It's one of the few Vietnam War movies that even comes close to portraying the war accurately. In May 1969, paratroopers from the 187th Parachute Infantry Regiment spent ten bloody days capturing

Hill 937. They called this awful place "Hamburger Hill." This movie tells that story, through the eyes of one beleaguered squad. The battle scenes are graphic and violent. Soldiers from both sides get blown to pieces. Mud is everywhere; so is blood. Sometimes the fighting is hand-to-hand. Death seems almost inescapable. The world seems confined to only this horrible hill and the death struggle with the North Vietnamese. Director John Irvin shows us this violence, not for cheap, ignorant entertainment value as in so many other films, but because this is the way Hamburger Hill actually was.

6. A Midnight Clear (1992)

If there is a better film that wrestles with the morality of war, I have yet to see it. Based on a novel by the same title, *A Midnight Clear* is the story of six youthful American soldiers in the Ardennes on the eve of the Battle of the Bulge during World War II. They are the survivors of a decimated intelligence and reconnaissance squad. They are all bright individuals, as evidenced by their high scores on Army classification tests. But the loss of their friends, along with the seeming endlessness and futility of the war have demoralized them. Nonetheless, their coldhearted battalion commander, Maj. Griffin, orders them to hole up in a house in no man's land to keep an eye on the Germans. Director Keith Gordon portrayed the European winter so effectively that you can almost feel the biting cold.

The sector is quiet, except for the presence of a quirky squad of German soldiers who seem to have no interest in fighting. The plot that follows is not as important as the combat-related themes that Gordon addresses, such as the camaraderie of American fighting soldiers, the struggle with the elements, the search for meaning in war, and the troubling question of who is a greater threat, enemy soldiers or one's own officers.

7. Memphis Belle (1990)

Memphis Belle tells the story of one American B-17 bomber crew's final mission over German-occupied Europe. During World War II, director William Wyler had immortalized this crew in a documentary by the same title. In 1990, director Michael Caton-Jones's fictionalized *Memphis Belle* retold that story by focusing on the men's 25th and final mission to Bremen (the real *Belle* crew flew its last mission to Wilhelmshaven).

If the crew can carry out the mission and make it back to its base in England, the men get to go home for good. In the course of the mission, nearly everything happens to these guys. German fighters attack them. Flak does terrific damage to their plane. They have engine trouble. Their oxygen system is on the fritz. One crew member gets badly wounded.

The excellence of Caton-Jones's approach is that he starkly portrayed the kind of things that routinely happened to World War II American airmen in Europe. Caton-Jones shows us the effect of intense cold at high altitudes, the claustrophobia of an oxygen mask, the helplessness of flying through flak, the intense superstition that infused airmen, the camaraderie among them, and the despair of seeing other planes go down. In filming the movie, he used the largest surviving collection of B-17s. To prepare for their parts, the actors paired up with their real-life counterparts who flew on the *Belle*.

8. Dances with Wolves (1990)

The most mythologized aspect of U.S. military history is the Indian Wars. In general, Hollywood filmmakers seem incapable of portraying the American West accurately. Not *Dances with Wolves,* though. The movie is the story of John Dunbar, an Army officer whose bravery in a Civil War battle earns him his choice of whatever posting he wants. He selects an assignment on the frontier in Lakota Sioux country (today's upper Midwest). At first, he thinks of the Indians as enemies, but over time, he befriends them, marries a white woman whom they have captured, and becomes a member of the tribe. To the Army, he is now a deserter, a wanted man. At the end of the film, Dunbar and his wife leave the tribe to become fugitives, so as not to attract unwanted Army attention on his tribal friends.

Kevin Costner produced, directed, and starred in *Dances with Wolves* as Dunbar. He used real Native American actors. They spoke in actual Lakota Sioux language. The movie shows little in the way of actual combat, which is quite true to the Old West. Costner portrays Lakota Sioux life as it actually was, warts and all, from a hunting party that eats the heart of a freshly killed buffalo to the interplay between tribal men and women. *Dances with Wolves* is the most lucrative western in film history, proving that audiences hunger not just for drama about the Old West, but authenticity.

9. A Bridge Too Far (1977)

From the late 1950s to the mid-1970s, Hollywood produced several World War II epics portraying big battles with lots of stars. *A Bridge Too Far* is the best of these epics. Based quite accurately on Cornelius Ryan's book of the same title, the film portrays Operation Market Garden, an Allied scheme to defeat Nazi Germany in the fall of 1944. The plan was to drop two American and one British airborne division behind German lines. The paratroopers were to capture key bridges and hold the main highway that led into Germany. Then, powerful British armored units were supposed to punch through enemy lines, hook up with the airborne units, and finally roar across the Rhine River bridges into Germany, all the way to Berlin.

The real-life plan failed miserably, but the same could not be said of this movie. *A Bridge Too Far* is loaded with acting talent. Every leading actor of the time was in this film, including James Caan, Sean Connery, Robert Redford, Michael Caine, Ryan O'Neal, Gene Hackman, Elliot Gould, Anthony Hopkins, Laurence Olivier, and Maximilian Schell.

The director, Richard Attenborough, didn't shy away from showing the grim realities of the battle — the burning bodies and vehicles at Arnhem bridge, the spine-tingling terror of the 82nd Airborne's Waal River crossing, and the shriek of artillery shells. His depiction of the airborne drop is breathtaking. He used actual C-47 transports like the ones the Allies employed in 1944. He also used real paratroopers to show the drop, putting cameras on some of the jumpers, creating a "you are there" immediacy to the movie.

10. The Dirty Dozen (1967)

The Dirty Dozen portrays a group of American misfits on the eve of the Normandy invasion during World War II. All of these men are in the stockade for serious crimes, including rape and murder. They have one chance for redemption, though, and it comes in the person of Maj. John Reisman (Lee Marvin), a hard-bitten Special Operations officer whose superiors have tasked him with a pre–D-Day, high-risk mission to kill German officers at a chateau in Brittany, France. If the convicts submit to Reisman's intense training and carry out his mission successfully, freedom beckons.

The movie is an entertaining blend of historical accuracy, humor, tension, and drama. The Army did actually offer convicts the chance to reduce their sentences if they volunteered for dangerous duty. The ensemble cast of Marvin, Ernest Borgnine, Telly Savalas, Robert Ryan, Charles Bronson, Donald Sutherland, and football star Jim Brown absolutely shines. World War II vets Marvin, Borgnine, Savalas, and Bronson all contributed their knowledge. What's interesting about this movie is that the villains are not just the Nazis but also U.S. Army senior officers. The film could not have been made in an earlier, more idealistic time. But in the 1960s, American audiences were ready for antiheroes like the misfits of *The Dirty Dozen*.

Index

Cuban Missile Crisis, 253–254
Custer, George (American commander), 166–168

• D •

Dai, Bao (Vietnamese leader), 281
Daiquiri, invasion at (1898), 175
Dakota War (1862), 25
Daladier, Edouard (French premier), 209
Dances with Wolves (movie), 162, 347
Danzig Corridor, 210
Davidson, Phil (historian), 296
Davis, Jefferson (Confederate president), 141, 155, 156, 338
D-Day, 234
de Rigaud, Pierre François (French governor), 75
deadly brotherhood, 63
Dearborn, Henry (American general), 114–115
death camps, 211, 214
Decatur, Stephen (American commander), 106
Declaration of Independence, 22, 94
deferments, 287
deficit spending, 241
Delaware, 73, 74
Delta Force, 44
demilitarized zone (DMZ), Korea, 274
Democratic-Republicans, 104, 108–109, 119
depth charges, 229
desegregation, 34
destroyers, 45, 199, 229
détente, 255–256, 260
determinists, 95
Detroit, 12, 112–113
Devil Dogs, 201
Dewey, George (American general), 180
Dickson, Keith D.
  The Civil War For Dummies, 137
  World War II For Dummies, 221
Diem, Ngo Dinh (Vietnamese leader), 281–282
Dien Bien Phu, Battle of (1954), 280
Dinwiddie, Robert (Virginia governor), 68
The Dirty Dozen (movie), 348
DMZ (demilitarized zone), Korea, 274
Dodge, Grenville (American general), 175
Dodge Commission, 175
dogfaces, 42
dogfights, 56
domino theory, 248, 283

Doniphan, Alexander (American commander), 131
Douglas, Stephen (senator), 139
draft
  Civil War, 155
  deferments, 195, 287
  Korean War, 271
  as reason for military service, 34
  Vietnam War, 287
  World War I, 195
  World War II, 215
drones, aerial, 61
Dulles, John Foster (secretary of state), 253
Dunkirk, evacuation of (1940), 213

• E •

East India Company, 82
Easton, Treaty of, 73, 74
Eaton, William (American diplomat), 106
economics
  American Revolution and, 95
  as reason for military service, 35
  as reason for war, 19–20
  of World War I, 193, 196–197
  of World War II, 241
Eisenhower, Dwight D. (president/general)
  as five-star general, 31
  George Patton and, 233
  New Look strategy, 252–253
  personal qualities of, 331
  tactics in World War II, 31
  in World War II, 231, 331–332
El Alamein, Battle of, 230
Emancipation Proclamation, 148–149
Embargo Act (1807), 110
enemies
  colonial European powers, 24–25
  Communists, 27
  continental, 24–25
  Fascists, 26
  hatred for, 63
  ideological, 26–28
  Native Americans, 25
  overseas, 26
  radical Islamic fundamentalists, 27–28
Enlightenment, 24
enlisted ranks, 35
entertainers, 12
escape, as reason for military service, 35
Espionage Act, 198

• *H* •

• *I* •

BUSINESS, CAREERS & PERSONAL FINANCE

0-7645-9847-3

0-7645-2431-3

Also available:
- Business Plans Kit For Dummies
  0-7645-9794-9
- Economics For Dummies
  0-7645-5726-2
- Grant Writing For Dummies
  0-7645-8416-2
- Home Buying For Dummies
  0-7645-5331-3
- Managing For Dummies
  0-7645-1771-6
- Marketing For Dummies
  0-7645-5600-2

- Personal Finance For Dummies
  0-7645-2590-5*
- Resumes For Dummies
  0-7645-5471-9
- Selling For Dummies
  0-7645-5363-1
- Six Sigma For Dummies
  0-7645-6798-5
- Small Business Kit For Dummies
  0-7645-5984-2
- Starting an eBay Business For Dummies
  0-7645-6924-4
- Your Dream Career For Dummies
  0-7645-9795-7

HOME & BUSINESS COMPUTER BASICS

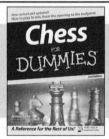

0-470-05432-8

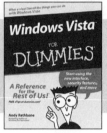

0-471-75421-8

Also available:
- Cleaning Windows Vista For Dummies
  0-471-78293-9
- Excel 2007 For Dummies
  0-470-03737-7
- Mac OS X Tiger For Dummies
  0-7645-7675-5
- MacBook For Dummies
  0-470-04859-X
- Macs For Dummies
  0-470-04849-2
- Office 2007 For Dummies
  0-470-00923-3

- Outlook 2007 For Dummies
  0-470-03830-6
- PCs For Dummies
  0-7645-8958-X
- Salesforce.com For Dummies
  0-470-04893-X
- Upgrading & Fixing Laptops For Dummies
  0-7645-8959-8
- Word 2007 For Dummies
  0-470-03658-3
- Quicken 2007 For Dummies
  0-470-04600-7

FOOD, HOME, GARDEN, HOBBIES, MUSIC & PETS

0-7645-8404-9

0-7645-9904-6

Also available:
- Candy Making For Dummies
  0-7645-9734-5
- Card Games For Dummies
  0-7645-9910-0
- Crocheting For Dummies
  0-7645-4151-X
- Dog Training For Dummies
  0-7645-8418-9
- Healthy Carb Cookbook For Dummies
  0-7645-8476-6
- Home Maintenance For Dummies
  0-7645-5215-5

- Horses For Dummies
  0-7645-9797-3
- Jewelry Making & Beading For Dummies
  0-7645-2571-9
- Orchids For Dummies
  0-7645-6759-4
- Puppies For Dummies
  0-7645-5255-4
- Rock Guitar For Dummies
  0-7645-5356-9
- Sewing For Dummies
  0-7645-6847-7
- Singing For Dummies
  0-7645-2475-5

INTERNET & DIGITAL MEDIA

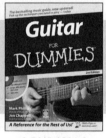

0-470-04529-9

0-470-04894-8

Also available:
- Blogging For Dummies
  0-471-77084-1
- Digital Photography For Dummies
  0-7645-9802-3
- Digital Photography All-in-One Desk Reference For Dummies
  0-470-03743-1
- Digital SLR Cameras and Photography For Dummies
  0-7645-9803-1
- eBay Business All-in-One Desk Reference For Dummies
  0-7645-8438-3
- HDTV For Dummies
  0-470-09673-X

- Home Entertainment PCs For Dummies
  0-470-05523-5
- MySpace For Dummies
  0-470-09529-6
- Search Engine Optimization For Dummies
  0-471-97998-8
- Skype For Dummies
  0-470-04891-3
- The Internet For Dummies
  0-7645-8996-2
- Wiring Your Digital Home For Dummies
  0-471-91830-X

* Separate Canadian edition also available
† Separate U.K. edition also available

Available wherever books are sold. For more information or to order direct: U.S. customers visit www.dummies.com or call 1-877-762-2974.
U.K. customers visit www.wileyeurope.com or call 0800 243407. Canadian customers visit www.wiley.ca or call 1-800-567-4797.

SPORTS, FITNESS, PARENTING, RELIGION & SPIRITUALITY

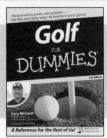

0-471-76871-5

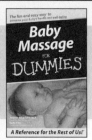

0-7645-7841-3

Also available:
- Catholicism For Dummies
  0-7645-5391-7
- Exercise Balls For Dummies
  0-7645-5623-1
- Fitness For Dummies
  0-7645-7851-0
- Football For Dummies
  0-7645-3936-1
- Judaism For Dummies
  0-7645-5299-6
- Potty Training For Dummies
  0-7645-5417-4
- Buddhism For Dummies
  0-7645-5359-3

- Pregnancy For Dummies
  0-7645-4483-7 †
- Ten Minute Tone-Ups For Dummies
  0-7645-7207-5
- NASCAR For Dummies
  0-7645-7681-X
- Religion For Dummies
  0-7645-5264-3
- Soccer For Dummies
  0-7645-5229-5
- Women in the Bible For Dummies
  0-7645-8475-8

TRAVEL

0-7645-7749-2

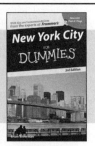

0-7645-6945-7

Also available:
- Alaska For Dummies
  0-7645-7746-8
- Cruise Vacations For Dummies
  0-7645-6941-4
- England For Dummies
  0-7645-4276-1
- Europe For Dummies
  0-7645-7529-5
- Germany For Dummies
  0-7645-7823-5
- Hawaii For Dummies
  0-7645-7402-7

- Italy For Dummies
  0-7645-7386-1
- Las Vegas For Dummies
  0-7645-7382-9
- London For Dummies
  0-7645-4277-X
- Paris For Dummies
  0-7645-7630-5
- RV Vacations For Dummies
  0-7645-4442-X
- Walt Disney World & Orlando
  For Dummies
  0-7645-9660-8

GRAPHICS, DESIGN & WEB DEVELOPMENT

0-7645-8815-X

0-7645-9571-7

Also available:
- 3D Game Animation For Dummies
  0-7645-8789-7
- AutoCAD 2006 For Dummies
  0-7645-8925-3
- Building a Web Site For Dummies
  0-7645-7144-3
- Creating Web Pages For Dummies
  0-470-08030-2
- Creating Web Pages All-in-One Desk
  Reference For Dummies
  0-7645-4345-8
- Dreamweaver 8 For Dummies
  0-7645-9649-7

- InDesign CS2 For Dummies
  0-7645-9572-5
- Macromedia Flash 8 For Dummies
  0-7645-9691-8
- Photoshop CS2 and Digital
  Photography For Dummies
  0-7645-9580-6
- Photoshop Elements 4 For Dummies
  0-471-77483-9
- Syndicating Web Sites with RSS Feeds
  For Dummies
  0-7645-8848-6
- Yahoo! SiteBuilder For Dummies
  0-7645-9800-7

NETWORKING, SECURITY, PROGRAMMING & DATABASES

0-7645-7728-X

0-471-74940-0

Also available:
- Access 2007 For Dummies
  0-470-04612-0
- ASP.NET 2 For Dummies
  0-7645-7907-X
- C# 2005 For Dummies
  0-7645-9704-3
- Hacking For Dummies
  0-470-05235-X
- Hacking Wireless Networks
  For Dummies
  0-7645-9730-2
- Java For Dummies
  0-470-08716-1

- Microsoft SQL Server 2005 For Dummies
  0-7645-7755-7
- Networking All-in-One Desk Reference
  For Dummies
  0-7645-9939-9
- Preventing Identity Theft For Dummies
  0-7645-7336-5
- Telecom For Dummies
  0-471-77085-X
- Visual Studio 2005 All-in-One Desk
  Reference For Dummies
  0-7645-9775-2
- XML For Dummies
  0-7645-8845-1